CANADIANS
IN THE
CIVIL WAR

CLAIRE HOY

McArthur & Company
Toronto

Published in 2004 by
McArthur & Company
322 King St. West, Suite 402
Toronto, Ontario M5V 1J2
www.mcarthur-co.com

Library and Archives Canada Cataloguing in Publication

Hoy, Claire
Canadians in the Civil War / Claire Hoy.

Includes index.
ISBN 1-55278-450-9

1. United States—History—Civil War, 1861-1865—Participation,
Canadian. 2. Canada—History—1841-1867. 3. Canadians—
United States—History—19th century. I. Title.

E540.F6H69 2004   973.7'089'11   C2004-904237-8

Composition & Design: *Mad Dog Design*
Cover photo: *National Archive Reproductions*
Printed in Canada by: *Friesens Corporation*

The publisher would like to acknowledge the financial support of the
Government of Canada through the Book Publishing Industry
Development Program, The Canada Council for the Arts, and the
Ontario Arts Council for our publishing activities. We also acknowledge
the Government of Ontario through the Ontario Media Development
Corporation Ontario Book Initiative.

10 9 8 7 6 5 4 3 2 1

CONTENTS

The Opening Salvo

THERE'S BEEN NO WAR LIKE IT IN AMERICAN HISTORY. Almost 140 years after the last shots were fired in the American Civil War (1861–65), tens of thousands of Americans – and several thousand Canadians – spend many of their weekends re-enacting the famous, and the not-so-famous, battles and skirmishes which marked that bloody chapter of North American history.

The Civil War marked the emergence of new and more powerful weapons, previously unheard of destructive techniques, and, yes, photography, to record the horrors and the triumphs of this most terrible war. Names such as Gettysburg, Shiloh, Manassas, Vicksburg, and Antietam, and General William T. Sherman's famous, and bloody, march to the sea still echo throughout the United States as critical battles in a war that saw more than 3 million Americans under arms and resulted in the death of more than 600,000 of them from both the North and the South. Men such as Abraham Lincoln, Jefferson Davis, Robert E. Lee, and Ulysses S. Grant, all of whom played key roles in the war, are better known even today than many contemporary political and military leaders.

But what of Canada in this epic struggle? Few Canadians realize that, although it was primarily an American tragedy, it also stands as a defining event in our own history.

For one thing, tens of thousands of Canadians (British North Americans at the time) fought in the war, many of them attracted by generous signing bonuses of $200 or considerably more offered by Northern authorities to replenish their depleted ranks. Others were youthful adventurers caught up in what they saw as the romance and excitement of it all. Still more were victims of squads of unscrupulous men who prowled the bars and streets of border cities and towns, using a variety of methods – from drug-laden booze concoctions to outright forcible kidnapping – to sell their victims to compliant U.S. Army recruiters. The war also marked the initial influx of draft dodgers – "skedaddlers" as they were called then – a phenomenon that upset settlers of the day just as it did a century later during the Vietnam conflict, when thousands of Americans escaped the draft by running across the border to a safe haven in Canada.

While it is not clear how many Canadians fought – estimates range from about 30,000 to 50,000, the latter likely being too high a number – an estimated 5,000 died in the struggle, and thousands more returned home lacking legs or arms or suffering from other dreadful injuries. Still more – nobody knows how many – decided simply to stay on in the United States after the war ended.

For me, the Civil War first entered my life when, as a young boy in the late 1940s growing up in Prescott, Ontario, directly across the St. Lawrence River from Ogdensburg, New York, I too was taken in by the latest marketing rage – the sale of both Union and Confederate caps. I wore a Confederate cap – not because I knew anything about the war, but because most of my compatriots were sporting Union hats. Even at that age, something about the rebel appealed to me above the establishment. That spark led to considerable reading about the Civil War and several trips to tour the war sites. Gradually I came to understand the importance of the conflict to our own history, its impact on the kind of government agreed on by the Fathers of Confederation in 1867, and why, all these years later, a significant element of Canadians still worry about an American takeover of our society.

When the war began in 1860, most Canadians were overtly sympathetic to the North. After all, slavery had been abolished years earlier in the colonies, and the geographical proximity between us and the Americans meant strong ties in trade between the two countries and considerable personal and family ties as well, as Canadians and Americans travelled freely and frequently back and forth across the border. As the war went on, however, and with a growing antipathy between Washington and Great Britain – which, on two distinct occasions, brought us within a whisker of all-out war against the Lincoln administration – Canadian sympathies underwent a dramatic transformation. Part of it was the Northern blockade of Atlantic ports, but there was also the social influence of thousands of wealthy, cultured Southerners living in Canada, moving in the most influential circles, and promoting the romance of their "lost cause" – a stark comparison to the crude, lower-class Northerners who populated the seedier sides of Canadian communities and left an unfortunate impression on the locals.

During the last two years of the war, in particular, Toronto, Halifax, Montreal, and St. Catharines hosted a well-financed network of Confederate spies, escaped prisoners, and soldiers of fortune whose raison d'être was to influence Canadian opinion in the South's favour and create havoc for Lincoln and his government. The war was brought much closer because these Confederate agents used Canadian soil to launch a series of organized raids along the Northern border states, ranging from a sensational attack on the village of St. Albans, Vermont, to the capture of two American ships on Lake Erie, as well as a failed attempt to burn down a group of hotels and public buildings in New York City – all in the hope of exacerbating Northern anger at the ongoing war in general and the heightened draft in particular. None of these forays into Union territory were particularly successful, but they certainly angered the Northern populace and helped fuel a powerful movement there, shared by some of Lincoln's most senior colleagues, to annex Canada. It was the fear of annexation, in fact, that convinced some of the most hardened Canadian opponents to Confederation to drop their opposition and accept the reality that there was greater strength in unity. And it was the American system of state sovereignty that Canada's founding prime minister, Sir John A. Macdonald, saw as the root of the problem and convinced him that Canada must adopt a strong central government, with the provinces as the weaker sisters.

The assassination of Abraham Lincoln also has a Canadian connection. The notorious John Wilkes Booth and a group of his Southern colleagues first laid out their plans leading up to the Good Friday, 1865, fatal attack on the American president when they met in Montreal's St. Lawrence Hall hotel – the place where so many Confederates lived that it offered mint juleps to its patrons.

In Halifax, where blockade-running continued to supply the South with personal materials and war munitions, several family fortunes were created. Southern sympathies ran so high there that many businesses openly flew Confederate flags and traded in Confederate currency. In Toronto – where a huge throng welcomed defeated Confederate President Jefferson Davis on the eve of our own Confederation (Davis and his family lived for a time in Montreal) – the swanky harbourfront Queen's Hotel became the Southern headquarters during the last two years of the war, the regular home for both the official and the unofficial representatives of the Confederate States of America, and a natural magnet for a small army of Northern operatives who spent their time spying on the Southern spies and agitators.

On the battlefields themselves, four Union generals had been born in Canada, and twenty-nine Canadians were awarded the Medal of Honor by the Northern forces. Most combatants fought for the North, but many did not. One of them was Dr. Solomon Secord, a surgeon with the 20th Georgia Volunteers and the grand-nephew of the War of 1812 heroine Laura Secord. His statue in Kincardine, Ontario, represents the only monument in Canada to a Civil War veteran.

Like all wars, however, the greatest direct impact of the Civil War was on the thousands of young men – and a few young women disguised as young men – who left their villages, cities, or farms north of the border and either trudged off to war or were duped into going. There they played their part in a cataclysmic event that, by virtue of its proximity to Canada and its overwhelming impact on the political, business, and cultural realities of the day, formed a part of Canadian history. Apart from a select group of academics and Civil War buffs, this war remains grossly underappreciated in Canada today. It's my hope that this book will help change that neglect.

ONE

A Family Affair

O N A WARM, BLUSTERY DAY on October 20, 1861, on a desolate hill overlooking the village of Wolverton in what was then Canada West, a solemn knot of mourners gathered around the family plot, quietly grieving as the body of 17-year-old Jasper Wolverton was lowered into its grave.

Among the mourners was Jasper's 23-year-old brother, Alfred, who, like Jasper and their youngest brother Newton, only 15, had already been serving as a teamster attached to the 50th New York Infantry in the Union Army. The three brothers had volunteered for service in July, just in time for the July 21 First Battle of Bull Run, Virginia (or the First Manassas, as the Confederates know it), where Confederate General Thomas Jonathan Jackson became immortalized as "Stonewall" Jackson for his stubborn defiance in the face of attacking Union forces. The battle, involving some 60,000 men from the North and the South, ended in an embarrassing rout for the overconfident Union men.

Also attending Jasper's funeral was another brother, Alonzo, 20, who returned to Washington with Alfred after the ceremony and became the fourth Wolverton brother to volunteer for service in the Union Army. A fifth brother, Daniel, had died at the age of 18 in 1858 from an accidental axe wound and was already buried at Wolverton Cemetery.

Jasper, like so many soldiers in that war, had contracted typhoid fever and died in a Washington hospital. He was buried eight days later, after Alfred, who was noted for his ability to memorize entire chapters of the Bible, had his brother's body embalmed and was granted a furlough to truck the body back by wagon over the arduous 600-mile journey to the family homestead for burial.

Also at the gravesite – which is today cordoned off by a black, decorative, wrought-iron fence – was the father, Enos Wolverton, who was born in 1810 and grew up in Cayuga County in upper New York state, but had moved first to Ohio and then briefly to Michigan. He emigrated to Canada West in 1826 with his father, Robert Wolverton, crossing the Detroit River into Canada between Detroit and Windsor, and setting up a lumber business on Governor's Road just east of Princeton.

In 1834 Enos married Harriet Newall Towl, and the couple moved farther east to the 5th Concession of Blenheim Township. They raised seven children, two daughters and five sons. In 1844 Enos bought the 200-acre Lot 8, Concession 8 (Blenheim), from the Crown, hoping to use the water power from the adjacent Nith River, which still snakes its way through the village, to erect lumber mills on the property. He also laid out a village plot in 1851, naming it Warsaw, but soon changed it to Wolverton, when, as the first postmaster that September, he discovered there already was a Warsaw. He cleared part of the land, first building a sawmill and later a grist and flour mill. He also helped construct the white-framed Baptist Church across the street from his home. By 1858 there were 200 people living there, not much different from the current population.

In 1854–55 Enos built the magnificent Wolverton Hall on the banks of the old mill race. Surrounded by lawns and gardens, it's a three-storey, fourteen-room, red brick, Regency-style home with casement windows on all floors. It originally had seven fireplaces on the ground floor alone, and it boasts beautiful red pine plank floors, some of the boards a foot wide. The centrepiece of the house, however, is a spectacular circular staircase, held in place by wooden pegs and supported by a single maple column extending from the spacious main-floor entranceway through three flights of steps to where the copula used to be. That copula, or windowed belvedere, afforded an eye-pleasing view of the Nith River and the gently rolling terrain of what is now Oxford County, about a ninety-minute drive west of Toronto. Although the copula is gone and the family no longer owns the house, Wolverton Hall, declared an official provincial historic site in 1970, still proudly guards the northwestern entrance to the village, perched majestically on a gentle curve on Wolverton Road directly across from the river and about half a mile east of the cemetery, where so many of the family members are buried.

The Wolverton Cemetery stands forlornly at the top of a long, skinny dirt road next to a farmer's field. It is a long, narrow piece of property, barren except for the tombstones, a few rock outcroppings, and a massive maple tree that has stood sentry as long as the Wolvertons have been in the area.

On December 17, 1856, Harriet Wolverton died of diphtheria and was buried in the village cemetery. A year later, during the depression that followed the Crimean War, business was so poor that Enos rented out Wolverton Hall and moved his family to Walsingham Township in adjacent Norfolk County. There he built and operated a steam sawmill, a novelty at the time which used to draw numerous onlookers when its 40-horsepower steam engine was in full flight. A year later Enos married Mariam Cline, but again his business failed and he returned to Wolverton in 1861. Early that year Mariam died and she, too, was buried in the cemetery, dressed in her wedding gown. Enos married again, this time on June 1, 1863, to Sabina "Binie" Bogart, who came from Napanee, a small town on Lake Ontario in eastern Ontario. She outlived her husband and ultimately returned to Napanee, living there until her death.

The family lumber business had brought Alfred and Jasper to Cleveland in 1858 for two reasons: to further their academic education by attending West High School; and to advance their business education by arranging for the ongoing shipments of shingles and other lumber products with Thatcher & Burt Co., a prominent development company there. Alonzo had stayed behind to help his father at the mill, but Enos decided that Newton should also get an education. Since there were no comparable schools near Wolverton, he sent Newton in the fall of 1859, at the age of 13, across Lake Erie in a small freight schooner to Cleveland, where he joined his two brothers in a boarding house. The next year they bought a lot on Franklin Street in the west end of the city for $240 and built a house on it.

Newton, who would become a famous educator after the war, took to his lessons instinctively. He was chosen as the class valedictorian at Eagle Street Grammar School and promoted to West High School. During the Secession crisis in 1861, Newton had begun training with the local cadets and Home Guards at the old Cuyahoga County Fairgrounds, which became Camp Taylor.

During this time, the family business was floundering and the boys were rapidly running out of money to continue their schooling and pay for their Cleveland house. Like most people in the North following the shocking April 13, 1861, Union surrender of Fort Sumter, they assumed that the war would be a short one. Because all three were experienced horsemen, having grown up in their father's lumber business – and Newton was an expert marksman – the prospects of earning good money in the service appealed to them.

In the wake of President Abraham Lincoln's call for 75,000 volunteers to put down the rebellion, the three Wolverton brothers approached the recruiters for the 50th New York Infantry who were in town looking for teamsters. While a soldier earned just $13 a month, teamsters were paid $25, and wagonmasters, which is what Alfred became as captain of a supply team of 100 six-horse teams, earned $40. Their combined income, then, was $90 a month, a significant wage for the period, which enabled them to send money home to help their father's struggling business interests and pay their Cleveland mortgage as well.

While most accounts have the brothers signing on as enlisted men, it is more likely that they joined as civilians under contract, a common pattern for teamsters at the time and an important adjunct to the ultimate success of the Northern forces. John Bessette, an American descendant of the Wolvertons who has researched the Compiled Military Records and other sources, concludes that they were almost certainly civilians under contract with the 50th New York. The history of this regiment coincides with the pattern of their experiences as described by Lois Darroch of Toronto, a granddaughter of Alonzo Wolverton, in her book *Four Who Went to the Civil War*. Bessette discovered that the unit arrived in Washington sometime before September 1861 and, by early 1862, had assumed mainly an engineering role, building bridges, repairing roads, and operating pontoon bridges. By October 1862 it had officially become the 50th New York Engineers, a title it retained for the duration of the war. In addition to deploying with different combat units in the field, the engineers, garrisoned near the Navy Yard in Washington, were engaged in a tremendous amount of military construction in and around the nation's capital, building the vast network of forts and batteries, as well as military camps for the numerous units stationed there and moving through the area.

Darroch, who bases much of her book on her extensive collection of family letters from the period, tells how Alfred was summoned to company headquarters outside Washington one night by Captain McCullough, handed a pistol and a rifle, and, despite his protests that he was a teamster and not a soldier, ordered to leave at midnight for a 6-mile horse ride through rain and mud to deliver a dispatch to the company's colonel. He arrived back in his camp about 2:30 a.m. In an August 31, 1861,

letter to his sister Rose, Alfred wrote: "The road was very dangerous and I was heavily armed. But a few nights afterwards nearly
a whole regiment was cut to pieces on the very same road." In a
letter to his father, Alfred wrote, "We still feel the war will be over
by Christmas and we can return to school."

They had reached Washington on August 24 and set up at
Camp Ross, about 5 miles from the capital on Bladensburg Road.
Alfred wrote that he and Newton were in good health, "but Jasper
has not been very well." A few weeks later, Jasper was taken to
hospital and, ten days later, he died of typhoid fever. An October
23, 1861, article in the *Cleveland Herald* called him "the best
scholar in the city . . . kind and affectionate to his friends, mod-
est in nature, and was respected by all who knew him as a model
young man."

Alonzo returned with Alfred after the funeral and, once
again, there were three Wolverton brothers serving as teamsters
with the Union. In a January 23, 1862, letter to Rose, Alfred complained: "We are frequently out in the rain long after night and
are thoroughly coated with ice by the time we reach camp. If we
had a comfortable place to go to after we get in it would not be
so bad." He said that Newton had been in hospital for three
weeks with a sore neck, but had since been released, adding, "We
have not received any money for the last two months but expect
to soon." In February, while Newton and Alonzo remained in
camp, Alfred was promoted to the Quartermaster's Department
in Washington located in Winder's Building on Seventh Street
opposite the War Department. In March he was offered a $50
bribe to approve a carload shipment of flour from Sloan's Mills
in Maryland – much of which, on his later inspection, turned out
to be mouldy. He not only turned down the bribe but signed a
rejection slip for the entire load.

Interest in the war reached a fever pitch in British North
America in November 1861, after what became known as the
Trent Affair, when the USS *San Jacinto* stopped the British mail

packet *Trent*, which was sailing from Havana to England, and arrested two Confederate diplomats and their secretaries who were on a diplomatic mission to England. The men were imprisoned in Boston, and the British, outraged by this breach of their sovereignty, demanded their release. In the meantime, as the prospect of war between Britain and the United States became frighteningly real, Canadian authorities called up the militia, and Britain dispatched some 14,000 officers and men to supplement the defence of the colonies in the event of war.

In the wake of this tension, and widespread agitation by many of President Lincoln's senior administration officials to wage war against Britain, Newton helped to organize a meeting of Canadians who were serving in the Union cause but who, like him, were worried about being caught in the middle between their duties for the North and their allegiance to Britain. In those days, Lincoln used to accept walk-in visitors at an office in the White House, and Newton, chosen as spokesman for the Canadian delegation, introduced himself and said: "We here are all Canadians. We are here to help in the war against slavery, but not to fight against either Canada or Britain. How serious is the danger of war with Britain, which would mean war with Canada?" Lincoln replied: "We are happy to have you Canadians helping the Northern cause and want you to stay. I am not in favour of war with either Britain or Canada. As long as I am president, there will be no such war, you may be sure of that. Good day, sir, and thank you for speaking up."[1]

In September 1862, about two weeks after the second Union defeat at Bull Run, Alonzo was assigned to drive a six-horse team to transport ammunition by the Porterstown Road to the artillery in General Ambrose Burnside's division.[2] It was a time of considerable action in the war. Early that month Union General George B. McClellan had defeated Confederate General Robert E. Lee at South Mountain and Crampton's Gap, but had not moved swiftly enough to save Harper's Ferry from being taken by

Confederate General Stonewall Jackson. Alonzo's assignment took him to Antietam Creek on September 17, the bloodiest single-day battle of the entire war, with 4,808 Union and Confederate deaths and 20,686 wounded. There was no clear winner, but because Lee withdrew to Virginia, McClellan claimed victory. This apparent turnaround in Union fortunes had another significant impact, of particular interest to the Wolvertons and to Canadians in general. Both Britain and France had been on the verge of formally recognizing the Confederacy, but, after Antietam, they decided to reserve their decisions. Lincoln, who had been holding back his preliminary Emancipation Proclamation, waiting for more encouraging results from the battlefields, was able to announce on September 22 that, effective January 1, 1863, all slaves in areas rebelling against the United States would be free.

Among the wounded at Antietam was Alonzo Wolverton, stabbed by a Confederate bayonet during the action around Bloody Lane. He spent the entire night lying semi-conscious on the ground before being found by some fellow teamsters in the morning. For a full week, Alfred and Newton did not know his fate. They were desperately searching hospitals in Washington hoping to find him among the wounded, and eventually Newton ran into Alonzo's friend Mose McBain, who had helped rescue Alonzo and was able to take the brothers to him. That February, Alonzo went back to Wolverton to recover.

In a letter in June to his father and sister Rose, Alfred wrote that Alonzo had written to them from Rolla, Missouri, where he had been sent by the quartermaster at St. Louis and was in charge of a wagon train and about forty men – at $60 per month – and was to start out the next morning for Springfield, about 300 miles southwest of St. Louis. That was the last letter Alfred would write. He contracted smallpox and died in Kaloramo Hospital on June 24, 1863. He was 24 years old. In a subsequent letter to Rose, Newton wrote: "Alfred is dead. He died about 11 o'clock last night. I saw him in the afternoon yesterday he seemed some better but when I went this morning he was dead. I cannot get his body under any circumstances whatever. He will be buried at the 'Soldier's Home' tomorrow. He died very easy. I can write no more now."

To protect others from infection, all smallpox victims were immediately put into rough wooden boxes. Alfred was no exception and was buried at Glenwood Cemetery in the paupers' burying ground, with no ceremony and a small board for a marker. In her account of the family, Darroch writes that Newton, just 17, bribed an undertaker to leave the cemetery gate unlocked that night. Four of the undertaker's employees, who, having recovered from smallpox, were immune to it, helped Newton recover Alfred's body, place it in a proper casket, and ship it to a plot he had purchased at Columbia Harmony Cemetery. After that, Newton decided to return home to Wolverton to help his father, leaving just one Wolverton, Alonzo, engaged directly in the war.

In January 1864 Alonzo took a train to Cleveland and volunteered as a private for the 20th Ohio Light Artillery. Even though he signed on for the low soldier's pay of $13 a month, he also received a $300 bounty, in $60 monthly instalments, for re-enlisting. Serving in the Army of the Cumberland (Tennessee/ Georgia), alongside his friend Joseph Fitzgerald, a Canadian farm boy from Millbrook, a town northeast of Toronto, he was soon promoted to corporal and assigned to the Commissary Department. He was subsequently captured at Dalton, Georgia, on October 13, 1864, after his company colonel agreed to a promise from Confederate General John Bell Hood, commander of the Army of Tennessee, that "all white officers and soldiers will be paroled in a few days." Black soldiers were sent south, with former slaves returned to their slave owners. Alonzo and his compatriots were lined up and forced to strip down to their underwear, then marched to Villanow, where, after signing a pledge not to bear arms against the Confederate States, they were paroled the next morning.

In a letter to Rose on December 4, 1864, in a camp 2 miles from Nashville, Alonzo said he had expected to be returning north but the government "would not recognize our parole so we were ordered to report for duty." He had rejoined his battery on November 6 at Pulaski, Tennessee, where they remained until the 23rd, when Hood flanked them and they were forced to evacuate the town. They marched to Columbia, fought for three days, and, still pursued by Hood, were again forced north, this time to Franklin, a small town that had been a Union military post since the fall of Nashville early in 1862. It is here that the Union decided to make a stand on November 30, resulting in a battle known as "The Gettysburg of the West," one of the few night battles of the war (fought between 4 and 9 p.m.) and also one of the bloodiest. Hood's ill-advised frontal assault against entrenched Union positions resulted in devastating losses for the Confederacy, thanks in part to the work of Montreal-born General Jacob Dolson Cox, commander of the 23rd Corps, Army of Ohio, and the Federal line commander during the battle. In just five hours of fighting the Confederates lost nearly 7,000 men, including six generals either dead or suffering mortal wounds, with some of their infantry units losing up to two-thirds of their men in vicious hand-to-hand fighting. The Union losses were about 2,300 men, with Major-General David Stanley, the corps commander, the only Union general injured.

In his post-battle letter to Rose, Alonzo wrote: "Our Battery was in the centre of the very hottest of the fight – we lost nearly half of our men and came out of the battle commanded by a sergeant . . . I never expected to come out alive but was fortunate. I was struck twice – once in the cheek – the ball just grazed my face and cut through the skin – it bled freely but did not amount to much, and once in the hip the ball cut through my pants, drawers and shirt and made a slight wound, but not enough but what I attend to my duty."[3]

Two weeks later, with the Union looking for white officers to command black regiments, Alonzo, now 21 years old, accepted a commission as a second lieutenant in Company D, 9th US Colored Heavy Artillery Regiment, at $75 a month. He was immediately involved in the successful Union battle against Hood at Nashville, this time effectively destroying his army and forcing the Confederate commander to flee the field down the Franklin turnpike. After the battle, with his company settled down in Nashville, Alonzo was again in charge of the commissary, where he served for the rest of the war. He was mustered out of the service on August 2, 1865, and returned to Wolverton, where he eventually married Helen McDonald and, together, they had six children. After his father's death, Alonzo took over the family business, changing the sawmill first to a grist mill and then to a flour mill. He also exported eggs and butter to England and, when the mill burned, he and his son J.G. Wolverton built an even larger mill and exported flour to both Cuba and Germany after the First World War. Alonzo applied for a U.S. government pension in January 1905, writing that he was "unable to earn a support by manual labor by reason of disability due to age," and, soon after, he began receiving $6 a month. By the time he died in 1925 his pension had reached $50 a month, and his widow received $30 a month until her death, at the age of 90, on October 11, 1939.

Although Newton returned from the war in 1863, it did not mark the end of his military experiences. While Alonzo was engaged in fighting Hood's forces in Tennessee, Newton volunteered for drilling and rifle practice with the Wolverton Rifle Company. This group, like several other volunteer militia groups, was responding to a Canadian government call stemming from the growing tensions between Britain and the United States, much of it caused by Confederate activity from Canada along the northern boundary. He spent some time stationed at Woodstock, Ontario, where he got to know Thomas Edison, who, long before he became famous, was working on the Grand Trunk Railroad trains in the area. After the war, during his frequent trips to Brantford as a supply Baptist preacher, Newton became friends with telephone inventor Alexander Graham Bell and sometimes assisted him with his work. Once he was allowed to speak over the famous 7-mile wire between Brantford and Paris, Ontario – the first long-distance wire in history.

Newton wrote to Alonzo on January 26, 1865, from LaPrairie, Canada East (Quebec), just 9 miles south of Montreal, to say he was now a private with No. 1 Company, Third Administrative Battalion, of the Canadian Volunteer Rifles. "The cause of this move (the militia call-up) is to put a stop to the raids which are conducted by Southern sympathisers for the purpose of bringing disturbances between the two government [sic] which would be the most effictual [sic] way of assisting the South."[4] They were paid 50 cents a day, plus board, and billeted in local hotels and private houses. On March 3 he again wrote to Alonzo and complained, "I was a fool for coming here at all for I could make as much if not more at home and besides be free."[5] A month later Newton was sent to Phillipsburg, just 2 miles from the Vermont border, and promoted to a full corporal, with a raise of 10 cents a day.

By chance, during his stay in Washington in 1863, Newton had lived for a time in a downtown boarding house where he had come to know a young actor named John Wilkes Booth. After Booth assassinated Lincoln, as the president watched the comedy *Our American Cousin* at Ford's Theater on April 14, 1865, American officials moved quickly to foil any attempt by Booth to escape to Canada, where he had spent considerable time leading up to the assassination. With records of the boarding house showing that Newton had also lived there, U.S. authorities contacted Canadian officials in Quebec City asking them to post Newton either at Niagara Falls or south of Montreal to "personally examine" every person crossing the border. He was to give particular attention to women, because Booth was an accomplished female impersonator in his theatrical roles. Newton was sent immediately to the Vermont border to begin his inspections, but Booth was shot long before he reached the Canadian border.

After the war, Newton worked as a journeyman carpenter in Wolverton and, in 1866, as a lieutenant in the 22nd Oxford Rifles during the Fenian Raids into Canada. The Fenians, radical Irish nationalists, were a ragtag army of Civil War veterans from both the North and the South who were initially, at least, aided and encouraged by President Andrew Johnson's administration. They actually launched three invasions against Canada from U.S. soil, first in 1866, then again in 1870 and 1871, believing that a victory over the British influence in British North America would win independence from Britain back home in Ireland. Newton, an expert enough sharpshooter to win a spot on the Canadian "Wimbledon" team (later changed to Bisley), was stationed for a year at Sarnia and then at Petrolia, where Canada's first oil wells had been struck in the 1850s.

Newton eventually returned to school, opting for the nearby Woodstock College because he couldn't afford the tuition in Cleveland. Later, he graduated from the University of Toronto with the highest honours in his class in mathematics and in five languages. In the summer of 1877 he was ordained a Baptist minister, and he rode by horse to different churches under his charge.

Destined to become one of Canada's foremost educators, Newton took over as principal of Woodstock College in 1880. He introduced new courses in astronomy, astronomical mathematics, and meteorology, and, despite protests from the board of directors that deviating from the classics was "undignified," he personally raised $10,000 and established the first manual training course in North America. He supervised the erection of the new manual training building and not only bought but installed the equipment needed for such trades as woodworking, black-smithing, and machine-shop work. He stepped down as principal in 1887 to run this department. In 1891 he became principal of Bishop's College in Marshall, Texas, a college for blacks, staying there for seven years. When he moved back to Canada, he headed west to Winnipeg, Manitoba, where he supplied churches, among them First Baptist Church. In 1899 he bought the old Clifford Sifton farm in Brandon, Manitoba, and became a successful farmer while also acting as treasurer of Brandon College. He moved again in 1906 to Nelson, British Columbia, and then to Vancouver, where he died at the age of 86 on January 31, 1932. His grandson, Harold Wolverton, lives in North Vancouver and remembers "Gramps" from the last years of his life. Even today, Newton's ceremonial sword hangs on his grandson's wall, a poignant reminder of a time long gone but still remembered.

TWO

Men at War

ON JULY 22, 1864, THE *Galt Reporter* published a letter sent eleven days earlier from Union Sergeant William Johnston in Washington to Mrs. A. Baird of Galt with the "distressing news" that her son Adam had been shot and killed on June 18. "He was quite sensible until the last moment," Johnston wrote. "He talked about his mother, and he wished me to write to you and tell you he would meet you in Heaven. I shed tears when he put his hand out to shake hands with me. We have been comrades for the last 16 months, with as much unity as any two brothers. He was a valiant little soldier as stood in the field. He was shot through the neck. I buried him about 9 o'clock that night. He is buried about 3 miles from Petersburg, and about 20 rods from the railroad. I would have wrote you sooner, but the day after Adam got shot I got shot through the right ancle [sic], which has since been amputated, and I have had a hard time of it, but am doing well now and trust soon to be able to see Canada, my native place."

Sadly, Baird's mother had died just a week before her son was shot fighting a foreign war. The *Reporter* wrote that young Baird "was very well known in Galt and neighborhood, having worked in the *Reporter* office for some time, and was a general favourite with his acquaintances. Poor fellow! Many a tear will rise unbidden when we think of his cheery laugh and hearty manner, and a sigh will arise at his sad fate when his name is mentioned."

It is impossible to know how many tears were shed throughout the length and breadth of British North America over the thousands of young men – some of them volunteers, many forced into service by unscrupulous predators – who left their homes and went off to war. Some went for the bounties, normally $200 or $300, but sometimes reaching $800 after Congress repealed commutation fees in 1864. In fact, the draft system was both unfair and inefficient. Because it allowed exemptions from service for a $300 commutation fee, only 7 percent of the men whose names were drawn for the draft actually served. At the same time, the war served as an irresistible draw for many young Canadians working for a few dollars a week. The chances of collecting this small fortune and returning home to buy a farm or pay off debts became particularly attractive in late 1864 or 1865, when it was clear the war would soon be over.

Not everyone went for the money, however. Canadian historian D.C. Bélanger in a booklet on Franco-Americans in the Civil War era[1] tells the story of Henri Césaire Saint-Pierre, later a judge and jurist in the Superior Court of Montreal, who joined the 76th New York Regiment and was active in the Grand Army of the Republic (the equivalent of today's Legion) out of his conviction to end slavery. Saint-Pierre believed that he and his comrades "were Christian soldiers fighting for a holy cause and, like the crusaders of old, who wielded their violent swords in their efforts to free their enslaved brethren moaning under the foot of a ruthless conqueror, we devoted all our courage, summed all our energy in the task of breaking to pieces the shackles by which three millions of human beings were kept in bondage."

Others, of course, went in search of old-fashioned adventure and the perennial pursuit of glory. Again, Bélanger recounts the experiences of the well-known French-Canadian journalist and writer Rémi Tremblay, who had moved with his family to Rhode Island at the age of 12 and later became a journalist and translator at the Canadian House of Commons. In his autobiographical

Civil War novel, *Un revenant. Épisode de la Guerre de Secession* (1884), Tremblay wrote that he had caught "war fever" as a young teenager. "[I] had witnessed the departure of the Woonsocket, R.I., company and was also present for the ovation they received upon their return [from the First Battle of Bull Run]. The spectacle of those brave men, their faces tanned by the Virginia sun, had gripped [my] imagination. The few injured men [I] had seen with their arm in a splint or walking with crutches inspired [me]. [I] believed that those soldiers who had lost their lives at Bull Run were martyrs to the cause of humanity. The dead, the injured and the survivors all seemed to be heroes. [I] would have enlisted immediately, but it was 1861 and [I] was only fourteen."

Two years after that, Tremblay left his job and his family and walked 72 miles from Contrecoeur, Quebec, to Rouse's Point, New York, and enlisted in the 14th United States Regular Infantry. During 18 months of service, writes Bélanger, Tremblay "would see very little money or glory, and plenty of misery." He fought at the battles at the Wilderness, Spotsylvania, and Cold Harbor and at the siege of Petersburg. He was captured and spent six months at the notorious Libby Prison in Richmond, Virginia. Paroled, then sent to a parole camp in Annapolis, Maryland, he went AWOL and fled back to Canada, where he fought as an officer in the Canadian Militia against the Fenians in 1866.

Young men in search of glory and excitement more often experienced what Bélanger characterizes as "the terror of battle contrasted severely with the monotony and boredom of camp life, with its endless and tedious drills and reviews as well as dirty, leaky and cold tents. Long marches carrying forty pounds of equipment, food shortages, contaminated water, parasites, improper nutrition, sanitation, lodging and medical care all weakened the troops' health and morale. Wearing the same uniform year-round, troops baked in the summer and froze in the winter. While the Union soldier was better fed than his Confederate counterpart, on the whole, the diet was utterly deficient. He lacked fresh meat, fruits and vegetables. Improper treatment of the wounded and the sick made soldiers fear the doctor. In fact, disease claimed twice as many Civil War soldiers as combat. In an era where germs were unknown to medical science, measles, especially in winter, malaria, venereal disease, dysentery, and the deadly typhoid fever were the soldier's worst enemies."

Despite these hardships, of course, thousands of Canadians came back alive, although many, like Sergeant Johnston, lost arms or legs or suffered other serious injuries in the fighting. Thousands more died, perhaps as many as 5,000, and were buried, usually in makeshift graves, under U.S. soil.

Most serious historians dispute the oft-repeated claim by Civil War buffs that some 50,000 Canadians served in that war – it's more likely about half that number. Still, there is no doubt that, whatever the precise number, many thousands of Canadians were directly involved in the fighting, largely for the Union, but not exclusively so. Record-keeping being what it was, though, it's impossible to say. What is known for certain is that four Canadian-born men became Union generals and twenty-nine won the U.S. Medal of Honor for outstanding acts of bravery. On the other extreme, eighteen Canadians were executed for a variety of crimes following capital court-martial trials.

The Medal of Honor wasn't created until the war was under way, being approved by Congress in December 1861 and applying only to enlisted men of the U.S. Navy and Marine Corps. Two months later, however, the Senate extended eligibility to include enlisted men of the U.S. Army, retroactive to the beginning of the war, and on March 3, 1863, army officers also became eligible. (Naval and marine officers, in contrast, didn't become eligible until 1915.)

The medal, intended to parallel England's Victoria Cross or Germany's Iron Cross, was for men who distinguished themselves by their "gallantry in action, and other soldier-like qualities." It was the only medal at the time that the United States awarded its armed services, and, as a result, some 1,500 were handed out. Congress tightened the eligibility rules in 1916. It also created a board of five retired generals to review all the previous medal recipients, and 911 of them, mostly Civil War veterans, had their names struck from the list.

Toronto-born Corporal John P. McVeane of Company D, 49th New York Infantry, was not among the men eliminated from the honour roll. According to Canadian Civil War historian Tom Brooks, McVeane was just 18 years old when he enlisted on August 21, 1861, at Buffalo. He was mustered in as a sergeant, but reduced to a private on November 18, 1962. Two months later he was promoted to corporal.

On May 4, 1863, at the battle of Salem Church at Fredericksburg Heights, Virginia, the colour-bearer of the 58th Virginia Infantry was wounded and dropped the standard. McVeane, at considerable risk to his own life, managed to recapture both the bearer and the colours. In the process he shot a Confederate colour-bearer and seized the flag and, all alone, approached a barn between the lines, demanding and receiving the surrender of several Confederate soldiers who were hiding inside. As a result of his heroism, McVeane was again promoted to sergeant and then, on October 16, 1863, to second lieutenant. On Christmas Day, 1863, he re-enlisted as a veteran volunteer, but on May 10, 1864, during the Battle of the Wildnerness, McVeane became the first Canadian of the 49th New York to die in battle.

In a short history of the 49th, Brooks writes that, of the 1,312 men in the 2nd Buffalo Regiment, sixty, or 5 percent of the total, were born in British North America, most of them being from Toronto, Hamilton, Queenston, and Niagara, although some came from as far away as Windsor, Chatham, Aurora, Whitby, and Kingston. In addition, four of them came from Canada East (Quebec) and one from New Brunswick. Twenty-five of the men enlisted in the late summer or fall of 1861 and only two of those – Torontonian Michael Fitzpatrick of Company C and Robert H. Taylor of St. George – survived four years of war intact to muster out with the regiment on June 27, 1865. Fifteen joined the regiment in mid-summer 1864, three of them as paid substitutes for Americans who did not want to serve.

One of those early recruits into the 49th who didn't survive the war was a prominent bookseller, Erastus D. Holt, a partner in the firm Campbell, Holt & Angell at 44 King St. E., Hamilton, who may have served briefly with a Massachusetts Militia regiment before joining the 49th New York as a 29-year-old first lieutenant in September 1861. He was promoted to captain on November 10, 1862, and then to lieutenant-colonel in August 1864, becoming the 49th's new commander. Holt and the 49th fought at many of the most famous, and bloodiest, battles of the war, including Malvern Hill, Antietam, Fredericksburg, Gettysburg, the Wilderness, Cedar Creek, and finally at Petersburg, where on April 2, 1865, just one week before General Robert E. Lee surrendered to General Ulysses S. Grant at Appomattox, he was severely wounded and died five days later.

Nearly half of these Canadian recruits were farmers or unskilled labourers – although there were eighteen skilled tradesmen – and more than half were 21 years old or younger. Seven of the sixty died in the war, and seven more were wounded, meaning they had one chance in five of being hit by a Confederate bullet. Six were taken prisoner, including John Dougherty of Company C, the only New Brunswicker in the regiment. He and John C. White of Hamilton were captured at Spotsylvania on May 12, 1864. White lived to tell about it, but Dougherty died of dysentery at the notorious Andersonville prisoner-of-war camp that August and is buried in grave 4650 in the National Cemetery there.

On the flip side, eleven of the sixty Canadians in the 49th deserted, one of them in 1863 while the regiment was headed towards Gettysburg. Two others were dishonourably discharged, one of them Perry Johnson of Company I, who, while home on sick leave, stole a horse and was caught, convicted, and sentenced to three-and-a-half years of hard labour.

Four British North Americans won Medals of Honor on the same day – August 5, 1864 – during the critical naval engagement of the Battle of Mobile Bay. Many historians see this battle as the beginning of the end for the Confederacy because it marked the first substantial success of General Grant's overall strategy to save Lincoln's troubled presidency by a military victory, rather than buckling under to growing pressure for a negotiated peace. Jack Friend, a management consultant in Mobile and the author of a history on the battle, wrote in the *Mobile Register*: "In a broader sense, the battle influenced the course of naval history well into the 20th century. It was the first engagement in which all the new technological developments of modern warfare were present: iron ships, sloping armor, rifled guns, explosive shells, revolving turrets, twin propellors and mines."

William Pelham of Halifax was a landsman aboard the flagship USS *Hartford*, a 220-foot screw sloop-of-war carrying forty-two guns and a crew of 304, under the command of the Glasgow-born flag officer David G. Farragut, the first admiral of the U.S. Navy. Farragut would gain fame in that battle by lashing himself near the top of the mainsail so he could see over the smoke of the battle and rally his men to victory by shouting "Damn the torpedoes! Full speed ahead!" During the heavy fighting against Fort Morgan, several rebel gunboats, and the famous Confederate ram *Tennessee*, Pelham's colleagues on his gun crew were either killed or wounded under intense enemy shellfire. Pelham, however, showed no fear but calmly helped to take the casualties below deck, then returned voluntarily and took his post at an adjoining gun, where yet another man had been struck down, and continued to fire his gun throughout the remainder of the battle. His Canadian colleague, 27-year-old coxwain Thomas Fitzpatrick, as captain of the number one gun aboard the *Hartford*, was struck in the face several times by splinters. When his gun was disabled by a rebel shell that landed between the two forward 9-inch guns, killing and wounding fifteen men, Fitzpatrick quickly had the gun in working order again, helped clear the area of the dead and wounded, and resumed fighting, acting, as his citation later said, "as an inspiration to the members of his crew" and contributing to the successful capture of the *Tennessee*.

Most Canadians who enlisted were from ordinary working families, predominantly farm families, reflecting the rural nature of the country at the time. But there were a few exceptions. Frederick Howe, for example, enlisted in the war and was severely wounded while serving in Sheridan's Cavalry. He was a privileged son of Nova Scotia firebrand Joseph Howe, the prominent politician and newspaper editor who led the fight for Nova Scotia to become the first self-governing colony in the British Empire (1848) and served as its premier from 1860 to 1863. Howe fought relentlessly against Canadian Confederation, but, after losing that battle, later served in Sir John A. Macdonald's Cabinet. Shortly before his death in 1873, he was appointed as Nova Scotia's lieutenant-governor.

Then there was Major David B. Bridgford, whose father, a British military officer, was lieutenant-governor of Upper Canada. Bridgford, a merchant shipper before the war, joined the Confederate 1st Virginia Battalion – nicknamed the "Irish Battalion" because of the large number of Irish immigrants who enlisted – as captain in April 1861. A month later he became commander of Company B and, in October 1862, was promoted to major and commander of the battalion. From June 1863 he served as an acting provost marshal after General Lee ordered the battalion to occupy the honoured position of Provost Guard of the Army of Northern Virginia, a position it maintained right up to the surrender of Lee's army at the Appomattox Court House on April 9, 1865. While Bridgford watched his general surrender there, another Canadian, Private John McEachern, was among sixteen soldiers serving as General Grant's honour guard at Appomattox, watching him accept Lee's surrender, and 22-year-old Alonzo H. Pickle, a native of Farnham, Quebec, after three years with the 1st Minnesota Infantry, was on picket duty outside the courthouse.

Another Canadian, Private John A. Huff of Company E, 5th Michigan Cavalry, gained considerable fame by shooting and mortally wounding the famous Confederate General J.E.B. Stuart during the Union victory at the Battle of Yellow Tavern, Virginia, on May 11, 1864. Huff, born in 1816 in Holland's Landing, Upper Canada, later moved to Michigan. A crack shot, he served with Borden's Sharpshooters before his transfer to the 5th Michigan Cavalry. His fame was short-lived: seventeen days after shooting Stuart, Huff was wounded at the Battle of Haw's Shop, Virginia, and eventually died of his wounds.

Two prominent Canadian editors – Augustus Toplady Freed and John Robson Cameron, both of whom, at different times, became editor the *Hamilton Spectator* – also fought in the Northern armies. Freed, a renowned author and orator, was born in Beamsville, near Hamilton, on October 8, 1835, and became an apprentice – or a "printer's devil" as it was called – at a Dundas print shop before beginning his journalism career as a reporter with the *Hamilton Banner*, a corporate organ founded to promote the interests of the Great Western Railway beginning in 1854. A well-read man, Freed became city editor and founded the *Literary Garland*, a publication dedicated to the poetic arts, eventually taking a job at the *Spectator* and then, in 1859, at Horace Greeley's *New York Tribune*. In 1862 Freed was offered a $300 bounty to take the place of a wealthy New Englander and he immediately accepted. Soon he found himself marching off to war with the 27th New Haven Regiment and fighting in several significant battles, including both Fredericksburg and

Gettysburg, without receiving any serious injuries. At the end of the war Freed went to Chicago to work at Lakeside Press, which was owned by an old friend, R.R. Donnelley of Hamilton. He returned to New York in 1871, but soon took a senior editorial job at the *Spectator*, only to return to New York in 1874 when the *New York Times* offered him a job. He again went to Chicago, then back to Hamilton, where, in 1880, he was associate editor of the *Spectator*. A year later he became editor, a position he held with distinction until his death in 1892.

Cameron, whose grandfather had emigrated from Scotland to Lanark County in Canada West in 1816, was born in Perth, Canada West, on April 19, 1845. His mother's half-brother, also named John Cameron, became the ninth premier of British Columbia. He, too, became a "printer's devil" and moved to Detroit, where, at the outbreak of the war, he joined the Union Army. Little is known about his actual experiences other than that he survived the war to become one of Canada's most prominent newspapermen. He founded the *Winnipeg Free Press* after he went to Manitoba with the 1st Ontario Rifles as part of the expeditionary force sent to the west to suppress the Red River Resistance in 1870. Métis leader Louis Riel had established the Republic of Manitoba, and Sir Garnet Joseph Wolseley, a distinguished British soldier who had been sent to Canada in 1861 over fear that the Civil War might lead to an American invasion of Canada, was assigned the task of putting down the insurgents. Because of his Civil War experience, Cameron became General Wolsley's aide-de-camp. He didn't see much fighting, but when he was mustered out in Winnipeg, he and a friend founded the *Free Press*. He went on to gain considerable notice through his humorous column "Noremac," which is Cameron spelled backwards. In 1883 he returned to Ontario, joined the *Spectator*, took over as editor-in-chief in 1894, two years after Freed's death, and held the post until he died on December 29, 1907.

Another prominent Hamiltonian involved in the war was Dr.

William D. Winer, whose father, John, moved to the city from Durham, New York, in 1830 and established a successful pharmacy. After graduating from the University of Toronto in 1851, Winer went to New York, where he passed his examination before the Medical Board and was appointed to the State Hospital, where he held the post of senior house surgeon. Three years later Winer went to Paris and studied at Imperial College. He moved to Chicago in 1856 and, according to a June 21, 1865, item in the *Chicago Journal* announcing his appointment as surgeon of the 23rd Illinois Infantry, he had made "quite a reputation in this city."

The 23rd, another "Irish Brigade," had been formed under the command of Colonel Mulligan in Chicago. Winer was formally mustered in on June 15, 1861, and, a month later, moved on to Jefferson City and then to Lexington, Missouri, where the garrison, with Mulligan in charge, was attacked by the Missouri State Guard under Confederate General Sterling Price. During the subsequent siege, which ended in the surrender of the 23rd, the brigade suffered 107 casualties – a setback that no doubt kept Winer busy tending wounds and amputating limbs. The regiment, including Winer, was then marched to Arkansas and paroled. It was mustered out by General John C. Fremont, but then reassembled by General George McClellan at Camp Douglas in Chicago. Winer's role after this time is uncertain, but it appears that he went back to civilian medicine and continued his practice until his death in Chicago in the early 1870s.

Of all the Hamiltonians who served in the war – and the city produced relatively prodigious numbers – Dr. Winer's nephew, William Winer Cooke, was likely the most famous. His lasting fame came eleven years after the war ended, on June 25, 1876, when he was regimental adjutant, or right-hand man, to Lieutenant-General George C. Custer in the battle against Sioux leader Crazy Horse at Little Big Horn. Celebrated as "Custer's Last Stand," it is one of the most famous battles in American history. Here the 31-year-old adventurer was one of the 264 soldiers of the U.S. 7th Cavalry – and about fourteen Canadians, mostly Civil War veterans as well – who died fighting. Born in Brantford, one of four sons of Dr. Alexander Cooke and his wife, Cooke was sent to Hamilton to live with his grandfather John Winer, a city alderman and owner of a successful wholesale drug firm at 56 King Street East, after the school he attended in the Brantford suburb of Mount Pleasant burned down. After attending Central School in Hamilton, Cooke returned home when Nelles Academy, a private school for young men, was built on his grandfather's farm. At 14 he went to a private school in Buffalo, New York, and in 1863, just 17, he enlisted in the 24th New York Cavalry, claiming to be 22, and quickly displayed his talents as a crack shot and skilled horseman. In April 1864 he joined the 9th Army Corps under General Ambrose E. Burnside and fought in several engagements in the Battle of the Wilderness around Richmond. He ended up in hospital that June after being injured in the leg at Petersburg. After returning to the Army of the Potomac, Cooke served two months as commissary of subsistence and later was put in charge of a commissary depot, but he rejoined his regiment in Sheridan's Cavalry Corps at the Battle of Five Forks.

After being mustered out as first lieutenant in June 1865, Cooke moved back to Brantford, but in October 1866 he was commissioned second lieutenant of the 7th Cavalry. Custer, at the time, was second in command. Cooke's mother, Augusta, had friends in high places, including President Andrew Johnson, and, in May 1868, she wrote to him, thanking him for his promise the previous day to look into her son's military record. When Custer, who had become Cooke's personal friend, recommended the young man for a captaincy – and Cooke applied on his own behalf to Secretary of War Edwin Stanton – General Grant said many other officers were more qualified for promotion than Cooke. Once President Johnson intervened on his behalf, however, Cooke became captain, major, and lieutenant-colonel by brevet, or honorary promotion, and from then on the War Department addressed him as lieutenant-colonel.

Cooke also had the distinction to write the last message sent by Custer, a plea to Captain F.W. Benteen, commander of troop H, several miles from the 4,000 Sioux warriors who were closing in on Custer: "Benteen. Come on. Big Village. Be Quick. Bring Packs. P.S. Bring Packs. W.W. Cooke." The message – now displayed in the library of the U.S. Military Academy at West Point – was given by Cooke to orderly trumpeter John Martin, who, riding off to find Benteen, took one last look back at Custer. He was the only witness, other than the Sioux, to the massacre. Cooke's body was found next to Custer's. Both had been stripped naked, and Cooke, noted for his flowing Dundreary whiskers, had been scalped twice – once for his hair, the other for his beard.

Cooke was buried on the battlefield, then exhumed and reburied in June 1877 in the Little Big Horn Battlefield National Cemetery. Finally, that August, his body was exhumed again and reburied in plot 63, Christ Church Section, of the Hamilton Cemetery.

In 1889 Colonel William Monaghan, a veteran of Hay's Brigade, 5th Louisiana, under Confederate General Jubal A. Early, was sent to Hamilton as U.S. consul, replacing another former Confederate officer, Captain Albert Roberts of Tennessee. Monaghan was instrumental in forming the Hamilton branch of the Grand Army of the Republic, Post 472, which was named in honour of William Winer Cooke. Beginning in 1891, and running well into the next century, members of the post honoured their fallen and deceased comrades each May 30 on "Decoration Day." It was common in both the northern and the southern United States to hold a solemn prayer service that day and to decorate the graves of the soldiers with wreaths.

On May 29, 1983, 106 years after his death, the *Hamilton Spectator* reported on a ceremony marking both the erection of a new headstone in Hamilton Cemetery for Cooke and the 100th anniversary of the first Memorial Day ceremony in that city – a practice that had been suspended for the previous forty years. "With a chorus of trumpets sounding The Last Post, and a lone piper wailing his lament, the memory of Colonel William Winer Cooke of Hamilton and other Canadian volunteers in American war history was rekindled," wrote staff reporter Gerry Nott, thanks largely to the efforts of Burlington historian-writer George Kush and Ranson Cooke, a great-nephew of Colonel Cooke. According to Kush, 250 Civil War veterans "are buried within a mile of this location in unmarked graves. It's a sad and unfortunate case."

The Civil War Web site produced by Private Church & Friends from the Ottawa Valley American Civil War Re-enactment Society tells the story of a family from Montreal. Five men – a father, two sons, and two first cousins – enlisted, two of whom died of their wounds. It began with Robert Gibson, a man who loved his booze, getting drunk with a group of "friends" on a business trip to Pittsburgh. Apparently thinking it a good idea at the time, he staggered off to join the 46th Regiment of Pennsylvania Volunteers, Company B, leaving behind his wife and children. When his two sons George and Joseph heard that their father had been killed in January 1863 at Harper's Ferry, they decided to enlist. George joined the 96th New York Volunteers, Company K, and was killed in March 1864. His two cousins, Thomas and William Moore, also joined the 96th New York Infantry, Company K, after William and his father found Thomas at the train station and tried to talk him out of enlisting. But Thomas was determined to fight, so William decided to go along with him. Both men, apparently, survived the war.

So, too, did Joseph Gibson, whose father and brother died in the conflict. He enlisted with the 16th New York Heavy Artillery and later transferred to the 1st New York Mounted Rifles. Although he was wounded twice, he was honourably discharged in August 1865 at Lynchburg, Virginia, and returned home to Montreal, where he lived until he was 80 years old.

On April 19, 1862, the *London Free Press* published a letter from Sergeant Jim Oates of the 9th Illinois Volunteers to his brother Joseph in London.

> Dear Brother:
>
> Before this reaches you, you will have received news of the battle of Pittsburgh Landing . . . I came through without a scratch, and am well at present . . . Sunday morning at 8 o'clock we did not know that the enemy were advancing. In our camp we were all busy cleaning up for weekly inspection . . . the first notion we had was the booming of cannon. In less than five minutes we were in line and ready to move to any part of the lines. We were not kept waiting long. The attack was so unexpected that several regiments were driven out of their camps before they could form, and the oldest and best regiments were sent out to hold the enemy in check.
>
> Our regiment engaged about 10 o'clock, and in less than an hour we lost one-third of our men, when we had to retreat. About two o'clock we again formed and went in, and were again driven back; when we fell back, I was the only officer left in our company.
>
> Both our lieutenants were wounded; the only sergeant besides myself was wounded. Our captain resigned some time ago and now I am the only one left in charge of the company . . . our company suffered less than any in the regiment as the regiment loss in killed is 61; wounded, 237; missing, I cannot state yet.
>
> Two strangers belonging to an Ohio regiment joined our company in the morning as they could not find their regiment . . . they were both killed, and will be reported missing from their own regiment, and their friends will not know what became of them. I could not

find anything on them to show who they were; when I was burying our boys, I buried them in the same grave.

I have been over a large part of the battlefield for two days; it is a hard looking sight; on some parts of the field I could count the bodies of hundreds without moving from one place. Several of the boys belonging to our regiment were set on fire by shells, and partly burned when we came to bury them.

We were badly whipped on Sunday, and if General Buell had not come up with reinforcements at the time he did, there would have been a defeat instead of a victory for the North . . . our regiment raised last fall was considered one of the finest raised in Illinois, but sickness and the fight at Donelson and here have nearly cleaned us all out . . . There are three companies out of ten where there is not an officer left to command them . . . I think you will yet see me back to Canada safe, as Beauregard, the Southern champion, has proved himself not to be invincible . . .

Your brother, Jim Oates.

Most Canadians likely aren't aware that, when they sing "O Canada," the national anthem, there is a direct connection to the Civil War. Calixa Lavallée, born in Verchères, Quebec, in 1842, moved with his family to Rhode Island in 1857 and then ran off to join a minstrel show in New Orleans. When the war broke out, he joined the 4th Rhode Island Regiment as a first-class trumpeter. Musicians, early in the war, were considered by the Union Army as a particularly important component of morale building. In an era before radio, television, or even gramophones, live music was the main public entertainment, and, when not marching, the regimental bands regularly gave concerts for the troops.

In 1861 each regiment was authorized to form a band, and in

September that year Lavallée, destined to become one of this country's most famous composers, enlisted. By mid-1862, however, with the war not going as well as hoped, the War Department cut back on regimental bands and Lavallée was transferred to combat duty. He was wounded in the leg at Antietam and given a full discharge. After the war ended, Lavallée moved back and forth between Canada and the United States, becoming one of the leading musicians of the day. Like many Americans at the time – and some Canadians, too – Lavallée believed that the United States should simply annex Canada. Lavallée is not a Canadian historical figure because of his war experiences or his political beliefs, however, but rather because he composed the music for "O Canada" in 1882. He died in Boston in 1891, aged 49, but his remains were brought to Montreal in 1933.

On September 25, 1861, the *Hamilton Spectator* published the following item:

> OFF TO THE WARS – We understand that some half dozen young men belonging to this city started for the States last night, with the intention of enlisting in the Northern army. It is a pity that any British subject should be so foolish and wicked as to interfere in a quarrel which does not concern them; but we expect that before they are three months in the army, they will be tired enough of its discipline, and be asking their friends to apply to Lord Lyons for their discharge. It is said that they are to join the regiment now being raised by Col. Rankin, in which one of the party has obtained a cornetcy. If this be so, and there is little doubt of the fact, it shows that Rankin has already commenced his operations to recruit in this Province, and the proper authorities ought, therefore, to look after him at once.

The reference here was to 50-year-old Arthur Rankin, an

overzealous politician from Windsor, Ontario, who recruited 683 men into a cavalry regiment, led them across the border to Detroit, and established the lst Michigan Lancers. The problem was that Rankin was an elected member of parliament for Essex, Canada West, and, since Britain had declared herself neutral, the last thing she wanted was any official from the colonies taking an active part in the conflict. Rankin's initiative immediately caused a flap in Quebec City, and he was charged with violating the British *Foreign Enlistment Act* of 1818, which made it illegal for British subjects to serve in or recruit for foreign armies, and also made it a criminal offence for foreigners to recruit British subjects. In addition, U.S. law made foreign recruiting illegal, and the War Department's General Order No. 45 in July 1861 – which was quickly rescinded and rarely enforced – banned the acceptance of recruits who did not speak English.

If officials on both sides of the border really meant to enforce those laws, they would be extremely busy. Rankin recognized the situation for what it was and, for a time, it appeared as though he was determined to lead his regiment into battle against the Confederacy. That notion had wide support in some circles. On October 5, for example, the Toronto *Globe* ran a previously published story about Rankin written by the Detroit correspondent for the *Milwaukee Daily Wisconsin*, describing Rankin as "a member of the Canadian Parliament, of great military experience in the British army, a gentleman of high social position and indomitable energy of character." It continued:

> He has been specially commissioned by the Secretary of War to raise, equip, and put in the field as quickly as possible, a regiment of Lancers, 1,600 strong. He has unlimited authority almost in furnishing the equipage and armament, as also in officering the battalion. He is authorized to proceed at once to Europe to purchase whatever can be procured there.

This will be one of the most splendid regiments on the continent when fully armed and drilled. It will be officered by men of known courage and experience. An officer of the U.S. army remarked to me today that he had rather be a private in this regiment of Lancers, under such Colonel as Arthur Rankin, than a First Lieutenant in a volunteer regiment of infantry. The Lieut. Colonel, J.W. Tilman, of Detroit, is a gentleman of considerable experience, and one of the most prominent businessmen in that city. The arms of the private consist of a formidable lance about 16 feet long, which is stepped in a strong socket attached to the saddle, a sabre, and a dragoon revolver with 300 yards.

A charge at full gallop of such a brigade upon infantry must be terrible – irresistible! The soldier, with his revolver in his left hand, his sabre in his right, guiding his lance mainly with his leg, and horse under good training, can deal out death upon the front and each flank at the same time. The recruiting for this regiment is going on rapidly, and it is thought that the quota will be doubled. Volunteers are flocking in rapidly from Canada, as our neighbors are anxious to serve under so well-known and popular an officer as Col. Rankin . . . The men if they desire it can furnish their own horses, and will be allowed to pay for the same at the rate of 40 cents per day, or $146 per year! Eight dollars per month, or $96 per year is also allowed for forage for horses when it is not furnished by Government. If not, the Government will furnish horses. The Lancers [will] be the crack regiment of the army.

Rankin formally enlisted for a three-year stint on September 4, 1861, and, despite the controversy, continued to raise "Rankin's Lancers." The October 18 *Hamilton Spectator* editorialized that Rankin, also an officer with the Great Southern Railway, "reached the height of folly in taking service under a foreign government, while a member of the British Legislature, a Magistrate, and the colonel of a military district. His idea of serving under two governments is probably the strangest that any man ever entertained; yet he is foolish enough to persist in saying that it is correct." Rankin proposed to serve in the U.S. Army and retain his seat in Parliament. The *Spectator* argued that he couldn't serve a foreign country "without violating his allegiance to his own country," and said charges should be brought against him by Canadian officials.

Rankin finally gave up his scheme, resigning on December 7, when diplomatic pressure made the Americans realize it wasn't worth the trouble. His unit was disbanded in March 1862, and most of the volunteers went to other Michigan regiments. The January 31, 1862, *Galt Reporter* published a letter dated January 16 from Colonel George D. Rugles, assistant adjutant general in Washington, ordering Rankin's Lancers to be "immediately mustered out of service." The *Detroit Advertiser* said the disbanded 800 Lancers were "as fine a body of men . . . as have been enlisted . . . It is hoped that their services will not be lost to the country."

In his booklet on Franco-Americans in the Civil War era, Bélanger cites various estimates ranging from 20,000 to 40,000 for Franco-Americans in the Civil War, concluding, sensibly, that it's really impossible to arrive at a specific conclusion. Those numbers include both French Canadians and French-speaking Americans, often of Canadian birth, who were living in the United States at the time. In 1860 the U.S. Census shows that 37,420 Franco-Americans lived in six northeastern states – Maine, New Hampshire, Vermont, Massachusetts, Rhode Island, and Connecticut – a number that nearly tripled over the next decade to 103,500, after French Canadians left their farms, forests, and quarries and headed for the industrial centres of New England in search of higher-paying jobs. French Canadians weren't the only colonists heading south during those years. By 1870 almost half a million Americans had been born in British North America.

Even those who weren't fighting were often directly affected by the war, especially by its impact on the American labour pool. As thousands of American draft dodgers, deserters, Copperheads, and escaped Confederate prisoners fled into Canada, wages in the northern provinces were driven down. In the United States, writes Bélanger, "the American leather and wool industries flourished in response to the military's endless demand for shoes, belts, harnesses, uniforms and blankets." And with so many young men fighting, the growth industries were desperate for workers, attracting thousands of Canadians from 1863 to the end of the war. One of these Canadians was Alfred Bessette of St-Grégoire-d'Iberville, Quebec, who got a job in a New England textile plant in 1865. Bélanger writes: "Orphaned at the age of twelve, he had come to the United States in order to escape desperate poverty. Bessette would return to Quebec in 1867 and join the Congregation of the Holy Cross as Brother André. He would go on to become Canada's most important faith healer and was beatified by Pope John Paul II in 1982. Today, Montreal's St. Joseph's Oratory, North America's only major urban shrine and an important pilgrimage site, stands as a testament to Brother André's intense spirituality."

While women of the era suffered extraordinary hardships from the war, the actual fighting, with a few exceptions, was strictly a male domain. Again, nobody is certain how many male impersonators there were among the soldiers – most historians estimate about 400 – but one of the more famous women who dressed as a man and enlisted was a New Brunswick farm girl named Sarah Emma Edmondson, later known as Emma Edmonds. She spent two years in the army as Frank Thompson and was the only woman soldier of the Civil War to receive a full army pension.

Born in 1841 on the family farm in the rural settlement of Magaguadavic, near Fredericton, one of five girls and a boy, she was an accomplished rider, crack shot, and strong swimmer by her early teens, but her tyrannical father – embittered that his only son was an epileptic – made life miserable for Emma and her mother alike. She recalled later that, when she was 9 years old, a peddler gave her a book on the adventures of Fanny Campbell, a teenage girl who disguised herself as a man and went on all sorts of adventures.

At 15, when her father announced that he had arranged for her to marry an older man, Emma ran off to live and work with a family friend making ladies' hats. Within a year she was co-owner of a Moncton millinery shop, but when her father found out where she was he demanded that she return home. Instead, she fled to Saint John, cropped her hair, stained her face a darker shade, put on a man's suit, and, as Frank Thompson, became an itinerant Bible salesman.

By 1861 she was selling Bibles in Flint, Michigan. When President Lincoln called for volunteer troops, she enlisted with a group of her male friends. At the time, there were no physical examinations: basically, if a recruit appeared to be alive, that met the standard required. But Emma – called the "beardless boy" by one officer – was at first turned down because, at 5 foot 6 inches, she fell just below the army's height requirement. A couple of weeks later, however, even that standard was reduced, and on May 25, 1861, she became Private Frank Thompson, Company F, 2nd Michigan Volunteer Infantry Regiment.

Nobody expected a woman to enlist, so the thought likely never occurred to a recruiting officer or anybody else. Many of the young recruits also qualified as beardless boys, so her complexion did not raise any suspicions. Nor did her loose-fitting uniform, because that style was not unusual, or the fact that she slept fully clothed and bathed in her undergarments, or wandered into the woods to take care of her personal needs. All these habits were common among soldiers in the field in those days, and they helped her to keep her remarkable secret.

Emma Edmonds's gender wasn't discovered until several years after the war, when she was trying to qualify for a pension. Even her 1864 best-selling book, *Nurse and Spy in the Union Army: The Adventures and Experiences of a Woman in Hospitals, Camps, and Battle-Fields*, a fictionalized account of her experiences as a soldier and a spy which sold an extraordinary 175,000 copies, was written from the perspective of a female nurse, making no mention of her disguise. There is little doubt that she grossly exaggerated her efforts as a spy, though her stories make for good reading, and she donated the proceeds to a charity providing relief for soldiers at the front. Still, despite the fact that no records exist to verify her spying exploits, the publicity she generated with this and a second book she wrote was enough to convince some people, and Emma Edmonds was inducted into the United States Military Intelligence Hall of Fame and the State of Michigan Woman's Hall of Fame in 1988. She was also elected to New Brunswick's Hall of Fame in 1990.

After a short basic training, she was assigned as a male nurse and postman for her brigade, and she served for a time as an aide to Colonel Orlando Poe, who would later testify that "her sex was not suspected by me or anyone else in the regiment." Her first experience with war was a bloody one, the Union rout at Bull Run on July 21, 1861, and she wrote later that "that extraordinary march from Bull Run (i.e., the Union retreat), through rain, mud and chagrin, did more toward filling the hospitals than did the battle itself." She also fought at Second Bull Run, Fredericksburg, and Antietam, and, according to her version of events, when a Union spy was caught and hanged, she volunteered to take his place, convincing a panel of high-ranking officers that she was suited to the task. She entered a Confederate camp at Yorktown, posing as a slave answering to the name "Cuff," having shaved her head, blackened her skin with silver nitrate, and put on a plantation suit and curly black wig. Moving about the camp as a water bearer, she heard a familiar voice one day and recognized a peddler, who regularly visited Union lines to sell newspapers and who was now describing the Northern camp in detail. Emma later said: "He was a fated man from that moment. His life was not worth three cents."

She managed to slip away into the darkness after three days, but not before making a rough sketch of the enemy fortifications which, she says, helped General McClellan successfully bombard the rebels, forcing them to abandon the camp. Another time she sneaked across enemy lines as an Irish immigrant woman, and, in March 1863, disguised as a Kentucky lad, she went to Louisville. Coming across a wedding, where the bridegroom was a rebel captain looking for recruits, she was immediately conscripted after stopping to ask for some food.

The next day, dressed as a Confederate soldier, the captain left Louisville in search of some Yankees. It didn't take long and, when a fight broke out between the rebels and the Union cavalry, Emma Edmonds rode her horse across to the Union side, where she was recognized. The captain charged directly towards her, his sabre drawn, and Emma calmly shot him in the face. She was praised for her efforts but stopped from spying in the area for fear of being recognized. She also claims, on another occasion, to have shot a Confederate farm wife through the hand after the woman had shot at her first.

In late 1863 Emma Edmonds went AWOL. While posted at a military hospital near Vicksburg, Mississippi, she explained, she contracted malaria, but couldn't seek treatment without having her gender discovered. So she travelled to Pittsburgh, donned a dress, and checked into a hospital there. Several weeks later, returning to her unit, she spotted an army bulletin posted in the window of a newspaper office that listed Frank Thompson as a deserter. The punishment, of course, was death, or at the very least a lengthy jail term, so she caught a train to Washington and, as Sarah Edmonds, worked as a nurse for the United States Christian Sanitarium Commission until the end of the war.

Emma Edmonds's close friend Jerome Robbins, who trained with her, then camped and marched into battle with her, kept a diary during the Civil War in which he wrote, "Though never frankly asserted by her, it will be understood that my friend Frank is a female, which accounts for the singularity of the use of pronouns."[2] Robbins also wrote that the sickness that prompted Emma to leave her camp had nothing to do with malaria and everything to do with a failed romance with a Union officer.

What is certain, however, is that she returned to New Brunswick after the war and married Linus Seelye, a carpenter. Their three children all died young and they adopted two boys. In 1882, after she and Seelye had moved several times with little success, she decided to tell her Frank Thompson story so she could qualify for a veteran's pension and erase her name from the list of deserters. She contacted several of her old soldier pals and former officers, who petitioned the War Department on her behalf.

On July 5, 1884, the same year her army buddies invited her to their reunion, she was granted an honourable discharge by a special act of Congress "for her sacrifice in the line of duty, her splendid record as a soldier, her unblemished character, and disabilities incurred in the service." She also received a small cash bonus and a veteran's pension of $12 a month.

She and her husband moved to La Porte, Texas, where Emma was accepted as a full member of the Grand Army of the Republic. In 1898, at the age of 56, she died of malaria and was buried with full military honours in the GAR Cemetery in Houston – the only woman there. Her tombstone reads: "Emma E. Seelye – Army Nurse."

THREE

Reach for the Top

T HROUGHOUT THE SUMMER AND FALL OF 1862, Confederate Colonel Joseph C. Porter and his newly recruited brigade of 2,500 men were creating havoc in northeastern Missouri while being pursued by a Federal force of about 1,000 men under the command of Colonel John McNeil. Born in Halifax on February 14, 1813, McNeil, who would later be responsible for one of the most notorious atrocities of the war, was one of four Canadian-born men to reach the rank of general. The other three are Henry Washington Benham, born in 1814 in Quebec City; Jacob Dolson Cox, born in 1828 in Montreal; and John Franklin Farnsworth, born in 1820 in Compton City, Lower Canada (Quebec). There is also some evidence that one of the war's most famous Confederate generals, Pierre Toutan de Beauregard, the man who commanded Confederate troops at Charleston and initiated the opening salvo in the war when he bombarded Fort Sumter on April 12, 1861, also had a Canadian connection. Some biographies argue that his grandfather emigrated from Trois-Rivières, Quebec, to New Orleans, where he acquired a personal fortune and became an influential leader among the French population of Louisiana, but it is more likely that his ancestors actually came directly from France to the New World.

McNeil, who, like the others, moved to the United States at a young age, apprenticed as a hatter in Boston before moving to

New York to set up his own business in the trade. He then went on to St. Louis, where he not only prospered as a hatter but was elected as a member of the Missouri legislature in 1844. He also branched out into insurance and, in 1855, became president of a local insurance company.

When the war began, Missouri found itself in an extremely awkward position. Perched on the border between North and South, the loyalties of its citizens were hopelessly split. Missouri had entered the Union on August 10, 1821, as a result of the Missouri Compromise. That meant, to maintain a balance of power in the Congress, Missouri joined as a slave state and Maine as a free state in order. Most of Missouri's American-born residents had come from Southern states and, naturally, sympathized with the South. Most of them lived on farms and many owned slaves. But Missouri had also attracted a large number of foreign-born settlers, most of whom strongly favoured the Union.

In hope of resolving the conflict, the Constitutional Convention of Missouri was held in St. Louis in March 1861, just three weeks after the Confederate forces had fired on Fort Sumter, and the delegates decided against secession and adopted a compromise position of armed neutrality, which didn't please either side. They thought that the state would raise its own army to protect itself against invasion from both the South or the North, and, in May, the pro-Southern General Assembly created the Missouri State Guard. Later, Northern sympathizers not in the regular Union Army formed the Missouri Enrolled Militia, which engaged in constant warfare with the Confederate Militia. With feelings running high in the state, and thousands of its citizens enlisting in both the Northern and the Southern armies, neutrality was out of the question. On August 14 Union officials declared martial law in St. Louis and, five days later, Missouri was formally admitted as a member of the Confederate States of America.

With 1,162 recorded official engagements, Missouri had the

third largest total of Civil War battles among all the states. The war in Missouri was particularly brutal, featuring large numbers of irregular troops and guerrilla operations. It was plagued by some of the most destructive guerrilla warfare in the war, including widespread bushwhacking, looting, and summary executions.

It was into this turmoil that McNeil quickly volunteered for service, where, as captain, he mobilized a volunteer company early in 1861. Once promoted to colonel of the 3rd Regiment, U.S. Reserve Corps, he commanded 600 men and defeated the Confederate General David B. Harris in a July 17, 1861, skirmish at Fulton, Missouri. After declaring martial law in St. Louis, U.S. Major-General John C. Fremont placed McNeil in command of the city and appointed him colonel of the 19th Missouri Volunteers. In 1862 he took command of a cavalry regiment and of the district of northeast Missouri, with orders to clear the area of Confederates. In a note to McNeil, Brigadier-General J.M. Schofield wrote: "I want you to take the field in person, with as much of your force as can be spared, and exterminate the rebel bands in your division. Don't rest until you have exterminated the rascals."

Just before noon on August 6, McNeil, commanding a combined force of about 1,000 men from the U.S. Cavalry and Artillery, caught up with Porter's rascals in Kirksville, Adair County, where the Confederates were hiding in homes, stores, and the crops in adjacent fields. After three hours of fighting, McNeil's men secured the town, captured about fifteen prisoners, and chased the remaining rebels away. In the process they helped to consolidate Union dominance in the region – and boosted McNeil to the rank of brigadier-general of volunteers.

But Porter wasn't finished yet. In the ensuing skirmish, McNeil gained everlasting fame – or infamy, depending on which side you were on – as the "Butcher of Palmyra" for ordering what became known as the "Palmyra Massacre."

In October, Porter entered the town of Palmyra and captured

a local Union supporter, Andrew Allsman, a former officer with the 3rd Missouri Cavalry. Union officials made much of the fact that Allsman was a "non-combatant" but said nothing about his activities spying on Confederates and reporting their whereabouts and activities to Union officials.

In a widely published notice to Porter, dated October 8, 1862 – with a copy also delivered to Porter's wife – W.R. Strachan, the provost marshal for the General District Northeast Missouri, warned that if Allsman was not returned unharmed to his family within ten days, then "ten men, who have belonged to your band and unlawfully sworn by you to carry arms against the Government of the United States and who are now in custody, will be shot, as a meet reward for their crimes, among which is the illegal restraining of said Allsman his liberty, and, if not returned, presumptively aiding in his murder."

Many Confederates believed that the notice was simply a scare tactic and that McNeil would not really execute ten prisoners, particularly because, earlier in the war, McNeil had been censured by headquarters for being too lenient towards the rebels. Although McNeil did order the execution of the Palymra prisoners, he was temporarily relieved of his command in October 1864 by General Alfred Pleasanton at the Battle of Westport, the decisive battle of Confederate General Sterling Price's Missouri expedition, for not attacking when ordered.

Back in Palmyra, the ten days passed. There was no word from Colonel Porter and no sign of Allsman, so McNeil drew the names of ten prisoners from a hat and told them that, unless Allsman was returned to his family by 1 p.m. the next day, a Saturday, they would all be shot immediately. The *Palmyra Courier* reported that most of the men "received the announcement with composure or indifference." A local clergyman, the Reverend James S. Green, stayed with them during the night as their spiritual adviser and, shortly after 11 a.m., three government wagons arrived at the jail, one carrying four rough board coffins and the others three each. The prisoners were taken from the prison and each one placed on top of his designated coffin. Accompanied by a large guard of soldiers, the cavalcade headed through the town and on to the fair grounds, about half a mile to the east.

With about a hundred people watching, the coffins were removed from the wagons and arranged in a row 6 feet apart in a line running north and south some fifteen paces east of the music stand in the centre of the amphitheatre. Thirty soldiers from the Second Missouri State Militia formed in a single line facing the coffins. The prisoners knelt on the grass between their coffins and their executioners while the Reverend R.M. Rhodes offered a prayer. After that, each prisoner sat on his coffin. Colonel Strachan and the clergyman each shook hands with the prisoners, offering them blindfolds – which only two accepted – and, as the *Courier* described it: "The stillness of death pervaded the place. The officer in command now stepped forward, and gave the word of command, 'Ready, aim, fire.' The discharges, however, were not made simultaneously, probably through want of a perfect previous understanding of the orders and of the time at which to fire. Two of the rebels fell backward upon their coffins and died instantly. Captain [Thomas A.] Sidner sprang forward and fell with his head toward the soldiers, his face upward, his hands clasped upon his breast and the left leg drawn half way up. He did not move again, but died immediately. He had requested the soldiers to aim at his heart, and they obeyed but too implicitly. The other seven were not killed outright, so the reserves were called in, who dispatched them with their revolvers."

The pro-Union newspaper then went on to editorialize: "It seems hard that ten men should die for one . . . but severe diseases demand severe remedies. The safety of the people is the supreme law. It overrides all other considerations. The madness of rebellion has become so deep seated that ordinary methods of cure are inadequate." But not everyone supported McNeil's actions. Confederate President Jefferson Davis put a price on McNeil's head; Nova Scotia's *Provincial Wesleyan* called him a "monster of inequity," and the London *Times* "denounced the act as beyond the rules of civilized warfare."[1]

In a lengthy defence of McNeil's actions written on December 10, 1862, and published in the *New York Times* in response to its harsh criticism of McNeil's "butchery," Strachan claimed that the Union had extended "every kindness and a degree of clemency" towards the rebels in Missouri, but "still treason continued rampant, traitors publicly held forth on the clemency with which they were treated, regarding it as proof and confession of the weakness of the Government . . . Union men and their families were forced to leave their homes and their all and fly for protection and for life to the loyal States." That was true, but it could equally be applied to Confederate supporters as well. But Strachan continued:

> What is war? Is it anything but retaliation? Must we allow our enemies, the enemies of liberty and republicanism, to outrage all the laws of war, and not take some steps to show them the propriety of adhering to those laws?
>
> . . . If you could have been a witness to many scenes that attended General McNeil's visit to the various posts of his district, made but two weeks since, when he traversed the whole country on horseback, attended by but two orderlies, when old men would come out of their farm houses, shake hands with the general, call down blessings upon him, ask him to delay so that their wives cold come out and thank him for executing justice . . .
>
> . . . Time and experience proved to him [McNeil] that in order to save bloodshed it was necessary to show some examples of severe punishment, and the

result, in giving security to persons and property of loyal men in our section, has amply justified the steps taken by him. Do you suppose that a rebellion that in this late day has ventured to employ the scalping knife of the savage in its service, that commenced in fraud, that has sustained itself from the commencement by robbery, that has practiced extermination and banishment and confiscation toward citizens that ventured to remain true to their original allegiance, can be put down without somebody being hurt? Let me ask you to do justice to a kind and brave officer, who has simply dared to do his duty, and in doing so has obtained the thanks and gratitude from every loyal man in Northern Missouri.

Strachan went on to say that since McNeil had the prisoners shot, "not a murder nor a single personal outrage to a Union man has been committed in Northeastern Missouri."

As for McNeil, he responded to a critical article in *The Century* magazine of July 1889 in these words: "Cherishing, as I do, the firm conviction that my action was the means of saving the lives and property of hundreds of loyal men and women, I feel that my act was the performance of a public duty."

Late in 1862 McNeil was transferred to southeastern Missouri, and in April 1863 he held Cape Girardeau with 1,700 men against Confederate Major-General John S. Marmaduke's force of 10,000 men in one of the major confrontations in the state. In 1864 McNeil was made commander of the district of Rolla and was directly involved in helping to save the state capital from General Sterling Price's army. In October 1864 McNeil led one of the five brigades that attacked the remnants of Price's army, which had been in full retreat but had stopped to rest about 2 miles south of Newtonia, Missouri, resulting in about 650 casualties and a Union victory. McNeil commanded central Missouri until April 12, 1865, when he resigned and was given the brevet rank of major-general of volunteers in recognition of his meritorious services.

McNeil became clerk of the criminal court in St. Louis County, then sheriff of the county from 1866 to 1870, then clerk of the criminal court again. In 1876 he was named commissioner to the Centennial Exhibition in Philadelphia and, between 1878 and 1882, he worked as an inspector in the U.S. Indian service. He then became superintendent of the U.S. post office, St. Louis branch, and died while holding that office on June 8, 1891. He was buried in St. Louis – still admired by those who supported the Union in Missouri, and reviled by those who didn't.

Like McNeil, the Quebec-born Brigadier-General Henry Washington Benham was also chastised for disobeying a direct command. Unlike McNeil, whose lapse of judgment was minor, Benham's folly cost the Union a significant potential victory, which would have been a major blow to Southern defences of one of their key cities. That being said, however, Benham's positive contributions to the war effort – and his strong personal relationship with Abraham Lincoln – make him an important figure in the U.S. history of that time.

Some biographies list Benham's birth on April 8, 1813, in Connecticut, but documents held by the New England Historic Genealogical Society show that Benham was born April 8, 1814, at the temporary business address of his father in Quebec City, Lower Canada. He was the son of Jared Benham, whose family ancestors were among the early settlers of Boston in 1630, and also among the first families to settle in New Haven. On October 3, 1843, he wed Elizabeth Andrews McNeil in Hillsboro, New Hampshire – and married well.

The bride's father was General John McNeil, who had won considerable distinction in the battles of Chippewa and Niagara during the War of 1812. Her mother, Elizabeth Andrews Pierce McNeil, was the daughter of New Hampshire Governor Benjamin Pierce. Her half-brother, Franklin Pierce, became the fourteenth president of the United States in 1853. His *Kansas-Nebraska Act*, which allowed residents of both states to vote on the slavery question, set the country on its tragic course towards civil war.

Pierce was considered a weak president from the outset, the product of a compromise between the stridently pro-slavery Southern Democrats and their anti-slavery colleagues in the North. The 1820 Missouri Compromise had banned slavery in the new territories, but, with the acquisition of vast new territories after the Mexican War, the issue heated up again. The compromise had abolished the slave trade in the District of Columbia, although slavery was still permitted there; it allowed New Mexico, Nevada, Arizona, and Utah to be organized without any mention of slavery (leaving it for the residents to decide when they applied for statehood); and, to pacify the slave states, it adopted the *Fugitive Slave Act*, one that had a significant impact on Canadian history because it prompted an estimated 20,000 blacks to flee to Canada on the Underground Railroad. When Franklin Pierce, a pro-slavery, one-term president who died an alcoholic in 1869, brought in the *Kansas-Nebraska Act*, in effect it repealed the Missouri Compromise. Almost overnight it turned Kansas into a war zone, resulting in the death of hundreds of people from both sides of the slavery issue, thanks in no small measure to Pierce's continuing reluctance to dispatch federal troops to restore civil order. His term was such a disaster that, in 1856, his own Democratic Party turned its back on him and nominated James Buchanan as its presidential candidate. Although Buchanan won the election, the damage had already been done, with "Bleeding Kansas" inflaming the irreconcilable differences between the pro- and anti-slavery politicians and setting the stage for all-out war.

Benham had spent 1832 at Yale College, before being appointed to the U.S. Military Academy, or West Point, where he graduated first in his class on June 30, 1837, and was named a brevet second lieutenant in the U.S. Corps of Engineers.[2] After serving with distinction as an engineer in the Mexican War – where he was wounded at the Battle of Buena Vista on February 23, 1847 – he was breveted to captain for gallant and meritorious conduct. Between 1848 and 1861 Benham was superintending engineer for sea-coast defence projects from New York to Florida. He also served for a time as assistant in charge of the U.S. Survey Office in Washington. He declined the chance to serve as a major in the 9th Infantry on the frontier in 1855, where he would have been rubbing shoulders with both Robert E. Lee and George B. McClellan. Six years later, after the outbreak of the Civil War, however, he became chief engineer under Brigadier-General T.A. Morris with the task of fortifying the strategic Union base at Cairo, Illinois, where troops met as they moved to and from the front lines. On July 14, just one week before the First Battle of Bull Run, Union forces under Benham's command defeated Confederate General Robert S. Garnett's forces at Carrick's Ford, West Virginia. Garnett died in the battle, and Benham was promoted to the rank of colonel.

Benham also served under Brigadier-General William S. Rosecrans against Lee's forces in West Virginia and, on September 10, 1861, he commanded the leading brigade at the battle of Carnifex Ferry, where the Confederates were forced to abandon an entrenched position on the Henry Patterson farm and retreat to the south side of the Gauley River and eastward to Meadow Bluff. That battle was important because the Confederates had wanted to regain control of the Kanawha Valley and, thereby, block the movement for West Virginia statehood. But when they were driven out of the area, the statehood movement went ahead without any more serious threats from them.[3]

In 1862 Benham was placed in command of the Northern

District of the South and, that spring, he took part in the siege of Fort Pulaski, a strategic fort on Cockspur Island about 15 miles east of Savannah, Georgia. When Georgia seceded, Confederate officials moved quickly to establish coastal defences before the Union forces could arrive and, with a force of 134 men, easily captured Fort Pulaski, which had been named after War of Independence hero Count Casimer Pulaski and virtually abandoned. The Union, too, wanting to enforce its naval blockade of Southern ports, also needed to control coastal fortifications. In early 1862 it began secretly constructing a host of artillery batteries in the area. When it opened fire on Fort Pulaski on April 10 – one of the first bombardments to use the new rifled cannons – it breached the fort within half an hour and forced the Confederates to surrender.

Shortly after that, however, Benham's lack of patience and insubordination played a significant part in a major Union setback. In June 1862 Benham, in command of the Federal forces on James Island, near Charleston, was told by Major-General David Hunter, commander of the Department of the South in the Battle of Secessionville, South Carolina: "You will make no attempt to advance on Charleston or to attach Fort Johnson until you are largely reinforced or until you receive specific instructions from these headquarters."

At the time, Charleston Harbor was virtually closed by the Federal blockade, and Union forces were searching for a way to attack this important southern city by land. They seemed to catch a break from a most unusual source – Robert Smalls, a slave working at a Charleston shipyard, who had been assigned as wheelsman aboard the 150-foot-long steamboat *Planter*, the designated flagship for Confederate General Roswell S. Ripley. On May 12 the crew went ashore to a ball at Fort Sumter, leaving the *Planter* in the hands of Smalls and the crew of eight other slaves, including his brother John. By 3 a.m., May 13, with Smalls in command – wearing the gold-braided coat and broad-brimmed straw hat of Captain C.J. Relyea, and waving at the various sentries as he'd seen Relyea do – they steamed up the Cooper River, past all the Confederate batteries, and finally made it to the Federal blockade fleet, where he surrendered to Lieutenant J. Frederick Nickels, captain of the USS *Onward* and a major player in the *Chesapeake* Affair in Nova Scotia. Along with the ship, Smalls brought news that the Confederates had abandoned Cole's and Battery islands, which opened the way for an assault by land on Charleston itself.

Hunter had already planned to attack Charleston from the south, so he assembled two divisions and landed them on the southeastern end of James Island on June 2, with Benham in charge. After meeting some resistance in several skirmishes over the next ten days, Hunter believed that he was outnumbered by the Confederates, under Major-General John C. Pemberton, who were defending Charleston and that he needed re-enforcements before making further assaults. He therefore told Benham to wait for reinforcements or specific instructions from headquarters. Pemberton, in the meantime, redeployed three batteries to James Island, and also ordered new earthwork defences, among them a fort at the tiny hamlet of Secessionville.

Despite Hunter's specific orders, Benham decided on June 15 that he would launch a "reconnaissance in force," or an early morning surprise frontal attack on the Secessionville fort, using about 3,500 men in two waves. Benham dispatched his forces, supposedly at double-quick time, but in the absolute darkness they had trouble negotiating two hedgerows and several open cotton fields. Instead, they found themselves knee-deep in weeds, bogged down in mud, and overtaken by their own second wave – all of which broke up the initial Federal lines, slowed their advance, and caused considerable confusion. They overran the Confederate advance pickets about 5 a.m., but Confederate Colonel Thomas G. Lamar, alerted by the noise, mounted the fort's parapet, saw the Union front closing in, and immediately dispatched couriers to send for reserves from Fort Johnson, about 5 miles away.

In the meantime, Lamar's 750 defenders began firing into the Union lines, stopping their advance long enough for Confederate reinforcements to arrive. The Union troops came under heavy fire from three sides and were ordered to fall back after suffering heavy casualties. The 79th New York had actually mounted the parapet and was engaged in hand-to-hand combat when the Union artillery opened fire on the fort, breaking up the attack and forcing its own troops to retreat. As the first Union wave collapsed and retreated, it made it impossible for the second wave to attack. The Union troops fell back to the hedge rows, reformed their lines, and Benham brought his other Union division up, making two more unsuccessful assaults on the fort, before a general withdraw was issued. The 3rd New Hampshire nearly succeeded in a flanking manoeuvre, but it, too, had to retreat when about 250 men from the 4th Louisiana Battalion arrived. By 9 a.m. the battle was over, with the Union suffering losses of 107 dead, 487 wounded, and 89 captured. The Confederates lost 52 killed, 132 wounded, and 8 missing.

An account of the battle on Charleston's Civil War Web site by Vincent J. Simonowicz underscores the significance of Benham's failure. According to Simonowicz, had the Union captured those Confederate batteries, "they would have flanked the harbor defenses and might have forced the abandonment of Charleston by the Confederacy, cut the Atlantic Coast Line Railroad and established a base for operations into the interior which might have ended the war two years sooner."

As a result of his own folly, Benham was informally charged with disobedience and mustered out of Hunter's command in August 1862. His contributions to the war effort were far from over, however, and he managed to redeem himself somewhat through his extraordinary engineering prowess.

From 1863 to 1865 Benham, commanding various engineer

brigades, "invented the method of laying pontoon bridges by simultaneous bays, thereby accelerating the movement of troops. He also invented a portable intrenching tool called a picket shovel, which was considered of great value to the efficiency of the army."[4] Benham's most famous action came while supervising the construction, under heavy enemy fire, of a bridge over the Rappahannock River near Fredericksburg, Virginia, in May 1863. The bridge allowed Major-General Joseph Hooker's defeated army to escape in the Battle of Chancellorsville, which many consider to be General Robert E. Lee's greatest military victory, and the battle in which the Southern General Stonewall Jackson was mortally wounded by his own men while making a night reconnaissance. Benham also served at Gettysburg under Major-General George Meade in July 1863 and under Lieutenant-General Ulysses S. Grant in the Richmond Campaign leading to Lee's surrender, and was breveted to brigadier-general for gallantry in that campaign. On March 13, 1865, Benham was made major-general, U.S. Army, as well as major-general, U.S. Army Volunteers. After mustering out of the volunteer force, he received a commission as colonel in the Corps of Engineers. He returned to duty on Atlantic Coast defences until his retirement from active service in June 1882, just two years before he died in New York City.

A.D. Bache, the superintendent of the Survey of the Coast of the United States, once described Benham as "a man of excellent judgment, of great kindness, yet firmness in dealing with his subordinates, and discreet in his management of officers and men, and with a faithfulness, energy and industry in the discharge of his duty which cannot be exceeded. His loyalty of character and devotion to the service in which he is engaged cannot be surpassed."[5]

Jacob Dolson Cox, a scholar, lawyer, soldier, and statesman destined to become one of Ohio's most famous citizens, was born on

October 27, 1828, in Montreal. He moved to New York City and apprenticed in law, but in 1846, opting for the ministry over law, the 18-year-old enrolled in the Prepatory Department and Seminary at Oberlin College (then known as Oberlin Collegiate Institute), a famous Christian college and colony set up in 1833 in a clearing about 35 miles southwest of Cleveland by two missionaries "to train teachers and other Christian leaders for the boundless most desolate fields in the West."[6] Oberlin had made its mark in the turbulent social history of the era when its trustees stated in 1835 that "the education of the people of color is a matter of great interest and should be encouraged and sustained in this Institution."[7] By the turn of the century in the United States, one-third of all black graduates of predominantly white institutions had graduated from Oberlin. And, in 1841, three women graduated from Oberlin, the first women in America to earn their bachelor of arts degree. As for Cox, he earned his BA in 1851 and his MA in 1854. While still a student he married Helen Finney Cochran, the eldest daughter of Oberlin president Charles Grandison Finney, a famous Presbyterian revivalist of the era.

Cox moved to Warren, Ohio, in 1851 as superintendent of schools and principal of the local high school. He also completed his legal training and entered a law practice. In 1853, as a member of the Whig Party, he lost an election for prosecuting attorney but, because of his strong anti-slavery views, he helped organize the Ohio Republican Party in 1855 and, three years later, was elected to the state Senate. There he became a close ally with other radical anti-slavery advocates, including James A. Garfield, who became the twentieth president of the United States in 1881.[8]

When the Civil War began, Cox was named a brigadier-general of volunteers in charge of training Ohio troops, but he quickly began active duty under General George B. McClellan in West Virginia and, later that spring, was given command of that state's Kanawha region, which he held until August 1862.

Cox was also engaged in the heat of battle as commander of Major-General Ambrose Burnside's 9th Corps at the Union victory at South Mountain, Virginia, on September 14, and, three days later, he fought at Antietam, a significant turning point in the war but also the bloodiest single day of the conflict. There, the Union forces under McLellan halted Lee's first invasion of the North along Antietam Creek near Sharpsburg, Maryland, but in twelve hours of combat, 23,000 men were killed or wounded. Five days after the battle, Lincoln issued the preliminary Emancipation Proclamation, promising that, after January 1, 1863, slaves would be "then, thenceforward, and forever free." Cox was promoted to major-general of volunteers, but his promotion subsequently fell through because the allotted quota of generals had been reached.

After commanding the Department of Ohio for most of 1863, Cox, as commander of the U.S. Third Division, 23rd Corps, took part in May 1864 in the Atlanta campaign, where the Union forces under General William Tecumseh Sherman finally captured the major Southern city on September 1 and ultimately burned it to the ground. These events inspired Margaret Mitchell's legendary American classic *Gone with the Wind* and the award-winning movie of the same name. But there was nothing Hollywood about the actual fighting, and Cox joined Sherman's famous – or infamous, to the Southerners – "March to the Sea." This bloody campaign ended with the capture of Savannah on December 23, splitting the Confederacy in two and hastening the end of the war a few months later. Along the way, Cox was again promoted to major-general of volunteers. This time his promotion stuck: he was given command of the 23rd Army Corps and was active in the battles of Franklin and Nashville.

At Franklin, located on a bend of the Harpeth River, Confederate General John Bell Hood, commander of the Army of Tennessee, ordered his 31,000 troops into a disastrous November 30 frontal attack against General John McAllister Schofield's 20,000 troops, desperately hoping to cut them off before they could reach Nashville, about 15 miles to the south, and hook up with General George H. Thomas's 20,000 additional troops there. After a horrific battle, which began at 4 p.m. and raged until 2 a.m., the Confederates suffered about 6,200 casualties, including 1,700 dead, six of them Confederate generals, compared to 2,700 Union casualties. By morning, Schofield had withdrawn his victorious army, which included Cox and his troops, and joined forces with Thomas in Nashville.

With the addition of Union General A.J. Smith's troops from St. Louis, Schofield now had 70,000 troops in Nashville, compared to the 25,000 men left in Hood's ill-equipped Army of Tennessee. The Battle of Nashville, the last major battle of the Western arena, began on December 14 when Thomas's Union forces, including Cox, attacked Hood's forces, routing the Southern general and forcing him to retreat to Tupelo, Mississippi. Confederate losses were estimated at 500 killed and 1,000 wounded, but Union forces captured some 13,000 Confederates, most of whom, recognizing the futility of fighting on, voluntarily surrendered. Sixteen weeks later Lee also surrendered, and the dream of the Confederacy was dead.

Cox spent the last few months of the war supervising the paroling of Confederate prisoners-of-war in North Carolina. After the war, he was nominated as the Republican candidate for governor of Ohio and published his infamous "Oberlin letter" where, much to the surprise of his pre-war allies in the anti-slavery movement, he openly advocated the segregation of freed blacks into "Negro reservations" and opposed giving blacks the right to vote. He served one term in 1866–67 but did not fare well. He failed in an attempt to resolve the dispute between President Andrew Johnson and the Radical Republicans in Congress over Reconstruction, and his support for the unpopular Johnson, plus his advocacy of forcible segregation, turned many of his former supporters against him. When the

Republicans refused to nominate him again for governor, he entered private law practice in Cincinnati.

But he wasn't finished with public office yet. He turned down Johnson's offer to serve as commissioner of internal revenue, but in March 1869 he was sworn in as President Ulysses S. Grant's secretary of the interior. He instituted a series of department reforms, including the first complete civil service examination, but resigned eighteen months later, in part because of widespread corruption in the Grant administration. Cox returned to his law practice and, in 1873, moved to Toledo as president of the Toledo, Wabash and Western Railroad. In 1876 he was elected to the U.S. Congress as representative of the 6th Ohio district and reunited with his friend Garfield, but he served only one term, leaving to resume his law practice. Between 1881 and 1897 he was dean of the Cincinnati Law School, and from 1885 to 1889 he also served as president of the University of Cincinnati. He became a noted writer of military history and lived in retirement in Oberlin from 1897 to 1900. Cox died on August 4, 1900, while visiting Magnolia, Massachusetts, and, four days later, was buried in Grove Cemetery, Cincinnati.

Of the four Canadian-born Union generals, John Franklin Farnsworth lived the longest time in this country and served the shortest time in the war. As one of the closest personal friends of the war's most famous personality, President Abraham Lincoln, however, he held the most influential position.

Farnsworth was born on May 27, 1820, at Compton, Quebec – hometown of Louis St. Laurent, the Liberal prime minister of Canada from 1948 to 1957 – the son of John Farnsworth, a surveyor, who had moved to Quebec from Maine with his father in 1812. His mother, Sally Patten, was the daughter of Colonel John Patten of Surrey, Maine. In 1834, at the age of 14, Farnsworth moved with his parents to Ann Arbor, Michigan, where he worked with his father for a time but ultimately studied law and was admitted to the bar in 1841. A year later he moved to the scenic Fox River town of St. Charles, Illinois, an hour west of Chicago, to practise law, and in 1846 he married Mary A. Clark and moved to Chicago. He was elected to the Thirty-fifth and Thirty-sixth U.S. Congresses (March 4, 1857–March 3, 1861) as a Republican, but did not win renomination in 1860. In the process, he quickly became one of Lincoln's best friends. Indeed, during Lincoln's 1858 senatorial bid against Stephen A. Douglas, Farnsworth acted as a key Lincoln adviser in the celebrated Lincoln-Douglas debates. Lincoln lost that election but won a national reputation for his debating skills, which helped him win his party's nod after Farnsworth nominated him as the Republican Party's presidential candidate in 1860. In that election, during which the Democrats were deeply divided over the slavery question, Lincoln defeated both Douglas and John C. Breckinridge, the Southern Democratic candidate. Breckinridge went on to become a leading Confederate general and minister of war, and Canada got to know him well after the war when he fled with his family to the Niagara area to avoid prosecution.

The debates, which pitted the relatively unknown Lincoln against the established Senator Douglas – the "Little Giant" as his supporters called him, one of the great orators of the day – opened in Ottawa, Illinois, of August 21, 1858, then moved to Freeport, Jonesboro, Charleston, Galesburg, Quincy, and finally to Alton, Illinois, on October 15. Not only did they capture the imagination of the entire nation by focusing on the major political schisms of the time – slavery, equality, Dred Scott, and the territories – but they were the forerunner to the very issues which, in just three years, would plunge the country into all-out war.

Lincoln ultimately went down in history as the Great Emancipator – and, as president, he put an end to slavery as a formal institution. During the debates with Douglas, however, Lincoln, supported by Farnsworth, argued that although slavery is "a moral, social and political wrong," he was not an abolitionist. He declared that the Republicans would "not molest it [slavery] in the States where it exists . . . but they will use every constitutional method to prevent the evil from becoming larger." During one debate, Lincoln said flatly, "I am not in favor of Negro citizenship." He also denounced the liberal doctrine of social equality for the races and refused to advocate the repeal of the 1850 *Fugitive Slave Law*, which gave slave owners the right to recapture escaped slaves (prompting thousands of blacks, many of them free people afraid of being caught by bounty hunters, to flee to Canada).

Farnsworth, despite his complete lack of military background, was named a colonel of the 8th Illinois Volunteer Cavalry in September 1861. In the spring of 1862 he fought with General George McClellan's massive Army of the Potomac during the unsuccessful Pennisular Campaign, aimed at capturing Richmond, which proved an embarrassment for Lincoln and the Federal forces because of McLellan's unwillingness to press his obvious advantages in manpower and equipment. During that campaign, Farnsworth had become friends with Major Alfred Pleasanton, who was to be an important figure in the U.S. Cavalry and in Farnsworth's own advancement. Farnsworth also fought against Lee's forces in the Maryland Campaign that fall, including the Battle of Antietam, which began just outside Sharpsburg, Maryland, in the early morning of September 16, 1862, and left 2,108 Union soldiers dead and 10,293 either missing or wounded. Lee's Confederates suffered 10,318 casualties, dead, missing, or wounded, fully one-quarter of his army. During the fall election of 1862, Farnsworth was again elected to Congress, and the War Department subsequently ordered him to raise the 17th Illinois Volunteer Regiment. His friend Pleasanton, now a general, promoted him to brigadier-general of volunteers on November 29, 1862, about three weeks after Lincoln had fired McClellan and placed General Ambrose Burnside in command of the army. Farnsworth commanded the First Brigade of Pleasanton's cavalry during the December 11–13 Battle of Fredericksburg, when the Union foolishly assaulted entrenched Confederate positions and suffered a humiliating defeat. Farnsworth escaped from that assault unscathed, but he was forced to resign from the army in March 1863, after receiving serious injuries on the battlefield.

Farnsworth's nephew Brigadier-General Elon Farnsworth of Green Oak, Michigan – the son of his older, Quebec-born brother James Patten Farnsworth – was killed that July at Gettysburg, just four days after being promoted as a political favour to his Uncle John, when he was goaded into a suicidal charge against the Confederate right flank. Farnsworth had been appointed first lieutenant and adjutant in his uncle's regiment in September 1861 and promoted to captain that Christmas. A fiery character, the young Farnsworth went to Saint Paul's Church in Alexandria, Virginia, on February 19, 1862, and, when the Reverand J.R. Stewart, a Confederate sympathizer who would later spend time in Canada, refused to read the required prayer for President Lincoln, Farnsworth ordered him arrested. Stewart was later released, but not without some unwanted public anger directed towards Lincoln.

In June 1863, after his unusually rapid advance through the ranks, the young Farnsworth was promoted, along with George Custer – who would become an American legend during the Indian Wars at Little Big Horn – and given command of the 1st Brigade, 3rd Division, Cavalry Corps, Army of the Potomac. Farnsworth fell under the division command of the notorious General Hugh Judson Kilpatrick, known by his men as "Kilcavalry," who, on the third day of the battle, ordered Farnsworth to charge the Confederate right flank, which was dug in behind a solid stone wall. When Farnsworth questioned the wisdom of the order, Kilpatrick directly questioned Farnsworth's personal courage, a grave insult at that time. As a result,

Farnsworth, leading the 1st West Virginia Cavalry, was struck by five bullets and killed in the charge, along with the bulk of his brigade. He was just 25 years old at the time of his death. Kilpatrick was later criticized for poor judgment. He earned even more notoriety in February 1864, when, assisted by Colonel Ulric Dahlgren, he attempted a daring, unauthorized cavalry raid on Richmond, hoping to burn the city and kill President Jefferson Davis and his Cabinet. The raid was a failure, Dahlgren was killed, and a scandal ensued when documents found in the colonel's possession were published.

As a clear measure of Farnsworth's strong relationship with Lincoln, the former general was also one of the select group of Lincoln friends, families, political associates, and doctors who gathered around Lincoln's deathbed for an all-night vigil. Following John Wilkes Booth's mortal attack, the president fought for his life, but was declared dead at 7:22 the next morning.

After leaving the army, Farnsworth moved back to St. Charles, Illinois, to resume his law practice, and he served again in Congress from 1863 to 1872. He supported the Radical Republic agenda, which included the Emancipation Proclamation, the Thirteenth Amendment (abolishing slavery), and the impeachment of Lincoln's successor, President Andrew Johnson. After failing in a renomination bid, he moved to Chicago to practise law, then moved again to Washington in 1880 and continued his successful law practice there until his death on July 14, 1897.

FOUR

Dixie Bound

W ITH MILITARY PRECISION, exactly at 8 p.m. every Saturday between the July holiday weekend and Labour Day, the thirty or so members of the Kincardine Scottish Pipe Band, founded in 1908, gather in Victoria Park on the south end of the downtown area overlooking Lake Huron and adjacent to the Penetangore River. The band and any guest pipers are all decked out in full regalia.

Dressed in their Kincardine tartan – black tunics, green and black plaid kilts, black tams with a fuzzy red knob on the top, and many featuring heavy, white, knee-length "Rose" stockings, hand-knit for many years by Rose Singerman, an elderly local woman now in failing health – they present an impressive picture as they march from the park and along Queen Street, where both sides are lined with residents and tourists of every age, description, and circumstance, along with dogs, cats, overhead birds, and even the odd squirrel chattering its approval of the passing parade from nearby trees.

It seems as though the whole town of 12,000 people is involved, as the band, music blaring, marches up the main street. At first dozens and then hundreds of spectators fall in behind, led by a group carrying a large banner emblazoned with the words "Friends of the Kincardine Scottish," many of them proudly wearing their own special lapel pins, which came with their $100 donation to join the "friends" and help pay the band's expenses.

When it reaches Quinn Plaza, just a few blocks up the street, the band takes a fifteen-minute "smoke break," only to turn around and march back down Queen Street and into Victoria Park, where it forms a wide circle in front of the bandstand and delights the assembled throng with a free half-hour concert.

On a particular evening in June 2003, as the fire-red sun sank slowly over the lake horizon, a guest piper – Bill Nicholson of Detroit, Michigan – was afforded the honour of playing the lead bagpipe in "Amazing Grace," a deeply moving rendition of former slave-runner John Newton's famous hymn, made even more beautiful when the crowd spontaneously began to hum along to the music.

Each Saturday, as the band marches up and down Queen Street, it comes within a few feet of an imposing 12-foot-high granite monument, perched on the grass between the old post office and the library and next door to the office of the *Kincardine News*, established in 1857. The monument honours Dr. Solomon Secord, the most famous and revered doctor in the 155-year history of the town. It is also the only monument in Canada dedicated to somebody who fought in the Civil War. And, unlike the majority of British North Americans in that conflict, Secord served with the Confederacy.

Secord was born in 1834 near Burlington Bay, not far from Hamilton, Ontario. He was the grand nephew of Laura Secord, the legendary American-born heroine of the War of 1812, who has her own place in Canadian history. On June 22, 1813, after overhearing American officers bragging about their plans for a surprise attack against a small British garrison at the village of Beaver Dam, she trekked for 19 miles, some of it through swamps and thick undergrowth, to warn British Lieutenant James Fitzgibbon. Armed with this information, Fitzgibbon, aided by a band of Iroquois Indians, attacked the rear of the American force. Not knowing the size of the attacking force and fearing annihilation, the 570 Americans surrendered – and the day was won.

In the late 1850s Solomon Secord went first to Walkerton and then to Kincardine to practise medicine. Next, acting against his father's advice, he moved to Georgia just before the Civil War broke out, believing, as many people did, that the political problems would be resolved without resorting to war. And just as most historians now believe that Laura Secord's real contribution to the War of 1812 has been massaged – there is evidence that both the Iroquois and the British already knew about the American plans – the local reviews of Solomon Secord's war service also lean towards the fanciful, particularly the explanations of how an alleged pacifist and strong anti-slavery advocate ended up in the Confederate Army.

In the April 28, 1910, edition of the *Kincardine Review*, Colonel Hugh Clark, the editor and a close friend of Secord, marked the death of the famous local doctor by publishing a series of stories on his life and times. There is no doubt that Secord was immensely popular. When he died the whole town shut down – the schools, stores, factories, everything – and there were few locals who did not show up at the funeral and honestly mourn his death.

The money for the granite memorial was easily raised through donations from local citizens. There was no canvassing, just an announcement in the local newspaper. The largest single subscription was $25, and more than $700 was collected. There is a sundial at the top and directly underneath is carved in capital letters: "I mark the sunny hours." Below that is a brief tribute to his life: "To Solomon Secord, 1834–1910. Our family physician for fifty years. This memorial was erected by his loving friends. Served as a surgeon with Southern Army during American Civil War. All that lived he loved, and without regard for fee or reward he did his work for love of his work and for love of his fellows."

The opposite side of the impressive marker contains a quote from Chaucer, one of Secord's favourite authors: "He knew the cause of eurich maladye were it a hoot or cold or moyst or drye. And where they engendred, And of what humour. He was a verray parfit praktisonr." The local citizens erected a marble shaft over his grave in Kincardine Cemetery from the same fund collected for the downtown memorial. It contains a bronze tablet outlining his particulars. The bottom line reads: "His last words were: 'Give my love to everybody.'"

Given the obvious reverence from those who knew him, Secord seems to have been a wonderful man. Always outspoken, he is reported to have told a leading Kincardine citizen, a man noted as a constant whiner who had come to the doctor's office in the local drug store with yet another complaint, that he should stick out his tongue. When the man complied, Secord said, "That looks like a tongue that has done a hell of a lot of lying in its day." He was not a man who ever went to church, an unusual stand at the time, but, although he enjoyed shocking clergymen, he treated them in his practice without charge. The February 1939 *Historical Bulletin* of the Calgary Associate Clinic tells the story of Secord's dealing with a retired Methodist Episcopal preacher named Hilts who had tried in vain to pay Secord for services rendered. Secord said, "I'll tell you what I'll do, Mr. Hilts. I'll make a bargain with you and call it square. You do all you can to keep me out of hell, and I'll do all I can to keep you out of Heaven."

In one oft-repeated story, Dr. Secord was literally dragooned into the Southern service, but historians agree that this account is highly suspect. According to Colonel Clark, Secord was a pacifist and an outspoken abolitionist when he moved to Georgia, two qualities that would not have been appreciated at that time, particularly by a foreign carpetbagger. "The doctor was an abolitionist," wrote Clark, "and, having the courage of his convictions, said so, a dangerous thing to do in a southern state. He was arrested and tried. The proceedings were wholly irregular and unauthorized by law but each district was a law unto itself in those days. Few men ever escaped hanging as narrowly as did Dr. Secord. At that time he had some friends who were armed to prevent it."

It certainly is true that Georgia and other Southern states had their share of ad hoc "trials," orchestrated by armed gangs and private militias, but it is doubtful that Secord ran afoul of them. Still, the local mythology has it that the brave Secord, in order to calm the standoff between those who wanted to save him and those who wanted to hang him – and because, as a surgeon, he wouldn't actually be shooting at anybody – agreed to join the Confederate Army. There is no doubt he did serve with the South, but his subsequent actions belie the notion that he was a reluctant Confederate. While his actual war records, like those of most Confederate soldiers, are incomplete, he did spend most of the war with the 20th Regiment, Georgia Volunteer Infantry, enrolling as an assistant surgeon for $110 a month.[1] He was promoted to regimental surgeon in September 1862 and paid $162 a month. On January 28, 1863, he was appointed as surgeon, equivalent to a major, of the 20th Regiment, Longstreet's Brigade, Van Dorn's Division, Beauregard's Corps, Army of Northern Virginia.

Records show that Secord was captured on July 5 and taken prisoner while tending the wounded after the Battle of Gettysburg (July 1–3), considered by most historians as the high tide of the Confederacy and the turning point of the war. It pitted General Robert E. Lee's Army of Northern Virginia against Major-General George Meade's Union Army of the Potomac, resulting in a horrible loss of life and the ultimate retreat of Lee's army back into Virginia.

The most famous military action at Gettysburg was Pickett's Charge on the third day of the battle, a disaster resulting in some 5,600 Confederate casualties, but Secord had no part in that. All told, Gettysburg resulted in about 23,000 Union losses and between 20,000 and 28,000 Confederate casualties. Secord was involved when his regiment fought at Round Top, Little Round Top, Devil's Glen, and Slaughter Pen, among the fiercest actions of the engagement. His immediate commander in the 20th Georgia, Colonel John A. Jones, was killed during that battle. Secord was in Benning's Brigade, assigned to Hood's Division, under Major-General John B. Hood, who was wounded at Gettysburg and replaced by Brigadier-General E. McIver Law.

Secord is registered among the sick and wounded Confederate soldiers in hospitals in and around Gettysburg after the battle. He had not been wounded, but was likely on the list because he had been captured while tending to wounded soldiers. In the custom of the time, defeated armies, unable to move their most seriously wounded soldiers from the field, left surgeons and other medical personnel behind to tend to them. Since medical personnel were not considered armed combatants, they were usually treated with considerable respect and, even though taken prisoner, they were allowed to continue to treat their sick and wounded. On July 5, two days after the battle ended, Secord was listed as a prisoner of war and transferred to the provost marshal. On July 28 he was admitted to the U.S. General Hospital, West's Buildings, Baltimore, and, a day later, "returned to duty" in Fortress Monroe, Virginia, the "Gibraltar of Chesapeake Bay." He was then sent to Fort Norfolk, Virginia, for confinement until further orders. Originally a coastal defence work, Fort Norfolk was built around 1810, but had been converted to a naval ammunition depot when the Confederates captured it at the beginning of the war. When the Union forces recaptured it, Fort Norfolk was used as a hospital.

From Fort Norfolk, Secord was sent on August 10, 1863, to Fort McHenry, Maryland, the historic fort where the valiant defence by 1,000 American troops against the British during the Battle of Baltimore in 1814 inspired the 35-year-old poet-lawyer Francis Scott Key to compose the poem "The Star-Spangled Banner," written to match the metre of an English hymn, which, in 1931, became the official American national anthem. Several key Maryland legislators had been imprisoned there in May

1861, when President Lincoln suspended the writ of habeus corpus. In the course of the war some 2,000 leading Southern sympathizers were jailed there under Lincoln's orders – often without the benefit of trials or the luxury of a defence – to prevent Maryland from joining the Confederacy. The U.S. Supreme Court subsequently found that Lincoln's actions in Maryland were in violation of the Constitution and issued a writ ordering him to free the prisoners. But Lincoln ignored the Court's order, telling Congress: "Are all the laws, but one, to go unexecuted, and the Government itself go to pieces, lest that one be violated?" Congress, somewhat reluctantly, eventually gave Lincoln authority to suspend the writ, since he had already done so in any event.

After Gettysburg, almost 7,000 Confederate prisoners were shipped to Baltimore and Fort McHenry. Secord, who was among them, had no intention of hanging around for long. He clearly was not singing patriotic Northern songs on October 10, 1863, when he and some of his comrades scaled the wall of the fort and escaped to New York. If, as the locals tell it, Secord was a reluctant Southern recruit, one wonders why he didn't take the opportunity of returning to Canada from New York. Instead, some Southern sympathizers helped him escape back to Georgia, where he rejoined the 20th Regiment. He became a medical officer, listed on a register of the Inspector of Hospitals Office, Richmond, Virginia, showing quarterly reports received from medical officers of the sick and wounded. His report was received on August 16, 1864, sent from a station near Gordonsville, Virginia. Secord may have also spent some time working at a four-storey cotton warehouse in Marietta, Georgia, the historic Kennesaw House, which had been turned into a hospital by the Confederates. The last known document containing his name was on a field, staff, and band muster roll for the 20th Georgia for September and October 1864, where it says "resigned" beside his name in the remarks section.

What is certain is that, after resigning from the Confederate service, Secord returned to Kincardine, where, with the exception of one year in the late 1860s which he spent in Sedalia, Mississippi, he lived the rest of his life. He married Elvira Crable, a local woman, and the couple had three children. Eventually they moved into a yellow-brick Gothic Revival home at 276 Durham Street, which still stands, not far from where the Kincardine Scottish Pipe Band takes its Saturday evening smoke break on Queen Street before heading back to Victoria Park and the concert.

Canadians like to think that their ancestors in the war all fought for the North. Although most of them did, that decision did not always stem from their opposition to slavery. In fact, as the war progressed, public opinion in Canada became decidedly pro-South, but the North was right next door and signing bonuses of up to $800 were a powerful attraction, as was the age-old notion of excitement and adventure.

There is no way of knowing precisely how many British North Americans fought for the South, although published estimates have ranged from 1,000 to 40,000. The likely number is far closer to the former than the later, though the available information is sketchy. Canadian Civil War historian Tom Brooks, for example, wrote in the *Camp Chase Gazette* in June 1991 that the number of Canadians in the Southern forces "can only be remotely guessed at" and mentioned the following examples: Halifax-born Thomas J. Devine, a district judge in Texas who served as Confederate commissioner to Mexico; John Orr, regimental adjutant for the 6th Louisiana Infantry; John Tolen and William St. Clair, privates in Company B of that regiment; George Osborne Elms, Company A of the 28th Louisiana Infantry; and E.A. McKenney, Company C, Texas Cavalry. How they got into those regiments, and why, and what happened to them has been lost to history.

Author Greg C. White writes that Andrew L. Ramsay, a marble cutter by trade, was born in Canada about 1831 and enlisted as a second Corporal with Company B, the "Muscogee Confederates," in the newly formed 31st Georgia Volunteer Infantry on October 5, 1861.[2] As part of Stonewall Jackson's Foot Cavalry, the regiment distinguished itself during its first year of action at Cold Harbor, Second Manassas, Sharpsburg, and Fredericksburg. At one point Confederate General Jubal Early – who would move to Canada for a time after the war – called it the bravest regiment he had ever seen. But Ramsay didn't live to see much of his regiment's heroics. He died at Beaulieu, Georgia, on March 8, 1862, just five months after enlisting.

Newspapers are a source for much of the available information, but the items on ordinary soldiers are usually quite brief. The December 7, 1864, *Niagara Mail*, for example, reports the death of William W. Johnson at Seabrook's Hospital, Richmond, on September 28 of wounds received in the charge on Weldon Road. Johnson, 29, was from Niagara, son of Isaac Henry Johnson and his wife, Annie Laing, and had joined the Sumter Guards of the Confederate Army.

Irish-born John O'Dowd, who migrated to Paris, Canada West, about 1846 and married Margaret Malay, signed up for the Tennessee Home Guards and fought for the Confederates. So, too, did two Adam brothers from Nova Scotia, who enlisted in Louisiana. One brother, Octave, liking it in the South, stayed on after the war and married a local woman. Major David B. Bridgford, a member of the Richmond Light Infantry Blues, was born in Canada, the son of a British officer and one-time lieutenant-governor of Upper Canada. He joined the 1st Virginia Battalion as captain in April 1861, became commander of B Company the next month, was promoted to major in October 1862, and given command of the battalion. From June 1863 until the war ended, Bridgford served as "acting" provost marshal for the Second Corps, then as provost marshal for the entire Army of

North Virginia. The Provost Guard, which also played a key role in the handling of prisoners, was temporarily assigned on provost marshal duty in 1863, but the "temporary" assignment lasted the rest of the war. After the war ended, Bridgford returned to New York and resumed his career in the shipping trade. He died in New York City on February 21, 1888.

On the popular Canadian Civil War Web site, Private Church & Friends, on behalf of the 2nd Michigan Volunteer Infantry, Company A, and the Ottawa Valley American Civil War Re-enactment Society, Church published a list of fourteen Canadians who fought for the South in Arkansas regiments. The list included Charles Jacques Boucher, born in November 1833 at Amherstburg, Ontario, who served as a private with Company E, 16th Arkansas Infantry Regiment, Confederate States of America (CSA), along with four of his relatives: three privates – G.L. Boucher, J.W. Boucher, and James T. Boucher – and Corporal Samuel K. Boucher. Another Canadian, Andrew E. Moore, a farmer, enlisted in "Crittenden Rangers," Company C, 6th Battalion Arkansas Cavalry, on June 3, 1861 – the same day that Canadian A.R. Anderson joined the unit – but he was killed in a fight with another private from the Rangers at Bowling Green, Kentucky, on October 12, 1861. Leslie Crook, born in Canada West around 1838, enlisted in the Ashley Light Infantry, Company F, 8th Battalion Arkansas Infantry, on March 15, 1862, then transferred to Company A., 12th Battalion Arkansas Sharpshooters, that June, an elite battalion of skirmishers organized from volunteers from other Arkansas units. He was captured at the fall of Vicksburg, Mississippi, on July 4, 1863, and paroled three days later.

Among a large group of men who volunteered on December 13, 1862, to form the Desha Rangers, an independent cavalry troop from rural Desha County, Arkansas, under Captain William S. Malcomb was John Cady, who had been born in British North America around 1833. The Rangers, although independent, were often attached temporarily to other regiments, such as the 5th Arkansas Cavalry Regiment and Carlton's Arkansas Cavalry Regiment, where they were usually detailed as advance scouts and sometimes as the commanding general's escort troop. Whatever convinced Cady to sign up, he apparently had second thoughts eight months later, since he was listed as a deserter at Redfork, Arkansas, on August 2, 1863, never to be officially heard from again.

The October 23, 1862, *Quebec Gazette* published a brief obituary of George Goldring, who had died a month earlier in Chicago "on his way home from the Southern army." He was the third son of Henry Goldring and son-in-law of George Hanson Gardener, both of Toronto.

James Law of Hamilton, Ontario, left his hometown and moved to New Orleans in 1860, enlisting with the CSA and serving for eighteen months before returning to Hamilton, where he died shortly afterwards. Albert Roberts, the U.S. consul to Hamilton between 1885 and 1889, spent most of the war as a captain with a Tennessee regiment and was instrumental, along with Colonel William Monaghan, who succeeded him as consul, in forming the Hamilton post of the Grand Army of the Republic. Another Confederate outfit with a significant connection to Canada was the 10th Louisiana. During the battle of Malvern Hill on July 1, 1862, Louisiana-born plantation owner Colonel Eugene Waggaman led them into battle. Waggaman's sister Christine was married to John Sanfield Macdonald, who became prime minister of the United Provinces of Canada on August 13, 1863, and, after Confederation, the first premier of Ontario. The 10th Louisiana was also chosen on January 27, 1985, in Toronto as the name of a new re-enactment regiment. Many of its members took part in the filming of the movie *Gettysburg*, and it is the only foreign "life member" of the Association for the Preservation of Civil War Sites. In addition, the 10th is also a member of the 4th Brigade, Army of Northern Virginia, commanded by Colonel

Don Taylor of North Carolina, and Canadian historian Tom Brooks is the color sergeant – a high honour for a Canadian to be recognized in this way by his American peers.

Brooks, along with Michael Dan Jones, a Texas-born U.S. Navy veteran and long-time Louisiana journalist, published a history of the 10th Louisiana, called *Lee's Foreign Legion*, which offers a detailed history of the men who served during the war. The authors also point out that, in addition to the fighting men of the 10th who had a Canadian connection, the French-born Jesuit who served as regimental chaplain, Father Louis-Hippolyte Gaché, died in Montreal in 1907. Of the regiment's 953 officers and men, 53 percent were foreign born, from twenty-two different countries (though about half of them were from Ireland). Among the regiment's members were eight Canadian-born volunteers. One of them, Private Jerry Cronan, was a 28-year-old bachelor when he enlisted on July 22, 1861, at Camp Moore. He was wounded in May 1863 at Chancellorsville and wounded again, and captured, at Spotsylvania. He was sent to the Judiciary Square U.S. General Hospital in Washington and, in an effort to save his life, his right arm was amputated. But, like so many amputees during the war, Cronan died on June 2, 1864. What makes his death historically significant for Canadians is that he was interred in the small Confederate section of Arlington National Cemetery, becoming the only Canadian Confederate to be buried there.

Quebec-born Captain Pierre Le Claire also died during the hand-to-hand fighting in the trenches at Spotsylvania on May 12, 1864. He had enlisted on July 22, 1861, and was just 27 and a bachelor. He had been wounded earlier at Second Manassas.

Another single Canadian labourer working in New Orleans was Joseph Labranche, who was wounded at Cold Harbor on June 3, 1864, and wounded again, and captured, at Cedar Creek on October 19. It is not known what became of Labranche. Canadian-born Henry Williams, a farmer from St. Landry Parish,

Louisiana, enlisted as a corporal at Camp Moore on July 22, 1861, but eventually deserted the 10th Louisiana to sign up with the Confederate Cavalry.

There were also two Canadian sergeants, Adolphe and Henry De Montigny, in the unit. Both clerks in New Orleans at the time, both bachelors, they enlisted at Camp Moore on July 22, 1861. Adolphe became ill during the winter of 1861–62 when the regiment was stationed at Lee's Mill, Virginia, and was confined to the Louisiana Hospital in Richmond. But he never fully recovered and was discharged in July 1862 because of his deteriorating health. Henry De Montigny stayed with the 10th Louisiana until May 31, 1864, when he apparently grew tired of the war and, like an estimated one Confederate soldier in nine (compared to one in seven for the Union), deserted.

Another category of soldiers listed by Brooks and Jones in their history of the 10th Louisiana are the "oath takers" – those who, when captured, saved themselves by swearing out an Oath of Allegiance to the United States. One of them was Canadian-born Henry Scott, a private, whose occupation was listed as sailor, the only Canadian in Company A. He was captured at Spotsylvania in 1864 and imprisoned at Point Lookout, Maryland, where he took the oath on May 28, 1864.

A third category are the "galvanizers," men who went one step beyond taking the enemy's oath and actually joined the Federal Army, exchanging their Confederate greys for Union blue, thereby becoming "galvanized Yankees." Brooks and Jones include them in the chapter "The Good, the Bad, and the Ugly," and they brand galvanizing "the most heinous of the three categories of malefactions." A total of forty-two regimental members switched sides in this fashion. Among them was 29-year-old Charles Holmes, a Canadian labourer living in New Orleans when the war broke out. He volunteered at Camp Moore on July 22, 1861, but spent most of the winter in the Louisiana Hospital in Richmond, thought to be the only Canadian wounded and captured at Culp's Hill at Gettysburg. In September 1863, two months after being sent to prison at Fort Delaware, Holmes became one of fifteen men from the 10th Louisiana to become "galvanized Yankees," signing up with the 3rd Maryland Cavalry. Ironically, their Maryland regiment was sent to New Orleans early in 1864 as part of what the locals considered an occupying army.

One of the most famous Canadians in the war was a telegrapher from the Ottawa Valley named George A. Ellsworth, known far and wide by the nickname "Lightning," who used his incredible telegraphic skills to disrupt Union activities and help spread the reputation of Confederate General John Hunt Morgan during his legendary cavalry raids throughout Kentucky.

Ellsworth met Morgan in July 1862 in Mobile and was one of the 800 men who followed Morgan some 1,000 miles from Knoxville into Kentucky in less than a month, capturing and patrolling 1,200 Union prisoners while losing only 100 of his own men. "A large part of this success was due to Ellsworth's shameless telegraphic fabrications, sent to various Union stations. Befuddled by these adroit fictions, the Federals rarely knew where Morgan was and never knew what he was going to do next ... his waggish wires served two vital military purposes. The messages he sent caused alarm, confusion, or delay among the Yankees. The messages he picked up by wire-tapping warned Morgan well in advance of what the enemy was doing or was going to do. Some of Ellsworth's telegrams, to be sure, served no military purpose whatever. They were sent for pure amusement, when the raiding cavalry was ready to move out and secrecy no longer mattered. Morgan found it just as diverting as Ellsworth did to send jocular telegrams to leaders on the other side."[3]

Before enlisting in Company A, Second Kentucky Cavalry, in Chattanooga on June 1, 1862, Ellsworth was assistant superintendent of the Texas Telegraph Co. He could tap a line without being noticed even when another operator was using it. He earned his nickname while part of a small detail of men led by Morgan near Cave City, Kentucky, close to the vital Union supply line along the Louisville & Nashville Railroad. Shortly after Ellsworth had tapped into the nearby telegraph wire, a severe thunderstorm broke out but, despite the obvious dangers and with lightning flaring all around him, he sat through the rain-soaked darkness and intercepted Union General Jeremiah T. Boyle as he sent orders from Louisville to Colonel Sanders D. Bruce at Bowling Green on troop movements to capture Morgan and his raiders. Thanks to Ellsworth, Bruce never received Boyle's orders, or a series of follow-up orders, although Ellsworth tricked Boyle into thinking that the messages had been received. The story goes that a Confederate scout named Ben Drake, seeing Ellsworth working despite the lightning flashing around him, exclaimed, "old lightning himself,"[4] a nickname that stayed with him throughout the war and made him the best-known telegrapher on either side of the war.

Author John Bakeless also writes at length about an August 10, 1862, raid on Gallatin, Kentucky, during which Morgan sent Ellsworth and a small party into town to capture regimental commander Colonel William P. Boone. Leaving their horses a mile outside the town and walking through the surrounding cornfields, the party arrived at dawn, finding Boone getting dressed in his room at the local hotel, a few hundreds yards from his troops. Ellsworth and a companion then went to the second floor of the railroad station, where they burst into the bedroom of telegrapher J.N. Brooks. Eventually Morgan and his cavalry arrived and Boone, recognizing the situation, ordered his troops to surrender. After breakfast, Ellsworth ordered Brooks to send a telegraph asking about train schedules, and the Confederates soon learned that the No. 6 bound for Louisville was on schedule.

At one point Ellsworth intercepted a message from the train

conductor confirming his orders to bring his train into Gallatin, but Nashville officials, suspicious of the telegraph Brooks had sent (since it was well before normal opening time), refused. Ellsworth, however, having tapped into this discussion, promptly sent the conductor a wire cancelling the previous order and instructing him to bring his train to Gallatin. When it rolled into town, Morgan and his men captured the twenty-four freight cars, many of them loaded with Federal supplies, including fifty fresh horses.

Realizing that even more suspicions would be aroused when the train didn't show up where it was supposed to be, Ellsworth pretended to be anxious about the train and wired Union operators, asking about its whereabouts. The Nashville operator, as a joke, replied, "Guess Morgan's got her." There were several telegrams back and forth all day but, finally, realizing they weren't likely to capture another train, Morgan decided to pull out of Gallatin. In response to a query from Nashville about who, exactly, was at the Gallatin key, Ellsworth replied, "I am Ellsworth." The Nashville northeast station replied, "You damn wild Canadian, what are you doing there?"[5]

In January 1863 Ellsworth spent two weeks living in a thicket near Cave City, Kentucky, listening to Union messages. On his way back to Morgan, carrying more than 300 copies of official Union telegrams – a hanging offence for sure – he was spotted by Federal cavalry. They gave chase, but Ellsworth managed to get back to Morgan. The telegrams, containing vital news of Union troop movements, were forwarded to General Braxton Bragg, commander of the Army of Tennessee.

Two months later Ellsworth was wounded in the ankle during a pistol fight with a Union soldier while on an all-night ride from Cave City to warn Morgan about a planned movement of Union troops. Ellsworth rode 2 miles with just one foot in the stirrup until he found Morgan. He was allowed to recuperate until June, when he was ordered to help with some raids into

Ohio, where Morgan, who was beginning to believe his own press clippings, violated Bragg's direct instructions not to cross the Ohio River. Ellsworth, along with Morgan and most of his men, were captured near New Liston, Ohio, on July 26, 1863, and sent to the Ohio State Penitentiary. Morgan escaped in November – along with Captain Thomas Hines, who would become a key player in Confederate operations in Canada – and was killed in a surprise raid at Greeneville, Tennessee, on September 4, 1864. Ellsworth passed several months in prison before being released, after which he spent the remaining months of the war as head of General P.G.T. Beauregard's telegraphy. He survived the war, but never returned to his native country.

One famous Confederate who was not a Canadian by birth but, late in the war, ended up living in Hamilton, Ontario, to escape a $10,000 bounty on his head was Frank Stringfellow. His full name, which he didn't use, was Benjamin Franklin Stringfellow, a notorious rebel spy who was described by his enemies as "the most dangerous man in the Confederacy." Weighing in at less than one hundred pounds on a 5-foot-8-inch frame, the beard-less, blue-eyed, curly blond-haired, and deeply religious Stringfellow, who also suffered from a habitual cough, hardly cut an imposing figure. Yet his scrawny figure – which led to four rejections before he was finally accepted into service by the Confederates – actually helped him succeed as a spy. "With a lit-tle suitable padding in the right places, it enabled him to enter the Union lines disguised as a girl and return with his masquerade unquestioned. It also led numerous confiding federals to under-estimate him – until it was too late."[6] His frail appearance, com-bined with his daring and cunning, made him a genuine star of General J.E.B. Stuart's network of southern spies. At one point, for example, he got close enough to General Grant to hear him talking to his troops, and he was such an important figure that, during the Wilderness campaign, he reported directly to General Robert E. Lee. His final assignment in the war – the one that forced him to flee to Canada – was given to him directly by Confederate President Jefferson Davis.

Stringfellow, who rose to a lieutenant in the Signal Corps, once held up a sutler's wagon at gunpoint specifically to rob him of his pass so he could penetrate enemy lines. On another occasion he bluffed his way past a Union outpost only to lead a cavalry raid against it, and, disguised as a woman, he even danced with unsuspecting Federal officers, men who were starved for feminine companionship and often remarkably loose-lipped in the process. One time Stringfellow actually hid under an elderly lady's hoop skirt while Federal agents, tipped off about his presence, searched the house in vain for him. He was captured and exchanged several times throughout the conflict.

In September 1864 Stringfellow sent a letter directly to General Lee, proposing that they kidnap Union General August Kautz. In February 1865 he again wrote to Lee, suggesting they kidnap Grant. When that letter was passed along to Davis, the president personally assigned Stringfellow to Washington to gather intelligence. His cover was that he would be a student of dentistry, using the name and papers of a Maryland soldier imprisoned by the Confederates. Arriving in Washington the day after Lincoln's second inaugural, it was never really made clear what his precise assignment would be, but, given his penchant for wanting to kidnap prominent Federals, and coming so close to Lincoln's assassination, his intentions certainly weren't good. Stringfellow actually boarded for a few days in the Kirkwood House, where Vice-President Andrew Johnson stayed. (Johnson, of course, would become president after Lincoln was assassinated.) "At another point he [Stringfellow] told of being 'in constant communication with an officer occupying an important position about Mr. Lincoln.'"[7]

On April 1, just two weeks before Lincoln was shot,

Stringfellow suddenly left Washington, he told Davis, "by the aid of a person whose name is linked in the history of these last dark days . . ." making "twelve miles the first evening."[8] William A. Tidwell writes: "There is no way to identify the person who aided him. But the wording is highly suggestive. John Wilkes Booth left Washington that day 'on the afternoon train,' as shown in the records of the National Hotel. Stringfellow's reference to 'the first evening' would also put his departure in the afternoon. Further, 'some twelve miles' is almost the precise distance from downtown Washington to the safe house regularly used by Confederate agents – Mrs. Mary Surratt's country tavern in Prince George's County, Maryland." Surratt was later hanged for her role in Lincoln's murder.

As for Stringfellow, he was captured in Maryland on April 2 by a Union patrol, but escaped two days later and headed for Canada, where he stayed until 1867 and was made exceedingly welcome by the large number of Confederate refugees already living there. Tidwell speculates that "a reasonable explanation for this extended Canadian stay is that Stringfellow feared to come home until he felt certain his Washington assignment had not been disclosed to the hated Yankees."

Stringfellow, whatever his role in Lincoln's death might have been, apparently kept a low profile in Hamilton. With the war over, there was no official work for him anyway, but it is clear that he regularly socialized with other prominent Confederate officials living in the vicinity for fear of being arrested on their return, particularly General Jubal Early and former U.S. Vice-President John C. Breckinridge. In 1867, feeling it was safe to leave Canada, he went to Wakefield, Virginia, and, after several months of preparation, entered the Episcopal Seminary of Virginia. There he graduated and was ordained, preached in a succession of churches, and, in 1898, became a chaplain in the U.S. Army. He died on June 8, 1913, from a heart attack.

Antipathy towards the institution of slavery was widespread in British North America when the war broke out. It created such initial sympathy for the Union cause that one "Highland" regiment raised in Boston in 1861 consisted almost completely of Nova Scotians. Some of them, writes Thomas Raddall, were "members of the Halifax militia; and their tales of battle appearing in letters to home newspapers were followed with all the avidity of a people actually at war.

"But the gathering of large armies across the border aroused misgivings in old men who remembered 1812, and their misgivings were increased by an astounding rumor from the States. It was said that Washington politicians were planning to unify their nation by a deliberately provoked war with a European nation or nations, preferably the British. The rumor was true. In April 1861, the U.S. Secretary of State [William H.] Seward had made this cold proposal to President Lincoln, and suggested himself as the man to conduct the provocation and the war. Lincoln quietly put it aside. But the impression was abroad and it was not lessened when Seward ordered the governors of the North states to take 'military precautions' on the Canadian frontier and adjacent coasts. Then came the Trent Affair."9

There is no doubt that, as the war dragged on and tensions between Britain and the United States increased – along with the disruption of Canadian trade caused by the coastal blockade – sympathies for the Southern cause dramatically increased in the Canadas. More and more Canadians, while perhaps not rushing to the South to enlist, were doing what they could from north of the border to support the South, ranging from extensive trading to offering financial and moral support to any and all Southerners who found themselves living north of the U.S. border.

W.H. Russell, the Canadian correspondent of *The Times* of London, a man of pro-Northern sympathies, travelled through-

out Canada shortly after the war began and wrote a widely published series of letters, which were reprinted in several Canadian
newspapers. He reported that, in Montreal, he found "a knot of
Southern families, in a sort of American Siberia, in a very comfortable hotel [St. Lawrence Hall], who nurse their wrath against
the Yankees to keep it warm and sustain each others' spirits. They
form a nucleus for sympathizing society to cluster around."

In a 1920 essay, historian Fred Landon wrote that once the
Southern states began to secede, "Canada had an influx of both
Northern and Southern elements. Canada had for some years
been a popular summer home for wealthy Southerners, and early
in 1861 many families began to arrive, the heads of the house-
holds being already in the Confederate forces." There were also
some Southern families who had sold everything and came to
Canada to make it their permanent home, at least until conditions straightened out in the South. These Southern refugees
were naturally bitter towards the North, and during the whole of
the war they tended to alienate Canadian sentiment from the
cause for which Lincoln was holding fast. "On the other hand, the
element that came in from the North was not of the type that
would counteract Southern propaganda. 'Skedaddlers' leaving
their homes in the North, to evade military service, depressed the
labour market in Canada and lowered wages in some trades.
There were pacifists as well who had left the country or been
driven out."[10]

One dramatic indication of the extent of Southern sympathies was outlined by W.T.R. Preston, a longtime Liberal back-
room organizer and senior federal bureaucrat, who wrote about a
"significant incident"[11] in the House of Commons shortly after
the Battle of Bull Run, or First Manassas, on July 21, 1861. Most
of Washington's society had come out to watch the Union Army
under General Irvin McDowell whip the Confederates under
General P.G.T. Beauregard. Instead of the expected easy Union
victory – and thanks largely to the historic resistance offered by

Confederate General Stonewall Jackson – the Union forces were routed, causing panic in their ranks and forcing many of them, literally, to run back to Washington.

Preston writes: "During the Civil War, a number of wealthy Southerners took refuge in Canada, and, mingling in Tory social circles, created a sympathetic Southern atmosphere, of which Northern spies kept Washington only too well informed. At the time of the battle of Bull Run, when the Northern armies suffered a very severe reverse, one or two Tory members, who had dined not wisely but too well, entered the Legislative Assembly with the news and, with a few sympathizers, started to cheer. At once the Speaker intervened. The great majority of the members on both sides were aghast. There was a moment of deadly silence, but the mischief had been done. To the horror of everybody, American papers published an account of the incident as, 'The Canadian House applauds the defeat of the Northern troops.' Whether or not George Brown might have overcome this acute prejudice that this created in the Washington Cabinet can never be known."

Even Sir John A. Macdonald, it seems, while fairly even-handed in his wartime dealings with the Americans, succumbed to the romance of the Southern cause, feeling confident enough in the popularity of Southern sympathies to betray his own personal feelings on the matter. Speaking on September 12, 1864, at a meeting in Halifax of delegates following the Charlottetown Confederation Conference, Macdonald openly praised "the gallant defence that is being made by the Southern Republic – at this moment they have not much more than four millions of men – not much exceeding our own numbers, yet what a brave fight they have made."[12]

Still, given the great distances between British North America and the South, it was extremely difficult, even for those so inclined, to make their way to a Confederate recruiter. That being said, there is no doubt that public opinion – while generally strongly anti-slavery – was severely split.

Norman Wade, of Bridgewater, Nova Scotia, in a series of 1861 letters to his parents and family – including his brother Fletcher Bath Wade, a prominent Halifax lawyer and Liberal MP for Annapolis County for many years – demonstrates that, just as many American families were split on the issue, so, too, were families north of the border. Wade, like many Nova Scotians of the time, left home as a young man and went to sea. He lived for a while in Liverpool, then in New York, then in Detroit – because wages on the Great Lakes were $90 a month – and finally in Boston, where, in a letter dated September 20, 1861, he told his parents: "Perhaps you will be surprised at the step I have taken now as belonging to Uncle Sam for one year, Captain of the forecastle and Captain of the gun on board the U.S.S. Young Rover," where he'd be paid $25 a month "besides the prize money."

Wade had come by his interest in the military honestly. An English coat of arms – azure on a saltire between four fleur-de-lis – was first granted to William Wade of Gloustershire, England, in 1604. His son, John Wade, was a major-general in Oliver Cromwell's Puritan army in the 1640s. The family first came to North American in 1632, when three Wade brothers arrived at Charlestown, Massachusetts, aboard the *Falcon* from England. Another offspring, Norman Wade – the great-grandfather of his namesake from the Civil War – was born in Bridgewater, Massachusetts, in 1725. A millwright and cabinet worker, he emigrated to Granville, Nova Scotia, in 1761 after wintering in Halifax, where he taught his trade to his sons and where many chairs and antique patterns manufactured by him are still in use. At the age of 33 he was appointed a captain and raised a company of troops to aid the British in the capture of Louisbourg. From there, Wade and his men ventured on to Quebec City, where he fought with General Wolfe in defeating the French on the Plains of Abraham in 1759, arguably the most important battle in British North American history.

In a November 25 letter to his father, Job, in which he described the capture of a prize worth $20,000, Wade wrote: "It seems that some of the people of Nova Scotia should sympathise with the Southerners. Several of them have been caught trying to run the blockade with arms and provisions for the rebels." He said they stopped a Lunenburg schooner two days earlier after he had fired the ship's cannon at her, and "some of the officers had the joke on me for firing at my own countrymen."

In a March 5, 1862, letter to his politician brother, Fletcher, the youngest son among the family's eleven children, Wade wrote: "I am not surprised to hear that your sympathies were wholly with the south, and do not see how it can be possible, considering the relation we bear with the northern people. You say that if three million people want their freedom they ought to have it, but is it freedom they are fighting for, or are they dupes of designing politicians? All know that there can be no freer form of government than the United States, and it is no wonder that Europe, a tyrant, should look upon her with an evil eye. You chose to look on me as a hireling, but I beg leave to inform you that not only my sword (for you must recollect that I wear one) but my whole heart is in the cause I have adopted. For where is a country where foreigners receive all the privileges of native born citizens? And persons receiving those privileges can not be called hirelings for trying to support her in times of trouble. But a truce to this for I see no reasons why we should quarrel about it for we may see the day when the Provinces will have a flag of their own yet, although it may be distant. I congratulate you on the success of the Liberal Party and I am glad to hear that Nova Scotia is shaking the rust of Toryism off once more."[13]

In a September 16, 1863, letter to Wade's sister Catherine, Norman's close friend John Leroach, who had originally talked him into enlisting, wrote to say that her 25-year-old brother had been killed two days earlier after falling from a loft on the *Young Rover* and was buried on an island near the shore. "We had laid

FIVE

Blacks and Brown

FROM THE OUTSET, Martin Robinson Delany defied the odds. From his birth into a slave family in Charles Town, Virginia (now West Virginia), Delany grew up to become a medical doctor, a confidant of radical abolitionist leader John Brown, a friend of President Abraham Lincoln, an international celebrity and world traveller, the first black commissioned military officer in U.S. history, a successful author and newspaper publisher, and the man widely recognized by historians as the father of black nationalism in the United States.

And along the way, he and many prominent American blacks – as well as the anti-slave zealot John Brown – had a significant Canadian connection. This link helped to lead the United States inexorably into war and to give ultimate freedom for Delany and his fellow African-Americans.

Born on May 6, 1812, just a month before the United States officially declared war against Great Britain in the War of 1812, Martin's father, Samuel, was a slave, but his mother, Pati Pearce, was a free woman who was both heroically courageous and determined to make the best of a bad situation for her family. Two years before Martin's birth, for instance, she walked 20 miles to the Winchester courthouse, carrying her two children with her, to defend her family successfully against an attempt by a local plantation owner to enslave them all. At some point, too, she managed to obtain a copy of *The New York Primer and Spelling Book* from a travelling peddler and used it to teach all five of her children to read. At the time a Virginia law made teaching enslaved blacks how to read a "crime" and, if discovered, the entire family would be sent into slavery or taken to a nearby almshouse, where they would be rented out as labourers to local farmers. One day a local sheriff happened by their small house on Charles Street and noticed the children reading. When they told their mother about the visit, Pati knew it was time to escape and, with the help of Randal Brown, a sympathetic banker, she got to Pennsylvania with Martin and his siblings before officials came back to arrest her. The family settled in Kernstown, a black community near Chambersburg, the site of two major battles in the Civil War.[1] To support the family, Pati worked as a labourer and seamstress while her mother, Graci, looked after the children.

In 1823, a year after the Delany family fled Virginia, a U.S. Circuit Court ruled that removing an enslaved person to a "free state" bestows freedom on them and that any malicious, cruel, or inhuman treatment of them is an indictable offence. Finally, at the age of 53, Samuel Delany was able to buy his freedom with the help of the proceeds from the sale of Pati's house and join his family in Kernstown. That same year, Martin began studying and worshipping at the black Methodist Episcopal Church, leaving briefly in 1828 to work in Cumberland County because the family could not support his education. In 1831 the 19-year-old lad walked to Pittsburgh and got a job as a barber, enrolling as a student under the Reverend Lewis Woodson in the cellar of Bethel African Methodist Church on Wylie Street. The next year he studied the classics, Latin and Greek, at Jefferson College. He was befriended by Dr. Andrew N. McDowell and, in 1833, during the cholera epidemic, he was hired as a physician's assistant, where he learned how to be a cupper and lecher. Eventually he upgraded his skills by studying medicine in the 1840s with McDowell and two other well-known abolitionist doctors, F. Julius LeMoyne and Joseph P. Gazzam.

Through his association with Woodson in particular, Delany began his lifetime involvement in social and political affairs. He attended his first Negro Convention in both Philadelphia and New York in 1836, about the same time that he set up his practice as a cupper and leecher at 40 Kerr's Row, between Liberty and Penn streets in Pittsburgh. He was barred because of his colour from the white literary societies, so Delany and a friend formed the Theban Literary Society. He also became secretary of the Philanthropic Society, a cover organization for the Underground Railroad, helping fugitive slaves escape to Canada. In 1836 he conceived the idea of leading an expedition to the eastern coast of Africa in search of a "Black Israel," and in 1837 he formed the Young Men's Literary and Moral Reform Society, a temperance response to the widespread whisky consumption among young blacks. (Twelve years later, Pittsburgh's mayor deputized society members as black police officers to quell the regular drunken riots.) That same year Delany toured the Mississippi River south to Louisiana, then over to Texas, to witness slavery first hand and to find a possible haven for freed blacks, a trip that inspired his semi-fictional novel *Blake: The Huts of America*. In 1843 he married Kate A. Richards, the mixed-race daughter of Charles Richards, a wealthy and influential Pittsburgh businessman and property owner. The couple had eleven children, seven of whom survived to adulthood, and named them all after African heroes.

By this time there were several successful black anti-slavery newspapers – the first, begun in 1827, was *Freedom's Journal* in New York – and in September 1843 Delany, with the help of some wealthy white backers, founded his own, *The Mystery*, the first black-owned newspaper west of the Allegheny Mountains. Delany's fame – or infamy in pro-slavery circles – grew when the renowned anti-slave publisher William Lloyd Garrison, a founder of the American Anti-Slavery Society, published some of his articles in his newspaper, *The Liberator*. Garrison, a white man from Massachusetts, was so unpopular in the South that Georgia offered a $5,000 reward for his arrest and conviction. Delany met Garrison and the even more famous abolitionist Frederick Douglass, the son of a white man and a black slave, when the two men visited Pittsburgh on an anti-slavery tour on August 14, 1847. They persuaded him to close *The Mystery* and co-edit *The North Star* with Douglass.

Delany began to travel constantly, lecturing, reporting, and selling subscriptions for the newspaper – a risky business for a black man, even in the North. In May 1848, for example, Delany and Charles H. Langston, travelling by horse and buggy to Marseilles, Ohio, had just checked into their hotel when a mob of angry men, gathered around a blazing fire in the middle of the street, threatened to tar and feather Delany and demanded that the hotel owner send him out. Expecting the worst, Delany armed himself with a butcher knife and a hatchet and stood at the head of the stairs, awaiting an attack from the mob. Fortunately, just after the mob voted to "break into the hotel, bring the nigger out, and burn him," a veteran U.S. soldier who had fought in the Mexican War chanced along and calmed them down. The two men left quietly very early in the morning.[2]

The next major event to affect Delany's life was the passage of the *Fugitive Slave Act* on September 18, 1850. It would destroy Delany's long-standing belief that a combination of reasoned argument and demonstrable merit could overcome prejudice against blacks, and it also led him directly to Canada, where he played a role in John Brown's ill-fated raid at Harper's Ferry. Billed as a compromise when the slavery issue threatened to dissolve the Union, the act allowed California to be admitted as a free state, while new territories in the southwest could organize as slave states if they chose that route. It also abolished the domestic slave trade in the District of Columbia. Although the white politicians believed they'd dodged a bullet, the act created terrible grief for the black population. In describing slaves as "property," it denied a slave any defence in court and gave slave-owners the right to return their property wherever it could be found. People suspected of being runaway slaves could be arrested without warrant and turned over to a claimant, based solely on his sworn testimony of ownership. As property, the suspects could not have a jury trial or testify on their own behalf. In practice, slave-owners now hired bounty hunters to track down escaped slaves, but the hunters weren't particular about whether the property they captured actually was an escaped slave or not, prompting many thousands of blacks to flee northward into Canada to avoid being forcefully removed to the South.

In a speech to a large crowd in Pittsburgh on September 30, Delany stated defiantly: "Sir, my house is my castle . . . If any man approaches that house in search of a slave . . . if he crosses the threshold of my door, and I do not lay him a lifeless corpse at my feet, I hope the grave may refuse my body a resting place, and righteous Heaven my spirit a home. O, no!! He cannot enter that house and we both live."

That fall, Delany applied to Harvard Medical School, along with two black Bostonians sponsored by the American Colonization Society. Delany had letters of support from seventeen Pittsburgh area physicians, but white medical students passed a resolution in December condemning the admission as "highly detrimental to the interests, and welfare of the Institution." The day after Christmas, following a 68 to 48 vote by the students, the faculty agreed to dismiss him. In March 1851 Delany left Harvard Medical School after completing just one of the necessary two, four-month terms.

Delany's first direct connection with Canada began when he met activist Henry Bibb in September 1851. Bibb invited him to attend the North American Convention of Colored Freemen at Toronto's St. Lawrence Hall, an anti-slavery gathering of several hundred freemen from Canada, the Northern states, and England. The convention resolved to encourage American slaves to resettle in Canada instead of returning to Africa (which was Delany's preference), on the grounds that Canada was the best place from which to organize anti-slavery activities. It held the convention in Toronto because "the British government was the most favourable in the civilized world to the people of colour and was thereby entitled to the entire confidence of the Convention."[3] Bibb, whose mother was a slave in Kentucky – and who had himself been sold by a slave-owner to a group of Native Americans and had subsequently escaped – had become one of the best-known anti-slave activists in the United States. In January 1851, just three years before his death, Bibb and Josiah Henson – the prototype for Harriet Beecher Stowe's controversial and highly influential anti-slavery best-seller, *Uncle Tom's Cabin* – formed the Refugees' Home Colony in Canada for escaped slaves. That same year, Bibb also established the *Voice of the Fugitive* in Windsor, Canada's first African-American newspaper, and Delany, encouraged by Bibb, soon became a regular contributor.

Delany's public challenges to the law, considered impertinent even by most white anti-slave people, made him and his family targets for bounty hunters – a situation that grew more serious when, in 1852, he published *The Condition, Elevation, Emigration and Destiny of the Colored People of the United States Politically Considered*, widely regarded as the first full-length tract of black nationalism. Delany not only criticized abolitionists but recommended that blacks leave the United States. He had become a champion of the notion of an independent black nation in Liberia, but in the meantime recommended that blacks, many of whom could not realistically make their way to Africa, should escape either to Mexico or to Canada. After touring Canada West in 1851, Delany wrote that it is "one of the most beautiful portions of North America."[4] He was less enamoured with Canada East (Quebec), "the climate being cold and severe in winter, the springs being late, the summers rather short, and the soil not so productive."[5]

While arguing that Canada West was a useful North American destination for blacks fleeing the United States, Delany warned that Canadians are descended from the same common parentage as Americans and tend to favour American interests: "The Americans are determined to, and will have the Canadas, to a close observer, there is not a shadow of doubt; And our brethren should know this in time . . . This we forewarn the colored people, in time, is the inevitable and not far distant destiny of the Canadas. And let them come into the American Republic when they may, the fate of the colored man, however free before, is doomed, doomed, forever doomed. Disfranchisement, degradation, and a delivery up to slave catchers and kidnappers are their only fate. Let Canadian annexation take place when it will. The odious infamous fugitive slave law will then be in full force with all of its terrors; and we have not doubt that fully in anticipation of this event, was the despicable law created.

". . . Continue to fly to the Canadas, and swell the number of the twenty-five thousand already there . . . Go on to the North until the South is ready to receive you, for surely, he who can make his way from Arkansas to Canada, can find his way from Kentucky to Mexico. The moment his foot touches this land South, he is free."[6]

In 1856, concerned for the safety of himself and his family, Delany moved to Chatham, Upper Canada, where, two years later, he and other black abolitionist leaders would become involved with John Brown in planning one of the most famous – or infamous – excursions in American history.

While most Canadians, with an air of moral superiority, can readily remonstrate about the history of slavery in the United States, in both the North and the South – few know about the shameful history of slavery in early Canada. Not that slavery in Canada ever reached U.S. proportions, but that had more to do with economics, cotton in particular, than with any widespread qualms about the morality of the institution. Canadians do know that in the years leading up to the Civil War, thousands of escaped slaves and "free" blacks fleeing the tyranny of slave laws came to British North America via the Underground Railroad. Although they were protected from the shackles of slavery here, they were not accepted as full-fledged members of society – a reality that prompted many of them to return to the United States after the war ended.

Black slaves were brought to Canada, or New France as it was called at the time, early in the 1600s. The first recorded slave purchase was in 1608, when sailor David Kirke brought a six-year-old boy to the country from Madagascar and sold him to a wealthy businessman. The boy was sold several times and eventually became the property of Father Paul Lejeune, who baptized him and gave him the name of Olivier Lejeune. He was finally freed in 1638, fourteen years before his death. Although slavery was forbidden in France, King Louis XIII, hoping to attract more settlers to New France, gave limited permission in 1629 for colonists to keep slaves. The colonists then began to buy slaves to clear their land, build their homes, and work as servants in the fields. In 1689 Louis XIV, the "Sun King," issued *Le Code Noir*, the "Black Code," allowing the full use of slaves in the colonies. The governor of New France, Intendant Jacques Raudot, issued a decree in 1709 regulating slavery in the colony, including heavy fines for anyone found guilty of helping slaves to escape.

In April 1734, when Marie-Joseph Angélique, the slave of a wealthy Montreal merchant, learned she was going to be sold to another family, she decided to escape – and, to cover her exit, she set fire to her master's house. Unfortunately, the fire spread rapidly and destroyed forty-six buildings, among them the Hôtel Dieu. Angélique was finally captured in June, cruelly tortured, paraded before angry mobs in the streets, hanged, and her body set on fire. In 1763, when the British took control of New France, there were more than 1,000 black slaves in New France, as well as a large number of aboriginal slaves. At the time, various Indian tribes also practised slavery, using men, women, and children captured during their frequent wars as slaves. In response to pleas from the wealthy, white colonists that slavery was an economic necessity, the 47th Article of Capitulation in the Treaty of Paris, ceding control of Canada to the British, guaranteed the maintenance of slavery in British North America. A 1792 bill to abolish slavery in Lower Canada (Quebec) was defeated, but in 1803 Chief Justice William Osgoode ruled that slavery was inconsistent with British law. That did not abolish slavery, but it guaranteed that any slave who left his or her owner did not have to fear being forcibly returned.

Slavery was also thriving in Nova Scotia, where many blacks were ruthlessly exploited by the local business and political elite, who imported them to help build Halifax – many were skilled tradesmen, others were needed for the grunt work – then re-sold them to the American colonies when their services were no longer required. A March 28, 1775, advertisement in the *Nova Scotia Gazette and Weekly Chronicle*, for example, advertised for sale "a likely, well-made Negro boy, about sixteen years old," while a January 1779 edition advertised "an able Negro wench, about twenty-one years of age, capable of performing both town and country work."

During the American Revolution (1775–83), when the Thirteen Colonies fought for and won their independence, the British promised freedom and land to any slaves – and to "free" blacks as well – who took up arms against the American colonists. When the war ended in defeat for the British, about 50,000 British Loyalists fled to the colonies, some 30,000 to Nova Scotia and New Brunswick alone, bringing about 2,000 slaves with them. Another 3,500 free blacks, who had gained their freedom through their loyalty to Britain, also settled, mainly in Nova Scotia and New Brunswick. Although these ex-slaves were freed from bondage, they were not freed from open discrimination in jobs, schooling, and the day-to-day social and political life of the colonies. For the most part, the British reneged on their promises of land ownership for the black Loyalists. Those who did receive land got smaller parcels than the white Loyalists, usually outside the white settlements and on rocky terrain that was difficult to farm. Many white Loyalists were so unhappy with the British that they soon returned to the United States, but this option was not open to their black counterparts. Because conditions were so poor for Nova Scotia blacks, the first Back to Africa movement emerged and the British Anti-Slavery Society offered black Loyalists passage on a boat to Sierre Leone, West Africa, in 1792. As a result, about 1,200 black Loyalists left Nova Scotia.

Even after the war ended, black slaves continued to be imported. An estimated 1,200 arrived in 1783–84, the bulk of them bought by Nova Scotians, but many were dispatched to slave-owners in New Brunswick and Prince Edward Island as well. During that same period, several hundred more slaves were bought by wealthy families in both Upper and Lower Canada. Slaves in Canada received only marginally better treatment than their U.S. counterparts. They weren't as likely to be lynched for minor transgressions, but, until slavery was outlawed, Canadian slaves were regarded as mere chattels, subject to arbitrary whipping, torture, and even death at the whim of their masters. Slave families were broken up at the convenience of their owners, with no consideration for the heartbreak it caused.

In 1796 more than 500 Maroons – escaped ex-slaves – who had been fighting slavery in Jamaica were captured, exiled, and sent north to Halifax. Four years later they, too, sailed for Sierra Leone to join the colony established by the disgruntled Loyalists. But long after slavery disappeared as an institution, blacks in Nova Scotia tended to be funnelled into ghettos and denied proper schooling and jobs. Until 1968, blacks were denied burial in some Nova Scotian cemeteries.

In Upper Canada (now Ontario) the Imperial Statute of 1790 made slave-owning legal, requiring owners only to feed and clothe their charges and placing a value of 40 shillings on each slave. There were a few hundred slaves in the province, and owners were allowed to free them, but only if they could support themselves financially – a rare circumstance in those days. Still, John Graves Simcoe, who in 1791 became Upper Canada's first lieutenant-governor, was an implacable foe of slavery and attempted to have the practice abolished. In 1793 Attorney General John White, with Simcoe's blessings, introduced "An Act to Prevent the Further Introduction of Slaves and to Limit the Term of Forced Servitude within This Province," the first of its kind in the British Empire. It ran into stiff opposition. Fully one-third of the members of the legislature, all prominent members of the local business elite, actually owned slaves, and a watered-down version of the law was approved. Even so, it was revolutionary at the time. While it decreed that existing slaves remain in bondage until their death, it banned the importation of new slaves into Upper Canada (though slaves continued to be bought and sold in Toronto until at least 1806) and offered automatic freedom to all slaves who were brought in or came on their own to Upper Canada. It also decreed that children of slaves born after 1793 would be freed after their twenty-fifth year, and their children would be born free. It was far from perfect, but, thereafter, the institution of slavery began to lose its social respectability.

By 1810 there were only about two dozen slaves left in Upper Canada. The March 1811 minutes of Toronto's magistrate's court, however, tell of a complaint from William Jarvis – who has a major street and a Toronto high school named after him – that two of his slaves, a young male and female, had stolen some of his gold and silver and eloped with the help of a free black named Coachly, who was sent to jail for his efforts. The court ruled that "said Negro boy named Henry commonly called Prince, be remitted to prison and there safely kept till delivered according to law and that the girl do return to her said Master."

Many more black Americans migrated to Canada during and after the War of 1812 and, during the 1837 Rebellions, black militia units were formed to help put down the rebels. They fought in 1837 less out of loyalty to Britain and more out of fear that a victory by the rebels would result in the annexation of Upper Canada to the United States and the reintroduction of slavery. In the town of York (now Toronto), several black settlers who had fought for the British in 1812 were awarded grants of land in recognition of their service. By the time of the Imperial Parliament *Emancipation Act* of 1834, which finally abolished slavery in Britain and the colonies, there were few, if any, slaves left to be set free.

Even so, blacks in 1837 weren't entirely confident that they were safe in Canada, and a troubling incident in Niagara that year showed that their reservations had some merit. With a population of 4,000, Niagara was one of Upper Canada's largest settlements, home to about 400 blacks, most of them former slaves. One of those escaped slaves, Solomon Moseby, had begun his perilous journey to Niagara by stealing his Kentucky owner's horse. After the owner tracked him to Niagara and demanded his return, Canadian authorities acquiesced and arrested Moseby for horse theft, even though he had let the horse go free once he was clear of the bloodhounds chasing him. When the local court ordered that Moseby be deported back to the United States, where he would almost certainly be hanged, about 300 people, mostly blacks, wielding pitchforks, sticks, stones, and other weapons, laid siege to the jail, foiling several attempts by the sheriff to sneak Moseby out. With several sympathetic white residents providing food for the protesters, the siege was in its third week when a wagon containing the handcuffed Moseby and six armed constables suddenly burst from the jail yard. Two men, Hubbard

Holmes and Jacob Green, each grabbed a horse, forcing the wagon to stop. In the ensuing scuffle, Holmes was shot dead and Green killed by a bayonet. Moseby somehow broke free, got to Montreal, and sailed to England.

Some three dozen black protesters were arrested and jailed as a result of the melee, but they were released that December when they agreed to join the white-led "Coloured Corps" of about 130 men serving along the Niagara frontier and Lake Erie shoreline during that winter. After the rebel threat subsided, the militia units were disbanded in the summer of 1838, but the men who had served in a corps under the command of Thomas Runchey were not paid for their service because Runchey had deserted to the United States with the money. By contrast, local businessman James Sears paid the men in his corps from his own pocket, waiting until 1840 to be reimbursed by the colonial government.

The early history of blacks in Canada is closely tied to political activities south of the border. The first significant influx began after 1793, when the U.S. Congress approved the first *Fugitive Slave Act*, providing that anybody who harboured or concealed an escaped slave must forfeit the slave and pay a $500 fine – a steep figure for the time. It also allowed slave-owners to retrieve their "property" in all the states and territories, even though some northern states (led by Vermont in its 1777 state constitution) had abolished slavery by then. In 1804, after slave-owner General Thomas Boudes of Columbia, Pennsylvania, refused to surrender an escaped slave to authorities, the Underground Railroad was first incorporated, although the Quaker Isaac T. Hopper had already begun an informal system for hiding and helping fugitive slaves.

The route network began slowly, but abolitionists were soon helping fugitive slaves and free blacks escape to Canada by way of a secret system of safe houses, voluntary guides, and a network of safe paths running through fourteen northern states and terminating in Canada. By 1850 at least 3,000 volunteers worked on the Underground Railroad, a system referred to in the old spiritual song "Follow the Drinking Gourd," reminding slaves to keep their eyes on the gourd – the Big Dipper – pointing the way north to "Heaven," or freedom in Canada. In 1838 the Underground Railroad was formally organized under the direction of Robert Purvis (1810–1898), the son of a wealthy South Carolina cotton broker, who had established the Library Company of Colored People, an anti-slavery society in Philadelphia in 1833. After a fundraising tour of England for the cause in 1834, he returned to lead the campaign to repeal a new Pennsylvania state law banning African-Americans from voting.

Indiana Quaker Levi Coffin – who was dubbed by slave-hunters as "President of the Underground Railroad" for more than thirty years – and his wife, Catharine, are also credited with helping get the system off the ground. The Coffins visited New Canaan, as Canada was often called, in 1844 and 1854 to see how the fugitives were getting along. Their home, now an official historic site in Newport, Indiana, provided a safe haven for some 2,000 slaves, one of whom was Eliza Harris, who went to Chatham in 1838. Her dramatic escape, jumping across the ice floes of the Ohio River carrying her young son in her arms, with the slave catchers and their dogs close behind, is described in *Uncle Tom's Cabin*.[7] Many years later Dr. Martin Luther King referred to nineteenth-century Canada, the terminus for the Underground Railroad, as the North Star for some 30,000 black Americans, both slaves and "freemen," who made their way across the border to escape persecution. They doubled British North America's existing black population: in Toronto alone, the black population grew from a few hundred to about 1,000 during the 1850s, largely in response to the 1850 Fugitive Slave Law. Between 1850 and 1852 an estimated 6,000 fugitive slaves and frightened free blacks entered Canada. In his 1967 CBC Massey Lecture, King said: "Canada is not merely a neighbor of Negroes.

Deep in our history of struggle for freedom, Canada was the North Star."

The Underground Railroad had several "conductors," people who went to the South and helped guide escaped slaves to safety. The most famous was Harriet Tubman, a former slave who made nineteen secret trips into the South and helped rescue more than 300 "passengers" (fugitives). She was so successful that slave-owners offered a $40,000 reward for her capture, forcing Tubman to take refuge in St. Catharines, Ontario, for a time. There a local Baptist clergyman, the Reverand Hiram Walker, had gained legendary status for his tireless assistance to runaway slaves and fleeing black freemen. Runaways were often transported by hiding in the false bottoms of covered wagons or carts as they made their way between "stations" – private houses owned by activists in the anti-slavery movement who risked heavy fines and even imprisonment if their role was discovered. Those stations were usually located about 20 miles apart, and runaway slaves hid during the day and travelled by night, eventually gaining their freedom by crossing into Canada at Niagara Falls or between Detroit and Windsor. Most runaways were men aged between 16 and 35, able to stand the incredible rigours of the long journey from the Deep South. Some women and children did escape but, because they were more likely to be caught, relatively few managed to gain their freedom in this way.

Although it is true that life for an escaped slave in Canada must have seemed like heaven compared to a life of bondage and brutality, the reality of daily life in the North Star fell far short of Eden. By the 1840s many schools had become flashpoints for anti-black prejudice, as white settlers increasingly pressured local officials, and provincial leaders either acquiesced to or, in many cases, were actively involved in movements that barred blacks from attending public schools. The *Common Schools Act* in Ontario created separate schools for blacks and Roman Catholics. The 1859 laws setting up segregated schools for blacks fell into disuse in the early 1900s but were not formally revoked until 1964. Blacks were also openly denied employment in many communities and refused service in local retail and entertainment establishments. Many local white farmers hired the runaways at low wages for the long, gruelling hours of fieldwork, shamelessly exploiting these people and creating deep resentment towards them in the local white community, whose members were unwilling to work for such wages and felt that the newcomers were stealing their jobs.

Still, life for escaped slaves in Canada wasn't all bleak – thanks, in particular, to people like Josiah Henson. Born into slavery in 1789 in Maryland, Henson had been sold three times before he was 18 years old. By 1830 he managed to save the $350 his master said would buy him his freedom, but when he presented the money, his master said the price was $1,000. That prompted Henson, with his wife and four children, to escape via the Underground Railroad to Canada, where they arrived on October 28, 1830, and soon partnered with Henry Bibb to teach other escaped slaves how to be successful farmers. Henson is also credited with single-handedly capturing an American steamer, the *Anne*, which was threatening the town of Sandwich during the 1837 Rebellion. Pastor of the British Methodist Episcopal Church at Dawn (now Dresden, Ontario) for several years, Henson was also an educational pioneer. In 1841, with financial help from the Quakers and other abolitionists, he bought 200 acres of land and founded the British North American Institute for Fugitive Slaves, the country's first educational system for blacks, and set about teaching skills such as blacksmithing and carpentry to former slaves. The next year he founded the Dawn Settlement of black farmers near Dresden, in Kent County, in what is now southwestern Ontario, and encouraged many blacks to settle in the area and create factories to employ their own people. Henson, whose Dresden home is now a museum known as "Uncle Tom's Cabin," once said of his escape to Canada, "When my feet first touched the Canada shore, I threw myself on the ground, rolled in the sand, seized handfuls of it and kissed them and danced around, till, in the eyes of several who were present, I passed for a madman."

The first organized black settlement in Ontario was the Wilberforce Colony, not far from London, where the Society of Friends (Quakers) had bought a 1,200-acre site in response to the 1804 Ohio law banning residents from employing any "colored man or colored woman to do any kind of work." The 3,000 blacks who found themselves suddenly unemployed feared they would soon be sold back into slavery, so J.C. Brown and some of his fellow blacks formed the Cincinnati Colonization Society and, thanks to the Quakers, sent two men to Upper Canada to negotiate the land purchase from the Canada Company in Biddulph Township. With the promise of freedom, several hundred settlers left Ohio and began clearing small plots, building cabins, and even erecting their own small sawmill. At one point they sent Baptist minister Nathaniel Paul to the United States to raise funds for the settlement, but when he returned to Wilberforce he had little money – although he did have a new English bride – claiming that he had given the cash he'd collected to an American abolitionist. In his 1857 autobiography, *Twenty-Two Years a Slave*, Austin Steward, who escaped to Wilberforce in 1815, wrote that the settlers there were, "in general, industrious and thrifty farmers: they cleared their land, sowed grain, planted orchards, raised cattle, and in short, showed to the world that they were in no way inferior to the white population, when given an equal chance with them." In the meantime, however, Ohio had relaxed its laws, several Irish settlers had arrived in the area and bought land the blacks had hoped to own, and, by 1852, most of the families had returned to the United States.

Richard Pierpoint was a 16-year-old boy in Bondou, now part of Senegal, when he was captured and shipped to the United States as a slave, where he was bought by a British officer. By

1780 Pierpoint was one of about a dozen Africans fighting at Fort Niagara with Butler's Rangers for the British in the American Revolution, having joined after the British promised freedom and land to slaves who fought with them. After the British defeat, Pierpoint and some of his colleagues received 200 acres of land and settled near St. Catharines. In 1794 Pierpoint and eighteen other Africans petitioned Lieutenant-Governor Simcoe to allow them to own land adjacent to each other to form an all-black community – among other things, they were concerned about ongoing American raids into Ontario to kidnap Africans and sell them as slaves – but the Executive Council of Upper Canada denied the request.

When war broke out again in 1812, many blacks feared that a U.S. victory would mean slavery for them, so they eagerly signed up to fight with the British. Pierpoint, about 60 years old at the time, sent a letter to the government suggesting that an all-African company of soldiers be formed. The government agreed, but put a white officer in charge. Still, Pierpoint and the others fought at the Battle of Queenston Heights and the siege of Fort George, and for the remainder of the war they were used for labour and garrison duty. Again, the British promised land to those who fought, but the payment was slow in coming. In 1822, after the government refused his request for money instead of land so he could go back to Senegal, Pierpoint received a land ticket, giving him ownership to a plot of land in Garafraxa, on the Grand River near the town of Fergus. He, along with several war veterans and other Africans, set up the Pierpoint Settlement. It is not known how many lived there – although Pierpoint did until his death at the age of 94 in 1838 – but eventually some Scottish settlers bought the settlement land and the black community dispersed.

Not far from Wilberforce, though closer to modern-day Guelph, the Queen's Bush Settlement became home by 1840 to about 2,500 blacks, most of whom were escaped slaves or free blacks who had left the United States because of various slave and anti-black laws. Among them was Thomas Elwood Knox, a free-born African-American who emigrated to Upper Canada in 1844 to escape discrimination in Pittsburgh. Three years later, when he established a farm in the Queen's Bush Settlement, he acknowledged that even though there was less racism in Upper Canada, he "would rather have remained in [his] native country."[8]

Building a settlement on the Canadian frontier was a difficult task. It meant clearing the land, planting and harvesting crops, building cabins and roads, and surviving the harsh winters. But the settlement grew and, by the early 1840s, there were several churches as well as a grist mill, sawmill, store, and hotel.[9] By this time, several American ministers had built schools – most slave-owners deliberately kept their charges illiterate and, during the 1845–46 school year, the community boasted 225 full-time pupils. Despite this progress, however, the blacks once again would be victimized by the system and, by 1850, most of the settlers had moved on. The problem was that the settlers, both white and black, were squatters without legal rights to the land. When the government sent in surveyors in the 1840s, the squatters were offered 100-acre parcels with payment over a ten-year period, but few could afford it and most were forced to abandon their homes and move on to Owen Sound and other surrounding towns.

The best-known and, arguably, most successful black settlement of the era was the Elgin Settlement, or Buxton as it came to be known, organized in 1849 by the Presbyterian-backed charitable body the Elgin Association. It had been formed, with the help of Toronto *Globe* publisher George Brown's Anti-Slavery Society of Toronto, as a response to American fugitive slave laws. That year the Irish-born Louisiana educator and Presbyterian minister, the Reverend William King, had brought fifteen U.S. slaves to the area, just outside Chatham.[10] King had attended Glasgow University and been influenced by the social reform work of the famous British abolitionist Sir Thomas Foxwell Buxton. With the help of both U.S. and Canadian abolitionists, King set up a community allowing the blacks to become self-sufficient landowners and successful businesspeople. While clearing and farming their lands, they earned money by helping build the Great Western Railroad through the area. In addition, they used $3,000 invested by blacks from Toronto and Buffalo to form a cooperative and build a factory for making pearl ash, a brickyard, a sawmill, and grist mill. It wasn't long before the town was producing lumber and barrel staves and selling corn, wheat, oats, tobacco, and other crops. Within ten years many of the former slaves had paid their government-held mortgages ($2.50 an acre) and earned enough money to send their children to college.[11]

In 1857, just four years before the Civil War broke out, some 300 blacks, most of them former slaves, hiked the 10 miles to the Chatham Court House to cast their votes in the provincial elections. "When the voting ended that day, the incumbent Provincial Parliament member from the area, who had won his seat two years previously on an anti-Negro immigration platform, had been defeated in the first demonstration of political black power on the North American continent."[12]

During the Civil War some seventy Buxton residents volunteered to fight for the North. Two of them, Jerome Riley and Anderson Ruffin Abbott, were among the doctors who set up the Freedmen's Hospital in Washington, DC, in 1863, the first public hospital for blacks in the United States. Abbott, whose parents had emigrated as freemen from Mobile, Alabama, in 1835, was the first Canadian-born black doctor. His father, W.R. Abbott, had first fled to the North, but, finding discrimination there, moved on to the town of York. Unable to read or write, he amassed a fortune in real estate and the tobacco business before his death in 1875. The young Abbott enlisted as an acting assistant surgeon, with the rank of captain, on September 2, 1863, serving for $100 a month ($113.83 plus transportation in the field), and, in 1864, he spent several months as chief executive officer of Freedmen's Hospital. During his time there he was warmly received by President and Mrs. Lincoln at the White House levee and came to be greatly admired by the Lincolns. After Lincoln's death in April 1865, Mary Todd Lincoln, as a token of friendship, presented Abbott with the plaid shawl that the president had worn to his inaugural ceremony. Once the war was over, Abbott returned to Canada, completed his medical education, practised in Chatham, and was appointed Kent County coroner – the first black man in Canada to hold such a position.

At its height, Buxton's population was close to 2,000 people, but after the Civil War it declined sharply when families returned to their former homes and young people moved south to help in Reconstruction. Among them, for example, was James T. Rapier, who served in the U.S. Congress from Alabama from 1873 to 1875, and Thomas W. Stringer, who became general superintendent of the African Methodist Episcopal Church in Mississippi and established thirty-five churches there. He also was instrumental in developing Negro Masonry in Mississippi and organized the Fraternal Life Insurance Benefit, the most successful black cooperative in the state. Another famous historical figure is Abraham Doras Shadd, a prominent founding member of the American Anti-Slavery Society and one-time Underground Railroad conductor, who settled in North Buxton in 1861 and was the first black to be elected to a political office as a counsellor of Raleigh Township. In 1994 the road through the heart of North Buxton was renamed A.D. Shadd Road in his honour. His daughter, Mary Anne Shadd, also a staunch opponent of slavery, taught school in Windsor and became editor of the anti-slavery newspaper *The Provincial Freeman*, the first woman editor in North American. A recruiting officer during the Civil War, she was also the first woman admitted to Howard Law School, at the age of 46, and the first black woman to be allowed to vote in a federal election in Washington, DC.

Another famous Buxton couple were the former slaves William Parker and his wife, Eliza Ann Elizabeth Howard Parker. They had gained international notoriety for their role in the 1851 Christiana Riots, which had a significant impact on Pennsylvania law, anti-slave resistance, and the Underground Railroad itself. Edward Gorsuch, a Maryland slave-owner and Quaker, was killed in the riot on September 11. At the time, Parker, who advocated the use of violence to eradicate slavery, was active in the Lancaster Black Self-Protection Society and leader of the local Freedom Society. He had had many fights with the Gap gang, a group of local kidnappers bent on capturing blacks and selling them to the slave market. Once he rescued a young girl from them and, on another occasion, he was involved in killing two white men in a shootout.

Although Gorsuch was known as a moderate – he did not beat his slaves, allowed them to earn wages when the wheat season on his farm was slow, and often let them go free during their twenties – he pursued four of his slaves to Parker's house in Christiana. The 1850 *Fugitive Slave Law* gave Gorsuch the legal right to retrieve his "property." He had discovered some wheat missing from his grain supply and learned that his slaves had sold it to a local farmer, prompting four of them to flee to Pennsylvania, a free state. After obtaining warrants for the arrest of his slaves, Gorsuch, U.S. Marshal Henry H. Kline, and a small posse arrived at Parker's house, where they were confronted by Parker. The exact circumstances are lost in the confusion, but what is certain is that about fifty people, mostly blacks, arrived at the house after the Parkers rang their warning horn. The verbal debate quickly degenerated into shots being fired. Gorsuch, who was unarmed, was killed on the spot after one of the escaped slaves, Sam Thompson, clubbed him on the head with a pistol and shot him as he tried to get up again. Other shots were fired and there were several injuries, none of them serious. As a result, thirty-eight people, both white and black, were charged with treason, but a jury of their peers that December found them not guilty.

The famous black abolitionist Frederick Douglass said while attacking the charges against the Christiana resistors: "This is to cap the climax of American absurdity, to say nothing of American infamy. Our government has virtually made every colored man in the land an outlaw; one who may be hunted by any villain who may think proper to do so, and if the hunted man, finding himself stripped of all legal protection, shall lift his arm in his own defense, why forsooth, he is arrested, arraigned, and tried for high treason, and if found guilty, he must suffer death. The basis of allegiance is protection. We owe allegiance to the government that protects us, but to the government that destroys us, we owe no allegiance. The only law which the alleged slave has a right to know anything about, is the law of nature . . . and his manhood is his justification for shooting down any creature who shall attempt to reduce him to the condition of a brute."

Although the Christiana incident may seem a minor historical blip at first blush, it had major repercussions and nudged the country a little farther along the road to war. The *Fugitive Slave Act* was supposedly a compromise to appease growing unrest among Southern leaders over what they saw as the political ascension of the free states. They were cynical from the outset at Northern promises that their right to recapture their slaves would be fiercely protected. When Gorsuch was killed in pursuit of his legal rights in Pennsylvania, and the killers, as they saw it, were subsequently freed by a jury, a maelstrom of bitterness swept through the South and strengthened the argument of those who saw Southern secession as the only legitimate way to maintain the institution of slavery. The *Mobile Daily Register* summed up the general feeling in the region when it editorialized: "Our country has been on the verge of a revolution. The elements of discord have scarcely subsided into sullen calm, the grieved and injured Southern States have barely yielded to the importunities and assurances of their patriotic citizens, that the hand of aggression would be stayed, and that the Compromise would be observed in good faith, when all this diabolical tragedy is enacted with all its vile and insulting circumstances."

In the aftermath of the trial in Pennsylvania, a law was passed preventing slave owners from capturing runaways in that state. Concerns over Christiana also prompted many blacks to emigrate to safety in Canada and, in early 1852, after the trial ended, Parker and his wife left for Buxton. Parker returned to the United States in later years, but his wife lived the rest of her life in the home they had built on the 12th Concession of Raleigh Township.

In the spring of 1854 the arrest and trial of escaped Richmond slave Anthony Burns under the *Fugitive Slave Act* sparked a series of riots and noisy protests by abolitionists and became another rallying point for opponents of slavery. Despite the protests, Burns was returned to slavery in Virginia escorted by armed marshals, but he ultimately escaped across the Canadian border to St. Catharines, where he died of consumption in 1862 and was buried in Zion Baptist Church cemetery, just one year before Lincoln introduced the *Emancipation Act*.

During the 1850s and early 1860s some slave catchers ventured into Canada, but because they had neither the legal right to kidnap slaves nor public support, they weren't very successful. Buxton historians, for example, tell the story of two Southerners, John Wells and T.G. James, showing up in Chatham in 1857 to recover "a smart, coloured lad named Joseph Alexander." A large crowd of blacks, including Alexander, gathered in front of the Royal Exchange Hotel to listen to the two white men speak. James told them that Alexander was "a good boy but too big and saucy," and added that he had beaten him only once after he had been drunk, smashed a carriage, and allowed some horses to escape. Then Alexander got up and told the crowd that Wells and James owned one of the biggest slave pens in the South, holding

500 slaves behind the St. Charles Hotel in New Orleans. When the slave catchers saw that the crowd was against them, they offered Alexander $100 to go to Windsor. Alexander replied: "I am positive from what I know of James that he would shoot me dead and then leave me, for he would just as soon shoot a man as a squirrel and a white man as a black man – and Wells is just like him." The crowd, clearly on Alexander's side, escorted the two Southerners to the train, and Joe Alexander became a free man.[13]

In 1841, however, the Americans had successfully won an extradition case against Nelson Hacket, a valet and butler who stole a beaver overcoat and a racing mare from his Arkansas owner, along with a gold watch and saddle from other people, and fled to Chatham, where his master caught up with him. Hacket was jailed, but Governor General Sir Charles Bagot refused a demand from the acting governor of Michigan that the prisoner be turned over to him on the grounds that the request should come from the state where the alleged offence occurred. In November the formal documents arrived from Arkansas, and Bagot, who had been admonished by Colonial Secretary Lord Stanley to restore good relations with the Republic – and also recognizing that Hacket had committed crimes not necessary for his escape – said he didn't want Canada to become "an asylum for the worst characters, provided only that they had been slaves before arriving here."[14] Bagot ordered Hacket's surrender and, during the night of February 8, 1842, he was rowed across the Detroit River. "For the first time," according to historian Robin Winks, "criminal extradition had brought a fugitive slave back from Canada West."[15]

The case caused considerable outrage among both Canadian and American abolitionists and was a factor in the 1842 Ashburton-Webster Treaty dealing with criminal extradition between the two countries. Six years later, Canada passed its own extradition law, and no other fugitive slave was ever surrendered to U.S. authorities.

The last and most famous extradition case involving a fugitive slave in Canada was the Anderson case – the Missouri slave Jack Burton who, on September 28, 1853, killed Seneca T.P. Diggs, a white cotton planter in Howard County, Missouri, after Diggs and four of his slaves tried to stop Burton from visiting his wife on a nearby plantation. Diggs, as the law allowed at the time, had detained Burton and ordered him to follow him. Missouri state law said that any black found more than 20 miles from his master's house without a pass should be arrested and returned. The capturer received $5 plus travelling expenses. The slave followed Diggs for a short time but then broke away, pursued by Diggs and his slaves, where they eventually overtook him near a fence. Diggs, brandishing a stick over his head, ordered Burton to surrender – at which point the slave produced a large dirk knife and threatened to kill anybody who touched him. When Diggs came closer, Burton stabbed him in the heart, knocking him backwards into a ditch. Burton headed north to Canada, where he changed his name to John Anderson. Diggs died two weeks later. In Windsor, Anderson met American missionary Laura S. Haviland, who wrote a letter on his behalf to his father-in-law, using a Michigan return address for protection. Haviland warned Anderson when a white Southerner arrived in Windsor looking for him, and Anderson fled first to Chatham and then to Brantford, where he found work as a plasterer and general labourer.

In April 1860, when Anderson was calling himself William Jones, he quarrelled with another former slave, who sought revenge by telling local authorities that Jones, aka Anderson and Burton, was wanted for murder in Missouri. Brantford Magistrate William Matthews issued an order for Anderson's arrest. He was jailed briefly, released, and then rearrested on a warrant sworn out by two Detroit police officers. Again appearing before Matthews, Anderson was ordered held in jail to await the arrival of evidence from Missouri, but when the witnesses, including two of Diggs's sons, didn't arrive, he was again released. Two days later they arrived, and Matthews issued another warrant for Anderson's arrest. He was caught in Simcoe after what the October 26, 1860, *Brantford Expositor* described as "a violent struggle, during which the officer alleges the prisoner tried to stab him." In December the Toronto Court of Queen's Bench ruled two to one that Anderson had committed murder and could be extradited, but added it would await an appeal to a higher court to resolve the matter.

There was no doubt where Anderson stood in Canadian public opinion. The January 12 *Montreal Gazette*, citing a story on the case in *The Times*, quotes that paper as saying: "The Canadians are full of sympathy. They have provided the prisoner with necessaries and with money for his defence . . . We suppose there will hardly be a man in England who will not hope for the success even of this forcible rescue, if things come to that extremity."

Large public meetings on Anderson's behalf were held in Toronto, Hamilton, and Montreal. A Montreal petition, asking the courts not to extradite Anderson, collected 2,726 signatures. In a January 17 editorial, the *Montreal Gazette* described slavery as "a state of war between the master and the slave," adding that the slave "as a prisoner of war . . . has a perfect right to take advantage of any negligence on the part of his enemy, or even to strike him dead in order to effect his escape."

In Toronto an angry mob outside the courtroom was dispersed only when Anderson's counsel, Samuel B. Freeman, asked them to leave. Four days later the mayor chaired a mass meeting at St. Lawrence Hall, during which, among a host of famous speakers, the fiery Irish-Canadian politician Thomas D'Arcy McGee condemned the court for its decision. In Hamilton, among 700 who showed up to protest the Anderson case, only two men in the audience defended the principle that treaties must be obeyed whatever the consequences.

At the packed Mechanics Hall meeting in Montreal,

Antoine-Aimé Dorion, a member of the legislature and future chief justice of Quebec, reminded the crowd that the extradition treaty was never meant to apply to fugitive slaves. "Is this man who committed no crime according to the common understanding of moral obligations . . . to be delivered up to the authorities of the United States?" he asked. "Now, sir, I maintain that it would be a crime on the part of our authorities – on the part of the people of Canada – to render this man up."[16]

In the wake of such public outrage over the case – and despite widespread anger in the United States that Canadian authorities were procrastinating on the issue – the Court of Common Pleas set Anderson free on a legal technicality. Its February 16, 1861, ruling in Toronto found that, because the second Brantford warrant had not specifically accused Anderson of murder, he could not be held.

While Washington authorities, still trying to resolve the growing animosity between North and South, were furious at the Anderson ruling, it quickly became a moot point when the Civil War broke out that April. Even so, not everybody in Canada was pleased with the court's decision to duck the issue by using a technicality. George Brown editorialized on May 31, 1861, in the *Globe*: "It will be remembered that the English Court of Queen's Bench issued a writ of habeus corpus, which, had it been enforced, would have removed Anderson beyond the jurisdiction of Canadian tribunals. Happily the discharge of the prisoner by our Court of Common Pleas prevented a clashing of authorities. Still, the legal point involved in the issue will remain in doubt."

By that time, however, Anderson had visited Montreal and thanked those who had supported him, then sailed for London, where he spent that summer speaking to a host of anti-slavery meetings. For a short time he enrolled in the British Training Institution in Northhamptonshire and, on Christmas Eve, 1862, sailed for Liberia, never to be heard from again.

It is impossible to say with any certainty how many slaves escaped to Canada and what the black population totalled. The formal 1861 census listed 11,413 "Negroes" in the Canadas, but most historians argue that, between 1850 and 1860, at least 20,000, both free and slave, entered the Canadas, bringing the black population in British North America to about 60,000.

There is no doubt, however, that slaves began escaping to the colonies in substantial numbers in the early 1800s, but this migration peaked in the 1850s. In the remainder of the century following the Civil War, between 60 and 75 percent of those blacks left Canada, many to fight in the war itself, and others to take advantage of opportunities created by Reconstruction. In any event, with Confederation in 1867, blacks were less welcome, as Canada concentrated on white European settlers to build the new country.

In 1911 Prime Minister Sir Wilfrid Laurier read the following statement in the House of Commons: "His excellency in Council, in virtue of the provision of Sub-section (c) of Section 38 of the Immigration Act, is pleased to Order and it is hereby Ordered as follows: For a period of one year from and after the date hereof, the landing in Canada shall be and the same is prohibited of any immigrants belonging to the Negro race, which race is deemed unsuitable to the climate and requirements of Canada." Few people objected.

While it is true that the first shots in the Civil War were actually fired at Fort Sumter on April 12, 1861, the sectarian violence actually became inevitable on October 16, 1859, when radical abolitionist John Brown and twenty-one men launched their attack on the Federal Arsenal at Harper's Ferry, Virginia. In this ill-conceived scheme they hoped to prompt an uprising by slaves and by white abolitionists to put an end to the institution of slavery.

While Brown became the subject of a popular marching song for the Northern forces during the war, his raid caused a sensation at the time, exacerbating the fears of both North and South and, at the very least, hastening what was likely the inevitable clash of cultures. And here, once again, Canada comes into the picture.

In the 1850s Chatham was a bustling regional centre of commerce, by far the most important place of black culture in the country. The town was about one-third black, most of them immigrants from the American South, although there were eighty Canadian-born blacks there too. They lived on King Street East, a street lined with small houses, log cabins, and garden plots. Many of the vegetable wagons at the Chatham market belonged to blacks, and some of the more successful black families built large, two-storey houses rivalling those of the white business class.

Martin Delany had come here to practise medicine in 1856, and it was only natural, given his reputation as a powerful black nationalist, that John Brown would ask him to co-chair what his May 5, 1858, invitation called "a quiet Convention in this place of true friends of freedom." In fact, however, the convention provided the platform to outline Brown's plan to overthrow the institution of slavery by encouraging an uprising of slaves and white abolitionists, including the thousands of refugees living in Canada, by establishing a military base in the Blue Ridge Mountains, both to assist runaway slaves and to launch armed attacks against slaveholders. Brown had also sent other invitations, dated April 29, 1858, for the same convention, co-signed by himself, Delany, and two other local activists, Charles L. Redmond and J.M. Bell.

Brown had been born at Torrington, Connecticut, on May 9, 1800. The family moved to Hudson, Ohio, in 1805, where his father, a tanner, was a voluntary agent for the Underground Railroad. Brown studied for a time for the Congregational ministry, but went back to work for his father. He was married twice, the father of twenty children, and he held a variety of jobs before settling in 1849 into the black community of North Elba, situated in the Adirondacks of Essex County, New York, on land donated by the noted anti-slavery campaigner Gerrit Smith. Smith was also active in supporting John Anderson, and he came to Canada on several occasions to offer his help and money. Among the donations to North Elba were $400 from two Canadian parliamentarians, who requested anonymity, and Glover Harrison of Toronto, a member of the Liberty League.

In 1854 Stephen A. Douglas introduced his Kansas-Nebraska bill to the Senate, allowing those two territories to enter the union with or without slavery – a bill that abolitionist leader Frederick Douglass warned was "an open invitation to a fierce and bitter strife." As a result of the legislation, both pro- and anti-slave groups poured into the territories, with preacher Henry Ward Beecher using his popular pulpit to condemn the bill and help raise money to buy weapons for those willing to fight against slavery in the territories. These rifles became known as Beecher's Bibles, and among the volunteers heading for Kansas to do battle in 1855 were John Brown and five of his sons. That year, Kansas elected its first legislature. While fewer than 2,000 people were eligible to vote, more than 6,000 actually voted, primarily Missouri slave-owners who had crossed the border to elect pro-slavery candidates. The result was a Kansas law imposing the death penalty on anyone helping a slave to escape and a two-year jail term for possession of abolitionist literature. In 1856 Brown's home in Osawatomie was burned and one of his sons was killed. With the help of Smith and others, Brown moved to Virginia and established a refuge for runaway slaves.

Brown's experience in Kansas had convinced him that the moral suasion tactics of abolitionists, what he called their "milk and water principles,"[17] would never end slavery. Revolution, he believed, was the only way. He had told some of his abolitionist backers in the United States about his plan and, while many felt it was futile, others contributed money. Brown raised $1,000 for his scheme and, in April 1858, he headed to Toronto, where he attended some anti-slavery meetings at the Temperance Hall and stayed with his long-time friend Dr. A.M. Ross, a noted naturalist and zealous abolitionist who had risked his life on several occasions sneaking into the South and helping slaves escape to Canada. Ross was such a good friend that Brown wrote him a farewell letter dated December 1, 1859, from the Charleston Jail, the day before his execution, thanking Ross for his help and his promise to provide for Brown's family. "In a few hours I shall be in another and better state of existence," he wrote. "I feel quite cheerful, and ready to die. My dear friend, do not give up your labors for 'the poor that cry, and them that are in bonds.'" He signed it, "Farewell, God bless you, your friend, John Brown." When Ross took Brown to a steamer bound for Niagara, Brown handed him a York shilling, saying, "Keep this, and whenever you see it, you'll remember John Brown."[18] From Toronto, Brown went to St. Catharines, also a major centre of fugitive blacks and anti-slavery activity, to see if he could round up some volunteers for his plan. Legendary abolitionist Harriet Tubman actually agreed to participate, but she was ill at the time of the raid. Brown wrote to one of his sons to say he was "succeeding to all appearance."[19]

Pleased with his reception in St. Catharines, Brown, with his son Owen, arrived in Chatham on April 29, 1858, where he stayed with merchant Isaac Holdenand on May 5 and issued his invitations to attend the organizing convention to be co-chaired by Delany and the Reverend William C. Munroe, a black minister from Detroit. Delany would say later that Brown ran into him on the street, and the two men went to a private parlour in the Villa Mansion Hotel to discuss his proposals. There were several preliminary meetings leading up to the convention, for the purpose of drawing up a constitution for the movement, the first at a frame cottage on Princess Street just south of King Street, then known as the King Street School. Other meetings were held at the First Baptist Church on the north side of King Street, with the organizers, to hide their true intentions, saying they were forming a Masonic Lodge of coloured people. The final pre-convention meeting, where the proposals were finalized, was held at a local fire station, "No 3 Engine House," a wooden structure near McGregor's Creek.

The convention itself, held May 8 and 10 at the Baptist Church and attended by forty-six men, only twelve of them white, chose Munroe as president and John Henry Kagi as secretary of war in Brown's provisional government. Brown was commander-in-chief. Kagi, a lawyer who helped draw up the constitution, was Brown's right-hand man in Kansas, Chatham, and, later, in Brown's raid into Missouri. He died at Harper's Ferry. Before debating the proposed action plan, entitled "Provisional Constitution and Ordinances for the People of the United States," a motion seconded by Delany called on everybody to declare: "I solemnly affirm that I will not, in any way, divulge any of the secrets of this Convention, except to the persons entitled to know the same, on the pain of forfeiting the respect and protection of this organization."[20] Delany, who later replaced Munroe as president, would disingenuously claim that Brown never suggested armed revolt but, rather, his plan to establish a Subterranean Pass Way to make Kansas, instead of Canada, the terminus of the Underground Railroad. But Kagi, along with Israel Shadd, publisher of the *Provincial Freeman*, not to mention the subsequent events, made it clear what the real intentions of the convention were. Brown left Chatham on May 29 and returned to St. Catharines, where he hired black printer Wentworth Higginson to print copies of the constitution for distribution.

Before the raid at Harper's Ferry, Brown paid one more short visit to Canada, on March 12, 1859, when he arrived in Windsor with a group of fugitives he had helped to escape from

Missouri. With donations from sympathizers in the eastern states, Brown had managed to organize a force and to buy supplies, arms, and provisions. In December 1858 he entered Missouri with two small companies of men. They freed eleven slaves, but in one raid a white man was shot and killed by Brown's lieutenant, Aaron D. Stevens. As a result, both Brown and Kagi were declared outlaws and had a price put on their heads, but they decided to take the freed slaves to Canada. They trekked through Kansas, Nebraska, Iowa, Illinois, and Michigan, but, at one point, just past Topeka, Kansas, they took shelter in an empty log cabin and were overtaken by a posse headed by a U.S. marshal. The marshal stationed himself with eighty armed men at Muddy Creek Crossing, and Brown was eventually joined by some sympathizers from Topeka. With only twenty-three white men and three black fugitives – the escaped women and children having been left in the cabin – Brown ordered his men to charge. The posse was in no mood to fight, however, and the men headed off in all directions.

Things didn't work out so well at Harper's Ferry, however. On the evening of October 16, 1859, Brown and twenty-one other men attacked the Federal armory at Harper's Ferry and captured the arsenal, but the next day they were surrounded by the Virginia militia under the command of Colonel Robert E. Lee, who, in less than two years, would be commander of the Confederate forces. Lee battered down the doors of the engine house and captured Brown, who was wounded, and six of his comrades. Ten of Brown's men were killed, five escaped, and all seven captives were later hanged. Historian Karen Whitman writes: "There is evidence also that several slaves and free Negroes from the Harper's Ferry region participated in the raid; those who were killed or captured were surreptitiously disposed of by the State of Virginia, and those who escaped went quickly and quietly back to their residences in order to avoid detection."[21]

Among those killed at Harper's Ferry were two Canadians –
William H. Lehman of Markham Township and Stewart Taylor, a
native of Uxbridge, also just north of Toronto. Lehman, 20, had
been the youngest member of the Chatham Convention and supposedly was shot by a militiaman after he'd surrendered. Taylor,
23, was a spiritualist who believed he could communicate with
the dead through a medium. A wagon-maker by trade, he was
also an accomplished stenographer. Two other raiders, Osborn
Perry Anderson, the only black man who escaped, and Shields
Green, who was captured and executed, were both fugitive blacks
who had been living in Canada before the raid. Anderson
returned to Canada after the raid, but joined the Union Army in
1864 and eventually wrote a book, *A Voice from Harper's Ferry*.
Another raider, Massachusetts native Francis Jackson Meriam,
also survived the raid and escaped to Canada. He returned to
fight in the war, where he became a captain in the 3rd South
Carolina Colored Infantry and was wounded in the leg while
serving under Grant.

The raid focused worldwide attention on the slavery question: Italian liberator Giuseppe Garibaldi, for example, declared
that Brown "was the instrumental precursor of the liberty of the
slave," and, in France, Victor Hugo wrote, "In killing Brown the
Southern States have committed a crime which will take its place
among the calamities of history." It also sparked fear and loathing
in the South that their worst fears of a slave insurrection were
possible, and it discouraged Northern moderates who had been
hoping for a peaceful solution to the growing schism between the
two parts of the country.

The raid also pointed fingers directly at Canada. For one
thing, news of the Chatham Convention, where the plan was orig-
inally codified, became widespread. In addition, Franklin
Benjamin Sanborn, George Luther Stearns, and Samuel Gridley
Howe, three members of the "Secret Six" – the group of
Northern abolitionists who helped finance Brown's activities –

immediately fled to Canada to avoid prosecution, although both Howe and Stearns returned after Brown's execution and testified before the Senate committee investigating the raid. At the committee, Stearns defended Brown's actions, and at a January 1, 1863, party celebrating Lincoln's Emancipation Proclamation, he unveiled a bust he had commissioned of Brown. Sanborn, in contrast, burned all the correspondence he'd had with Brown and steadfastly refused to testify before the Senate committee. As for Gerrit Smith, he had a nervous breakdown on hearing the news, was placed in an asylum, and, when he was released, conveniently forgot that he had known Brown.

In his message to the Virginia legislature, Governor Henry A. Wise thundered: "One of the most irritating feature of this predatory war is that it has its seat in the British provinces which furnish asylums for our fugitives and send them and their hired outlaws upon us from depots and rendezvous in the bordering states."[22] In a December 28, 1859, speech in Detroit, he said, "With God's help we will drive all the disunionists together back into Canada. Let the compact of fanaticism and intolerance be confined to British soil."[23] The *New York Herald* quoted Wise as demanding that the president notify the British government to stop Canada from offering asylum to fugitive slaves, fostering disunion and dissension in the United States. "The war shall be carried into Canada," he said.[24] And *De Bow's Review* wrote that abolitionists were a "vile, sensuous, animal, brutal, infidel, superstitious Democracy of Canada and the Yankees."[25]

Three of Brown's sons – Oliver, Owen, and Watson – were also in the raid. Both Oliver and Watson died, but Owen escaped and is the only one of the five survivors who did not join the Union Army during the Civil War. He died at his home on "Brown's Peak" near Pasadena, California, on January 9, 1891.

As Fred Landon wrote in *The Canadian Magazine* in 1919: "In a purely material sense the Harper's Ferry raid accomplished nothing; indeed, for the moment it seemed a setback to the abolition cause. After events, however, showed that it played a very important part in precipitating the conflict between slavery and freedom. John Brown made the North come face to face with the problem that Lincoln enunciated when he questioned if the nation could long endure half slave and half free. When the North elected Lincoln its purpose had been declared. Within a year and a half after John Brown died, the Civil War had begun and the first regiments that went to the front sang as they marched,

> John Brown's body lies mouldering in the grave,
> But his soul goes marching on."

After Harper's Ferry, Delany busied himself with his plans to set up a colony for blacks in Africa and was much in demand as a speaker. His most prestigious appearance came on July 16, 1861, at Somerset House, before the International Statistical Society, chaired by Queen Victoria's husband, Prince Albert.

The strident abolitionist Lord Brougham, then 82, chaired the event, which included a delegation from the United States headed by jurist and author Augustus Baldwin Longstreet. U.S. Ambassador George Mifflin Dallas was also seated on the dais when Brougham said, "I call the attention of Mr. Dallas to the fact that there is a Negro present, and I hope he will feel no scruples on that account." After Brougham sat down, and the minister from Spain was seated, Delany rose in his place to say: "I rise, your Royal Highness, to thank his lordship, the unflinching friend of the Negro, for the remarks he has made in reference to myself, and to assure your royal highness and his lordship that I am a man."

The enthusiastic applause – described by *The Times* as "the wildest shouts ever manifested in so grave an assemblage" – was too much for Longstreet, who jumped up and led the entire American delegation from the hall, leaving Dallas sitting, silent, on the dais. The meeting ended immediately. The next day, Dallas refused to see Lord Brougham, who was attempting to be conciliatory, and U.S. Secretary of State Lewis Cass criticized Dallas for not walking out with the U.S. delegation in the face of this "insult." As for Delany, he instantly became an international celebrity.

Delany quickly returned to the United States and began recruiting black enlistees throughout the Midwest, including his eldest son, Toussaint Delany. In 1865 Delany met with Lincoln to complain about the poor conditions for black soldiers and to suggest that the president appoint black officers to oversee the black regiments. Lincoln commissioned Delany as a major, making him the first black commissioned officer in U.S. history, and assigned him to the 104th Regiment, United States Colored Troops. After the war, Delany returned to Wilberforce, Ohio, with his wife and family. When he died in 1885 at the age of 73, he was buried at Massie Creek Cemetery there and widely heralded as the father of black nationalism.

Delany was not the only black man with Canadian connections to sign up for the Union in the Civil War. In his three-part 1995 feature article entitled "All Men Are Brothers," published in the historical quarterly *Lest We Forget*, Canadian Civil War historian and Confederate re-enactor Tom Brooks of Gravenhurst, Ontario, wrote that, of the 180,000 freemen or former slaves who served in the Union Army, as many as "a thousand or more" were free men of colour born outside the United States, most of them in the British North American colonies. There were also several thousand fugitives – both freemen and former slaves – who had escaped to Canada but returned during the war to fight for the Union.

Brooks writes that the most famous of the coloured regiments was the 54th Massachusetts Infantry, formed in May 1863, which "actively recruited in Canada West." In addition to several former slaves enlisting and going south to join the regiment, at least eighteen free men of colour born in British North American also enlisted. Three were born in Nova Scotia, three in Toronto, two in Hamilton, one in Chatham, another in London, one in Galt (now Cambridge, Ontario), and another in Woodstock. Two more gave Montreal as their place of birth, and the remaining four simply gave "Canada" as their birthplace. The men ranged from 18 to 39 years old and listed such occupations as farmer, cook, glass-maker, sailor, and waiter.

Several Internet sites also contain lists of 348 names, compiled from information available on the Civil War Soldier and Sailor System's Web site, of blacks born in British North America who served in the U.S. Navy during the war. Brooks reports that there were sixty-two soldiers born in British North America in the 20th United States Colored Troops alone, most of them from Canada West but with a few from Nova Scotia and New Brunswick and one from Montreal. At least six of those men died in the service of a foreign country and are buried in the coloured section of the Union military cemetery in New Orleans, Louisiana.

There are no reliable statistics to show how many fugitive slaves who had been living in Canada decided to join the Union Army, but it is likely that several thousand of them did. A typical story is that of Abraham H. Galloway, a slave from Wilmington, North Carolina, who escaped on a ship bound for Philadelphia in 1857, made his way to what is now Ontario, and became a noted spokesman for abolition. When the war broke out, Galloway, like so many of his fellow escapees, returned home to fight in the war.

On July 8, 2003, U.S. President George W. Bush, standing at Goree Island, Senegal, the exact spot where hundreds of thousands of Africans were bought and sold for the American slave trade, called American slavery one of history's greatest crimes. "At this place, liberty and life were stolen and sold," he said. "Human beings were delivered and sorted, and weighed, and branded with the marks of commercial enterprises, and loaded as cargo on a voyage without return. One of the largest migrations of history was also one of the greatest crimes of history.

". . . My nation's journey toward justice has not been easy and it is not over. The racial bigotry fed by slavery did not end with slavery or with segregation. And many of the issues that still trouble America have roots in the bitter experience of other times."

In Canada, Bush's speech was greeted generally by cynicism and complaints that he didn't actually offer an apology for slavery. It is a typical reaction from a country that, while never involved in slavery to the same extent, has little reason to prolong its widespread sense of moral superiority. Unfortunately, Canada's record on slavery isn't as pristine as we like to pretend.

SIX

Skedaddlers, Deserters, Crimps, and Assorted Rogues

IN NOVEMBER 1864 A 25-YEAR-OLD FRENCH-CANADIAN man named Lapiere left Montreal to visit his 21-year-old sweetheart in Ogdensburg, New York. As often happens to the young and foolish, however, Lapiere fell in with some bad companions – in this case, "crimps" actively seeking out young men just like him – who were intent on befriending him and getting him intoxicated. As a result, he woke up the next morning in the local lock-up, where he was informed, much to his shock and horror, that he was now a soldier in the United States Army and would soon be sent to the front.

Panic-stricken, he sent for his sweetheart and, after "an earnest colloquy,"[1] the pair decided to get married. The bride-to-be begged the local military commanding officer to grant her intended a one-day leave so they could get married.

The leave was readily granted, and the relieved couple proceeded to her mother's house, where the marriage ceremony was performed that day by a magistrate. During the subsequent festivities celebrating the event, the newlyweds sneaked off and boarded the ferry for Prescott, directly across the St. Lawrence River on the Canadian side.

Unfortunately, they took the wrong ferry. Getting off, and

thinking they were in Canada, they began strolling along the railway tracks towards what they thought was the Prescott station when, on meeting a passerby, the groom announced that he was a deserter. "A deserter from what army?" asked the stranger. "From the American army," replied Lapiere. "Then, sir, I have to inform you that you are on American soil and are going directly to Ogdensburg. You had better go to the woods until you can find a good chance to get over."

With that, however, the bride insisted on returning to her mother's house, and the couple arrived just about daylight, some thirty minutes before the local recruiting sergeant knocked on the door looking for his newly inducted soldier. Thinking quickly, Lapiere explained that, since it had been his wedding night, he'd been up partying the whole night and pleaded for time to wash and shave himself, promising to turn up at the base within half an hour. The sergeant agreed.

At this point his wife dressed him in her own clothes, spirited him off to the ferry boat – this time, the one actually going to Prescott – and about half an hour later she followed him. The newlyweds then bought tickets for the Ottawa and Prescott Railway Co. and were last heard of arriving in Ottawa the same day.

For untold thousands of British North Americans, however, their stories didn't end as happily. While there are no official records of just how many young men were "crimped" – cajoled, drugged, kidnapped, or otherwise tricked or forced against their will by military procurers into the Northern Army – the practice was a thriving cottage industry along the northern frontier during the Civil War years. These unwilling recruits were usually sent directly to the front, with little, if any, military training, and, often, they did not live long enough to tell their tale. The recruitment of British regulars was not dissimilar, as they were attracted by the relatively high pay of the Union service. This problem caused considerable strain between the Americans and the British and Canadian governments.

Another product of the war was the significant influx into Canada of "skedaddlers" – the original draft dodgers – mainly from the border states of Maine, New Hampshire, New York, Wisconsin, and Minnesota, who, along with outright deserters from the Northern armies, flooded across the borders to avoid the draft. The community of Pemberton Ridge, New Brunswick, in the Mapleton district of Carleton County, for example, sits on a hill overlooking Grand Lake and Spednic Lake, about 20 miles by water and 30 miles by road from Danforth, Maine. In the early 1860s it was called Skedaddle Ridge because of the American settlers who fled there to avoid the draft. For the same reasons, there was also Skedaddler's Reach on Campobello Island. At most, Skedaddle Ridge had a population of about twenty families, or a hundred people, but it was just one of several similar communities that sprang up all along the Restigouche River in New Brunswick after Lincoln introduced the draft in 1862. Many other skedaddlers found their way to Montreal, Toronto, Niagara, and Windsor as well.

Before the Civil War changed attitudes forever, the whole concept of a standing professional army was anathema to Americans – a result of the actions of the British to rule from across the sea by using their army as enforcers and an instrument of outright oppression. When the British landed in Boston in 1768, for example, statesman Andrew Eliot wrote: "To have a standing army! Good God! What can be worse to a people who have tasted the sweets of liberty!" The Continental Congress was so apprehensive about the military that, even during the Revolutionary War, it insisted on regular reports from commanding officer George Washington. The Congress appointed his staff officers and forced him to consult with his generals in council before making any major military decisions. Despite the urgency of the war, Congress had no power to conscript soldiers directly into the Continental Army. Even when the states were asked for quotas of troops, Congress had no power to force them to deliver. The Philadelphia Constitutional Convention, which began in May 1787, gave Congress limited powers to raise a small standing army and, during the War of 1812, an attempt by the federal government to implement universal conscription met with such strong opposition that it didn't make it to the voting stage.

But as the Civil War dragged on, and despite having set aside money for bounties to induce volunteers to enlist – many Canadians signed up for bounties ranging from $200 to $800 – in 1862 Lincoln brought in the *Civil War Enrolment Act*, giving each state a quota of men needed for the service. Based on the 1860 census, each state, in turn, assigned a quota to each town. Even so, the act allowed a drafted man to hire a substitute to take his place or to buy an outright commutation from the draft, a provision that also had a major impact on Canadian participation in the war, since thousands of colonists signed up for the money. The 1864 Adjutant General's Report, for example, lists 1,043 Maine soldiers as being Canadian born. One of them, New Brunswicker John Dalton of Company C, 2nd Maine Cavalry, signed on as a substitute and was listed under "Quota of Vassalboro, Maine." He was randomly credited to a town that needed more men to fill its quota requirements.

Even with such liberal provisions – which allowed only wealthy people to escape the service, since the average working man could hardly afford a $300 fee – public sentiment against conscription led to numerous protest riots, many of which were aided by Southern agitators headquartered in Canada. The worst, in New York City in July 1863, resulted in 1,200 deaths and millions of dollars in property damage. The rioters, predominantly middle- and lower-class Irish immigrants, often targeted African-Americans, because they blamed the war on slavery and accused blacks of taking their jobs. Among other things, they burned down the Colored Orphan Asylum and lynched several black men on the spot.

Just how many Canadians signed up for the bounties or

became substitutes is not really known, although they certainly numbered in the thousands. As for the skedaddlers, again, precise numbers don't exist, but credible estimates range up to 20,000 Americans who fled to Canada by the end of the war. The vast majority of them returned home when the war ended.

The oft-repeated claim that some 50,000 men from the colonies fought in the war is highly suspect, based more on the political rhetoric of the times than any hard evidence supporting it. One source of the inflated number came from a February 1865 speech by Saint-Constant parish priest Hercule Beaudry at a memorial service in Montreal for French Canadians who had died while serving in the Northern armies. There he claimed that 40,000 French Canadians fought and 14,000 died. Historian Robin Winks postulates that Beaudry's figures may reflect the number of Franco-Americans living in the United States combined with the French Canadians from Canada East, but Beaudry "could have had no firm foundation upon which to base what undoubtedly was an estimate."[2] Winks points out, for example, that Edmond Mallet, the most famous French Canadian to serve – he was a major in the New York Volunteers and went on to become a local historian and leader of the French-Canadian nationalist movement after the war – "had lived in New York since he was five and could hardly speak French."[3] At one point, however, so many French Canadians signed up to receive their bounties that three leading Roman Catholic bishops in Canada East issued letters to the parish priests ordering them to warn their parishioners against the practice.

John A. Macdonald claimed that 40,000 British Canadians had served in the Northern armies, but again that appears to be a number pulled out of a hat. Canada didn't keep records – for one thing, joining a U.S. army violated the British *Foreign Enlistment Act* – and neither the Northern nor the Southern armies kept accurate accounts of how many British North Americans fought in the war. That having been said, it's likely that at least 20,000 British North Americans, perhaps more, were actively engaged in the conflict. Although some joined up to fight for a principle or in search of adventure, most were in it for the money.

The deserters and draft dodgers were initially welcomed by Canadians, but that changed to hostility when they began working on farms for $10 a month, well below the going rate for locals. They provided cheap labour for farmers, who found their products in great demand and their prices inflated because of the endless needs of the two warring armies south of the border. Some even formed gangs and roamed the countryside, indulging in petty thievery, exacerbating existing anti-American feelings. They were deeply resented in towns close to the border, where they were blamed for causing unemployment. There were so many deserters heading north that, in 1862, Lincoln issued an order forbidding all foreign travel to citizens of military age unless they had special clearance papers from Washington. In the colonies, however, a flourishing international trade developed in discharge papers, making Canada the promised land for draft dodgers and conscripts who wanted to escape the war. Legitimate Civil War veterans would sell their discharge papers to traders, who, in turn, would bleach out the name and sell it at a profit to somebody who could substitute his own name. In addition, there was another class of profiteers, the bounty jumpers, who would voluntarily go to the United States to join the service, receive their bounty – a signing bonus ranging from $200 to $800 – then desert, taking their money with them. While the penalty for this practice was death, some bounty jumpers completed the exercise several times and lived to talk about it and enjoy their ill-gotten gains. General H.B. Carrington, the British commander of the Great Lakes frontier, reported that, to stop the bounty jumpers, he had court martialled and shot several Canadians who had collected three bounties each.

Crimping was a big business. With bounties being offered to

both the recruiter and the enlistee, they provided an open invitation to scoundrels everywhere to profit at the expense of young, vulnerable men. The *St. Catharines Constitutional*, for example, wrote about what it called the "thriving business of crimps and bounty jumpers" between that town and Buffalo, preying on three classes of boys: "country boys, Negroes and drunkards." The crimp dupes them, it explained, by offering to pay their passage to the United States, sell them to a broker, split the proceeds, "then follow them up with their old clothes which they have exchanged for a 'suit of blue' and help them escape. But when the crimp reaches that part of his programme where the spoils are divided, he abandons his victim who, after being satisfactorily secured with a pair of 'bracelets,' is hurried off to a recruiting depot" and, after a week or two of training, "is sent off to the front for 'seasoning,' and many don't survive beyond a month or two."[4] According to the *Constitutional*, "the bounty-jumper, compared to the crimp, is a prince, for the only life he risks is his own . . . although no one but a depraved person could break his oath with the same indifference that the bounty-jumper does."

One of the more infamous crimps working the frontier was George Briggs, a resident of Wolfe Island, near Kingston, who ran an organized gang which plagued Kingston to the point that, as the *Brockville Recorder* described it, "scarcely a night passes without a soldier or civilian being spirited away from the precincts of the city to the other side of the lake."[5] There was considerable excitement, then, in Kingston when Briggs was formally charged with enticing soldiers to enlist and driving them to Cape Vincent on the American side. Briggs appeared in court on Monday morning and, for two-and-a-half days, a large number of witnesses testified against him. Things looked bleak for Briggs, when, just before noon on Wednesday, the magistrate said he would return at 1 p.m. with his verdict.

In the meantime, Briggs was taken back to the police station, where Constables Lynn, McDermott, and Milan were on duty. After the prisoner's lawyer left his cell, his father arrived, carrying some apples for his son. But the two policemen, Lynn and Milan, who were in charge of the door, neglected to lock it when the elder Briggs entered and, in moments, the prisoner rushed out, tripping one policeman, who stood guard at the door, and rushing past the other two, who, it seems, had been bribed by Briggs. He jumped into a waiting horse-drawn sled and sped off into the afternoon, causing what the *Sarnia Observer* describes as "much indignation and excitement." Two policemen began an immediate pursuit towards Garden Island, but later returned without finding any trace of him.

Briggs waited for much of the night near Kinghorn Wharf, then, accompanied by a strong bodyguard in his own sleigh, he crossed Simcoe Island to reach Cape Vincent about daybreak. There his friends greeted him by firing their guns in the air and hosting him at a special supper.

To make matters worse for the local officials, a few nights later a carriage, driven by William Neville, arrived at the local jail and some men sneaked inside and "liberated" four prisoners. One was a soldier of the 47th Regiment named Kelly, who was awaiting his departure to England on a charge of desertion. The other three were all members of the Briggs gang – William Cochran, arrested for procuring soldiers for the American army; Murphy, awaiting trial for perjury; and Austin, also for enticing soldiers to desert.

Crimpers recruited soldiers and sailors in various ways. There were "crimping houses," where young men were beguiled into signing enlistment papers while drunk or in the arms of a prostitute or both. Many prostitutes had their own crimping business going, where they'd entice a man to sign up, drug him with chloroform, a drugged tea concoction, or Mickey Finns – whisky laced with a dollop of opium. With the help of an assistant, the victims were transported in crimping boats across the Niagara,

St. Lawrence, or Detroit Rivers, or one of the Great Lakes, to recruiting stations just inside the U.S. border. Potential recruits were often just promised the bounty for signing up and told by the crimps they would help them escape with their money, only to find themselves without either their money or their promised helper, but wearing a Union uniform. Despite several statements from leading American officials decrying the practice and promising to crack down on it, recruitment stations didn't care exactly how their recruits had come to be members of the Union Army, as long as they had a warm body to fill their quota and send off to the battles. More often than not, local recruiting officers were only too happy to accept a bribe and look the other way.

The practice was, of course, illegal. But the reward for catching a crimp was only $50 – raised to $200 in 1864 – and convicted crimps usually got six months of hard labour, though one particularly notorious crimp received five years. But not many crimps were caught, and those who were often bribed local officials into letting them escape. Still, some were caught. In February 1865 Edward St. Michael of Montreal was fined $160, under the *Foreign Enlistment Act*, and sentenced to six months for enticing a private from the 60th Regiment to desert.

In Quebec, Montreal, Kingston, Toronto, London, Sarnia, Sandwich, and Hamilton, each of which had significant British garrisons stationed there, the crimps – who called themselves "substitute brokers" – preyed on the regular soldiers. They were easy targets because the pay in the British Army was low, discipline was harsh, and life in the northern colonies was difficult. What's more, the troops from the Old Country were overwhelmingly Irish boys from Belfast, many under 18, and often illiterate, using "His Mark" as a signature. The opportunity of making more money, meeting adventure, and escaping the current dreadful conditions was more than thousands of British regulars could resist.

According to the April 23, 1862, *Huron Signal* in Goderich, for example, "our chief article of commerce now-a-days is a commodity known in the market as substitutes." And Marguerite B. Hamer of the University of Tennessee writes: "Of the 22,261 foreign-born troops in Michigan regiments, 19,341 were British or Canadian born." These figures are likely overstated, but they provide an indication of how brisk the trade was at the time. A military dispatch in 1864 to a Captain Hall in London, Canada West, read: "The inducements to desert are too much for the 'virtue' of any British soldier. I should be glad to have authority to remove from Windsor men who are evidently meditating a trip across the river. Length of service is apparently but a slender tie on the soldier under the temptation held out. Any detachment near Detroit will melt away; the facilities will be nearly as great at Sandwich for there also is direct communication across."[6]

In Hamilton, crimps operated openly out of Hutton's Inn on York Street, Egeners on John Street, and the Rob Roy Tavern and McCarthy's Saloon on King William Street. In Kingston, crimps plied soldiers with booze at Cockran's across from the Dublin Inn; and in Sandwich, Mears Tavern became headquarters for the activity.

Hamer holds that the crimps "made ample use of the anti-British prejudice of the Irish soldiers." She cites the approach of Kingston crimp James Miller to three Irish soldiers: "You are all Irishmen, why did you enlist in the bloody English service? Come along, I will take the whole lot of you." During the April 1865 trial of a Montreal crimp, Sergeant James Campbell of the 63rd Regiment testified: "While walking in Notre Dame Street, I was accosted by Edward Kelly. He asked me what countryman I was. I told him I was from Ireland when he remarked that he pitied me for wearing the coat I did. I asked him why and he answered that there were two hundred fifty thousand of my countrymen over in the United States, and as soon as the war now raging between the Northern and Southern states was over, would go and free Ireland, and come to Canada where they would hang every

British soldier that would not join them – and that General [George B.] McClellan was an Irishman himself."

Then, of course, there was the money. Non-commissioned officers in the militia earned only 40 cents a day, while a sergeant made $1 and a sergeant-major $1.60. Privates earned five or six pence, making the promise of hundreds of dollars in bounties hard to resist.

Crimps also posted false and misleading posters in the various taverns to catch the interest of prospective enlistees. Hamer cites one that read: "Five hundred men wanted at Detroit, Michigan. Steady employment will be given to active young men of good habits and character accustomed to farm labour and the care of horses. I will pay good wages, thirteen dollars a month and upwards, with good board and clothing and will allow to all employed, traveling expenses to this place. Apply at my store, No. 44 Jefferson Avenue, Detroit, J.H. Tillman, Detroit, September 1861." Others promised good jobs in brickyards and quarries, but they were part of organized scams to entrap young men into the Union service. If the victim failed to cooperate, the crimps simply resorted to drugging and kidnapping. The practice was so common that the British consul at Buffalo said that a "regular system" was organized in which men were "passed over the frontier and . . . stupefied with liquor" until they enlisted in the service. And the head constable of Niagara reported that he had "a man in gaol for four days, who in that time had not sufficiently recovered his senses to be able to give an account of himself, and that he had been rescued from a man who was leading him over to the American side of the river."

The August 20, 1862, *Hamilton Spectator* reports under the headline "Another Yankee Swindle" that "O.E. Ballou & Co. of Bay City, Michigan, advertises for fifty men acquainted with saw mill work; ten or twelve carpenters, eight or ten frame hands, and ten or twelve coopers, to all of whom tempting wages are offered, while the absurdity of the requirements makes the fraud more palpable. The above quota just makes a respectable military company, and would be very acceptable just now in any one of the new, or depleted regiments of the Michigan soldiers. A Yankee, named Wisner, who resides at present in Brantford, is the Canadian agent to whom recruits should apply for further information, and as his business leads him through a large portion of the country, we presume he will hold out the bait in other places than in this locality. We ask our contemporaries to expose this dodge to entrap Canadians into the army of the North, and give Jesse O. Wisner the benefit of a gratuitous notice. This gentleman is only pursuing the same scheme that the blackguard Marx did in Hamilton a few weeks ago, and still more lately pursued by other scoundrels of the same type in Canada. We warn this Yankee recruiting agent in disguise that he had better not attempt to inveigle any of our citizens by honied words or false promises, or he may repent of his folly by finding himself in the grasp of the law that will deal justice out to him, as the rascality of the case demands."

A month later, on September 12, 1862, the *Spectator* again attacked the local enlistment efforts by U.S. Federal agents, who "still continue their endeavours, and in a manner the most objectionable possible. Not content with flaunting the Federal uniform in our faces, and trying to seduce our young men to fight in their behalf, the Northern agents have attempted to seduce our soldiers from their allegiance to Queen Victoria . . . yesterday . . . we saw one of the soldiers of the [Prince Consort's Own] Rifle Brigade, [under the influence of liquor] in the company of a person, clothed in the uniform of the Federal army, who took him to a disreputable house on King street. The soldier seemed to wish to go away, but his companion appeared to insist on his accompanying him. No one, under the circumstances, can have any doubt as to the motive of the Yankee, and it would be well if a strict look-out were kept on those recruiting agents. We make this incident public because we believe the intention was to induce the soldier to desert, and to put the military authorities on their guard against similar proceedings."

The July 16, 1863, *St. Catharines Constitutional* reports on the plight of a Mrs. Nyland, a Montreal widow, who, with tears in her eyes, pleaded before Judge Coursol – who, a year later, would gain infamy for his role in the St. Albans raid – that her only son, aged 14, had been conned by an American named E. Clapper, "who made it his business to come to Montreal to decoy young Canadian boys into the U.S. under pretence of employing them on canals and railroads."

Clapper's ad in local newspapers read: "500 boys wanted to drive for the W.T. (Western Transportation Co.) on the Erie Canal – wages $12 a month, and board. Application to be made at West Troy. Signed, N. Kelsay, Superintendent." The newspaper claimed that Clapper "wheedled about 100 boys from Montreal on Wednesday (July 15), paying their fares to the States by Rouse's Point. We learn that this business has been going on for six months, and several hundreds Canadians have already been sent off to the States, the intention no doubt to make them enlist in the federal service. It would be well if an inquiry were made by the authorities with a view to putting a stop to this business of recruiting Canadian neutrals for Uncle Sam's unpopular service."

On December 11, 1862, the *Brockville Recorder* published a letter to a "Dear H" of Brockville from C.A. Hammond, an old friend from Montreal, saying he was soon heading to the United States and was looking for recruits, who would receive a $125 bounty on enlistment, plus $75 after their service expired. Hammond wrote that his friend's knowledge of Brockville, Prescott, Ogdensburgh, and Cornwall would be helpful, "trusting that you will do this for your old friend and well-wisher." He added a PS: "$5 is given to any agent for every man."

Accompanying that letter was a note from Amos A. Lawrence of the prominent Boston law firm Lawrence & Co., saying an acquaintance had just received his $200 bounty as a "sharpshooter" and "proposes to bring it to me tomorrow to give to his wife . . . In order to avoid a draft for men, our towns are paying huge bounties to induce enlistments. Several towns have placed large sums of money in my hands and requested me to obtain men for them to fill the quotas . . . As I cannot legally send into Canada, I have thought these men might come across the boarder and I would send an agent to meet them and bring them here . . . $5 for the person who brings them, for each man."

In November 1864 a letter was presented in a Quebec City court dated October 28, written by a detective stationed by Canadian authorities in the Eastern Townships to prevent crimping. It made the astounding claim that up to two hundred young men had been forcibly "carried away" by crimps, fifty of them from the small village of Coaticoke alone. The *Quebec News* reported: "About 80 were first drugged and made insensible before they were conveyed and sold across the lines. About 40 of them had been taken by force and many of these had been seen passing on the highway in wagons, with their arms tied. About 10 had been carried off through the effects of chloroform, which was given them in their sleep by parties entering their rooms through windows. Houses had been frequently broken into and the inmates carried off by force. Several parties have been attacked on the highway by gangs of men and carried away. In one instance a man was taken out of a wagon by the side of his wife and she threatened with a revolver if she attempted to make the least alarm. The husband was carried off and has not been heard from since . . . others have been gagged and put out of the way, and others still have had sacks put over their heads to prevent them shouting; and in this manner thrown in a cart and driven off. Some have been decoyed to the vicinity of the lines, where the ingenious dodge of slipping something into their pockets and then bringing a charge of robbery against them, where the alternative of enlisting or going to prison is presented to them."

In May 1863 workers with the lake steamer *Cataract*, which

carried passengers and goods between Kingston and Sackett's Harbor on the American side, loaded a large oblong box bearing the following message: "With care. American Glass Co. Pearl Street. New York. From: Wm. Hunter & Co. Napanee." Later, while the box lay on the wharf at Sackett's Harbor, the ship's engineer pulled out some hay from it to wipe his hands on. When, to his astonishment, the box fell onto the deck, two of Her Majesty's soldiers jumped out, sprang to their feet, and headed for the nearby embankment. They stopped briefly, as the *Rochester Democrat* delicately put it, to "commence their toilet," but when several deck hands came towards them seeking an explanation and hoping to collect the freight charges, the soldiers – one a private, the other a sergeant – headed off to the nearest recruiting office. An examination of the box found it was owned by William Cassons, 4th Battery, 10th Brigade, Royal Artillery, Kingston.

Another soldier who deserted and joined the Union Army in January 1863 was Michael Benson, 28, an Irishman who had fought in the Crimean War and was stationed with the 63rd Foot Regiment at London, Canada West. Late one night, dressed as a woman, Benson left his post and began walking west along the old stage-coach road, sleeping in abandoned farmhouses at night. At Chatham he left the road and took to the railroad tracks. Near Belle River he met a Canadian man and the two began talking. According to the *Detroit Free Press*, Benson "revealed his gender" and offered the Canadian $20 to take him across the river at Windsor. The Canadian accused him of being a deserter, but Benson, who apparently had the gift of the gab, convinced the other man that he had married in London against his father's wishes, his wife was already in Detroit, he had stolen $1,000 from his father, and he had adopted the disguise to elude pursuit.

His companion, who knew the area, took him to Walker's Mills, less than 2 miles from Windsor, where a boatman with a skiff was procured to ferry them across the river to safety. Once on the other side, the Canadian demanded his $20, and Benson assured him he would get it as soon as he found his wife. The man took Benson's shawl as security, and "Michael went directly to the recruiting office of Captain Lee and enlisted in the 28th Michigan Regiment, still wearing his petticoats."

Crimps and others involved in shady profiteering from the war weren't exactly citizens of high moral character. About 6 p.m. on February 12, 1865, for example, local rowdies John Cavanagh, a known bounty jumper, his brother-in-law Anthony Connolly, along with their wives, and an elderly man named McMahon, all from Sarnia, had been drinking at the local taverns and were walking along Francis Street across from the *Sarnia Observer*, when Connolly and his wife got into a fight. Newspaper editor W.G. Gemmill, who was also warden of Lambton County – and who had recently published an editorial critical of crimps and bounty jumpers – stepped out of his office and asked them to move along, only to be met by considerable abuse. When Gemmill threatened to send them to jail for disorderly conduct if they didn't leave quietly, they attacked him and his foreman, James Allen, who had come to his aid.

Gemmill laid an information against Cavanagh before Alfred Fisher, a justice of the peace. Warrants were issued for his arrest, and Chief Constable William G. Harkness and Constable W.J. McEtheron headed to Cavanagh's house on Davis Street, a house of ill repute, to arrest him. There they were assaulted by heavy bludgeons from the two younger men and their wives, with Cavanagh yelling, "Kill them . . . Strike them on the head." Harkness, who had been clubbed as he lay on the ground, lay motionless, while the injured McEtheron returned to the station for help. Cavanagh and Connolly fled, and the mayor offered a $100 reward for their capture. Harkness was unconscious and in critical condition for several days and, at the March 27 trial before Mr. Justice John Wilson of Cavanagh and Connolly, doctors testified he would never fully recover. On the same day these two men were in court, three other cases involving crimps were on the docket. Both men were sentenced to five years in the Provincial Penitentiary.

On August 14, 1862, military police boarded the lake ship *Madison*, which was docked at Toronto and about to leave for Oswego, New York, and found two privates from Her Majesty's 30th Regiment of Foot hiding in the forward hold, lying in a dark corner of the compartment. In addition to the two deserters, they arrested the ship's captain, Victor Myers, an American, along with his second mate, William Innis, and engineer Simon Muirhead, both Canadians, on charges under the *Foreign Enlistment Act*. Deserters were usually dealt with more harshly than crimpers – they sometimes had the letter *D* tatooed on their foreheads – and on occasion were condemned to death.

Even when locals were obviously involved in enlisting for the Union, however, it was not always easy to convict. In December 1864 a local Fredericton man – who had fought for the North – was acquitted by his friend Mayor J.A. Beckwith on charges of enlisting men for the North after the mayor concluded there were not sufficient grounds to convict. New Brunswick Governor General Gordon, after calling the mayor in for a meeting in his office at the Governor's Mansion, furiously charged that "every man in the province is a traitor." There were "hundreds" of Yankee deserters living in the province, he claimed, and the British soldiers were not to be trusted either. The mayor felt at first that it had been a private conversation, but he discovered that the governor had been repeating the same accusations elsewhere, and the story had become somewhat twisted. In due course he received a letter from Major Sewell, the commander of the 15th Regiment, demanding that he substantiate the accusations, followed quickly by another letter from a Colonel Cole saying that the mayor was subject to libel.

It was now Beckwith's turn to be upset, and he raised the matter at the next city council meeting. That resulted in a strongly worded censure motion against the governor. Council called

Gordon's remarks "a direct insult to every British subject residing in New Brunswick . . . [we] cannot allow the citizens of this province to be branded as traitors without giving it our unqualified denial."

In the meantime, the brisk trade in human cargo continued apace. In December 1863 a case was brought before a Montreal police magistrate after the arrest of a man named George Washington Waitt, who had been staying at the Eagle Hotel on College Street. He had been at the wharf awaiting the arrival of a man named Hamlin, who had agreed to go to the United States with him and enlist in the Northern Army. Waitt was subsequently convicted – he got six months and a $200 fine – mainly because police discovered a letter in his pocket, dated November 23, 1863, from William P. Merrill, a businessman in Portland, Maine. Merrill wrote: "I can't take men unless they understand and speak some English. I can give $500 per man and even $600 for some towns, and can give in cash from $300 to $480 cash down when mustered in; and if hard pushed can go for some places – that is, to fill some town's quotas - $400 cash.

"Send such men as can speak English, and are sound, and of suitable age, along, and I will muster them right in without delay. I can find a place for 1,000 men as fast as the papers can be made out. I can also, for men that want to get cash and not wait for government . . . find a market for $500 cash down. If you find any veterans there from our own army with a regular discharge paper, I can get for them $750, and $425 cash down.

"P.S. If you should start with any, send a telegram and call them boxes of medicine, or say if you have 10 men that you sent $10, so that I can know and Canadians won't know."

In February 1863 the *Globe* reported the story of six soldiers of the 60th Regiment who had been taken in a freight car from Point St. Charles to Island Pond. "There, the American customs officer opened the door, and the soldiers were received by a party evidently waiting for them. Where they entered or who assisted them is a mystery." A week later the *Globe* reported that the 60th Regiment had lost fifty men in this way, and the officials on the train had been suspended.

In August 1864 the *Niagara Mail* reported that three men of the 63rd Regiment from Grimsby, near Niagara Falls, had left at midnight by boat, with both arms and ammunition, heading for the United States. Six privates from the Royal Canadian Rifles under Sergeant McKenzie had been dispatched from Niagara in pursuit. After rowing for two hours, the pursuers saw the boat, and the sergeant ordered it to stop. But the deserters fired, missing from just 10 yards away, and the sergeant ordered his men to fire a volley over their heads to intimidate them. It didn't work, and the deserters fired again, slightly wounding one rifleman who, in a return fire, hit one of the three deserters in the head with a bullet. The two boats came into close contact and, after a brief scuffle, the deserters were arrested. Once the wounded man had been treated at the hospital, they were taken before the Grimsby mayor, who committed them to jail until the proper authorities could be contacted.

In January 1864 the *Chatham Planet* reported that two black men, Willis Hosey, who owned land near Buxton but was then living in Detroit, and Isaac Washington, who owned land and lived near the Elgin Settlement, had decided to go into the business of recruiting for Colonel Barnes for the Colored Regiment at Detroit. The two men were brought before the police magistrate charged with enticing at last one man to "go for a soldier." It seems they had conned 15-year-old Mordecai Morris, the only son of widow Emilene Crose, "a poor simple-minded body living near Buxton." The report said Morris was seduced by Hosey to go with him on the pretext that constant work and good wages could be found for him on a Michigan farm. Instead, he was taken to Detroit and enlisted, leaving his mother no way to support herself and the rest of her family.

After the circumstances in the case were reported, Hosey

sent Washington $120 in greenbacks from Detroit to be given to the widow, but she declined, saying she'd rather have her son than the money. The two men were fined, but, that September, Hosey was back in front of Police Magistrate Thomas McCrae again, charged, along with Frederick T. Backenstose, a white man, with violating the *Foreign Enlistment Act* after they'd tried to enlist James Graham, a Chatham shoemaker.

Graham testified that he had been in Detroit on Friday night and met Hosey, as well as a man named John Durkin, who had recently moved to Canada from Dunlinthe, Illinois, after enlisting in and then leaving the army. The next day the three men went to Windsor, where Hosey promised them $600 as substitutes in the U.S. Army. Both agreed, and Hosey said he was going to "see the man." He returned, eventually, to say that the other man had changed his mind, but they could go to New York to enlist and he would pay their expenses in Windsor for the night and for the ticket on the Great Western Railway. Hosey paid for their breakfast and had them wait in a barber shop until Backenstose showed up, told them they would get the $600 the next day, and said he and Hosey were in business together. When the train was about to leave, Backenstose handed Hosey three tickets on the train heading east – Graham's was ticket No. 436, first class, Detroit to Paris – and they rode to Chatham, where Durkin and Graham got off to have some drinks while Hosey and Backenstose went to the Rankin House together. When they returned, Backenstose assured them they would have their money the next day in New York. Even though Backenstose said he was authorized by the U.S. government to recruit soldiers, Graham and Durkin were getting suspicious. But before they left Chatham, Police Chief John Goodyear arrested Backenstose, after intercepting a telegram confirming the first-class rail tickets. He didn't believe Backenstose's story that he was hiring the men to work in a nursery. Neither did the court, as it turned out.

The ultimate results of flouting the law and recruiting young

Canadians was often tragic. The August 12, 1864, *Quebec Mercury*, for example, republished an article from the *Brantford Courier* reporting the death of 16-year-old H.A. Graham, the youngest son of Michael Graham of the township of Brantford, Canada West, from typhoid fever in a hospital at Alexandria, Virginia. "The above youth was enticed away from his parents by a strolling Yankee Company who were exhibiting, in Brantford, pictures of the American war. He was taken to Lockport, and there enlisted on the 9th [of] June last. He was then ordered to Washington, where he was taken ill, and in a few days died . . . We deeply sympathise with the bereaved parents in the loss of their young son, and trust it will be a warning to young Canadian boys to remain at home, and let the Yankees get men in their own country to prosecute their murderous war; for there is not doubt, had young Graham remained at home, he would have been alive to-day."

In June 1864 the *Sarnia Observer* reported the story of three men newly arrived from Adelaide, Scotland, looking for work. Two of them – John Keays and Richard Ashton – went to Point Edward, where they were warned by a local man to watch out for crimps and not to drink, advice they opted to ignore. Both men became drunk, assisted by local crimps, and Ashton found himself locked up in a room overnight. The next morning, waking with a hangover, he was coerced into enlisting on the pretext that he had committed a crime the night before and enlisting was the only way to avoid being sent to jail. The story was made more believable because it was told him by a local Port Huron police constable who, unfortunately for Ashton, was in on the scheme from the outset. The next day, Ashton was dispatched to the battlefield as a new recruit. "This, in all likelihood, is the last that will ever be heard of him," wrote the *Observer*.

As for Ashton's pal Keays, he also got drunk and was locked up in the Port Huron jail, where he was plied with arguments to enlist but steadfastly refused. Fortunately for him, a friend heard of his plight, went to the sheriff, and arranged to get him discharged from jail and safely back onto the Canadian side.

In the same town in the summer of 1864, well-known crimp Levi Merrick once escorted five Canadian deserters into a local saloon and offered them for sale at $40 each. Around the same time another local crimp, envious of his rival Joseph Porter, tried to entice two of Porter's substitutes – privates named Flynn and Coleman – when Porter challenged him, saying, "These are my men. I brought them from the other side." The ensuing argument attracted a large crowd of local rowdies and a scuffle broke out, attracting the attention of a U.S. marshal. He at first arrested Flynn and Coleman as deserters from the U.S. Army but let them go when they showed him the mark of the 47th Regiment on their underwear – crimps usually supplied a new set of clothes for the soldiers, including socks and underwear, which acted both as an added bonus for their recruit and as protection from detection by the authorities. As a result, with the help of the crowd, Porter was arrested and sent back to Canada for trial – six men shared in the $200 government reward for his capture and conviction – and Porter spent the next six months in a Sarnia jail.

The October 13, 1864, *Brockville Recorder* tells the sorry tale of an unnamed young man from Camden Township who left his home for the first time a few weeks earlier to look for work in the United States and, shortly after arriving in Rochester, was befriended by two young men. His newfound "friends" took him on a tour of the city, eventually ending up in a bar, where one of them asked what time it was. The other male made a motion to produce his watch but, to his mock horror, announced that it was missing. Great consternation ensued and a "policeman" was called. He searched the three men and "found" the watch on the Canadian, whereupon he immediately arrested him and told him he was facing five years in prison. But there was a way out: if he'd enlist in the army, he could be saved. With that, the necessary papers were produced on the spot, the young Canadian signed, and was immediately marched off to the local military headquarters, which is the last that was heard of him.

While both governments made token efforts to stem the practice, Lord Richard B.P. Lyons, the British ambassador at Washington from 1858 to 1865, wasn't convinced they were trying all that hard. In a note to Earl Russell on August 9, 1864, Lyons wrote: "I have no ground for asserting that any one in the service of the United States Government is directly concerned in these practices, nor do I doubt that the higher authorities at Washington would give due redress in any case where positive proof can be produced; but I think that it is difficult to deny that in their eagerness to fill up the ranks of the army, some subordinate recruiting officers connive more or less at the nefarious practices of brokers and agents, and I cannot believe that an earnest determination on the part of the supreme authorities here to put down these iniquities would be ineffectual."[7]

On more than one occasion, U.S. troops chasing deserters who fled for safety into Canada created some sovereignty concerns for Canadian officials. On September 21, 1861, for example, a U.S. captain from the 8th Michigan Regiment in Detroit, along with five men – three in uniform and two in civilian clothes – arrived on horseback in the community of Gosfield, near Windsor, in pursuit of four deserters from their regiment. In a lengthy statement dated October 2 to Essex County Sheriff John McEwan, local Justice of the Peace W.H. Billings explained that, about 5 p.m., a man named Nagle, who owned the local tavern, came to see him. He reported that the Americans had entered his tavern hunting for deserters, left their horses in his barn, and gone into the bush in search of the men who, they knew, were working on a nearby farm. Nagle asked if it was legal for them to take the deserters, and Billings said it was not, unless the men were willing to return to the United States on their own accord. Nagle said he didn't know how to stop them because he had been told they were all armed with several shooters and the captain had threatened to take the men back "dead or alive."

At this point Billings went to see local constable John Noble, instructing him to call out all the neighbours he could find and instruct them to bring their rifles to the tavern. As a result, several men showed up, all carrying rifles and all drinking beer, until the American soldiers emerged from the bush about 9 p.m., escorting the four deserters, all of whom were still wearing their U.S. Army uniforms. Billings asked the captain by what authority he had arrested the men, and the captain said he hadn't arrested them but had asked them to return – and they had agreed. He also showed Billings an order from his colonel empowering him to recapture any regimental deserters. "I told him we did not acknowledge his colonel's orders this side of the river," wrote Billings. "It might be good enough on the other side, but these men were now under the protection of the British flag." Billings then asked each deserter if he was returning willingly, and each said no. Asked why they had come out of the bush with the captain, the men said he had not threatened them but "they thought they had too." When Billings told the deserters they were at liberty to go, they thanked him and left. "The captain then asked me if we thought they were all wild beasts, as my men were all armed with rifles and so excited . . . I told him I had been told that they were all armed with seven shooters and bowie knives and that they had said they would take the deserters back dead or alive . . . I thought the rifles might be very useful if they attempted to carry out their threats."

The captain denied having made any threats and offered "his word of honour" that they were not armed. Billings could search them if he chose. "I declined to do so, telling him that as he was a military man of rank and, I supposed, a gentleman, I would take his word. He said he should complain of me to my government for discharging the men and that he would be down next week with fifty men and an order from our governor."

The case attracted the attention of Canadian officials, resulting in a September 30 telegraph from the attorney general's department in Quebec to Sherrif McEwan, which read: "Is it true that United States soldiers have lately come over the line into Upper Canada to arrest persons? If so, where and when and what are the particulars? Answer at once." McEwan responded the next day with some details, but said he would ask Billings to forward the complete story.

Nothing came of it except for an October 16 letter from Lieutenant-Colonel E. Backus in Detroit to McEwan: "I am anxious to see you relative to a matter connected with an alleged apprehension of American deserters in Canada by a United States officer and four unarmed men. But I am an invalid and have but once left my room in a week. I can not do myself the honor to call and see you at your office. Will it be asking too much if I request you call and see me as early as you can make it convenient at the Michigan Exchange, room No. 4?" But McEwan did not respond.

The February 13, 1862, *Globe,* from an earlier story in the *Montreal Gazette*, reported that ten American soldiers crossed the border at Malone from New York State, broke into a house near Dundee, and took a Federal deserter back with them. Canadian officials promptly complained to General Thorndyke, the U.S. commander in the district, and he ordered that the deserter be given up and compensation paid for damage to the home.

Because Canada offered protection for deserters, some rather unsavoury characters made their way across the borders. One such man was George Hill, described in the March 24, 1864, *Tillsonburg Observer* as "a big strapping fellow, brakesman on the Milwaukee & Mississippi Railroad." Hill enlisted in the 1st Wisconsin Regiment, but was soon discharged on some pretext, so he returned to Milwaukee – and to a $150 bounty for enlisting in the 24th Wisconsin. Just past Louisville, Hill and five others deserted and, over the next two months, he enlisted in two more regiments, getting a bounty from each one, before heading off to Fort Wayne, where he got a job on the Fort Wayne & Toledo Railroad. In July 1863 he was arrested in Toledo and taken to Columbus, Ohio, but managed to get away after presenting the officers with phony discharge papers. The trick was quickly discovered, however, and he was again arrested and sent down the Mississippi River to Memphis. Once again he escaped, fled to eastern Indiana, was captured once more and sent to Chattanooga, where his original regiment was, but again escaped. Not short on nerve, Hill made his way to New Jersey, enlisted, got another bounty, then deserted, went to New York City, enlisted again, this time for a $500 bounty, then fled to Canada, where, according to a *Chicago Tribune* story about his exploits, "he is now enjoying his bounty."

Despite the ongoing horrors of crimping, desertion, and bounty-jumping, Canadian authorities took little action to combat it, beyond increasing the fines and offering regular rhetorical flourishes about the evils of the practice. In the fall of 1864, the Grand Jury of York and Peel, showing considerable frustration over the situation, offered the following public comment: "A great many bills have been before the jurors for enticing soldiers of the regular army to desert – a crime of such frequency that, in the opinion of Grand Jurors, demands increased severity in the punishment of those concerned in it, and greater vigilance on the part of peace officers; and, otherwise, the large bounty offered for able-bodied soldiers on the other side of the line induces that pest of society, the crimp, to ply his unlawful and disgraceful traffic in human beings successfully and profitably, to the utter ruin of the soldier.

"And it cannot be too often repeated that the man who, in a moment of weakness, is enticed or persuaded to leave the standard of his country in the hope of bettering his condition and of pocketing a large sum of money, meets with disappointment, and not only perjures himself, but ends his life in misery and wretchedness, and, when too late, finds that he is treated by his betrayer and purchaser as a slave.

"In no case that we remember do we find that the British soldier who has deserted is ever promoted, no matter how faithfully and zealously he may perform the duties assigned to him, no matter how superior his knowledge of military discipline may be.

"This warning has been time and again repeated; nevertheless, the Grand Jurors are induced again to raise their voice in the hope that this warning, so often repeated, may be the means of restraining even one soldier from committing that one great crime of desertion, and placing himself in the humiliating position of perjurer and traitor, beyond the hope of advancement even in the service of the foreign government under which he may have enlisted."

Despite all such warnings, and the efforts – albeit somewhat meagre – of Canadian law enforcement officials to clamp down on the crimps, thousands of Canadian boys – and thousands of British regulars – were taken from their homes under false pretenses and thrown into a foreign battle, many of them not living long enough to tell their tale to anybody. The only thing that stopped this dreadful practice was the end of the war itself.

SEVEN

To the Barricades

A T 1:15 P.M. ON NOVEMBER 8, 1861, Captain Charles Wilkes of the USS *San Jacinto*, a sloop-of-war carrying thirteen guns, fired two shots that, literally, were heard around the world. Wilkes, in clear violation of international law and acting against direct orders from Washington, accosted the British mail packet the *Trent* in international waters in the Old Bahamas Channel, 300 miles east of Havana, Cuba. Firing two shots across the *Trent*'s bow, Wilkes forced the unarmed British ship to stop, then dispatched an armed boarding party onto it and demanded the surrender of two Confederate diplomats – James M. Mason and John Slidell. The men were on their way to Europe as commissioners-designate to Great Britain and France, assigned the task of convincing those European powers to bestow formal recognition to the Confederate States of America.

The two Southerners had boarded the *Trent*, a neutral ship, at Havana, a neutral port, and Wilkes had no legal authority to arrest and detain them – but he did. Even worse, after allowing the *Trent* to continue on its way to England with the diplomats' families, Wilkes transported the captured men and their secretaries to Fort Warren in the Boston harbour. There, despite their diplomatic status, the four men were immediately thrown in jail and Wilkes "was welcomed as a conquering hero."[1] In *Murdering Mr. Lincoln*, best-selling author Charles Higham argues that

French documents show that the Confederacy staged the seizure by paying Wilkes, in the hope it would provoke the British into a declaration of war against the United States. He says the deal was consummated between Wilkes and Sara E. Brewer, the Confederate agent at Havana.[2]

Whatever the truth, for a time Wilkes was the toast of the nation. Congress thanked him for his "brave, adroit, and patriotic conduct in the arrest of the traitors," struck a gold medal in his honour, and adopted a resolution calling on President Lincoln to keep Mason and Slidell confined in prison as convicted criminals. The *New York Times* advocated that a second Independence Day be declared in Wilkes's honour, and the City of Boston presented him with a jewelled sword. Charles Francis Adams, the son of the American ambassador to Great Britain and a young law student in Boston at the time, would later write: "I do not remember in the whole course of the half-century's retrospect . . . an occurrence in which the American people were so completely swept off their feet, for the moment losing possession of their senses, as during the weeks which immediately followed the seizure of Mason and Slidell."[3]

While celebrated at home, however, Wilkes's high-handed actions actually exacerbated a split within the Lincoln administration – where some senior officials clamoured for war against Britain, while others wanted to avoid it at all costs, certainly until the Civil War was won. The seizure of the diplomats also caused a brief but intense sensation throughout Europe and all North America, and, most important, brought Britain within a whisker of declaring war against the United States. The London *Times* summed up the widespread public outrage there, writing that Wilkes was "an ideal Yankee . . . Swagger and ferocity, built on a foundation of vulgarity and cowardice, these are his characteristics . . . the most prominent marks by which his countrymen . . . are known all over the world."[4]

In the colonies, had cooler heads not prevailed, British

North Americans would have found themselves transformed from interested sideline spectators to frontline participants in a war against their Yankee neighbours, a war they were ill prepared to fight. There would be other tense moments between Britain and the United States during the Civil War period, but none would come as close to sparking all-out war as the 1861 *Trent* Affair did.

On April 13, 1861, one day after the Civil War began, Queen Victoria proclaimed British neutrality. It was no secret that Britain, the leading world power at the time, was sympathetic to the South. Britain's huge textile industry depended on Southern cotton and, besides, elite British public opinion still bristled over the upstart Americans having won the American Revolution less than a century earlier, and many still remembered the hostilities between the two countries in the War of 1812.

On April 16 President Lincoln announced a naval blockade of Southern ports, a move that infuriated business interests both in Britain and in the colonies, particularly Nova Scotia and New Brunswick, which, while enjoying stronger trading ties with Boston and other northern ports, also did considerable business with the South. The next day, Confederate President Jefferson Davis, hoping to capitalize on this anger and on anti-American attitudes generally, announced that would-be privateers could apply to his government for letters of marque – an effort to bolster the fledgling Confederate Navy. Lincoln announced that privateers would be treated as pirates, and he expected all countries to take the same approach – a position the British rejected when, in effect, their neutrality proclamation implied the existence of two belligerent parties in the conflict. As historian Francis Jones explains: "Britain was determined to remain aloof from the conflict. The South persisted in attempting to incite Britain to declare war on the United States. Britain insisted on protecting its commerce while at the same time respecting the blockade. These factors, combined with the inducement to adventure and profit offered by privateering, would ensure that the Royal Navy, and therefore Halifax, would play a pivotal role in the conflict which was to last until the Confederate surrender at Appomattox Court House on 9 April 1865, four years later."[5]

The Queen's immediate declaration of neutrality was not exactly what either the North or the South had hoped for. The North was deeply upset because the declaration, while appearing to be even-handed, in fact formally recognized the Confederacy as a belligerent – conferring wartime privileges on rebel invaders – a position the North viewed, correctly, as tacit British support for the South. The South, in contrast, was disappointed that it hadn't received outright recognition from the British. It remained hopeful that it eventually would because of Britain's cool attitude towards the North, the early Southern victories on the battle-fields, and the long-term impact of the blockade on trade. For the British, their declaration of neutrality would keep them out of the war itself, while still allowing them to trade with the North and, pending a way around the blockade, the South as well.

While these diplomatic negotiations were unfolding, many of the colonists living in British North America were fearful of an American takeover. Though not initially widespread, these concerns were compounded by the belligerent, anti-British expansionist attitude expressed by several senior U.S. officials, particularly Secretary of State William H. Seward. The British were certainly worried about it. Lord Lyons, Britain's ambassador to Washington, recommended that the surest way to avoid an American takeover of the colonies was "manifest readiness to prevent one,"[6] a position supported by the British North American governor general, Sir Edmund Head. And so, within weeks of the Confederate attack on Fort Sumter and the subsequent outbreak of the war, Britain announced that it was sending major reinforcements to the colonies to bolster its existing defences. At the time, there were only 4,300 regular imperial troops in the colonies, and, although all the provinces began forming local militias, they were not only ill-trained but desperately short of weapons and supplies, should the war spill over into Canada.

In the summer of 1861 the British naval squadron stationed at Halifax featured just thirteen ships, a motley collection of steam and sailing craft – its flagship was the wooden three-decker *Indus*, armed with the old-style smooth-bore cannon. Within a year, however, the harbour, besides teeming with various private blockade-runners, was home to twenty-four British men-o'war, all steamships. "The twilight of the windjammer had begun," which had little to do with the war, "but a great deal to do with Nova Scotia's future."[7] The city's entire defence system, which had been redesigned in 1829 and expanded at enormous cost ever since, had suddenly been rendered obsolete by the appearance of the rifled cannon in U.S. warships. That led to an immediate revamping of the system – an expensive operation that continued throughout the war but would never be tested in battle.

In July 1861, responding to the hostilities to the south, the *Great Eastern*,[8] a behemoth 19,000-ton steamer, six times larger than any ship that had ever been built, was quickly commissioned by the imperial government in London, converted into a troop ship, equipped with the powerful new Armstrong gun, and dispatched from England amid considerable fanfare. It carried 2,144 officers and men of the Royal Artillery (plus 473 women and children), the most reinforcements ever sent abroad by Britain at one time, and it crossed the Atlantic in a record eight days and six hours. Another 900 troops were also sent over on the *Golden Fleece*. The June 27, 1861, *Globe*, commenting on the British announcement that troops would be dispatched over the next few weeks and on American reaction to the news, wrote: "The Americans may consider their advent 'an insult' to the United States if they like. That will not go far towards removing them." Troops were headed for Quebec City, Montreal, Toronto, Kingston, London, St. Catharines, Niagara, and Amherstburg.

Given the enormous sudden strength of the Northern armies and the U.S. Navy, and the vast expanse of the British North American boundaries, the actual number of British troops – reinforced even more in the months ahead, particularly during and immediately following the *Trent* Affair – represented a pittance in practical defence terms. It served, however, as a strong message to Washington that Britain was prepared to fight, if necessary, to defend its colonies against American expansionism.

Among the colonists themselves, much of the pro-Confederate sympathy was muted at the outbreak of the war, given the popular sentiment against slavery, but it rapidly came to the fore after the embarrassing Union defeat at Bull Run in July. It continued to grow, fed by business concerns over the naval blockade and by a general feeling among the business and social elite that the Southern cause was more romantic and more legally justified. The social impact on public opinion cannot be overstated. Throughout the war, while the Southern gentry mingled with the local gentry, making a great and generally positive impression on them, the only Northerners the colonists came in regular contact with tended to hail from the lower classes or were outright rogues, such as Yankee bounty-hunters seeking to trick British North Americans into signing up with the North. As for Britain, which had not enjoyed warm relations with the Americans, it was furious at the Northern blockade of Confederate ports and the impact that had on the cotton trade, so vital to England's textile industry. But public opinion was widely split. Many Britons, having read the disturbing series on slavery by the *Times* foreign correspondent W.H. Russell, at a time when that newspaper carried enormous weight on both public and political opinion, were not inclined to favour the pro-slave Confederates. Then again, in his March 4, 1861, speech, Lincoln essentially announced that the war was not about slavery: "I have no purpose, directly or indirectly, to interfere with the institution of slavery in the States where it exists. I believe I have no lawful right to do so, and I have no inclination to do so." One newspaper editorialized in reply that if the North was not fighting to free the slaves, England was "relieved from any moral consideration in their favour."[9] Lincoln's statement allowed Southern supporters to focus on trade and other issues, such as the 1861 *Morrill Tariff Act*, which the South saw as an unfair tax on its products, one that made European imports more expensive. That act, as Robert A. Toombs, the first Confederate secretary of state, put it, "extorted millions . . . from our people to foster Northern monopolies." He said secession was "separation from associates who recognize no law but self-interests and the power of numerical superiority[10] – arguments that seemed to find considerable resonance among the British elite.

When the Confederacy set out to be a separate country in 1861, one of its major concerns was how it would be perceived abroad. Like any country, it needed formal international recognition to strengthen its own case, and the way to do that – although the South didn't do it very well – was to send diplomats abroad in the hope of convincing other countries to extend their official recognition to it.

On March 16, 1861, even before the first official volleys of the war at Fort Sumter, President Davis ordered Toombs to appoint a three-man commission to send to Europe seeking official recognition. Toombs named William Lowndes Yancey, Pierre A. Rost, and Ambrose Dudley Mann, all former politicians, with instructions to convince Europeans of two propositions: that the war was not a revolution but a legitimate expression of freedom under the existing U.S. Constitution; and that there would be serious economic consequences from the sharp reduction in the supply of Southern cotton. But even the impressive and unexpected Confederate victory at Bull Run in July 1861, while garnering some public sympathy for the South, wasn't enough to convince the Europeans, the British in particular, that officially recognizing the Confederacy was worth the risk of alienating the United States. Moreover, the fact that the Southern diplomats, like the ones to follow, were all ardent pro-slavers continued to make recognition a more difficult sell in Europe, where slavery was universally unpopular. Lord John Russell, the head of the British Foreign Office, met "unofficially" with the Confederate commissioners on May 3, but told them beforehand that he would "under present circumstances, have little to say."[11] In October, unhappy with the lack of concrete progress, Davis scrapped his diplomatic triumvirate and replaced it with two new men – Mason and Slidell – neither of whom, as it turned out, was a good choice.

Slidell, the junior partner, had been born in New York but fled to Louisiana after a duel, where, as first a congressman and then a senator, he became an outspoken advocate of states' rights. In New Orleans he had operated a successful commercial law practice with Judah P. Benjamin, who was to become the Confederacy's secretary of state and, besides being the only Jewish official in either administration, was widely seen as "the brains" of the Confederacy. As for Slidell, he had only limited diplomatic experience – as special commissioner to Mexico in 1845 during the border dispute leading up to the Mexican War. His job was made easier when the French emperor, Napoleon III, told Confederate officials that France would officially recognize them, but only if Britain, the dominant European power, did so first.

That recognition wasn't likely to happen, given the political realities in Britain at the time. Lord Henry Palmerston, the prime minister, a Whig, was desperately trying to retain power by leading a tiny majority, thanks to a shaky coalition with the Tories. He worried that intervention on the side of the slave-owners would

upset the working class. More to the point, having closely followed the march to Southern secession and anticipating the
worst, Britain had stockpiled a two-year supply of cotton,
enabling it to wait and watch the progress of the war before taking a definitive position. On the personal level, "Slidell was
rumoured to be a drunkard, however, and would come to be
hated by practically all the Confederate agents in Europe."[12]

The Union diplomats in Europe, while more experienced
and polished than the Confederate representatives, had their lives
made more difficult by the constant bellicose public threats
against Britain by William Seward – described by the Duke of
Argyll, for example, as "the very impersonation of all that is most
violent and arrogant in the American character." In 1860 the
Duke of Newcastle had reported that Seward, perhaps as a joke,
had quipped that if he became secretary of state, it would
"become my duty to insult England, and I mean to do so."[13]
Following the meeting between Russell and the original
Confederate diplomats, Seward dispatched a note to Charles
Francis Adams, the U.S. minister in England, saying that any further contact between England and the South would result in a
break of diplomatic relations between the two countries and
threatening war "not unlike . . . at the close of the last century."
Adams was confused, writing: "The government seems ready to
declare war with all the powers of Europe . . . I scarcely know how
to understand Mr. Seward."[14]

Even with Seward's help, however, Mason turned out to be a
diplomatic disaster in his own right. His father, George, had been
a famous Virginian patriot and friend of George Washington, and
he himself was a lawyer and veteran politician. As chair of the
Senate's Foreign Relations Committee for ten years, he drafted
the *Fugitive Slave Law* of 1850 and served as U.S. minister to
France. Once in England, however, "he did much to undermine
the British stereotype of the South as populated by dignified,
chivalrous gentlemen such as General Robert E. Lee or those

found in Sir Walter Scott novels. Historian Howard Jones describes him as 'rude and obnoxious.' He recalls how Mason chewed tobacco, which was anathema to the British. Moreover, he spat the tobacco in Parliament and, more often than not, missed the spittoon and left it in a heap on the red carpet."[15]

In October 1861 Mason and Slidell, along with their secretaries, George Eustis and James McFarland, Eustis's wife and Slidell's family and servants, left Richmond for Charleston, South Carolina, hoping to run the blockade. Their departure was delayed by tides, weather, and the appearance off the coast of more Federal ships, but finally, on October 11, they boarded the *Gordon*, a shallow-drafted vessel later renamed the *Theodora*, which had run the blockade before. They arrived at Nassau three days later, but, on learning there was no direct steamer service to England, proceeded on to Cuba. They arrived at Cardenas, 100 miles from Havana, on October 15, only to learn they had just missed a British mail ship and would have to wait three weeks for the next one. They decided to wait.

In the meantime the 62-year-old Wilkes, who had been born in New York City, was busy setting a trap for them. Before the war he had been a famous explorer and, as head of the U.S. Exploring Expedition from 1838 to 1842, had circumnavigated the globe and, on January 19, 1840, discovered Antarctica. He had also explored Puget Sound, helping to establish Oregon and the Sound as new prizes in America's self-declared Manifest Destiny. He had joined the navy as a midshipman in 1818 and steadily worked his way up the chain of command. But he was such an arrogant, disagreeable man, whose harsh discipline was notorious, that he became the inspiration for Herman Melville's character Captain Ahab in the novel *Moby Dick*. In 1864 he was court-martialled for insubordination and conduct unbecoming an officer – among other things, he had disobeyed orders and

publicly rebuked the Navy secretary. He was found guilty, publicly remanded, and suspended for three years, a sentence later
reduced to one year. In 1866, commissioned a rear admiral, he
retired, and lived in Washington until his death on February 8,
1877.

On May 14, 1861, Wilkes was ordered to sail to Fernando
Po, on Africa's west coast, to take command of the warship *San
Jacinto* and, except for stopping to pick up supplies, sail it direct-
ly back to Philadelphia. But when he took over the ship in late
August, he spent the next month sailing along the African coast
searching for Confederate privateers. He didn't find any. In late
September, however, hearing that the Confederate cruiser *Sumter*
had run the blockade from New Orleans and was harassing
Union shipping in the West Indies, he headed off to the
Caribbean, reaching St. Thomas on October 13 and taking command of two other cruisers. He then left for Cienguegos, Cuba,
where he learned that Mason and Slidell had arrived in Havana,
getting ready to sail to London. Wilkes sailed immediately to
Havana, intent on capturing the *Theodora*, as the *Gordon* had now
become, but, after learning it had a two-week head start, he sent
two of his officers to meet with Mason in hopes of discovering
their intentions.

That tactic didn't work, but Robert Shufeldt, the U.S.
consul-general in Havana, a former naval officer, told Wilkes that
the Confederates had booked passage for November 7 on board
the *Trent*. And so, on November 2, announcing that he was headed back to the United States, as he had been ordered to do,
Wilkes set sail from Havana, doubling back towards Key West
that night, intent on finding some Navy vessels there to aid in his
capture of the *Trent*. When he discovered there were no USN
ships at Key West, Wilkes ordered the *San Jacinto* towards the
Bahama Channel, where, shortly before noon on November 8, his
lookout spotted the *Trent* some 10 miles in the distance.

Some of Wilkes's own officers had expressed concerns that

stopping a British ship in neutral waters could spark a war with Europe, but Wilkes was not the sort of man to entertain doubt. He arrested some of his own men and placed them under guard – the same sort of high-handed treatment of his staff that had brought him an official reprimand some twenty years earlier during his exploration days – while he selected a boarding party under the command of his executive officer, Lieutenant Daniel Macneill Fairfax. In a four-page, December 1999 essay entitled "Charles Wilkes and the *Trent* Affair," writer Jonathan L. Mahaffey cites Wilkes's biographer, John Sherman Long, claiming that Fairfax, who had initially expressed concerns to Wilkes about the plan, had been ordered to seize the *Trent* as a prize of war, along with the two diplomats, but, "disobeying the orders, Fairfax departed the *Trent* without making it a prize. He was able to convince Wilkes, however, to overlook that fact by claiming that put[ing] a prize crew on the *Trent* would inconvenience its innocent passengers and would also impair the *San Jacinto*'s fighting ability."

To explain the extraordinary and instantaneous jubilation in the North over what really was a pretty minor incident, albeit highly illegal, it's necessary to remember the mood of the general public at the time. When the war had begun six months earlier, most people in the North expected to put down the Confederacy quickly and easily. Since then, Bull Run had been a major embarrassment and psychological set-back; the Europeans, particularly the British, had not endeared themselves to Americans by their appearance of favouring the South; and, in essence, Northern morale had hit a low point and was badly in need of a boost. The actions of a "brave" navy captain, unfettered by bureaucratic bumbling in Washington, seemed to be just what the North craved.

In Richmond, while Confederate officials hotly decried the act, they were, in fact, thrilled – suddenly hopeful, as Jefferson Davis would say, that the British would not "submit quietly to the insult." Davis told the Confederate Congress on November 18: "These gentlemen were as much under the jurisdiction of the British government upon that ship and beneath its flag as if they had been on its soil, and a claim on the part of the United States to seize them in the streets of London would have been as well founded as that to apprehend them where they were taken." If Britain were to declare war against the United States – a Confederate hope that suddenly appeared possible – it would almost certainly break the blockade and give the Confederacy official recognition in the process, not to mention making it a whole lot easier for the Southern forces to defeat the Union on the battlefield.

In British North America the November 19 *Ottawa Citizen* reported that the incident had "set the whole country ablaze." It had an immediate impact on public opinion, undercutting widespread Northern sympathy – most of which came from long-time trade and personal ties to the Northern states and Canadian abhorrence of slavery – and making the Southern "cause" more popular. Governor General Lord Monck, less than a week into his new office, immediately ordered Sir Fenwick Williams, the British military commander in North America, to stop using the telegraph to send important or secret information abroad and to prepare to strengthen his forces and local militias in a way that was "as quiet as possible, not on account of the Americans but lest an alarm and panic should be excited amongst our people."[16]

The Canadian government, also fearful of an American attack even before the *Trent* Affair, had asked the British for a report on proposed British military strategy for defending the colonies in the event of war, and a captain from the Royal Engineers had been assigned the task. The *Trent* Affair brought a renewed urgency to the question and, on November 19, just eleven days after the incident, the report was handed over to the government. It recommended large troop concentrations near the Beauharnois, Cornwall, and Welland canals, where it predicted much of the fighting would occur. It also resulted in the creation of a Department of Defence – headed by John A. Macdonald, who would later become Canada's founding prime minister – and suggested that colonial and imperial troops would, if war were declared, go on the offensive and capture Fort Montgomery at Rouse's Point and Fort Niagara, to protect Montreal and Toronto against invasion. Within a month, construction of new defensive batteries had begun in Toronto and Kingston.

In New Brunswick, Lieutenant-Governor Arthur Gordon met Charles Hastings Doyle, commander of the British troops in Nova Scotia, and was told that both Saint John and Woodstock were defenceless, which meant that most of the province west of the Saint John River would be surrendered to the invaders so that the interior, primarily the land approaches to Nova Scotia, could be defended. Doyle felt the Maritimes could be defended by issuing letters of marque and mounting guns at strategic points along the Nova Scotian coast. "According to Joseph Howe, leader of the liberals in Nova Scotia, who offered every able-bodied man in the province for military service, the major weakness in Maritime defence was that the frontier could not be armed quickly due to the lack of railroad connections. However, Howe had an ulterior motive, for he wrote from London whence he had gone on a mission to obtain Colonial Office support for the Inter-colonial Railway project."[17]

In Halifax, U.S. consul Mortimer Melville Jackson, who would play a key role throughout the conflict reporting rebel movement in and out of Nova Scotia, began to fear for his personal safety when angry anti-American mobs, egged on by incendiary newspaper stories, took to gathering in front of his house, shouting insults and threats. The fact that the local police showed up was not entirely comforting, since most of them were equally outraged that the dreaded Yankees had violated British sovereignty in the affair.

In early December Monck, who still had heard nothing from

Britain about the matter, received the colonial Cabinet's approval to issue arms to local troops and form several companies of artillery and engineers, although he still didn't have enough arms to supply to those men who had already volunteered for service. Monck, with the agreement of Lord Russell in Washington, wanted all these preparations made as quietly as possible so as not to panic the locals or tip off the Americans. For this reason, he did not exercise his right to declare a national emergency under the *Militia Act,* which gave him the power to do so in case of "war, invasion or insurrection, or imminent danger," the last provision of which was the obvious issue here.

Unlike today's instant communications, where the entire world knows everything the moment it happens, it took considerable time in the 1860s for word to get abroad. It wasn't until the *Trent* arrived at Southampton on November 27, nearly three weeks after the event, that the British learned what had happened. The British reaction was instantaneous. An angry Lord Palmerston, despite the weak political position of his government, told his Cabinet, "You may stand for this but damned if I will." The British government immediately began dispatching even more troops to Canada, and it sent an ultimatum to Washington demanding the surrender of Mason and Slidell and an apology – otherwise it would declare war against the United States. France agreed, and its minister in Washington was instructed to convey that message to American officials. As for the U.S. Cabinet, only Postmaster General Montgomery Blair and Lincoln himself were openly opposed to war with the British. Seward remained officially noncommittal, although he did say that the British wouldn't go to war over a "couple of slave envoys." He openly advocated the bizarre theory, supported by many other senior American officials, that the North should provoke a war with Europe in order to reunite the divided country, believing that the South would set aside its internal quarrels and side with the Union to defeat a common foe. Lincoln wasn't buying this theory and cautioned Seward, "One war at a time." As the clouds of war darkened over England and the British North American colonies, Seward kept Adams, his minister in London, in the dark for several weeks while the government debated how best to handle the crisis.

In the meantime, an American living in London wrote to his friend Seward: "There never was within memory such a burst of feeling as has been created by the news of the boarding . . . the people are frantic with rage, and were their country polled, I fear 999 men out of a thousand would declare for immediate war."[18] Another American wrote to his New York uncle from Edinburgh: "I have never seen so intense a feeling of indignation exhibited in my life. It pervades all classes, and may make itself heard over the wiser theories of the Cabinet officers."[19] The *London Morning Chronicle* summed up the prevalent British view: "Abraham Lincoln, whose accession to power was generally welcomed on this side of the Atlantic, has proved himself a feeble, confused, and little-minded mediocrity; Mr. Seward, the firebrand at his elbow, is exerting himself to provoke a quarrel with all Europe, in that spirit of senseless egotism which induces the Americans, with their dwarf fleet and shapeless mass of incoherent squads, which they call an army, to fancy themselves the equals of France by land and of Great Britain by sea. If the Federal States could be rid of these two mischief-makers, it might yet redeem itself in the sight of the world; but while they stagger on at the head of the affairs, their only chance of fame consists in the probability that the navies of England will blow out of the water their blockading squadrons, and teach them how to respect the flag of a mightier supremacy beyond the Atlantic."[20]

On November 29 the British Cabinet announced that the seizure of the *Trent* "was illegal and unjustifiable by international law." Two days later, Cabinet ordered an immediate prohibition of the shipping of arms, ammunition, military stores, and lead to the United States, a serious issue because Britain was the main source of military arms and supplies to the Union forces. It also authorized 30,000 men to stand in arms for Canada, along with officers to assist in local organization, a full battery of artillery, and 10,500 troops as reinforcements. In addition, there would be significant increases in naval activity in the North Atlantic.

On December 15 the *Europa* arrived in Halifax with the Queen's messenger on board, carrying dispatches for Lord Lyons in Washington. They demanded the return of the prisoners and a formal apology. Two weeks previously both the First Lord of the Admiralty and the secretary of state for war had travelled by special train from London to Windsor Castle to attend a special Cabinet meeting on the crisis and, underscoring the gravity of the situation, had formed a special war committee (for only the fourth time in its history) to oversee strategic planning and war preparations. The *Melbourne*, a large ship, was being loaded at Woolwich with Armstrong guns, 80,000 Enfield rifles, ammunition, and other stores intended for the Canadian military, along with heavy reinforcements of field artillery.

Finally, on December 16, with the Civil War on the brink of becoming a world war, Adams received a dispatch dated November 30 from Seward saying that Wilkes, "having acted without any instructions from the Government, the subject is therefore free from the embarrassment which might have resulted had the act been specially directed by us. I trust that the British Government will consider the subject in a friendly temper, and it may expect the best disposition on the part of this Government." On the same day, British foreign affairs secretary Earl Russell wrote to Lord Lyons in Washington, characterizing the incident as "an outrage on the British flag" and saying he hoped it had not been authorized by the government: "Her Majesty's Government, therefore, trust that when this matter shall have been brought under the consideration of the Government of the United States, that Government will, of its own accord, offer to the British Government such redress as alone could satisfy the British nation, namely: the liberation of the four gentlemen and their delivery to your lordship, in order that they may again be placed under British protection, and a suitable apology for the aggression which has been committed." Lyons was told that, unless the Americans "unconditionally accepted" the British demands within seven days, he was to ask for his passports and leave the United States. "What we want is a plain Yes or a plain No to our very simple demands," wrote Russell, "and we want that plain Yes or No within seven days of the communication of the despatch."

The British government, which really didn't want a war with the Americans, nonetheless felt it had no choice if the Americans refused to back down. It resorted to big-stick diplomacy, believing that being conciliatory would only embolden the hawks in Washington to mount increasing challenges to British interests, including the invasion and annexation of Canada. As Lord Edward Hyde Clarendon said: "What a figure . . . we shall cut in the eyes of the world, if we lamely submit to this outrage when all mankind will know that we should unhesitatingly have poured our indignation and our broadsides into any weak nation . . . and what an additional proof it will be of the universal . . . belief that we have two sets of weights and measures to be used according to the power or weakness of our adversary."[21] In addition to ratcheting up the rhetoric, by early in the new year the regular British Army troops in Canada had jumped from 5,000 to 17,658, while the Royal Navy forces in North American waters increased from twenty-five to forty warships, with 1,273 guns, nearly three times the number just before the *Trent* crisis.

The *Trent* Affair also prompted the Canadian officials in Quebec to issue a general order on December 20 calling for significant increases in the militia, and reports of men volunteering could be found in newspapers right across the colonies. The December 31 *Globe*, for example, reported that four companies of the Toronto Active Force, about 150 men, had drilled the night before in the Exhibition Building under the command of Lieutenant-Colonel Durie. A week later it reported that twenty new recruits had joined the Toronto Highland Rifles and received their first lesson in drill from Commanding Officer A.T. Fulton in the private drill room of the company on Front Street. Also, members of the newly formed University Rifle Corps had turned out in full force the previous Saturday for their inaugural drill in the University of Toronto's Convocation Hall, while about fifty members of the Toronto Field Battery had met for drills at the artillery barracks and then marched through the streets with their band. There were even more drills by members of both the Number 4 and Number 7 Sedentary Militias at the St. Lawrence Hall in Toronto. This same level of militia activity, aimed at preparing Canadians for a possible American attack, was being carried out in every major community in the colonies at the time.

Even when British troops arrived in Canada to bolster defences against a possible U.S. attack, moving them into position along the frontier was a major challenge during that winter of 1861–62. The January 30, 1862, *Hamilton Spectator* reported that about one hundred British regulars had been arriving each day at Rivière-du-Loup on their way to Montreal, having left Halifax by steamer to the Bay of Fundy, where they had to board a train at St. Andrew's, New Brunswick, to the village of Canterbury, then proceed by sleigh to Woodstock, 23 miles away, then on the next day the 49 miles to Tobique, then 24 miles to Grand Falls, 36 miles to Little Falls, and, finally, 80 miles to Rivière-du-Loup – a total of 212 miles by sleigh at an average of some 40 miles a day. It took the whole regiment more than a week to get through, living off their daily rations of a pound and a half of bread, the same weight of beef, along with rice, coffee, tea and sugar, and "a gill of rum." About 7 a.m., after breakfast, they were mustered into their sleighs, halting for dinner at mid-day and completing their afternoon stage between 4 and 5 p.m. One soldier died when he got drunk and fell through the ice on a lake, and three deserted to the United States near the Maine border.

Another story in February reported that 400 men and sixteen officers of the 63rd Royal Regiment left Montreal for London by special train on the Grand Trunk Railway but, at Vandreuil, just 15 miles west of Montreal, they ran into a large snowdrift and had to work until the afternoon of the next day clearing the snow. They eventually reached Brockville, but the train slipped off the tracks because many rails had been broken by frost. Three days later, running short of food, the men put the cars back on the track and reached Kingston the next day. After resting and eating, they left Kingston for Toronto, and, just 6 miles below the Don Station, one of the wheels of the Great Western engine broke. After arriving in Toronto and resting a day, the men left for London, but again ran into several more snowdrifts, and finally reached their destination some ten days late.

In the United States there was strong anti-British sentiment throughout the North – including the Congress and Lincoln's Cabinet, where most ministers were hawkish about taking on the British lion. In January 1862, in the wake of tensions from the *Trent* Affair, the U.S. Congress authorized spending $750,000 to repair and strengthen fortifications along the Canadian border at forts at Oswego, Niagara, Buffalo, and Detroit. Adding to Lincoln's political difficulties during the affair was the fact that Wilkes, the man who caused the whole furor by taking precipitous action on his own, was still being feted as a hero for his act, making it tougher to accede to British demands without upsetting the voting public. Just as the British public was in an uproar over the affair, so were the Americans, caught up in the jubilation of patriotic pride at a time when the war at home had not been proceeding well.

Although Lincoln for a time considered holding the prisoners and seeking an arbitrated settlement of the affair, he fully understood that the British were serious about going to war. Making matters worse, France also made it clear that it supported the British position. The European superpowers, if they launched a war, would effectively be on the side of the South. Given that the Union was having more trouble than it could handle trying to subdue the rebels, the last thing Lincoln needed was the presence of another one or two major military powers lobbing cannon balls in his direction.

On Christmas morning, 1861, two days after Lord Lyons, the British envoy, had formerly presented the British demands to Seward, with its deadline of seven days, the Cabinet met to consider its response. Joining the meeting was Senator Charles Sumner, the influential chairman of the Senate Foreign Relations Committee, who would have a significant impact on the outcome. Sumner, a Boston lawyer, had been the Senate's leading opponent of slavery. He will be forever recorded in the history of American politics as the man who, in 1856, was beaten unconscious by South Carolina Congressman Preston Brooks, after he'd given a speech attacking pro-slavery groups in Kansas. He was so badly injured that he could not attend the Senate for the next three years. Sumner, who strongly opposed going to war with the British, was one of the leaders of the "Radical Republicans" and was never shy about speaking his mind. That August he had clashed openly with Lincoln over the president's dismissal of Major-General John C. Fremont, commander of the Union forces in St. Louis. Fremont proclaimed that all slaves owned by Confederates in Missouri were free, but Lincoln ordered him to modify his order and free only those slaves who were owned by Missourians actively working for the South. When Fremont refused, Lincoln fired him. Sumner wrote to Lincoln to complain, saying how sad it was "to have the power of a god and not use it godlike."

At the meeting, Sumner read two letters he had received from important pro-Union British MPs, Richard Cobden and John Bright, letters that Lincoln would later concede had a significant influence on him and many of his ministers. Cobden wrote,

"Three-fourths of the House [of Commons] will be glad to find an excuse for voting for the dismemberment of the Great Republic." And Bright wrote: "If you are resolved to succeed against the South, have no war with England; make every concession that can be made; don't even hesitate to tell the world that you will even concede what two years ago no Power would have asked of you, rather than give another nation a pretence for assisting in the breaking-up of your own country."

Attorney General Edward Bates argued that Britain wanted a war to break the Northern blockade of Southern cotton ports, adding that the United States "cannot afford such a war . . . In such a crisis, with such a civil war upon our hands, we cannot hope for success in a . . . war with England, backed by the assent and countenance of France. We must evade it – with as little damage to our own honor and pride as possible."[22]

Lincoln knew they had no choice, and the only question was how to placate the angry British while not upsetting the celebrating American public. He said: "We fought Great Britain in 1812 for doing just what Captain Wilkes has done. We must give up the prisoners and apologize." Seward locked himself in his office for two days and drafted the dispatch that many historians have described as a "masterpiece," an effort to turn the American defeat into a diplomatic victory. He argued that Wilkes, while acting on his own, had not acted improperly but had made the mistake of failing to take the *Trent* as a prize, where its fate would have been decided by an international court – an "oversight" he described as an act of "prudence and generosity." According to Seward, British anger at the incident indicated that the old argument between the two countries over the legalities of seizing instruments of war had been decided, since Britain was now obviously agreeing with the American position. While the British pooh-poohed much of Seward's twisted logic, there was widespread relief that the crisis had passed without another shot being fired.

Not everybody felt generous about the deal. The December 28 *New York World* wrote, "The simple fact is that Canada hates us,"[23] and there was a popular belief that war between the two superpowers had merely been deferred. In the House of Representatives, Illinois Representative Owen Lovejoy, who was a confidant of Lincoln, "shouted that Great Britain would pay for her arrogance when the domestic crisis was over, for the United states would aid Irish rebels, inspire the French Canadians to revolt, and encourage Chartist insurrection throughout England."[24]

On December 31 the pro-Confederate *Toronto Leader* published an editorial that had run earlier in the *Buffalo Express*, a popular newspaper widely read throughout both sides of the border along the Niagara frontier: "Out of this Trent affair has come one permanent good. The old, natural, instinctive and wise distrust and dislike for England is revived again in the American heart, and will outlive all the soft words and sniveling cant about international brotherhood and reciprocity. These are 'our Canadian brethren,' these suckling Britons to whom, like fools, we have opened our ports . . . These reciprocal brethren of ours have been ready to fly at our throats from the moment when they felt it safe to be insolent."[25] For its part, the *Leader* scoffed that the American eagle "which soared, and soared, and soared almost out of sight, [had] descended like the stick of an exploded rocket."

Even George Brown's Toronto *Globe*, the most stridently pro-Northern newspaper in Canada – had originally reported the *Trent* Affair that November in a story headlined "Outrage on the British Flag!" and demanding an apology and the immediate release of the prisoners. Further exacerbating the tensions between the Americans and Britain, the United States in November, without any warning and as a show of anger over what it saw as British support for the South, suddenly imposed a new passport system requiring all foreigners leaving U.S. ports – including British North Americans, who had been exempt from visa requirements – to first obtain a visa from Washington, a move that threatened considerable harm to cross-border business between the two countries. On November 25, 1861, the *Globe* again attacked its Washington friends, writing: "The vigilance of the American envoys here should be a sufficient guarantee against improper persons getting passports, and if there be rebel agents in Canada desirous of proceeding to Europe, the most rigid passport system will not prevent them from accomplishing that objective – by taking the overland route they can get to Halifax and take ship there."

On December 10, under a headline "War!" the *Globe* again published a lengthy editorial claiming that talk of war with the United States over the *Trent* Affair was "at the corner of every street," adding that the sitting government in Quebec wanted a war "to prop up its own sagging fortunes." Brown had consistently attacked both the *Leader* and the *New York Herald*, accusing them of trying to provoke war, but he himself was so distraught over the *Trent* Affair that he wrote on December 17: "In spite of all our efforts . . . war may be forced upon us . . . Not only is it needful that Canadians should be ready, drilled, armed and equipped – to meet the foe at every point should his temerity tempt him to touch our shores – but it is our duty to show . . . we are a united people on this issue."

The *Buffalo Express*, in contrast, reflecting widespread American opinion, saw the *Trent* Affair as "a pretext anxiously awaited for by England as an excuse for an interference in our affairs, for the recognition of the Southern Confederacy, the raising of the blockade, and the opening of the cotton ports. If this be true, and we see no reason to doubt it, then our government may as well meet the issue now as to negotiate or apologize." The *New York Times* concluded bluntly, "We are on the brink of war with England."

In early January 1862 the HMS *Rinaldo* left Halifax for Fort Warren in Boston Harbor to pick up Mason, Slidell, and their two secretaries. They had planned to return to Halifax, where the diplomats would take a Cunard steamer to London. Plying through the bitterly cold weather, the *Rinaldo* came within 50 miles of Halifax, but, with a thick mass of ice forming around the ship's hull and on her deck, Captain Hewett reluctantly turned back and set sail for Bermuda. On their arrival there, Admiral Sir Alexander Milne, the naval commander-in-chief, feted Hewett and the four Southerners at his Clarence Hill residence. The *Rinaldo* left the next day for St. Thomas and, from there, the commissioners boarded the *Royal West India*, a mail steamer headed for London.

Ironically, Mason and Slidell's biggest impact on European opinion came as they sat in a Boston prison, before they even set foot in Europe. Although they worked throughout most of the conflict to convince Europeans to recognize the South, they would never again come as close to achieving their hopes as they had when they were seized illegally by Wilkes from the *Trent*. And, while relations between Britain and the colonies, on one side, and the United States, on the other, calmed considerably in the aftermath of the *Trent* Affair, the hostile attitudes and deep lack of mutual trust it highlighted would have a significant impact on future border incidents and would colour U.S.-Canadian relations long after the Civil War ended.

One immediate impact of the *Trent* Affair was the introduction of the Militia Bill by Sir John A. Macdonald: "We lately have been rudely awakened to the full consequences of any danger which may beset us by reason of our position in relation to the neighboring country," he said. "If that country should ever unhappily come into collision with the British Empire, we should no doubt be subject to all the desolating effects of war." Then, offering an argument that he and other advocates of Canadian Confederation would later offer as a reason for uniting the provinces to make them stronger, Macdonald continued: "From the geographical formation of Canada – a country with a long and extended frontier, and having but a sparse population – we are liable to invasion at innumerable places. We are in the near vicinity of a nation whose strength and power and whose resources, recent occurrences have shown, to be beyond all example; and we know, therefore, that even although we place the fullest confidence, as we have a right to do, in the assurances of the Imperial Government, that the whole power of the British Empire will be exerted on our behalf, in case of an attack from a foreign foe, yet in the face of our present militia organization, or rather want of organization, we must know that so far as ourselves are concerned we should be utterly helpless in such an event . . . had war come on, as it unquestionably would but for the fortunate termination of the *Trent* difficulty, we should have been utterly unprepared to meet the foe."

A military preparation report by Sir John Burgoyne, supported by Macdonald and his government, called for a 50,000-man active service and 50,000 in reserve, a total of 100,000 able-bodied men out of the population of the two provinces of just 2.5 million. "In case of war with the United States," Macdonald said, "England will undoubtedly be willing . . . to expend her last farthing and her last man in our defence. But while it is the duty of England to do so, and while we receive from her the exercise of all her power, still it is plainly and obviously our duty to provide a large and efficient force for the purpose of fighting upon our own soil, for our own possessions, our own privileges and our own liberties."

Maybe so, but in May 1862, when Finance Minister Alexander Galt proposed a $850,000 expenditure for the militia out of his $12.526 million national budget – saying, "for the first time almost in our history we had to contemplate the possibility of war and make suitable preparations against such an evil contingency" – the Militia Bill was defeated 61–54 by the Clear Grits

EIGHT

The *Chesapeake*

O N SATURDAY, DECEMBER 6, 1863, the coastal steamer *Chesapeake* and her crew of seventeen men left New York City on what appeared to be her standard thirty-six-hour commercial run up the Atlantic coast to Portland, Maine. It was destined to become one of the most sensational international incidents in the entire Civil War period.

In addition to a substantial $180,000 cargo of sugar, cotton, wine, tobacco, tinfoil, leather, augers, and other dry goods, the vessel also carried sixteen special "passengers," led by Lieutenant John C. Braine, who had fraudulently obtained letters of marque from Confederate President Jefferson Davis. Braine's passengers were all New Brunswickers or Nova Scotians – except Lieutenant Henry A. Parr, a native of Canada West (Ontario) and an apprentice apothecary, who had moved to the South and become a commissioned officer of the Confederate Navy. Braine said he had been born at Ball's Point, Islington (a London suburb), in 1840 and, a decade later, had emigrated to the United States with his parents on a Liverpool packet, but his penchant for lying makes his true history uncertain.[1]

What was certain, however, is that the subsequent seizing of the *Chesapeake* was no random act. Braine and Parr had both been commissioned for the project by Vernon G. Locke, a Canadian citizen who had lived for several years in South Carolina and was using the name Captain John Parker, taken from a man who had recently died in Richmond. He also used the alias Thomas B. Power, which is the name the letter of marque from Davis had been made out to. In any event, the three men had held several meetings that summer and fall in Lower Cove, Carleton, a village across the harbour from Saint John, home to seven of their crewmen, where they recruited and drilled men to help with their plan to claim a ship as a prize of war on behalf of the Confederacy. Braine had raised most of the money for the venture earlier that summer in Halifax, where he spent several weeks scamming local merchants by selling advertising for a business directory of Canada and the Provinces, promising them free copies of this book he never intended to publish. Braine had also gone to New York beforehand to scout the *Chesapeake*, which apparently was singled out in retaliation for the local fame it had garnered that June after being chartered and used to capture a Confederate privateer that had attacked the revenue cutter *Caleb Cushing*.

The plan was to capture the *Chesapeake*, take it for re-coaling to Saint John, New Brunswick, where they would be joined by Parker (Locke), the scheme's main organizer and a former commander of the Confederate privateer *Retribution*. Then they would sail her through the blockade to safety – and glory, they hoped – in Wilmington, North Carolina.

The *Chesapeake* passengers had travelled by steamer to Boston and then taken the train to New York, pretending to be recruits for a regiment stationed there. On the way they displayed so much patriotism by singing Union songs that a Worcester citizen treated them all to refreshments when the train stopped there. Unfortunately, the two engineers they'd recruited from New Brunswick indulged to excess and became so drunk they had to be left behind. Adding insult to injury, Braine didn't even pay for his *Chesapeake* fare but wrangled himself a complimentary pass by posing as an agent of a British steamboat company.

After midnight on Sunday, some 20 miles north-northeast

off Cape Cod, the passengers suddenly brandished their weapons, which they had carried aboard in a large trunk, and shot and killed Orin Schaffer, the second engineer. Some accounts say Schaffer was shot without warning; others say he died in a shoot-out. Like many Civil War events, the telling depends directly on the bias of the teller. In any event, Schaffer was definitely killed and his body, weighted down by chains, was later dumped overboard.

Many of the crew members were sleeping at that hour and, because the *Chesapeake* was not involved in a war operation of any kind, the Confederates caught them completely by surprise. Still, after Braine announced that the ship was now in the hands of the Confederacy, there was a short exchange of gunfire with the crew, during which the first engineer, New Yorker Patrick Connor, was slightly wounded, as was the first mate, Charles Johnston, wounded in the knee and arm, and the Irish-born chief engineer James Johnston, who was shot in the chin. *Chesapeake* Captain Isaac Willitt and some his men were soon put in irons. But, because Braine's engineers had been left behind in their drunken stupor, Connor and four other crewmen were forced under guard to continue stoking the fire and tending the engine while the ship steamed up the coast of Maine towards New Brunswick.

Waiting for them there was Parker – Locke. He had been born in 1827 at Sandy Point, Shelburne County, Nova Scotia, but had lived in the United States since 1840, the last three years in Fayetteville, South Carolina. He had amassed a disreputable record on the *Retribution* for capturing Northern schooners and selling the confiscated cargo, frequently using aliases and wantonly violating British neutrality and revenue laws by disposing of captured goods in the Bahamas. When Union officials complained of his activities, Locke was arrested and charged, but, after posting bail, he quickly left the island on a ship headed for New Jersey.

Meanwhile, heading north on the stolen *Chesapeake* during that cold December, Braine had commandeered passenger Robert Osburn, a former master of a Saint John ship, to act as his pilot. They first made their way to Mount Desert Island to establish their bearings, then to Grand Manan Island, where a few of the privateers got off at Seal Cove. When they finally arrived safely in the Bay of Fundy, Braine fired a distress signal to alert Locke of his whereabouts. Locke had been waiting in the locally owned pilot boat *Simonds* and, after the signal, came alongside and boarded, by some accounts taking command of the expedition.

After Locke boarded, Captain Willitt and some of his crewmen were loaded into the *Simonds*, which the *Chesapeake* towed to within 6 miles of shore before casting it off – a foolish move that allowed Willitt to row to Saint John and, about four o'clock on the morning of the 8th, alert U.S. Consul James Q. Howard. By later that day – the same day President Lincoln issued a Proclamation of Amnesty and Reconstruction offering pardons to any Confederates who would swear an oath of loyalty to the United States – a fleet of Union ships in the area had been ordered to pursue the *Chesapeake*. News stories – portraying the event as either a compelling example of Southern audacity and courage or a disgraceful case of piratical cowardice and murder – created a sensation throughout British North America, particularly after Captain Willitt's version of events was published first in the *Saint John News* and subsequently by major American newspapers, after the ship's owner, H.B. Cromwell and Co., told New York journalists about the incident. It created a major international flashpoint which, for a short, tense time, threatened to bring Great Britain into the war against the United States. The *Halifax Herald* wrote that the "news of the audacious piracy and murder had roused the fury of the people of the North and stimulated the pride of the people of the South in the daring and pluck of Lt. Braine."

While much of the pro-Southern media coverage of the affair portrayed the main combatants as noble defenders of the Southern cause, there wasn't much nobility in either Braine or Locke. Braine, 23 at the time, claimed to be a New Brunswick native. He is said to have developed an intense hatred for the North when he was jailed, without trial, for six months in Indiana in 1861, after being accused of committing seditious acts against the United States as a member of the Knights of the Golden Circle – a charge he always denied and which apparently was false.[2] Braine met Locke in New Jersey in 1863, after Locke had fled from the Bahamas to avoid prosecution, and the two rogues seemed to be a match.

Posing as John Parker, Locke had obtained control of the CSS *Retribution* from Thomas B. Power, along with a letter of marque issued by Confederate Secretary of State Judah P. Benjamin to Power. He subsequently captured the *Hanover*, a Northern ship, and sold her cargo in the Bahamas. After that he was arrested, released on his own recognizance, and quickly skipped town, taking the letter of marque with him for future use.

The *Chesapeake* had left New York carrying 30 tons of coal, but, because it needed half that amount to reach Saint John, its bunkers had to be replenished for the proposed trip to Wilmington. In Saint John, Locke had arranged to buy several small lots of coal, purchased illegally at premium prices from local merchants, many of whom were Southern sympathizers, some of whom were not, but none of whom were burdened by any concerns over the morality of it all. Locke had paid the owner of a local schooner for the clandestine venture of delivering the coal to the *Chesapeake*, but, when the time came, he failed to show up. The privateers made new plans to buy coal at Halifax or Sydney, but a gale came up, which lasted two days, and they hovered along the Eastern Shore. They put in at both Petit Rivière and Shelburne, about 150 miles west of Halifax, where they sold some of the stolen cargo in exchange for a few tons of coal and other supplies. Although they renamed the ship the *Retribution*, they generally made their presence known, allowing Union spies to keep track of their whereabouts and notify U.S. Consuls Howard in Saint John, J.M. Merrill at Yarmouth, Cornelius White in Shelburne, and Judge Mortimer Jackson at Halifax. The consuls, in turn, kept Federal officials abreast of the *Chesapeake*'s route.

While anchoring off Petite Rivière on December 14, Braine went ashore and was almost arrested by Dr. Joseph Davis, the vice-consul at Liverpool, escaping only when a group of anti-Northern citizens intervened on his behalf. Braine then escaped overland and headed for Halifax, while Parr took over the task of sailing the *Chesapeake* and set off for the LaHave River, roughly half way between Shelburne and Halifax, taking her as far up the river as New Dublin, spending two days there, and exchanging some cases of stationery, bales of leather and cotton, and port wine for provisions. John Harley, the collector of customs from nearby Lunenburg, showed up, but, he said, he was unaware that the *Retribution* was actually the hunted *Chesapeake*. Although the local citizens certainly knew who their visitors were, Harley made no move to stop the unloading. Several hours later, however, when he realized it was the stolen *Chesapeake*, he ordered a halt to further unloading. In the meantime, the privateers, greeted as celebrities by the locals, even donated a cask of wine to the managers of a local Church of the Redeemer, along with a large church bell that had been meant for a congregation in Maine. (After the war, at the insistence of U.S. officials in Halifax, the bell was returned to the church in Maine.)

But the *Chesapeake* needed fuel, and Parr planned to take her to Lunenburg to buy some coal from a schooner sitting in the harbour. In the meantime, two Union warships, the speedy side-wheeler *Ella and Annie*, moving south from Halifax, and the USS *Dacotah*, coming north from Shelburne, were closing in. Parr spotted the *Ella and Annie* at the mouth of the LaHave River, turned all the lights out on the *Chesapeake*, and ran her behind Spectacle Island without being discovered.

Parr subsequently went into Lunenburg, 25 miles to the east, hoping to arrange for some coal and to send a telegram to Braine in Halifax. The telegraph office and post office were both in the same building, owned by Mrs. William Randolph. Parr was inside the post office when somebody knocked on the locked door of the adjacent telegraph office. Mrs. Randolph, before answering the knock, raised the curtain and saw it was a Union Navy officer – Lieutenant J. Frederick Nickels, captain of the *Ella and Annie*. Quickly spiriting Parr off into another room, she admitted Nickels, calmly assisted him in sending his telegram, and then, after he'd gone, told Parr the way was clear.

Parr had narrowly escaped detection, but, despite having taken on some coal at Shelburne, the *Chesapeake*, with at least a dozen Union ships closing in, was still in desperate need of coal to make it to British territorial waters in Halifax. Leaving the approaches of Lunenburg to avoid detection, the *Chesapeake* worked its way slowly along the coastline towards Halifax, first entering Mahone Bay and then St. Margaret's Bay, where even more of the privateers left the ship. By the evening of December 16, ten days after leaving New York, she arrived at Mud Cove harbour at Sambro, just west of Halifax at the head of Halifax harbour, well within Nova Scotian territorial waters. There, Locke left Parr and the *Chesapeake* and went into Halifax to arrange for some coal.

Later accounts would claim that Locke promised engineer James Johnston and the other captives from the *Chesapeake* that he would find two engineers to replace them and relieve them from their forced labour. Locke did, in fact, arrange for the delivery of some coal by hiring master mariner Thomas Holt, who claimed to be the owner and operator of the *Investigator*, a small, two-masted schooner, even though up until the day before this incident the legitimate owners had been listed as B. Weir and Co., not coincidentally the main commercial agents for the Confederacy in Halifax – a company that, for a time, flew the Confederate flag outside its office and accepted Confederate money for its goods and services.

Early in the morning of December 17 Holt's *Investigator* pulled up alongside the *Chesapeake* and began transferring its load of coal. Locke had also managed to hire two new engineers, Scottish immigrants William and Alexander Henry, both residents of Halifax, who, according to their later testimony, were allowed to sleep in the state room while the *Investigator* was transferring its coal to the *Chesapeake*.

Before the job was done, however, the *Ella and Annie* appeared at the entrance to the harbour. Parr, realizing that the jig was up, quickly abandoned the *Chesapeake*, along with most of his crew, leaving only two of the original crew onboard, the Henry brothers, and New Brunswicker George Wade, one of the privateers, who, in a commonplace occurrence at the time, seems to have been in the captain's cabin of the *Investigator* sleeping off the effects of too much grog.

After boarding the *Chesapeake* and freeing the captive engineers, a group of armed Americans arrested the Henry brothers and took charge of the ship. Lieutenant Nickels, completely ignoring the legalities of territorial waters – in what the *Halifax Herald* later called "a gross outrage upon international law" – then sent six armed men onboard the *Investigator*. U.S. Navy Acting Master William M'Gloin demanded that Holt, who was unaware that Wade was in the cabin, turn over any of the privateers who might be on the ship. When Holt reminded the American that they were in British territorial waters and asked under what authority they wanted to search his ship, M'Gloin put his hand on his pistol and said, "This is my authority." With the other sailors aiming their guns at him, and M'Gloin's threat that if he didn't cooperate he'd be arrested and carted back to Boston to stand trial, Holt had little choice but to accede to their demands. M'Gloin and his men found Wade during this illegal search, arrested him on the spot, and carried him back to the *Ella and Annie*. They also took some sea chests and other valuables owned by the Henry brothers, along with property that had been left behind by Locke and his associates.

Wade and the Henry brothers, in heavy irons, were held incommunicado aboard the *Ella and Annie* for more than fifty hours, while Nickels re-coaled the *Chesapeake* and made preparations to take her and the prisoners back to Boston. Shortly before Nickels was ready to leave, however, Commander A.G. Cleary arrived in the sloop *Dacotah*, which had also been involved in the search for the *Chesapeake*. Cleary, who understood the implications of international law, ordered Nickels to take the *Chesapeake* and the prisoners into Halifax to obtain British approval for his actions. Cleary also sent a telegram to Washington informing authorities of his decision, and Gideon Welles, the secretary of the navy, replied that the *Chesapeake* had to be delivered to colonial authorities because she had been captured in British waters.

While all this was going on, Braine and some of his fellow privateers were openly strolling around Halifax bragging about their exploits, much to the delight of a large group of Haligonians who were ardent Confederate sympathizers. Upset by Braine's brazen bravado, the U.S. vice-consul, Nathaniel Gunnison, who was temporarily replacing the consul, Mortimer Jackson, in Halifax, asked Provincial Secretary Charles Tupper and Premier James William Johnston to issue a warrant for the arrest of Braine and his gang. They refused, demanding more evidence – as if Braine's own public boasting wasn't enough. Gunnison could not have had a more unsympathetic pair to deal with.

Tupper and Johnston, along with Joseph Howe, were the most important political leaders in the colony at the time. Tupper, a Conservative, who took over from Johnston as premier on May 11, 1864, was later knighted and served as high commissioner to London. A medical doctor, he was leader of the Nova Scotia delegates at all three Confederation conferences (Charlottetown, Quebec City, London) and a leading Father of Confederation in 1867. He was one of Sir John A. Macdonald's chief lieutenants, serving in several Cabinet posts over twenty-six years. In 1896 he became Canada's shortest-serving prime minister, being defeated in a general election after just ten weeks in office. Johnston, who in addition to being premier doubled as attorney general, was proud of his United Empire Loyalist history (his grandfather was a British officer who had left Georgia as a Loyalist) and had married Amelia Elizabeth Almon. He was therefore a relative, by marriage, of Dr. William J. Almon, a major Confederate sympathizer and activist in Halifax, of whom we will soon be hearing a great deal.

Gunnison was determined to bring the pirates to justice, so he hired a private detective to investigate Braine's activities. When he presented this additional evidence to the government, Chief Justice William Young (himself a former Liberal premier) issued a warrant signed by Johnston and Lieutenant-Governor Hastings Doyle for the arrest of Braine and ten others. The warrant was given to county constable James Monteith to serve. Tupper also instructed two Halifax police officers to assist Monteith, but when the officers attempted to arrest Braine at Sambro they were surrounded by a group of armed local men who, firing their pistols into the air and shouting threats, forced the police to retreat, allowing Braine to escape. Gunnison wrote to his State Department that Braine "boasted that he was perfectly safe in Halifax." And so it seemed.

Meanwhile, the *Ella and Annie*, the USS *Dacotah* with the *Chesapeake* in tow, and three other American warships entered Halifax harbour about 2:30 p.m. on December 17, drawing huge crowds to Citadel Hill and the various wharves to witness the event. But, much to the chagrin of Lieutenant-Governor Doyle, "a stickler for protocol,"[3] the Americans ignored the usual procedures of formally notifying local officials of the purpose of their visit and receiving official clearance. The Irish-born Doyle, a

Crimean War veteran and former inspector of militia for Ireland, was not a man given to quiet contemplation. As commander of British North America's Atlantic region during the 1861 *Trent* crisis, Doyle had openly advocated the occupation of strategic border points in Maine to counter what he saw as brazen U.S. aggression. As dinner time came and went that day and there was still no official word from the Americans, Doyle dispatched a letter to Commander Cleary through Tupper asking just what, exactly, the American warships were doing in British territorial waters. Cleary, apologizing for his tardiness, claimed that the U.S. Navy would comply with "all the proprieties required in British ports," explaining that his goal was to turn the *Chesapeake* over to British officials or "to the owners, upon faith." He also apologized for the *Ella and Annie*'s earlier excursion into British waters at Sambro, claiming she was responding to a distress signal sent by the five original crew members still on board. One significant fact Cleary did not mention at the time, however, was that the Americans were holding three British subjects – two Nova Scotians (the Henry brothers) and a New Brunswicker (Wade) – incommunicado. It wasn't until word leaked out that Cleary acknowledged the presence of his prisoners, an oversight that did not improve Doyle's disposition towards the American claims.

U.S. Secretary of State William Seward, who was no diplomat himself, told British Ambassador Lord Lyons in Washington that he wanted the *Chesapeake* returned immediately to her rightful owners, and he considered local authorities should throw Braine and his crew of "pirates" into jail pending the arrival of formal affidavits containing various criminal charges against them from the United States. From Seward's perspective, it was a clear case of piracy and murder, and the perpetrators needed to be punished. Many Nova Scotians, however, sympathized with the argument that because the *Chesapeake* had originally been captured in open waters by Confederate officers, it was an act of war, not piracy. To them, the Americans were the ones acting like pirates, by violating British sovereignty when they recaptured the *Chesapeake* within Nova Scotian waters.

With tensions mounting, Doyle summoned Tupper for a meeting. Tupper advised that Cleary must be told not to leave the harbour until there had been a full investigation. When Doyle raised the possibility that Cleary might ignore the order, Tupper told him, "In that case, you must sink his vessel from the batteries."[4] After the original note was sent, the rabid pro-Southerner Dr. William J. Almon showed up with Captain Holt of the *Investigator* and Mrs. Susan Henry, wife of one of the captured local engineers, and heard the entire story about the boarding of the *Investigator* and the capture of three prisoners. Nova Scotia then dispatched another, sharper note, stating that the Americans had deliberately withheld information about the arrests and had made a "forcible entry" onto a Nova Scotia schooner. Doyle accused the Americans of "a grave infraction of international law."[5] To add even more confusion, when U.S. Navy Secretary Gideon Welles was told that the *Chesapeake* had been taken at Sambro, he wired the Halifax consulate ordering it to hand the steamer over to colonial authorities. In addition, more American vessels arrived in Halifax harbour, including the gunboat *Acacia*, which carried several members of the original *Chesapeake* crew, assuming they would be needed as witnesses in the expected criminal proceedings against the Confederates.

Doyle, while upset with American high-handedness and aware that most Haligonians were siding with the privateers, appreciated why the Americans were demanding justice for the crimes against their property and citizens. When he met with W.A.D. Morse, the lawyer for the U.S. consul, the two men agreed that the *Chesapeake* could be turned over to colonial authorities, pending a full investigation, and that criminal charges would be laid against Wade, seeking his extradition to the United States to face charges of murder and piracy, but only after he was formally released from the *Dacotah* by Commander Cleary. As things stood, Doyle felt that the Americans had no right to take Wade with them because their arrest of him on board a Nova Scotia schooner was illegal. They decided that Wade would be delivered by the Americans to the Halifax wharf and set free, after which local officials, acting on a new warrant, would rearrest him immediately and extradition proceedings could legitimately begin.

It was a good plan, and it may have satisfied both British sensitivities about their territorial integrity and American anger over what they saw as high-seas piracy. What no one had anticipated was the inventiveness of Dr. Almon and his zeal for the Southern cause.

The Almons were among the most prominent social families in Halifax at the time. Their remarkable history in medicine in the city began in 1780, when Dr. William James Almon emigrated from England and set up a medical practice in Halifax. He began an unbroken string of Almon family physicians which lasted for 160 years, until the death in 1940 of Dr. William Bruce Almon.

William Johnstone Almon, the third doctor in the line, had been born in Halifax in 1816 and had attended King's College – established by United Empire Loyalists in 1788 after the original King's College in New York had been renamed Columbia College (now Columbia University) after the Revolutionary War. It was British North America's first college and also the birthplace of ice hockey, Canada's national game. Almon was extremely well connected. He attended King's with a host of the colony's most distinguished citizens and retained life-long friendships with most of them, including Sir Charles Tupper; Sir Edward Cunard, founder of the Cunard Lines steamship company; John A. Gray, chief justice of British Columbia; T.S.H. Sutler, bishop of Aberdeen; and General Sir John Inglis, who would later command the British garrison at the 1857 Siege of Lucknow, a critical battle in the Indian Mutiny of that year. Almon earned his medical degree in Glasgow in 1838, did postgraduate work in Edinburgh and London, returned to Halifax to operate a drug business at Cronan's Wharf, and eventually succeeded his father as physician and surgeon to the Halifax Alms House.

In February 1846, while amputating a woman's thumb, he made the first use of chloroform as an anaesthetic in Nova Scotia. He also challenged Nova Scotia's most famous historical figure, politician and newspaper owner Joseph Howe, to a duel for remarks Howe had made about his father, then a Cabinet minister. But the duel was cancelled when Almon couldn't find a suitable second, and he and Howe, who had first brought responsible government to Nova Scotia, became such good friends in later life that Almon was a pallbearer at Howe's funeral in 1873. Almon, the first president of the Halifax Medical Society (1853) and a founder of Dalhousie University's faculty of medicine, was later elected to the House of Commons as a member of Sir John A. Macdonald's Conservative government. In 1879 he became the first doctor to be appointed to the Senate, where he shared an office with Senator Sir James A. Lougheed, whose grandson Peter became one of Canada's most prominent political leaders as Alberta premier from 1971 to 1985. Almon retired from medical practice in 1890 after fifty years of service and died at his Halifax mansion, "Rosebank," at the age of 85 in 1901.

During the Civil War, however, Almon was generally regarded as the unofficial Confederate consul in Halifax. He constantly harboured Confederate "refugees" and hosted numerous prominent Confederate officials, who were automatically welcomed at "Rosebank" during their stay in town. He was a friend and correspondent of Confederate President Jefferson Davis, two of his sons served on blockade-runners, and another, Dr. William Bruce Almon, lost his life while serving as an assistant surgeon in the Confederate Army in Florida. On May 24, 1864, James P.

Holcombe, the special commissioner of the Confederate States of America, wrote to Almon "on behalf of President Davis," thanking him for "the disinterested sympathy which you have so frequently and effectively manifested on behalf of our people and cause."

When American officials brought Wade and the Henry brothers ashore at the Queen's Wharf about 1 p.m. on December 19, Almon had paid Paul Woods, the owner of the fastest horse in the county, to wait with his horse next to the wharf in the hope that he could spirit Wade away as quickly as possible to avoid any possible repercussions against the prisoner. Almon had brought along a group of Southern sympathizers, including his colleague, Dr. Peleg W. Smith, who later became sheriff of Digby County, and Alexander "Sandy" Keith, a disreputable rogue who would do anything for money and who, at one point, operated his own blockade-runner, the *Caledonia*. Keith has often been mistaken by historians for his uncle, the respected beer baron Alexander Keith. But Captain John Wilkinson, a legendary Confederate blockade-runner who settled in Halifax after the war, described Keith this way: "By dint of a brazen assurance, a most obliging manner, and the lavish expenditure of money, he ingratiated himself with nearly every Southerner who visited Halifax, although he was a coarse, ill-bred vulgarian of no social standing in the community."[6]

When Almon noted that J.J. Sawyer, the high sheriff of Halifax, was among the crowd of dignitaries at the wharf, he asked Sawyer what he was doing there. Sawyer replied that he had a warrant for Wade's arrest, which had been quietly obtained from Mayor P.C. Hill by Vice-Consul Gunnison. Sawyer showed it to Almon, explaining he had ordered Constable Lewis Hutt to serve the warrant on Wade. The plan, he said, was that the Americans would first surrender their prisoners to British authorities, and then, an hour later, surrender the *Chesapeake* to British revenue officials to await adjudication in the colonial Admiralty court. The prisoners were to be declared free – and the Henry brothers were, in fact, to be let go – but Wade was to be rearrested and extradited for trial on charges of murder and piracy. That way, British sovereignty would be completely complied with, and the demands of the United States would also be satisfied. At least, that was the plan.

Almon, realizing it would now be impossible to get Wade over to Woods and his horse, spotted two well-known local rubes, Jerry Holland and Bernard Gallagher, sitting in their whaler near the fish market on an adjacent wharf. As the U.S. boat carrying the three prisoners from the *Dacotah* moved closer to shore, Almon rushed over and offered Holland and Gallagher one pound if they would row over to the Queen's Wharf, allow Wade to jump into their boat, and take him to Ketch Harbour. They agreed immediately.

About fifty spectators had gathered on the wharf to witness the event, including Tupper, Solicitor General W.A. Henry, Captain H.W.C. Clarke (the aide-de-camp to Governor Doyle), and many others, a crowd described by the *Halifax Herald* as "respectably dressed persons – the only class of people that the governor would permit to be present." There wasn't anything respectable in the dress or demeanour of Holland and Gallagher, but, as the excitement grew while the Americans and their prisoners advanced, nobody paid attention to them and their whaler bobbing about in the chop next to the wharf. It had not occurred to local officials that Wade would be able to escape his fate.

The prisoners, in leg irons, were brought onto the wharf by Ensign Coghlan, a junior American officer from the *Dacotah*, but Sheriff Sawyer refused to accept their surrender until the leg irons had been removed. As Sawyer announced that the men were free to go their own way, Almon immediately went up to the Henry brothers, hugging them and congratulating them, thereby demonstrating to Wade, whom he didn't know – and who, of course, knew nothing of what had been planned for him – that he was a friend. Almon then turned to Wade and whispered, "Your life depends on your jumping into that boat and going with those men. Now jump, quick." Wade jumped. Soon after, Gallagher and Holland began rowing him away. At the time, City Marshal Garret Cotter was speaking to Gunnison and, as the boat pulled away from the wharf, Cotter, attracted by the commotion, said, "Who's that in the boat?" Gunnison, white with rage and mortification, hissed out: "It's Wade."

At that point, Constable Hutt, dressed in civilian clothes, rushed to the edge of the slip, pulled out his Colt revolver, and shouted, "Gallagher, stop, I want that man!" While Almon and his colleagues shouted to them to keep going, and other vessels in the area, including the American boats, strangely ignored the whole thing, Hutt, who had been a sailor in the U.S. Navy, told Gallagher to "come back or I'll shoot."[7] Just as he raised his arm to point his pistol at Gallagher's boat, however, Almon jumped on Hutt's back, quickly joined by Smith and Keith, and the three men wrestled the constable to the ground, allowing Gallagher and Holland to row Wade away. Another constable tried to get into a boat sitting next to the wharf, but Keith, a big, burly hulk of a man, physically stopped him. The *Evening Mail* reported, perhaps apocryphally, that Wade shouted back to the cheering throng, "Thank God and Queen Victoria for my freedom." Actually, Wade owed his freedom to Almon, who had also sent Woods and his speedy horse to Ketch Harbour to pick up Wade later that day and take him overnight to Hantsport in the Annapolis Valley between Windsor and Wolfville, never to be heard from again by the American officials.

The Americans were outraged. Secretary Seward wrote to British Ambassador Lyons: "It would be necessary for the U.S. government to seriously consider whether or not it would be necessary to adopt extraordinary precautions with respect to intercourse with Nova Scotia." This threat resulted in the imposition of controls on Northern exporters to the Maritimes: henceforth, cargoes had to be bonded as security against their sale and trans-shipment to the South. The *New York Herald* reported on "the rescue of the pirate and murderer by a Halifax mob," and published the news item that a ciphered telegram addressed to Keith had been intercepted by the New York City postmaster and sent to the war secretariat. The letter, from agent J.H. Crammock to Confederate Secretary of State Judah Benjamin, told of a shipment of 1,000 muskets on their way from New York to Halifax "to be used for rebel purposes," one of which, according to the newspaper, was that the Confederates "would attempt to steal the *Chesapeake* out of Halifax harbor." Of course there was no such plan, but the *Herald* readers didn't know that. This story, along with others of a similar nature and the fact that the "pirate" had escaped, helped to generate considerable animosity against the colonies.

Realizing that they had to counter the American anger, local officials arrested Almon, Keith, and Smith, charging them with "interfering with the police in the discharge of their duties." The three men appeared before the city's Magistrate's Court, with the mayor, P.C. Hill (who would later become premier), and Alderman Roche, both pro-Southern sympathizers and friends of Almon, sitting as the judges. Almon defended himself, claiming he could not sit idly by while a Nova Scotian was sent to the United States, where the "law was a mockery."[8] Almon's close friend and noted Halifax lawyer-politician J.W. Ritchie volunteered his services, too, arguing before the court that Almon had actually prevented murder because Hutt's intention had been to kill Wade. After Hutt had testified that he had been jumped by Almon and Smith and held down by Keith, all of whom knew he was a police officer, Roche declared that Hutt, who had not been wearing his policeman's uniform, had acted "highly improperly" and that Almon had "only done what the feelings of humanity would dictate any good citizen to do under the circumstances." The mayor, who also had high praise for Almon, said there was enough evidence to raise the presumption of guilt but, under the law, the offence was a misdemeanour and, as a magistrate, he had no authority to deal with it. Anyway, it had already been sent to a grand jury, which, for its part, soon returned a "no bill," and the three men were released and never convicted of anything in the incident.

During the peak of local excitement over the affair, Thomas L. Connolly, the Roman Catholic archbishop of Halifax and a noted Confederate sympathizer – who dismissed American abolitionists as ranking with P.T. Barnum, the famous circus huckster – invited both Almon and Governor Doyle to a dinner party. Almon, concerned that the hot-tempered Doyle might make a scene if he saw him there, wrote to the archbishop asking to be excused. The next morning, Connolly showed up at Almon's house and insisted that he attend the dinner. "I have asked you to be my guest, and if Governor Doyle chooses to leave my table because you are there, that is an affair of his own. But you must come!"[9] Almon, who had a quick temper of his own, did attend, and the dinner reportedly turned out to be a pleasant affair. Besides Connolly, the other leading Nova Scotia churchmen of the day, Church of England Bishop Howard Binney, was also there, a man who regularly opened up his heart, his house, and his purse for any Southerners who happened to be in Halifax seeking solace or support.

In the meantime, Doyle, attempting to fend off growing resentment from American officials over the affair, had issued an arrest warrant for Braine and his crew. Responding to these events, Confederate Secretary of State Judah H. Benjamin sent James P. Holcombe, a University of Virginia law professor, and ardent secessionist, to Halifax as a special commissioner to prevent the extradition of the privateers who had taken the *Chesapeake* and to make a claim that the steamer, as a legitimate prize of war, belonged to the Confederacy. Holcombe wrote back to his officials saying that the expedition did not have legitimate

Confederate authority but was organized by "men, who, sympathizing with us in a righteous cause, erroneously believed themselves authorized to act as belligerents against the United States by virtue of Parker's possession of the letter of marque issued to the privateer *Retribution*." Holcombe was also assigned to organize the repatriation of several hundred Confederates believed to be living in the colonies at the time. He was given $8,000 for expenses ($3,000 of which was his salary for six months) and told to hire Benjamin Wier of Halifax and inform him that a letter of credit for $25,000 was being forwarded from Liverpool to provide emergency funds to help with the repatriation issue. Holcombe didn't do much work on that file either. He seemed otherwise engaged most of the time: a June 21, 1864, report from the U.S. consul's office in Montreal noted that Holcombe, who settled for a time in a house in St. Catharines, Ontario, was constantly accompanied there by "a vixen named Stansbury." (Later in that same year, on October 1, Holcombe would be involved with another woman in one of the most publicized events of the war – the drowning death of famous rebel spy Rose O'Neal Greenhow.)[10]

On January 14, 1864, Judge Alexander Stewart of the vice-admiralty court in Halifax ruled that the seizure of the *Chesapeake* was "undoubtedly a piratical taking." He said the vessel should be returned to its rightful owners, but he added some harsh words for the Americans as well. "It is not for me to deal with the gross outrage on the liberty of our fellow subjects, and the contemptuous and coarse violation of Her Majesty's proclamation and her territorial rights perpetrated by officers of the Navy of the United States . . . these are safe in the hands of Earl Russell . . . I do not doubt that His Lordship will promptly demand that ample reparations be made by the Government of the United States and I confidently anticipate that the Government will as promptly disavow and apologize for the conduct of their officers and make full reparations to the sufferers." He also dismissed the captors, saying, "This court has no prize jurisdiction, no authority to adjudicate between the United States and the Confederate States, or the citizens of either of those States."

Braine was still a wanted man, but that didn't seem to trouble him. Just before Christmas he had checked into the Lawrence Hotel in Saint John, New Brunswick, basking in the glory of celebrity status. He even gave an interview to the *Morning News*, offering several complete fabrications, including the claim that he and his cronies had shot Second Engineer Orin Schaffer in self-defence when he had tried to scald the privateers with hot water from the boiler. He also denied that the captured engineer from the original crew had been kept in chains and forced to tend the boiler on the voyage to Sambro.

This bravado was a bit much even for local officials, and on December 26, under intense pressure from U.S. Consul James Howard, New Brunswick Governor Arthur Hamilton Gordon issued a warrant for the arrest of Braine and his gang for piracy and murder under the 1842 Ashburton-Webster Treaty between the United States and Britain. But even that initiative was botched. The announcement was made in Saint John, but the warrant issued in Fredericton – a delay that allowed Braine time to get out of Dodge. He was subsequently pursued by Saint John police officers, but they ended up slinking back into town empty-handed. Not surprisingly, Braine left without paying a tailor for the new Confederate uniform he had commissioned. The search for Braine became almost a Keystone Kops caper as police chased down one reported sighting after another without any success – much to the delight of the local newspapers and pro-Southern groups. At one point the British dispatched two companies of redcoats to Richmond, Nova Scotia, acting on information from American officials in Halifax that Braine was on the evening train to Truro in that province. But when the train arrived, there was no sign of Braine – only lots of fodder for the pro-Southern press to use to ridicule local officials and further infuriate the Americans.

While officials never did catch up to Braine, he was to be

heard from several times before the end of the war. On September 24, 1864, Braine, dressed in his Confederate uniform and leading a group of ten "passengers," seized the U.S. mail-steamer *Roanoke* about 25 miles off the coast of Cuba. After an exchange of gunfire, these pirates placed the captain and the crew in irons, killing the ship's carpenter in the exchange, and, ultimately, they burned the ship off the coast of Bermuda. Braine was arrested there by British authorities but immediately released, after he produced documents showing his lieutenant's commission and letter of instructions from S.R. Mallory, the secretary of the navy of the Confederate government.

Braine was back again on March 31, 1865, when he seized the 115-ton schooner *St. Mary's* out of Maryland, which he and his raiding party boarded and captured off the Patuxent River in Chesapeake Bay. Braine and his crew, wearing civilian clothes, came alongside the schooner in a yawl – essentially a sailing yacht – pretending that their craft was sinking. After capturing the *St. Mary's*, Braine took her to sea, where he also took the New York–bound schooner *J.B. Spafford*, which he released after putting the *St. Mary's* crew on board, but not before stealing their personal effects. He told the captured crews he was headed to St. Marks, Florida, but in fact they put into Nassau on April 22, where U.S. Consul Thomas Kirkpatrick reported the arrival to U.S. Rear Admiral Cornelius Stribling, commander of the East Gulf Blockading Squadron. Once again, British authorities apprehended the vessel, but Braine and his companions were allowed to put to sea after being adjudged a legitimate prize of war by British authorities there.

Braine sailed the *St. Mary's* to Kingston, Jamaica, where he abandoned it after learning of the final collapse of the Confederacy. On June 22, 1865, he booked passage to Liverpool, England. When he returned to the United States in 1866, he was arrested for murder and piracy and held in jail, without trial, for three years. After his release, he earned his living giving lectures throughout Florida and Texas. But Braine never did change his ways. In 1903, just three years before he died, he was arrested and convicted for defrauding a Maryland hotel. At the time, he claimed to be president of a fictional fertilizer company in Birmingham, Alabama.

Although police in Saint John did not manage to bring Braine to justice, they captured three of his gang. Two days after Christmas, Police Chief John Marshall arrested David Collins and James McKinney at the home of George Wade's father at Loch Lomond, a rural area just east of Saint John. Marshall also arrested Linus Seely when he arrived in town on a trading schooner from Windsor, Nova Scotia.

On January 4, 1864, the three men were brought before local Magistrate Humphrey T. Gilbert, who was charged with deciding whether there was sufficient evidence against them to warrant extradition – an act he knew would result in death for all of them. The courtroom was full of spectators, with the crowd overflowing down a long hall and out into the street. Public opinion was overwhelmingly on the side of the prisoners, to the point where, in mid-January, Governor Gordon telegraphed the Colonial Office to say that he feared the public would attack the jail if the men were convicted.[11]

To demonstrate the significance of the case to U.S. officials, the Crown did not conduct the prosecution. Instead, the U.S. consul hired two prominent local lawyers, William H. Tuck and Andrew Rainsford Wetmore – who would become New Brunswick's first premier after Confederation – to carry the prosecution's case. The defence also hired two equally prominent lawyers, Charles Weldon and John Hamilton Gray, a New Brunswick Cabinet minister and Confederate sympathizer who, after the *Chesapeake* case, was dubbed "The Honorable Member from Richmond." Gray's brother, Captain A.B. Gray, had died in the Confederate service near Memphis, Tennessee. Gray attended both the Quebec and the Charlottetown conferences as a member of Samuel Leonard Tilley's

New Brunswick government delegations, and he became one of Canada's illustrious "Fathers of Confederation."

Gray opened the initial examination by challenging the magistrate's authority to oversee a case involving such serious charges, arguing that imperial law required a special commission for a trial of piracy. He even threatened to subpoena New Brunswick Governor Gordon; claimed the warrant was improperly framed; and added that, since the men were charged with both murder and piracy, authorities had failed to issue separate warrants for each charge. Gray's bombast as a celebrated orator, plus his standing in the community, moved Gilbert to publicly question his own jurisdiction in the case, but he decided to continue in any event.

Indeed, on February 24, Gilbert defied public opinion and dismissed defence arguments that the men had shot the engineer Schaffer in self-defence and were belligerents engaged in a legitimate act of war. He said the letter of marque for the *Retribution* was not legally transferred to the *Chesapeake*, and, therefore, the capture was an act of piracy. The magistrate called the raid "the work . . . of a coward and a villain, which ought to be considered against all law – Human or Divine." He ordered the prisoners to be held over for extradition to the United States.

An editorial in the *Saint John Telegraph* captured the prevailing public mood in the Maritimes, expressing complete outrage that two "respectable British subjects" – McKinney and Collins, both New Brunswickers (the third prisoner, Seely, was from Upper Canada and apparently didn't rate) – could be sent to certain death in the United States on the strength of a police magistrate. Once the verdict was announced, that was precisely what the defence argued too, when it announced that it would apply for the release of the prisoners on a writ of habeus corpus and the right to take the matter to the provincial supreme court.

South of the border, where the war was going well for the Union, the mood was different. On March 3, government officials dispatched the revenue cutter *Miami* from New York to Saint John, along with two U.S. marshals, in the expectation that the British authorities would hand the prisoners over to them. Most Maritimers may have been unhappy with the court ruling, but the *New York Times* reflected the general view among Northerners in the United States, proclaiming, on March 5, that the decision by Britain's colonial courts was "so satisfactory that our own Government will hardly find cause in it for complaint."

As things turned out, the American expectations were premature. Defence lawyers Weldon and Gray may have been stung temporarily by Gilbert's decision, but they were still feeling relatively confident when they approached New Brunswick Supreme Court Justice William Johnston Ritchie and he agreed to hear the case on behalf of their clients – who, by this time, also included Henry Parr and Vernon Locke, aka Captain John Parker, the two men who, along with the still-absent Braine, were the chief organizers of the expedition and who, subsequently, had been captured by the Saint John police. The Nova Scotia–born Ritchie, who would later become Chief Justice of Canada, was anything but neutral on the subject. Like his brother, Halifax lawyer John W. Ritchie, who would later join him as a Supreme Court justice, he was a known Confederate sympathizer. At the time, John W. Ritchie was Nova Scotia's solicitor general and government leader in the provincial upper house, or the Senate. After refusing to accept financial compensation for his work on behalf of the Confederacy before the vice-admiralty court in Halifax in the *Chesapeake* case, he was given a silver tea service by Confederate commissioner Holcombe. The father of these two men, Boston-born Thomas Ritchie, had moved to Annapolis Royal, Nova Scotia, and become a charter member of both the Anglican elite and Nova Scotia politicians, a man who had worked tirelessly to secure legislation to protect the property of Nova Scotia slave-owners before the practice was outlawed in the Maritimes by the Imperial Parliament *Emancipation Act* of 1834, which finally abolished slavery in the British Empire.

Also, both brothers were close personal friends and associates with Gray. In 1859 Ritchie sat with Gray (and Joseph Howe) on a commission in Halifax appointed by the Colonial Office to adjudicate a dispute on Prince Edward Island between tenant farmers and absentee landowners. Their uncle, James William Johnston, was Nova Scotia's premier. And, to complete the circle, in 1836 the Halifax Ritchie married Amelia Rebecca Almon, sister of the infamous Dr. W.J. Almon, making Almon not only a kindred spirit but a brother-in-law too.

In Halifax on January 5, 1864, J.W. Ritchie wrote to Benjamin Wier, the Confederacy's business consul there, "broadly hinting that the *Chesapeake*'s captors, if Confederates acting under Southern orders, could be freed." Ritchie argued that the act was piracy only if the majority of the privateers were not Southerners, prompting Wier to write to Confederate Scretary of State Benjamin "asking for a copy of Locke's commission and a Confederate affidavit that would show that Parr was acting with proper authority."[12]

On March 10 Judge Ritchie threw out Gilbert's decision and released all the *Chesapeake* prisoners on the writ of habeus corpus. He found that the warrant for their arrest had not been properly requisitioned from U.S. authorities; that, since the alleged offence was piracy against the United States, the proceedings should have begun there; and that Gilbert had no jurisdiction in the matter, or, even if Gilbert had such jurisdiction, the warrant he issued for the commitment of the prisoners was "bad on its face and insufficient to warrant their detention."

And so the men were free, a decision that prompted local U.S. Consul Howard to write to Seward, enclosing a copy of Ritchie's decision. He complained that the "rotten rubbish . . . of the dregs of society" must be punished or else "any notorious offender may murder the Governor . . . of Massachusetts, may take the steamer to this province, and walk the streets of St. John [as Saint John was commonly called then] . . . with impunity, there being no power to arrest him for an offense within the Extradition Treaty."[13]

Governor Gordon, desperately attempting to assuage American anger at the outcome, suggested that the privateers could be tried for violating the *Foreign Enlistment Act*. New warrants against them were sworn out in the United States, but, because of confusion among provincial officials, the prisoners were released three days before the proper British warrants could be sworn and, once again, the men escaped.

The fallout from the affair had a significant impact for several months on the actions of Americans living near the Canadian border. With rumours flowing that the Confederates planned to seize more ships, rob banks, and burn towns in the northeastern United States, many ships along the coast began searching all male passengers, with the help of local police, before departing. All passengers leaving New York harbour were now required to obtain special passports, and, over the next several months, extra warships were brought in to examine the ships and detain anyone without proper credentials. On Christmas Eve, responding to a hot rumour that Confederates were planning to cross the bridge from New Brunswick and raid Calais and Eastport, several armed men spent the night guarding the bridge. When a fire broke out during the night, the men refused to fight it, believing it was a decoy to lure them away from the bridge. It wasn't – and the building burned to the ground.

During the early months of 1865, Governor Gordon ordered the sheriffs of each New Brunswick county to arrest the privateers, but, for all their efforts, only Linus Seely was caught and rearrested, primarily because he had contracted syphilis in 1864 and had become legally incompetent. Even so, and despite the end of the war and the victory of the North, Seward demanded that Seely be brought to trial. In June 1865, with Judge Ritchie again presiding, Seely appeared before the Court of Admiralty. Destitute, he was again defended by Weldon and Gray. They argued that, because Seely had a weak mind, he honestly believed that Braine's mission was a legitimate act of war on behalf of the Confederacy, as Braine had claimed. After Ritchie charged the jury that Seely could not be found guilty if they believed he had joined the raiders in the belief that he was acting under proper authority from the Confederate government, Seely was, once again, acquitted. He died a few months later when he was shot in a bar-room brawl in the south end of Saint John, just a few blocks from where Braine and Locke had hatched the *Chesapeake* adventure in the summer of 1863.

As for Locke, he was arrested in Nassau in February on the complaint of the American consul. While the State Department believed that Locke could be extradited over the *Chesapeake* incident, Lord Earl Russell in Washington advised U.S. officials that the British would extradite him on offences he had committed on British soil – engaging in the slave trade. Even here, however, Locke seems to have stayed out of jail, and the next we hear of him was in the summer of 1890, as skipper of the sailboat *Marion* out of a Boston yacht club, when the vessel hit a rock off New Hampshire and forced Locke and two companions to take to a small boat. When the boat capsized in the ocean's swell, Locke and his companions drowned. Another of the raiders, George Robinson, also drowned in 1865 when a boat he was on in Halifax harbour overturned.

In July 1865 Henry Parr sailed from Cuba to Nassau, having first helped Braine capture the *St. Mary's*. Two years later he became a naturalized British subject at Yarmouth, Nova Scotia, where he married, set up a thriving drug and medicine trade, expanded into dentistry, and, several years later, relocated his practice to New York. There he beat a charge for the murder of Orin Schaffer and prospered in his chosen field of apothecary.

NINE

Lake Erie Rebels

ON AUGUST 11, 1864, Confederate Captain Charles H. Cole, dressed as a private citizen, registered in Room 66 of the West House, a five-storey hotel in Sandusky, Ohio, not far from the waterfront, at the southwest corner of Columbus Avenue and Water Street. He was within sight of Johnson's Island, the prison home to some 2,000 Confederate officers, about 30 miles directly across Lake Erie from Point Pelee, Ontario. Among the prisoners were seven generals and the son of Confederate General John C. Breckinridge, the former U.S. vice-president, who would become the Confederate secretary of war and flee to Canada to avoid prosecution at war's end.

Cole, who had recently served in Confederate General Nathan Bedford Forrest's cavalry, knew the island well. He had escaped from the prison the year before and fled to Toronto, where he hooked up with the Confederate commissioner, Jacob Thompson, and the city's burgeoning Confederate community. His pockets bulging with cash, Cole was subsequently sent back to Sandusky, a bustling city of 25,000 people, to help orchestrate a mass prison break, with specific orders not to infringe on the neutrality laws of Canada.

Posing as secretary of the Pennsylvania-based Mount Hope Oil Company, Cole opened accounts in several local banks and began lavishly wining and dining officers from the prison and from the USS *Michigan*, the first iron-hauled warship in the U.S. Navy and the only warship allowed on Lake Erie at the time under the terms of the Ashburton Treaty between the United States and Great Britain.

Johnson's Island sits not far from Put-in-Bay, the site of a major naval victory by U.S. Commodore Oliver Hazard Perry against the British Commodore Robert Hariot Barclay on September 10, 1813, when the entire British fleet surrendered. This decisive win not only gave the Americans control over all the land and inland waterways in the area, which became vital to shipping and the growth of the American economy, but it spawned two of the most famous battle cries in U.S. history. First, just before the battle began, Perry unfurled the motto "Don't give up the ship," and, after the victory, he announced, "We have met the enemy, and they are ours."

While the climate and harsh living conditions on the island prison resulted in the death of many Confederate officers, most of whom were accustomed to warmer climes and ill-prepared for the northern winter, one significant American legacy from Johnson's Island is that some Confederate officers learned from the locals how to play a popular new sport called baseball. After the war ended, many of these returning officers introduced the game to the South. The rest, as they say, is history – just as, eighty years later, baseball became an important game in Japan. During the American occupation after the Second World War, the Americans played baseball and taught the Japanese to play, and again it quickly grew in popularity and stature there.

Sandusky had also been a rendezvous site for the Canadian "patriots" during the ill-fated Rebellion of 1837–38. It became a launching point for an unsuccessful winter skirmish against the British cavalry, fought on the Lake Erie ice off Pelee Island.

But Cole's interest in that summer of 1864, with the war going poorly for the South, had nothing to do with baseball or the Canadian patriots. While the Confederate scheme to capture the

USS *Michigan* and use it first to free the Johnson's Island prisoners and then to attack several northern cities along the lake ultimately failed, the rebel capture of two Lake Erie ships, the subsequent high-profile "piracy" trial of the main combatants, and the heightened U.S.-British tensions in provoked went down in history as the *Philo Parsons* Affair, adding another significant chapter to the Canadian connection to the war.

It wasn't the first time the Confederates had tried to liberate Johnson's Island.

In February 1863 Lieutenant William H. Murdaugh of the Confederate Navy approached several fellow officers with a plan for a surprise raid to capture the USS *Michigan* and use it to wreck havoc on the largely undefended cities bordering the lake. Secretary of the Navy Stephen Mallory liked the idea immediately and ordered several officers, under the command of Captain Robert D. Minor, to prepare for the assignment, approving $25,000 to finance the expedition. But the Confederate Cabinet had concerns and the plan was ultimately vetoed by President Jefferson Davis because it would compromise the Confederacy's good working relationship with England and jeopardize completion of several iron-clads and other vessels being built in numerous private shipyards in England for the Confederates.

In September, however, Major Y.H. Blackwell forwarded an unsigned letter to Confederate Secretary of War James A. Seddon from Brigadier-General James J. Archer, a prisoner at Johnson's Island, claiming there were 1,600 prisoners there, including 1,200 officers: "We can take the island, guarded by only one battalion, with small loss," it continued, "but have no ways to get off. A naval officer might procure in some way a steamer on the lake and with a few men attack the island and take us to Canada."[1] This letter seems to have been enough to convince Davis that the idea would work and, within days of its receipt, both Mallory and

Seddon asked Minor to organize an expedition to free the Lake Erie prisoners.

Minor immediately turned to his good friend Captain John Wilkinson, arguably the most famous Confederate blockade-runner of the war (who later lived in Nova Scotia for several years), to lead the expedition. The Navy Department forwarded $35,000 in gold, plus a cargo of cotton – which subsequently sold for $76,000 in gold at Halifax.[2]

Wilkinson, Minor, and two dozen officers and men left Smithville, North Carolina, on October 7 on board the blockade steamer *Robert E. Lee*, sailing for Halifax. At one point a U.S. cruiser spotted them and fired several shots, one of which hit a cotton bale on the port side, set fire to it, and wounded several men. But the danger quickly passed as the burning bale was tossed overboard. Finally, having passed precariously within hailing distance of a U.S. southbound man-of-war by flying American colours, they arrived safely at Halifax on October 16 and consigned the cotton to the pro-Confederate local firm of B. Wier & Co. Wilkinson would later write that the island "was supposed to be easily accessible from Canada . . . but it was left to the judgment of the officer in command how the details were to be arranged, his sole explicit instructions being not to violate the neutrality of British territory. How this was to be avoided has never seemed possible to me, but having been selected to command the expedition, I resolved to disregard all personal consequences, and to leave the responsibility to be borne by the Confederate Government."[3]

It would be the last of twenty-one times that Wilkinson successfully ran the blockade commanding the *Lee*, during which he had carried abroad a total of 6,000 to 7,000 bales of cotton, worth about $2 million in gold, and returned equally valuable cargo to the Confederacy. On the way southbound, however, under the command of another officer, the *Lee*, with a full cargo, was captured off the coast of North Carolina.

With so many Confederate and Union spies and freelance informers watching the Halifax docks, the arrival of any blockade-runner in Nova Scotia was immediately noticed. After all, the clandestine activity out of Canada was nothing new. The U.S. consul in Halifax had reported the first arrival of a blockade-runner there on August 6, 1861. In December the U.S. consul in Quebec asked Washington officials for a confidential agent to help him keep track of Confederate activities there, and in January 1862 the U.S. consul in Montreal hired detective Henry Howes to spy on Confederates in that city. About the same time, Union officials reported that about twenty Confederates were living permanently in Toronto, with many others coming and going at regular intervals, many of them staying at the Rossin House, a classy hotel at what is now King and York streets. The owner, G.P. Shears, also ran the Clifton House in Niagara Falls, another favourite haunt for big-name Confederates both during the war and in its aftermath, when some of these Southerners spent time in Canada to avoid prosecution before the amnesty.

On September 13, 1862, Major William Norris, an Irish immigrant, Yale-educated lawyer, and prominent Baltimorean who was head of the Confederate Signals Corps, asked the secretary of war for permission to set up a system of Confederate couriers and secret routes through the North, including "a proposition to station a reliable officer in Quebec; his duty to convert into cipher, and the reverse, and forward all dispatches of the president to and from our agents and ministers abroad. It is believed that this could be accomplished with but little delay beyond that of regular mail and with no possibility of discovery."[4] The proposition was approved – although the Canadian part of the proposal had been sent to President Davis for his personal acquiescence first – and Norris was given authority to set up what became known as the "Secret Line," a system of transmitting official correspondence to and from Confederate officials in Canada and Europe, as well as Southern agents in the Northern states.

For their part, Union officials and spies were always alert for Southern activity to and from Canada, so the Johnson's Island raiders took precautions to avoid detection. They divided the party into groups of three or four men, directing them, under top secrecy, to rendezvous in Montreal. Travelling under assumed names, the rebels used two separate routes: the first via Saint John, New Brunswick, through Fredericton and Grand Falls and into Quebec through Rivière-du-Loup, then on to Quebec City and into Montreal; the second taking men through Pictou, Nova Scotia, then the Northumberland Strait to the Bay of Chaleurs, via the Gaspé, next up the St. Lawrence River to Quebec City, then on to Montreal by train, where they all congregated on October 21. In Montreal Wilkinson met with a "Captain M.," whom he describes in his book as "a zealous and self-sacrificing friend to the cause, and to whom I had been accredited." Wilkinson claimed it would have been easy to sign up hundreds of recruits for the project from among the assorted local sympathizers, Southern refugees, and escaped prisoners living in Canada, "but it was not considered prudent to increase the size of the party to any extent."[5] They did, however, recruit three men who had escaped from Johnson's Island and who knew a lot about the prison and the surrounding territory. Wilkinson also dispatched a sympathetic retired British Army officer, posing as a duck hunter, to Sandusky, where he gathered daily intelligence on conditions there and reported back by telegraph.

The raiders included Colonel W.B. Ball of the 15th Virginia Cavalry and Lieutenant-Colonel W.W. Finney, formerly of the 15th Virginia Infantry, who volunteered to serve the expedition as acting masters' mates. Finney was an interesting character himself. A longtime friend and business partner of Major B.F. Ficklin, the man credited with convincing Robert E. Lee to opt for the Confederacy, they had graduated one year apart from the Virginia Military Institute and, together, had organized the famous Pony Express.

Another problem was how best to notify the prisoners when the breakout would be attempted, a challenge they solved thanks to Patrick C. Martin, a former Baltimore liquor dealer and blockade-runner who, in addition to assisting the Confederates, helped himself to huge profits through an informal partnership with the notorious Alexander Keith Jr. of Halifax, buying and shipping contraband. Martin, who moved to Montreal in 1862, sent his wife to visit a Southern friend, the wife of an imprisoned Confederate general, and convinced her to obtain permission from Washington to visit her husband at Johnson's Island, so she could hand him a paper telling him that the date would appear in the *New York Herald* "personal" advertisements section using particular initials meaningful only to the general. Given the strong sense of chivalry that characterized the upper classes of the day, a reality the South put to good use on many occasions, it was relatively easy for women to indulge in espionage activities. After all, no real gentleman would ever search the personal effects of a lady or suspect her of being involved in anything wicked or underhanded.

All seemed to be proceeding well. The party, now numbering fifty-four men, having sent off its last "personal" to the *Herald* announcing that "the carriage would be at the door on or about the tenth," had purchased 100 navy Colt revolvers, two small nine-pounders, powder, bullets, butcher-knives in lieu of cutlasses, and grapnels for scaling the *Michigan*. A man was sent to Ogdensburg, New York, to buy passage for a large group of "mechanics and laborers" bound for Chicago. They planned to assemble at St. Catharines, board the steamer, and, once past the Welland Canal and therefore clear of British jurisdiction, overpower the crew, seize the ship, mount the two nine-pounders, and surprise the *Michigan*. Then, commandeering several private steamers docked at the Sandusky wharf, they planned to load the 2,000 prisoners and transport them safely to Canada, after which they would use the *Michigan* to attack commerce and various cities along the lake, most of which were virtually defenceless from the water.

In his subsequent formal report to the Navy, Captain Minor wrote that they were so confident of their success that they had all assembled at St. Catharines, waiting for the steamer, "when the storm burst upon us."

That "storm," which aborted the venture, was a telegram from U.S. Secretary of War Edwin M. Stanton warning local officials about the planned Confederate raid. Canadian Governor General Lord Monck had learned through intelligence from the American consul at Halifax or indirectly from the British consul in Baltimore that Confederates in Montreal were trying to buy military supplies. The consul was friendly at the time with Baltimore's former police marshal, George P. Kane, a shadowy figure with Southern sympathies who was arrested by American authorities in 1861, then fled to Montreal. Kane had been in Canada since 1862, mostly in Montreal, where he worked with Martin, the secret service operative. Kane was involved not only in the Johnson's Island caper but also in some anti-Union activity with Lincoln's assassin, John Wilkes Booth. He moved to Richmond in early 1864 and was an adviser on Confederate operations in Canada. In any event, Monck telegraphed Lord Lyons in Washington on November 11 asking him to warn U.S. Secretary of State William H. Seward about "a serious and mischievous plot." Lyons immediately informed Seward by special messenger and, the next day, Michigan Governor Austin Blair notified Stanton about an expected raid. For his part, Stanton telegraphed the governors of all the lake states, and the mayors of the major cities, plus the military commanders in New York, Pennsylvania, and Ohio, ordering extra troops to Sandusky. Stanton warned that "there is reason to believe that a plot is on foot by persons who have found an asylum in Canada to invade the U.S. and destroy the city of Buffalo." He said they also planned to burn Ogdensburg, take over some steamboats on Lake Erie, surprise

Johnson's Island, "and free prisoners of war confined there." He said that Canadian authorities pledged to "use every means in their power to prevent any breach of neutrality."

To demonstrate his concern and placate the Americans, Canadian Prime Minister John Sandfield Macdonald made a point of going to Buffalo to meet with U.S. officials there. Some prominent Americans were suspicious of Macdonald, however, because his wife, Christine, hailed from a prominent secessionist Louisiana family and his brother-in-law was a celebrated Confederate lieutenant-colonel. Macdonald, to counteract these suspicions about his real sympathies, went to Buffalo to reassure both U.S. General John A. Dix, who had spent several years in a Montreal school, and Buffalo Mayor William Fargo that Canada would not be a party to extraterritorial activities against its neighbour – even though Canadian officials continued to turn a blind eye most of the time to Confederate activities along the border states. Monck, also to placate American concerns, ordered troops to Port Colborne and St. Catharines. Because of a rumoured attack against Detroit, which never was planned, officials there sent about 1,000 men to Belle Island on the Detroit River, paying them the handsome sum of $2 a day to chop down trees near the shore and build an emergency barricade.

Although Monck's warning about Johnson's Island subsequently proved to be accurate, it was not widely believed in Canada. Several newspapers, and most Canadian politicians, pooh-poohed the whole escapade. The November 18, 1863, *Niagara Review*, for example, criticized the "flaming order" from Washington about an expected attack from Canada, concluding that there was "no truth" to such "rumours," lamenting that it "caused panic" along the frontier, and accusing Macdonald of "compromising the personal safety of a great number of persons here." The pro-Confederate *Toronto Leader* dismissed the accusation on November 13 on the grounds that Southerners were too "manly and honourable" to engage in such a nefarious plot.

On the same day, however, the *Montreal Gazette*, which also tended to be pro-Confederate, published an unattributed letter – undoubtedly written by a senior Confederate official in Canada – saying: "The Washington government, having refused to continue the exchange of prisoners of war under the cartel, sent the Southern officers, accustomed to a tropical climate, to Johnson's Island . . . it was in fact, an attempt to commit murder without publicly incurring the odium of slaughter. In these circumstances, the Confederate government determined to make an attempt to rescue the doomed officers."[6]

While accusations flew back and forth for some time – and rumours of "planned" Confederate invasions from Canada grew like Topsy – the fact was that the Johnson's Island scheme was now in shambles. The rebels retreated to Halifax, making much of the arduous journey on sleighs because the ground was already covered in snow and the river steamers had closed for the season. After a brief respite with friends and supporters in Halifax – where Confederate sympathies were so widespread that some businesses flew Confederate flags and others, to their ultimate chagrin, accepted Confederate money in payment for their merchandise – Wilkinson and most of his men sailed to Bermuda aboard the steamer *Alpha*.

As for the Johnson's Island prisoners, they would have to wait for Plan B.

Confederate sympathizers had been active in Canada since the early days of the war. By 1863 they were operating so openly that C.S. Ogden, the U.S. consul at Quebec City, sent a plea to Washington asking the government to implement measures to protect the border states and to "prevent the consummation of contemplated deeds of wreckless wickedness."[7]

After several appeals from Canadian-based sympathizers – many of them Southern refugees and escaped prisoners, as well as locals who profited by dealing with the South or simply sided with the Confederacy – President Davis decided in April 1864 to formalize opposition from Canada. He was greatly encouraged by consistent reports – which proved to be highly exaggerated – that opposition against President Lincoln in the North, particularly through a secretive "peace" organization known as the Knights of the Golden Circle (also known as the Sons of Liberty and Knights of America), had some 490,000 members. With a little well-placed encouragement and the aid of some weapons from the Confederacy, these men were ready to break from the Union and set up a northwest republic friendly to the South, forcing Lincoln from office and negotiating an honourable and equitable (Southern-friendly) end to the war. Many of Davis's advisers were more enthusiastic than he was about using the northern "peace" movements to foment rebellion in the Northern states, but Davis liked the idea of formalizing opposition from the safety of Canada.

On March 26, 1864, the *Montreal Gazette*, based on an article nine days earlier in the *Saint John Telegraph*, reported that Captain D.U. Barziza of the CSA 4th Texas and two other Confederate officers had arrived in Saint John after jumping from a railroad car 90 miles west of Harrisburg, Pennsylvania, while being conveyed with several other officers from Johnson's Island to Point Lookout. Barziza had gone to Montreal, "where he was kindly provided for and sent on his way rejoicing."

Many Confederate officials felt they had considerable cause to rejoice at the possibilities of unrest in the North and the potential of secret operations from Canada. Acting on this optimism, Confederate Secretary of State Judah P. Benjamin, after a secret session of the Confederate Congress had allocated money for the Canadian project, invited well-known Virginia politician Alexander H.H. Stuart to Richmond to run the Canadian operation. Stuart, a Whig, besides a long career in state politics, had also served in the House of Representatives and as secretary of the interior under Millard Fillmore. Described as "a reluctant secessionist but outspoken defender of slavery," Stuart turned down the offer, explaining later that the job was to "foster and give direct aid to a peace sentiment which it was understood was then active along the Border States." After listening to Benjamin he concluded, presciently as it turned out, that the secretary "was laboring under a remarkable delusion as to the peace sentiment in the north, as well as about the probable efficiency of such a Commission as he proposed."[8]

Undeterred, Davis turned to two old friends in April 1864 – Jacob Thompson and Clement C. Clay – to advance the Southern cause in Canada. Thompson, who was Davis's first choice, had served six terms as a Congressman from Mississippi and was secretary of the interior under James Buchanan. A powerful Democratic power broker, he was a personal friend of the prominent peace promoter, or Copperhead, Clement Vallandigham, at one time a serious presidential hopeful, of whom we will be hearing much more. A lawyer, Thompson had migrated from North Carolina to Mississippi in the 1830s, organized courts of law in ten new state counties, married the daughter of a wealthy planter, and built a huge estate and cotton plantation in Natchez, near the University of Mississippi, in 1843 – the same year he was elected to the U.S. House of Representatives, where he would serve on the Mississippi Congressional delegation with Jefferson Davis. Thompson had played a major role in both the 1852 and 1856 national conventions and had opposed secession, but when war broke out he volunteered for the Confederacy and rose to the rank of colonel as a volunteer aide-de-camp for prominent Confederate Generals P.G.T. Beauregard and Joseph E. Johnston. At one point the Union commander on the Missouri wrote to his subordinate complaining: "I understand noted rebel ex-officers, including the arch-traitor Jacob Thompson, have been at Helena (Ark.) without being hung. Any such monstrous breaches of military law and reason will be severely noticed."[9]

Clay had been assistant editor of the Huntsville (Ala.) *Democrat*, a family newspaper. He had served in the U.S. Senate from Alabama from 1853 until the war began in 1861. Davis, who had respected Clay as a Senate colleague, had offered him the initial post of secretary of war in the Confederate government, but Clay opted to serve in the Confederate Senate instead. He had lost his bid for re-election in 1863 and was searching for an assignment when the call came from Davis to meet him and Thompson in Richmond. While Thompson, as chief, reported directly to both Benjamin and Davis, Clay was head of the War Department contingent to Canada. Clay loved good food and wine, but his health was not great. "A frail, sickly man, racked by a hacking cough which made him feverish, impatient and impulsive, he hated the biting cold of the Canadian winter and longed for his beloved Alabama."[10]

In a subsequent order to Thompson, Davis wrote: "Confiding special trust in your zeal, discretion and patriotism, I hereby direct you to proceed at once to Canada, there to carry out such instructions as you have received from me verbally, in such manner as shall seem most likely to conduce to the furtherance of the interests of the Confederate States of America which have been intrusted to you."[11] In his own published memoirs, Davis offered a rather benign explanation for his move, writing that he sent the agents to Canada "with a view to negotiation with such persons in the North as might be relied upon to aid the attainment of peace. The commission was designed to facilitate such preliminary conditions as might lead to formal negotiations between the two governments, and they were expected to make judicious use of any political opportunity that might be presented."[12]

But Benjamin, much more a bull on the subject than Davis, sent a secret dispatch to John Slidell (of *Chesapeake* Affair fame) in Paris, saying the agents were sent "to Canada on secret service in the hope of aiding the disruption between Eastern and Western states in the approaching election at the North. It is supposed that much good can be done by the purchase of some of the principal presses of the northwest." In other words, the agents "interpreted their instructions to authorize support and encouragement to peace groups and disaffected elements, direct meddling in northern politics, an attack on the northern monetary system, efforts to release confederate prisoners of war, and schemes otherwise to wreck havoc and destruction behind enemy lines."[13]

Given that Thompson and Clay were well-known public figures, it was remarkably naïve of Davis and Benjamin to think they could get into Canada unnoticed by the plethora of Union officials and spies who were also working there. Both men used phony names at times – Thompson called himself Colonel Carson, and Clay used the names Hope, Tracey, and Lacey at various times – and slipped through the federal blockade out of Wilmington, North Carolina, on the *Thistle*, a speedy Clyde-built steamer capable of 14 knots per hour, and then to St. George, Bermuda. They left there on May 10 aboard the British mail steamer *Alpha* and arrived in Halifax on May 19, where they hooked up with law professor James P. Holcombe, who had been sent there earlier by Davis to represent some Confederate legal interests and had become the third Confederate commissioner. With Clay taking sick, Thompson and his secretary William Cleary left Halifax on May 21 for Montreal, crossed the Bay of Fundy to the St. John's River, then went overland to Rivière-du-Loup, where they took a train to Montreal and arrived about 10 a.m. on May 29, 1864.

Thompson, who considered himself a legitimate representative in Canada of a foreign power, formally notified Lord Monck of his presence in Canada and established his headquarters at the St. Lawrence Hall in Montreal, a grand, expensive, 700-room Victorian hotel on St. James Street which was operated by Henry

Hogan, a Southern sympathizer. With about one million dollars to work with, opened an account for $95,000 at the Montreal branch of the Bank of Ontario. He sent Cleary on to Toronto to set up a more permanent headquarters in the upscale Queen's Hotel, the epicentre for Confederate activities for the remainder of the war, where about one hundred Confederates were renting the entire hotel. Cleary, a Kentucky lawyer, had fled to Canada in 1862 to avoid being arrested for anti-Union activities and had moved first with his wife, Ann (née Wherritt), into the Clifton House in Niagara and then to the Queen's Hotel. He returned to Kentucky that September when he heard that General Braxton Bragg had launched a successful assault there, and he took a job in the auditor's office in Richmond. In the spring of 1864, however, Davis asked him to go back to Canada with Thompson and Clay.

Clay and Holcombe arrived in Montreal, then a thriving metropolis of about 75,000 people, about two weeks late, just as Thompson was getting ready to leave Toronto for a meeting with Vallandigham and others in Windsor. A secret society called the Knights of the Golden Circle, featuring an elaborate system of oaths and rituals, had existed before the war, essentially in opposition to the Republican Party. By 1862, however, it had stagnated, so Davis sent Captain Emile Longuemare of Missouri to revive it, beginning with the inaugural meeting of the Order of American Knights in early 1862 in St. Louis. The movement kept no records and transmitted all message orally, following a strict code of secrecy. It also had various degrees of membership and an inner circle, the Sons of Liberty, which Vallandigham headed. Organized by state, county, and townships, it recruited membership ostensibly to save the Democratic Party, although the Confederate aims were to organize it into a military force operating behind Union lines. Vallandigham, a supporter of both states' rights and slavery, had become one of Lincoln's leading opponents. With the help of New York City Mayor Fernando Wood –

who would also visit Canada during the war to meet with Lincoln's enemies – he had formed the Peace Democrats, or Copperheads. In May 1863 soldiers acting under Lincoln's orders burst into his home in the dead of night, arrested him for making "treasonable utterances" by urging citizens not to cooperate with Federal recruiting efforts, summarily tried him before a military commission, and sentenced him to prison for treason.

Responding to criticism from leading Democrats over the heavy-handed use of the military to muzzle a critic, Lincoln said: "Long experience has shown that armies cannot be maintained unless desertion shall be punished by the severe penalty of death. The case requires, and the law and the Constitution sanction, this punishment. Must I shoot a simple-minded soldier boy who deserts, while I must not touch a hair of a wily agitator who induced him to desert? . . . I think that in such a case, to silence the agitator, and save the boy, is not only Constitutional, but, withall, a great mercy."[14]

Lincoln didn't shoot Vallandigham, but he commuted his prison sentence and banished him to the South. Vallandigham soon moved on to Canada, where he stayed mainly at St. Catharines and Windsor and even ran unsuccessfully on the Democratic ticket for governor of Ohio. He certainly had his supporters in Canada. Responding to an anti-Vallandigham editorial by George Brown in the pro-Union Toronto *Globe* on August 5, 1863, the *Niagara Review* dismissed Brown's work as a "foul, malignant and unprovoked attack upon that eminent American refugee now in Canada." Calling the *Globe* "a subsidized advocate of the Lincoln Government," the *Review* wrote that Vallandigham's "honest advocacy of peace in the interests of our common humanity is what has brought upon [his] head the vengeance of the mad, blood-stained despot at Washington, and of his military satrap in Ohio."

Vallandigham returned to Hamilton, Ohio, in June 1864, after a carefully scripted publicity campaign announcing his intentions. "But I warn also the men in power that three is a vast multitude, a host whom they cannot number, bound together by the strongest and holiest ties, to defend, by whatever means the exigencies of the times shall demand, their natural and constitutional rights as freemen, at all hazards and to the last extremity."[15] Vallandigham had yearned for martyrhood, but Lincoln, wisely concluding that Vallandigham was now a spent force, simply ignored him.

After meeting Vallandigham and others, Thompson wrote his first formal report to Benjamin on July 7, announcing he had become a member of the secret order in the Western states and "I was much pleased with it . . . it is now fixed that this movement shall take place on the 20th [of August]." Thompson claimed that the order had 85,000 members in Illinois, 56,000 in Indiana, 40,000 in Ohio, plus an unknown number in Kentucky, all of whom could be used to free prisoners at Chicago, Rock Island, and Springfield and seize and hold Indianapolis. He also said that "the people of Canada generally sympathize with us."[16]

Clay and Holcombe stayed on in Montreal for about two weeks, with Clay busily contacting all the Confederate operatives and sympathizers he could find, while Holcombe, who had earlier been sent to Canada ostensibly to expedite the return of Confederate refugees, spent much of his time entertaining what his associates described as his "vixen," a woman named Stansbury whom he had first met in Halifax, then had ensconced in a country hotel just outside Montreal. It is not known what happened to the woman when Holcombe and Clay left Montreal, but, after a brief stay in Toronto, they moved into a house in St. Catharines, another significant hotbed of Confederate activity and much closer to the American border, where they entertained an endless string of "peace" advocates and others discontented with Lincoln or the progress of the war. Clay, who did not get along with Thompson, later established a headquarters at Montreal's St. Lawrence Hall and deposited $93,000 in the local

Bank of Ontario for his own purposes. (Later in the war the second Doneganasp Hotel, built on Notre Dame by Confederate sympathizers, also became a hotbed of Confederate activity. After the war, it was taken over by the Roman Catholic Church and turned into Notre Dame Hospital.)

In St. Catharines, Clay and Holcombe moved into a house in the Merchants' Block owned by Robert E. Coxe, another wealthy Southern refugee from Alabama who had gone first to Europe and then to Canada in 1862. Coxe was active in several anti-Union schemes and, in 1865, was arrested and briefly jailed on suspicion of being involved in Lincoln's assassination. Also sharing the house was former Virginia Governor Beverly Tucker, another early suspect in Lincoln's death, who stayed on in St. Catharines after the war and won local plaudits for reopening the Stephenson House hotel and spa, a fashionable resort that catered to wealthy tourists from the South, including Jefferson Davis and Confederate Generals Jubal Early and John C. Breckinridge and their families. For a time, the Stephenson House was the centre of social activities for the well-to-do citizens of St. Catharines and the surrounding Niagara area. Tucker, a former U.S. consul in Liverpool who was widely seen as a true Southern gentleman, shocked his many supporters in October 1871 when he and his son skipped town, leaving behind unpaid bills of $23,000 – including $7,000 he had borrowed from Lieutenant-Governor Howland. His staff were in such dire straits that the October 14 *St. Catharines Evening Journal* reported: "The bartender had to invest his last dollar to prevent his fellow employees from starving, begging or stealing." Clay, Tucker, and Coxe set up a regular system of clandestine meetings at the Niagara Falls Museum, just a few miles south of St. Catharines and on the border with the United States, a place where they wouldn't be noticed because many people were constantly coming and going.

St. Catharines, in fact, was a perfect spot from which to

carry on such activities. Situated close to the Canadian railway system, it was just a few miles from Buffalo, itself centrally located on the northern U.S. railroad system, affording relatively easy access to New York City, Pittsburgh, Cleveland, and Detroit. It was also close to Niagara Falls, with its many tourist hotels on both sides of the border, where, unlike many towns, strangers were not likely to draw any attention. Ironically, St. Catharines was also a main Canadian centre for black Americans who had escaped slavery or the *Fugitive Slave Law,* although the ex-slaves obviously travelled in different social circles from the wealthy Southern fugitives and spies.

The Clifton House, a large and luxurious hotel, was a favourite for Southerners, but many also stayed at the Table Rock House, a much smaller hotel nearby which shared the same building as the Barnett Museum, one of the few establishments at the time open seven days a week. A post-war examination of the signed registers at the hotel and the museum shows that Coxe, for example, visited in September 1863, and a Confederate courier made twenty-one visits in a fifteen-month period. "It would have been very easy for a courier or other agent to visit the museum and sign the register, thus reporting his presence to a local agent, who could inspect the register at frequent intervals. Meetings or exchanges of messages could follow in accordance with previously arranged procedures. With St. Catharines less than an hour away by train or two or three hours by horse, Confederates living [there] . . . could meet visiting agents or northern Copperheads among a crowd of strangers in which they would not be noticed. At the same time, the visitors would not know the permanent location of the Confederates they met."[17]

Another piece of the Confederate Canadian operations puzzle was Cassius F. Lee of Alexandria, an uncle of Robert E. Lee and a staunch Episcopalian who was forced out of his home in late 1863 because of his strong pro-Southern opinions. He set up shop in Hamilton, at the western end of Lake Ontario between

Toronto and Niagara, where, according to Tidwell, he acted as a message centre. "Messages could be sent to him, and he would know where the agent was currently located and could forward the message to the correct address . . . His name was listed on the Confederate cipher keys on a ledger contained in the Confederate Secret Service record book."[18]

Still another prominent, although unofficial, member of the Confederate's Canadian commission was George N. Sanders, a controversial and dangerous figure who had been U.S. consul in London under President Franklin Pierce and a drinking companion of Victor Hugo. Sanders had little regard for concerns about Canadian neutrality, and passionately believed that the Confederacy had every right to retaliate against the North for its sins. He "was probably the only man who made J.W. Booth believe that political assassination was a permissable action."[19]

Sanders, described by historian Charles Highham as "the most furious and dangerous anti-Lincoln of all," had been born in Lexington, Kentucky, on February 21, 1812. The family moved to Grass Hills, Kentucky, a few miles up-river from Madison, Indiana, where his father became a highly successful cattle breeder. He moved to New York, where he became an active Democratic Party propagandist, and then to Europe, where he was involved in arming revolutionaries in a radical Democratic Party group known as the "Young America" movement. This group held that democracy was the best form of government, and it was the destiny of the United States to help people then ruled by monarchies and dictatorships to achieve democracy – by force if necessary. Sanders gained considerable notoriety in 1853 when, as U.S. consul to London, he hosted a dinner attended not only by U.S. Ambassador James Buchanan, who became president four years later, but by many leading English political figures and, most controversially of all, several well-known revolutionary figures including Italy's Giuseppe Mazzini and Giuseppe Garibaldi, Hungary's Lajo Kossuth, France's Alexandre-Auguste

Ledru-Rollin, and Russia's Alexandre Herzen. The dinner caused considerable diplomatic difficulties for the United States because it left the impression that America supported the European revolutionary movement in place of the existing governments there.[20]

The impetuous Sanders went even further in 1854 and published a letter addressed to the "People of France," urging them to get rid of Louis Napolean and restore democracy. In 1859, back in Kentucky, he organized the "New Mississippi Valley Movement" around the themes of states' rights and free trade. While negotiating a scheme with Benjamin in 1863 to set up a courier system between Europe and the Confederacy, Sanders is credited with being the first to suggest the idea of establishing a Canadian operation to work with the Northern Peace Democrats. "Davis didn't like it at the time, but did take it under advisement."[21]

Sanders has been called "an evil figure," but the personal descriptions of him tend to be conflicted. Biographer James Horan described him as "a tall, debonair, smiling man . . . never without money or beautiful women . . . a friend of presidents and kings."[22] He, too, was ensconced at the Queen's Hotel, where historian Robin Winks writes he was "constantly unkempt and unshaven, but living affluently in a room overlooking the bay, working to obtain the release of his son from a Northern prison and trying to convince Thompson that robbing the banks of Buffalo would be a legal act of war."[23] Sanders also lived some of the time with Coxe, Clay, and company in St. Catharines and was instrumental, along with Thompson, in organizing a controversial "peace conference" with famous *New York Tribune* editor Horace Greeley in Niagara Falls in 1864.

Also part of the Queen's Hotel contingent, and an important member of the Confederate commission, was Captain Thomas Hines, a dashing Kentucky cavalryman who was the first Confederate officer selected by Davis for service along the Northern borders for the release of prisoners. By some accounts,

Hines – who hated Sanders – looked enough like John Wilkes Booth to be his twin. He reached Toronto on April 20, 1864, with $5,000 in gold and an additional $70,000 from a shipment of cotton he had sold to finance his operations in Canada. He had travelled north by train through Cincinnati to Detroit, where he crossed the river by ferry to Windsor and then took the train to Toronto. His first stop was a small boarding house, but once he discovered the Queen's Hotel, "he established his headquarters at once in the bar."[24]

Hines, of the 9th Kentucky Cavalry Regiment, earned his spurs when he was sent by Kentucky General John Hunt Morgan in the summer of 1863 to contact the Northern Peace movements to see if they were willing to offer military support for a Confederate raid into Ohio. In July, before anything substantial could be worked out, Morgan was captured in eastern Ohio, near the Pennsylvania border. He and his officers, including Hines, were taken to the Johnson's Island prison, but the next day, as a display of Union anger at Morgan and his raiders, they were treated as common criminals and dispatched to the "East Hall" of the Ohio State Penitentiary. "This situation, however, may have worked to Morgan's advantage. In October, Morgan and six of his officers, including Captain Hines, escaped . . . It is possible that money and local political influence may have been of help . . . which would have been harder to arrange if Morgan had been in a prison controlled by the military."[25] Hines, whose Cell 20 was situated in the centre of the first-floor block, was credited with planning and executing the escape. Figuring out there was an air chamber below the floor, he used stolen dinner utensils as shovels, and he and his colleagues spent several weeks taking turns digging an escape route, and the six escapees – Morgan and five captains, including Hines – finally used a rope and a bent poker to scale two walls. Splitting into pairs, Hines paired Morgan and caught an express train to Cincinnati, which took them right by the prison, and, on the outskirts of Cincinnati, they jumped off the train and made their way to Newport, Kentucky. According to Horan, "their escape had electrified the South."[26] At another point, Hines was recaptured and a noose tossed around his neck, but he talked his way out of that, was placed under guard in a log house, escaped, was caught again, and once more escaped. Hines would say that his role in Morgan's escape prompted Confederate officials in Richmond to pick him for the Canadian operations.

A March 16, 1864, letter from Confederate Secretary of War James A. Seddon assigned Hines – who later claimed he was commissioned a major-general *pro tempore* – for "special service to proceed to Canada" to meet with Holcombe and gather men "who are willing to return" and "while passing through the United States confer with leading persons friendly or attached to the cause . . . [and] induce our friends to organize and prepare themselves."[27] Hines had already made contact with the Sons of Liberty and others, so he was Davis's natural choice to continue this work from Canada. To that end, Hines met Vallandigham in Windsor, Ontario, on June 9, the day before Clay and Holcombe arrived in Montreal, and two days before Thompson reacquainted himself with the Peace Democrat leader, who was grand commander of the Sons of Liberty, to discuss the use of the secret order to instigate a northwestern rebellion. While the other commissioners were more concerned with promoting their cause on a diplomatic front, Hines had the specific task of organizing a band of Confederate soldiers in Canada who could be used in future military strikes against the North and, with the help of Vallandigham's group, overthrow the Washington government.

On July 22 Hines and former 2nd Kentucky Cavalry officer, Captain John B. Castleman, Hines's second in command, along with the Confederate commissioners, met in St. Catharines with delegates from the upcoming Chicago Democratic Convention to discuss a proposed August 16 northwest uprising. The Confederates pushed strongly for that date, fearing, correctly as it turned out, that delays would increase the chances of the Union hearing about their plans, but the Northerners, fearing it wouldn't work because the Confederate Army was not faring as well as it had hoped in Kentucky and Missouri – Confederate successes would divert the Union Army – wanted a postponement. They agreed to another meeting in London, Ontario, on August 7, but it, too, was postponed until August 29, the day of the national convention in Chicago. Although Hines was quite enthusiastic about the capabilities of the Northern dissenters, as a military force they were impotent. Most were armed and they did participate in twice-monthly military drills, but they were not military men. They talked a good game and had a large membership roll, but Hines and others, in just looking at the sheer numbers, "did not take into consideration the willingness of the individuals to be shot at."[28] Before long, it became painfully obvious to the Confederate hopes that the secret Northern orders were, as they would have been described in Texas, all hat and no steer.

While Cole was still playing the role of Mr. Money Bags in Sandusky, doing his best to win friends and influence Union officers for the planned Johnson's Island outbreak, Hines led a team of sixty-two men from Canada to Chicago ready to assist in what they hoped would be an armed uprising sponsored by the Copperheads on August 29 at the Democratic National Convention. Hines's plan was, first, to release 8,000 Confederate prisoners at Camp Douglas and then to capture Chicago itself, helped by large numbers of the Sons of Liberty from Kentucky, Missouri, Indiana, and Illinois (commanded by Brigadier-General Charles Walsh) who had come armed to the convention. Colonel G. St. Leger Grenfell, Morgan's former chief of staff, who had also come to Toronto and hooked up with Hines, was part of the Chicago-bound force, which had armed itself with pistols at Toronto and, divided into smaller groups and dressed in civilian clothes, travelled via a number of different routes to Chicago.

The night before the convention opened, Hines and Castleman hosted a meeting in their room at the Richmond House in Chicago, hoping to ascertain precisely what military help could be expected from Vallandigham's group for the planned prison break-outs and the northwest rebellion. John Maughan, an Englishman, had lived the previous two years in Windsor, Ontario, where, as a teller and clerk at the Bank of Upper Canada, he had become acquainted with most of the senior Confederates – he knew Jacob Thompson, for example, as Colonel Carson. At a later hearing in Cincinnati into the Camp Douglas affair, Maughan testified that he had left Windsor on August 16, 1864, planning to run the blockade and join the Confederate Army, but, because his sympathies were known by Confederate refugees there, he was asked to join the Chicago project. He was sent to Toronto to meet with Thompson at the Queen's Hotel and then, after a few days, given a package containing $10,000 and a letter to take to Chicago to give to Castleman. In Chicago he delivered the package to Castleman at the Richmond House, where he met Hines and several other Confederates, but almost immediately the Confederates, fearing they'd been found out, left Chicago.

The Democratic Convention nominated General George B. McClellan as its candidate for president on August 31. The only "victory" that Vallandigham and the Southerners could claim was the convention's adoption of the "peace" plank: "That this convention does explicitly declare, as the sense of the American people, that after four years of failure to restore the Union by the experiment of war . . . justice, humanity, liberty, and the public welfare demand that immediate efforts be made for a cessation of hostilities, with a view of an ultimate convention of the States, or other peaceable means, to the end that, at the earliest practicable moment, peace may be restored on the basis of the Federal

Union."[29] But eight days later, after Atlanta had fallen, McClellan rejected that plank, which had not dealt with slavery, and demanded a series of preconditions from the South before peace talks could begin. In a subsequent letter to Confederate leaders in Richmond, Clay wrote that he had seen McClellan's turnabout with "mingled feelings of surprise, indignation and regret," and that McClellan's candidacy now offered "no hope for the South."[30] Clay had also become convinced that the Northern secret orders were of little use to the South. On September 12 he wrote to Benjamin from St. Catharines saying: "Perhaps our true policy is to keep our own counsels, withhold any further declaration of purpose, and let the so-called peace party of the north have no excuse for laying its defeat at our door, if Lincoln should be elected."[31] Lincoln was indeed elected, defeating McClellan on November 8, 1864, by 228 electoral votes to 21. (The popular vote was much closer, 2,206,938 for Lincoln and 1,803,787 for McClellan, but still a one-third increase over Lincoln's 1860 popular support.)

In any event, given the efficiency of the Union spy network in Canada – and the propensity of many Confederates to boast, as well as the utter lack of discipline among the secret orders – the Union knew all about the Chicago plot. It had dramatically increased the federal garrison in Chicago to about 3,000 troops, more than enough to deal with the Confederates and their Sons of Liberty supporters. Castleman, heading back to the South, was arrested by federal officials in Indianapolis. Hines sent Maughan there "to see what was going to be done with him." Maughan checked into the Palmer House but did not try to meet Castleman, so he eventually returned to Canada, met Clay and Hines in St. Catharines, and suggested a plan to take Union hostages and hold them as ransom until Castleman was released. "Clay promised to hold hostages for the safety of Castleman."[32] Like so many of the Confederate plans, however, this one didn't materialize either.

With the complete failure of the Chicago operation, the Toronto-based Confederates then turned their full attention to the Johnson's Island caper. Cole was still living in the West House at Sandusky, ingratiating himself with everybody he could. He not only entertained officers from the USS *Michigan* to sumptuous dinners at his hotel but was frequently a guest aboard the warship and had carte blanche to visit Johnson's Island, where he told the prisoners of the plans for the escape.

On the evening of September 19, when the escape was to take place, Cole had arranged for the officers to be his guests at a champagne dinner aboard the ship, during which he planned to drug them. He and a fellow rebel would each wield two pistols and guard the onboard armory until a small band of armed Confederates, led by Acting Master John Yates Beall of the Confederate Volunteer Navy, who had been involved in the *Chesapeake* incident, would bring a boarding party alongside the *Michigan* in a captured civilian vessel and take control of the U.S. warship. Beall, born January 1, 1835, at Walnut Grove, Virginia, one of seven children of English settlers, had joined the 2nd Virginia Infantry Regiment as a private at the age of 26 and fought in the First Battle of Bull Run as part of the Stonewall Brigade. Later, on October 16, 1861, he was badly wounded in the chest while leading a charge of a company of General Turner Ashby's cavalry in defence of Harper's Ferry Gap and was given a medical discharge. After a long convalescence, Beall convinced the War Department to appoint him an acting master in the Confederate States Navy so he could raise a band of partisans to raid Union ships in Chesapeake Bay, their only payment being a share of the captured booty. After successfully capturing four ships in September 1863, Beall and his eighteen-man crew were captured that November, strapped in irons at Fort McHenry, Maryland, and held as pirates. When Confederate authorities seized Union prisoners and put them in chains to protest Beall's capture, Beall was freed in a prisoner exchange on May 5, 1864, and immediately came to Canada to sign up with Thompson's organization.

Beall would write in his diary that he met with Thompson in Toronto as soon as he had arrived in Canada, where he learned about the Johnson's Island plan and volunteered for it. Thompson sent him to Sandusky to meet Cole – having cautioned both men to "carefully abstain from violating any laws or regulations of Canada or British authorities in relation to neutrality."[33] After meeting with Cole, the project leader, Beall went to Windsor to round up the men he needed for the job.

As usual, word leaked out. In Toronto, Beall had recruited Godfrey J. Hyams of Arkansas, who had been working undercover for U.S. Lieutenant-Colonel Bennet H. Hill, the assistant provost marshal general at Detroit responsible for the draft, general security, and counter espionage. On September 17 Hyams walked into Hill's office in the Detroit Armoury Building and told him about the plan. Rumours of borders raids had been so common that Hill was sceptical, but Hyams said he would return the next day with more details, after a planned meeting with the conspirators, so Hill telegraphed Captain J.C. Carter, commander of the *Michigan*. Carter replied, "Thanks for your dispatch. All ready . . ." The informant returned as promised and told Hill that the rebels planned to take passage on the steamer *Philo Parsons*, a wood-hull, 136-foot sidewheeler at Malden (now Amherstburg, Ontario), and take possession of her before reaching Sandusky.[34]

The next day, at 6 a.m., Monday, September 19, Hill, having concluded the threat was real, went to see the *Philo Parsons* at her Detroit dock. He concluded she was too small to be a danger to the *Michigan*: it would be wiser to leave her and have Carter on guard so the entire rebel party could be captured. He telegraphed Carter again with more details, saying, "Both Commodore Gardner and myself look upon the matter as serious."

On Sunday evening a man later described as thick-set, below medium height, with light hair and a thin, light-coloured beard, with "the bearing of a gentleman," boarded the *Philo Parsons* in Detroit to speak to Walter O. Ashley, part-owner and clerk of the ship, to say that he and his friends planned a pleasure trip the next morning to Kelley's Island, near Sandusky, and wanted the ship to stop at Sandwich, on the Canadian side, to pick up some more friends. Ashley said the skipper, Captain Sylvester F. Atwood, would likely agree, but because there was no custom house on Kelley's Island, they could not take on any baggage there.

The stranger, it turned out, was Bennett G. Burley (also spelled Burleigh in several accounts), one of the most colourful men in the Civil War saga, who, along with Beall, was destined to become a household name in both Canada and the United States. A Glasgow-born newspaper correspondent and adventurer, he had fought both with and against Garibaldi in Italy. He went to Richmond in 1861 to sell marine torpedoes patented by his father to the Confederacy, where he joined the CSN as a lieutenant and was involved in several clandestine operations. He is credited with having cut the U.S. cable to Delaware's Delmarva Peninsula, blowing up a U.S. lighthouse, and burning several U.S. ships on Chesapeake Bay. He was captured in May 1864, while laying torpedoes in the Rappahannock River, but soon escaped Fort Delaware by wading through the sewer system which flowed into the Delaware River. Two of his companions drowned, two were recaptured, but Burley and another man swam out into the river and were picked up by a ship, whose captain believed his story that they were fishermen whose boat had capsized, and taken to Philadelphia. From there, Burley made his way back to Toronto.

At 8 a.m. on September 19, with forty passengers, including Burley, the *Philo Parsons* left Detroit and picked up Burley's four friends at Sandwich, then made its regular stop at Malden, where about twenty men boarded, carrying with them a large black trunk filled with ropes. Ashley would testify later that he saw nothing unusual in that, since the ship often carried "skedaddlers" back to Ohio and he assumed that's what these men were. Each man paid his own fare in greenbacks and had no contact with those already onboard.

The boat continued with its regular stops at the various Lake Erie islands, including Middle Bass, where Captain Atwood lived, and where, as was his weekly custom, he went ashore to spend the night with his family. Up until that point, nothing unusual had happened.

As they approached Kelley's Island, however, Ashley reminded the men who had come on at Sandwich, but after speaking with four men who came onboard from the island dock, they told Ashley they were going on to Sandusky. When the *Philo Parsons* left Kelley's Island about 4 p.m., with mate D.C. Nichols in command in Atwood's absence, Ashley still had no reason for concern. But that quickly changed.

Shortly after passing within 300 feet of the steamer *Island Queen*, a clean-shaven man in a Kosuth hat (a soft hat with a low crown and medium brim) accosted Nichols on the hurricane deck, pulled a revolver, and announced he was one of thirty Confederate officers on board. He demanded that Nichols pilot the ship as directed. At the same time four armed rebels confronted Ashley, telling him he'd be shot if he offered resistance, and the old black trunk from Malden was opened, revealing a cache of revolvers, hatchets, and several other weapons. Two guards were left with Ashley, and others moved into the cabin, threatening to shoot anyone who resisted and frightening many of the women passengers.

Wheelsman Michael Campbell heard some shots and yelling and ran onto the deck, where he saw a man with a cocked revolver chasing the fireman and ordering him to the main hatch; otherwise, he would be shot. As Campbell scrambled up the ladder to the upper deck, a ball from the rebel's revolver passed between his legs and, when he reached that deck, he was confronted by five armed men who were ordering the passengers into the cabin. He was forced into the fire-hold with them, which was weighted down with pig iron, but later allowed to come up on the deck again when the rebels asked where the pilot was. In the meantime, the deckhands were ordered to toss the cargo of pig iron overboard.

Engineer James Denison, on hearing the commotion, arrived on the deck just as the man was shooting at Campbell. Denison, along with his fireman, was ordered at gunpoint to return to his engine room and obey orders.

The operation lasted about thirty minutes and, under Beall's orders, the *Philo Parsons* was taken to the entrance to Sandusky Bay, within easy view of the *Michigan*. When Beall learned that the ship did not have enough fuel to run the seven hours or so he had planned, he ordered her returned to Middle Bass Island, where its unscheduled reappearance sparked considerable fuss, particularly when the rebels fired at the local wood-yard owner and two other men who had refused to board. A local boy, alarmed that the rebels were shooting at his father, ran to Atwood's house, about a mile away, and when the captain arrived on the dock he was immediately taken prisoner.

At this point, the *Island Queen*, another wooden sidewheeler, arrived on its scheduled stop and several of the rebels immediately jumped on board, one of them shooting engineer Henry Haines through his nose, left cheek, and ear. He too was taken aboard the *Philo Parsons*, but, despite his injuries, was returned to the *Island Queen* when the rebels learned he was the engineer. All the *Island Queen*'s passengers – including about twenty-five soldiers from the 135th Ohio Volunteer Infantry who had gone to Toledo to be mustered out – were put aboard the *Philo Parsons*. After the captured deckhands loaded wood on the *Philo Parsons*, most of the prisoners were freed by Beall, including the unarmed soldiers, after agreeing not to fight against the Confederacy until they were properly exchanged and not to notify mainland officials for twenty-four hours. The island did not have telegraph service at the time.

Beall and Atwood went to the captain's quarters on the *Philo Parsons*, where Atwood was asked on his word of honour to stay on the island for twenty-four hours and take charge of the released prisoners. He promised to take the women to his home, where they would be more comfortable.

About 8 p.m. the *Philo Parsons*, towing the *Island Queen*, set off once again. A certain Captain Morgan had smashed the main injection valves of the *Island Queen*, allowing water to flood in, and the ship was set adrift between Middle Bass and Kelley's Island. (She was easily raised and repaired and was back in service within a week.) Next, the captives, except for the engineer and wheelsman of the *Parsons*, were ordered into the ship's hold.

Beall was still determined to complete the plan, but seventeen members of his crew, fearing they'd been found out, presented him with a protest, written on the blank side of a bill of lading and dated September 20. It expressed their "admiration of [Beall's] gentlemanly bearing, skill and courage" but continued: "Believing and being well-convinced that the enemy is already apprised of our approach, and is so well prepared that we can not by any possibility make it a success, and having already captured two boats, we respectfully decline to prosecute it any further."

Beall, given no option, ordered the ship back to the Detroit River, where it reached Malden about 4 a.m. He proceeded up the Canadian channel for about 3 miles, then sent a small boat laden with goods taken from the *Philo Parsons* ashore. Further along, about 8 a.m., all the passengers and all but three of the crew went ashore in two boats onto Fighting Island. The rebels finally docked at Sandwich and unloaded their booty before cutting the valves to sink the ship, though she, too, was back in service in less than a week. The two captives, Campbell and

Denison, immediately set foot for Windsor. Two of the rebels who had been caught making a hole in the cabin so they could remove the piano were arrested by Canadian customs officers for importing goods without a permit. They were arraigned before a justice of the peace, but, released on their own recognizance, they quickly disappeared.

While all this excitement was happening on the lake, Cole was faring even more poorly at Sandusky. He was arrested on September 19 and taken aboard the *Michigan* about 4 p.m., where his papers were examined. They revealed he had been a captain in the rebel army, had taken the oath of allegiance to the United States and been paroled at Memphis by General Stephen A. Hurlbut, and had corresponded with rebels in Windsor, Niagara Falls, Toronto, and other Canadian communities. When confronted, he apparently confessed to the whole plot, including the involvement of six prominent Sandusky men, all members of the Sons of Liberty, who were promptly arrested.

On September 20 Secretary of War Edwin M. Stanton telegraphed Major-General John A. Dix in New York about the "recent piracy on Lake Erie," ordering him to Buffalo to "make an official examination and report of the facts." Among other things, Dix later told Canadian authorities that Jacob Thompson had been staying at Sandwich with a Southerner named Colonel Steele – a Kentucky officer who was never positively identified – and recommended that Thompson be extradited under the Ashburton-Webster Treaty.

Thompson learned of Cole's capture from Annie Davis, Cole's companion in Sandusky, who had been registered in the hotel as Lady Harrisburg. She was, in fact, a prostitute named Emma Bison, whom Cole had met in Buffalo. Typically, given the chivalry of the times, her luggage was seized for inspection, but she was not arrested, even though she had been working with Cole, so she immediately left Sandusky for Toronto. On September 22 Thompson and Clay reported the fate of the project to President Davis, saying, "the scheme was admirable laid, and promised success" but was foiled "by some treachery." They asked Davis to intercede on Cole's behalf, claiming he had "violated no law or regulation of the enemy" but was being court-martialled as a spy. As a result, on October 12, Davis ordered War Secretary Benjamin, "through the commissioner of exchange or otherwise, as may be indicated," to "let all practicable efforts be made in behalf of Mr. Cole." Ironically, Cole was imprisoned at Johnson's Island. After attempting to escape on July 24, 1865, he was put in close confinement and, in September, transferred to Fort Lafayette in New York Harbor. He was discharged on February 10, 1866, following a writ of habeus corpus filed by sympathizers on his behalf.

As for Beall, he made a full report of the affair to Thompson, then went further north into Canada for a two-week hunting and fishing trip. After the *Globe* criticized the Confederate operations in Canada, Beall, in a published letter to the editor, wrote that the Confederates "have the right to retaliate, provided they can do so without infringing your laws." He said the United States is "carrying on war on Lake Erie against the Confederate states . . . by transportation of men and supplies on its waters; by confining Confederate prisoners on its islands; and lastly, by the presence of a 14-gun steamer patrolling its waters." Beall added that they did not break any Canadian laws because the plan "was matured, and sought to be carried out in the U.S., and not in Canada; there was not a Canadian, or any man enlisted in Canada, no act of hostility was committed on Canadian waters or soil." This claim, clearly, was not true.

After his holiday ended, however, Beall went back to work. On December 16, 1864, he and two Confederate companions, including a 16-year-old boy who turned state's evidence against him, were arrested on the American side near the Suspension Bridge separating Canada and the United States at Detroit, after an unsuccessful attempt to derail an eastbound passenger train and rob the express money on board. He was taken immediately to the Mulberry Street police station in New York City, then to Fort Lafayette in the harbour, and brought before a military court-martial on February 21, 1865, presided over by Brigadier-General Fitz Henry Warren, charged with being a spy and violating "the law of war" by carrying on an irregular or guerrilla war against the United States. Despite a letter from President Davis saying Beall was acting under his authority and that it was a legitimate act of war, Beall was found guilty on eleven charges and sentenced to be hanged on February 24.

The Confederacy had certainly tried to save Beall. Lieutenant Samuel Boyer Davis, an infantry officer who had been wounded in Pickett's charge at Gettysburg and subsequently placed briefly in command of the infamous Andersonville prison, happened to be at a party in Richmond's Spottswood Hotel on December 26, 1864. There he met Harry Brogden, a Marylander with the Confederate Signal Corps, which included the espionage service under its aegis, who told him he was headed for Canada to supply Thompson and Clay in Toronto with documents showing that Beall was a Confederate officer acting under orders in the Lake Erie raids. Brogden was loath to go, but Davis jumped at the chance, "and within 25 hours, carrying a British passport, with his hair dyed, and in civilian clothes, was on his way north . . . under the cover names of Willoughby Cummings and H.B. Stephenson, and at his capture gave his name as Stewart."[35]

Establishing Beall's bona fides never made any sense, since he was captured without his uniform and was considered a common criminal, forfeiting the normal protections of warfare afforded to combatants. The best they could hope for was to encourage some Canadian diplomatic protests, but, given American disdain for what they saw as continuing leniency, even compliance, by Canadian officials towards Confederate operatives, that wasn't likely. In any event, Davis made his way north, crossing the Potomac at Pope's Creek, Maryland, reaching Washington, and arriving at Toledo, where he stayed in a hotel lobby while his train was delayed. There, he listened to a U.S. Navy officer reading aloud from a newspaper telling how federal authorities were searching for a Confederate secret agent who was carrying the papers Davis had in his bag. He continued on and reached Detroit via Columbus, crossed over at Windsor, and met with Thompson.

When Davis left for the South many weeks later, he was carrying several secret messages, some of them written on white silk and sewn into the lining of his jacket – a sophisticated technique that Colonel George Taylor Denison of Toronto bragged about introducing to the Confederates. The advantage of silk is that, unlike paper, it did not rustle under prying hands. Denison, a wealthy military historian and prolific author, went on to become Toronto's chief police magistrate and, later, a prominent federal member of parliament, heading the Canada First Movement, a pro-British/anti-American/anti-Catholic group. He was an unabashed Southern sympathizer during the war, a fact that didn't hurt his later political career. His mansion, "Heydon Villa," occupied a huge section of what is now west Toronto, where Denison Avenue is named after him, and was "built as a replica of a southern mansion with a neoclassical columned verandah."[36]

When Davis boarded a southbound train near Newark, Ohio, two Union soldiers who had recently been exchanged from Andersonville recognized him. Despite his British passport and his denials when they confronted him, they posted themselves at the door and got the conductor to telegraph the provost martial, who met Davis on the platform at Newark and marched him off to jail. The officer, however, failed to find the secret messages, and Davis was placed in a large room with several other prisoners. The room had a stove, which Davis promptly used to burn the incriminating silk messages. Obviously, the reports from the U.S. consul in Toronto telling the secretary of state that Confederate spies were carrying messages in coat pockets and "making highly reduced photographic reproductions of other messages and concealing them in coat buttons, a very modern touch in that day, when photography was in its infancy" had not been heeded.[37]

Davis was court-martialled, condemned to death, and sent to Johnson's Island for execution. He was such a gentleman that, after the trial, the members of the court martial all shook hands with him and expressed their personal regret at his situation. On February 1 he was shown a newspaper clipping announcing his execution for sixteen days hence. "Fighting Joe" Hooker, the local Federal commander, reportedly said of Davis "he's no spy" but approved the sentence anyway. And Lieutenant Lewis A. Bond, the judge advocate who had prosecuted him, wrote to compliment Davis on his "manly conduct and heroic bearing." On February 9 he was told by a guard that he would not be hanged, and the same thing was repeated two days later. On February 13 Lincoln telegraphed officials asking that Davis's life be spared, but his telegram was so ambiguously worded that it almost had the opposite effect. "Is it not Lt. S.B. Davis, convicted as a rebel spy, whose sentence has been commuted; if not, let it not be done." Officials were not sure what that meant, and on February 15 Davis had a clear view of the gallows being erected. When he awoke on hanging day, he could see the rope being tested and the large crowds gathering to watch, at which point the commanding officer entered his cell and said, "I have a commutation for you; your sentence is commuted." Davis was sent to Fort Delaware in irons, where he was beaten by guards for saying he had handled more prisoners than the fort commander and had never put one in irons. After six weeks in an Albany cell, he was sent to prison hospital after several citizens protested his treatment, and then on to Fort Warren in Boston. He was released on December 4, 1865, prompting Stanton to grumble that he should have been hanged.

Beall wasn't as lucky. Widely celebrated as a hero and martyr in the South, he was allowed a visit from his mother and, about 1 p.m. on the appointed day, his arms were pinioned, a military cape thrown over his shoulders, and a black cap put on his head. Beall, a former lay member of the Episcopal Diocesian convention of Virginia, was marched to the scaffold with a soldier's guard, while an Episcopalian minister read a commendatory prayer. Showing no outward signs of fear or nervousness, Beall was asked if he had anything to add. "I protest against the execution of the sentence," he said. "It is absolute murder – brutal murder. I die in the defence and service of my country." Asked if he wanted to say anything else, Beall replied: "No. I beg you to make haste." At 1:13 a.m., February 24, 1865, with the black cap drawn over his face, the signal was given and Beall, his neck broken, died instantly.

The March 13, 1865, *Montreal Gazette* carried a story from the *Richmond Examiner* on "the murder, by hanging, of Capt. John Y. Beall, under the signature of and by authority of Lincoln." It reported that the Confederate Senate had unanimously approved a resolution calling for "such steps as may be necessary for retaliation" and praising Beall as a martyr and hero.

Burley's story, however, is something else again.

Another little-known Canadian connection to the Lake Erie adventures involves a Canadian-built freight propellor ship called the *Georgian*. It also involved a prominent family in Guelph, Ontario, headed by Scottish immigrant Adam Robertson, who established two iron foundries there, including one in partnership with the Inglis family (famous for appliances), and opened his own factory in 1852 on Eramosa Road. Robertson's cousin Bennett Burley also played his role in the affair.

It was common knowledge in Guelph at the time that the Robertson and Son foundries were manufacturing much more than ploughs for local farmers. They were, in fact, making munitions, specifically cannons and cannonballs, for the Confederates.

This illegal activity in no way hurt Robertson's popularity. A long-time town councillor and respected employer, Robertson later became mayor and successfully lobbied the provincial government to pick Guelph over competing sites for the Ontario School of Agriculture and the Experimental Farm, forerunners of the Ontario Agricultural College.

Also living in Guelph at the time and helping to facilitate Confederate activities there was the Reverend Kensey Johns Stewart, an Episcopalian minister who had resigned as chaplain in General Winder's command in Richmond and, along with the Reverend Stephen F. Cameron and others, gone to England, ostensibly to arrange for publication of prayer books for the Confederacy but, in fact, to be trained by the British in spying techniques and sent to Canada to help the cause.

In 1864, after the failure of the Johnson's Island caper, two Canadian businessmen, George Wyatt and A.M. Smith, had just purchased the newly constructed 130-foot, 377-ton *Georgian*, built at the Potter shipyard at Port McNicoll at the mouth of the Severn River in Georgian Bay. Both men were well-known Confederate supporters and had sold at least one ship to rebel blockade-runners. When they learned that Colonel Thompson was still determined to launch an armed ship on the Great Lakes, they met Thompson and Kentuckian Dr. John Bates, a former Mississippi River pilot, in Toronto and, on November 1, sold them the *Georgian* for $17,000. They planned to fit the *Georgian* for military purposes and, with Bates as captain, to cause havoc to U.S. commercial vessels. If things went well, they would use the *Georgian* to capture more ships and create a fleet of "commerce raiders."[38] On the downside, the *Georgian* had only a 70 horsepower engine, which meant a top speed of 8 miles per hour. Still, because the vessel was built to carry heavy loads at a shallow draft, she was solid and could venture into areas of the lake where the deep-drafted USS *Michigan* couldn't go.

Having bought the *Georgian*, the next move was to transform her into a fighting vessel. Part of the plan was to strengthen her bow so she could be used to ram U.S. commercial vessels. Thompson and Bates also wanted her armed, which is where Robertson and his cannons entered the picture. Stewart, Burley, and others met with Robertson, likely in his Mitchell Street home in Guelph, to arrange for the cannon and cannonballs.

Although the Johnson's Island plan had failed in practical terms, it had created a stir among Americans living along the lakes, generating a host of widely published stories about supposed Confederate attacks from Canada and prompting several Northern cities to form citizen militias to defend themselves against the impending raids. In Buffalo, for example, rumours of a large Confederate force gathering in Toronto and Hamilton and preparing to attack that city caused outright panic, leading local officials to place cannons on two local tugs to fend off the marauders and prompting Union officials to dispatch four regiments of soldiers to the lake.

It was into this atmosphere on November 3 that Bates docked the *Georgian* at Buffalo. The next day Mayor William Fargo telegraphed the USS *Michigan* to say the *Georgian* was bent on freeing the prisoners at Johnson's Island, prompting U.S. Navy Secretary Gideon Welles to order the *Michigan* to seize the ship on any pretext it could.

Buffalo officials boarded the ship, but when they failed to find any weapons or contraband, they had to let her go. After stopping at Amherstburg for repairs, then lying to at Amherstburg, the *Michigan*, responding to Detroit media reports of an impending attack on that city, cruised nearby keeping a cautious eye on what crew members were convinced was a rebel privateer. The *Georgian* left Amherstburg, only to be stopped first by U.S. customs house officials and then by two revenue cutters (tugs with mounted cannons) under the command of Lieutenant-Colonel Bennet Hill of Detroit – a player in the *Philo Parsons* Affair. Again, since they could find no contraband, the *Georgian* was allowed to sail on to Sarnia, where Bates went ashore to order that a new propellor be sent ahead to Collingwood and where Canadian authorities, responding to American pressure, seized her on the grounds that she was a shipping hazard. But this charge didn't stick either, and the *Georgian* once again headed off, this time to Bruce Mines on Georgian Bay, intent on laying up for the winter for repairs.

In the meantime, Robertson was busy making the cannons for her in Guelph. Union officials, believing that Beall was overseeing the operation – when, actually, it was Burley who was superintending the job – demanded that Canadian authorities arrest the fugitive, so police raided the plant and seized some cannons and a large quantity of cannonballs. Apart from a stiff lecture and soliciting a promise that the factory would not make any more munitions for the rebels, the police did nothing to the Robertsons. (The family managed to hide one cannon until 1892, when Adam Jr., to celebrate his mother's birthday, had it mounted on the front lawn of their home. When the home was sold in 1920, the cannon went to another relative in Guelph, but it was finally shipped to British Columbia when the family moved west. Today the cannon overlooks Vancouver's Horseshoe Bay.)

In light of widespread American panic over the Johnson's Island plot, and with Union spies reporting the Confederate activities at Guelph, U.S. officials continued to push Canadian officials to make some arrests in the case and to extradite the criminals to stand trial in the United States. Finally, in late November, detectives were dispatched from Toronto to Guelph, where they arrested a Captain Bell – whom they thought was Beall but was, in fact, Burley. They brought him to Toronto to stand trial, where it took some time to establish his identity, and charged him with taking part in the attack and trying to murder the engineer of the *Island Queen*.

Burley appeared for a preliminary trial on November 22 before a two-man panel in Police Court, where his defence lawyer, M.C. Cameron, pointed out he had been arrested under an improper warrant. Police had used information from a woman who had been on board the steamer *Island Queen*, so the court released him. As he left the court with a group of his cheering friends, he was arrested again. Back in court the next day, he was identified by Gertrude Titus of Detroit as one of the pirates on the *Philo Parsons*, although she thought of him as "Colonel Bell," testifying that "after the seizure he did all the ordering and commanding and was very active."

Following a remand, on December 7 Burley, who by now was known to officials by his proper name, appeared before Toronto Recorder George Duggan in a courtroom crowded with Southern refugees, many of whom were then living in Toronto. They testified on Burley's behalf that, as a member of the Confederate Navy, he was legally authorized to do what he did. One of the defence witnesses, Captain Robert Kennedy of Louisiana, who had escaped from Johnson's Island and had been living in St. Catharines, London, and Toronto "for several weeks," was committed for contempt for refusing to answer a question from Crown consul R.A. Harrison about where he had been living since October 4 – no doubt because he, too, was one of the Lake Erie pirates.

In an affidavit sworn on December 8 before Duggan and presented to the court, Burley, claiming his commission as a naval officer was taken when he was imprisoned on May 13 at Fort Delaware, asked for a one-month postponement to allow him to produce documentation from Richmond that "the capture of the *Philo Parsons* was an act of hostility against the Federal Government of the United States, under due authority, and was not made with any design to plunder or commit piracy, but for the express purpose of aiding in the capture of the Federal vessel of war *Michigan* and the release of Confederate prisoners on Johnson's Island . . . I claim the privilege of a belligerent and protest against my being sent out of the Province of Ontario."

After lengthy legal debates, lawyer Alfred Russell, representing the U.S. government, said on December 10 that he was prepared to admit that Burley held a commission as master in the navy of the "so-called Confederate states," but felt the extradition trial should continue. The judge disagreed and adjourned the trial for a month, sending Burley back to jail in the meantime. The *Globe* story reported that Jacob Thompson was among the large crowd on hand that day and "during the proceedings Mr. Cameron frequently consulted with him and other friends of the accused."

On Christmas Eve 1864 in Richmond, President Davis issued a proclamation that the expedition in which Burley participated in "was a proper, and legitimate belligerent operation, undertaken during the pending public war between the two Confederacies . . . and that the Government of the Confederate States of America assumes the responsibility of answering for the acts and conduct of any of its officers engaged in said expedition, and especially of the said Bennett G. Burley, an acting master in the Navy of the Confederate States.

"And I do further make known to all whom it may concern that in the orders and instructions given to the officers engaged in said expedition they were specially directed and enjoined to 'abstain from violating any of the laws and regulations of the Canadian and British authorities in relation to neutrality . . .'" The custom at the time was that once a government had assumed responsibility for an individual's actions, the action became national in character and therefore not subject to jurisdiction of the criminal courts. But in trying to protect Burley, Davis actually hurt his case, since it was obvious that Burley had disobeyed direct orders against violating the laws of Canada regarding neutrality.

The case resumed on December 31, again before a packed courtroom and amid much excitement both in Canada and the United States, with Burley facing a new charge of robbery against Walter O. Ashley of Detroit, the clerk and part owner of the *Philo*

Parsons. Again, Burley had been allowed to walk out of court because a witness had not appeared, but as he left he was re-arrested on the theft charge and the case was adjourned for twenty-four hours.

The next day Ashley testified that a man calling himself Captain Bell, who actually was Beall, had made the arrangements the previous September for himself and a group of friends to travel on the *Philo Parsons*, but, after taking over the ship, "Bell" and two others had pointed their revolvers at him and taken $2,000 from his office, plus another $20 when they made him empty his pockets. Russell, this time representing the state of Michigan, argued that, under the *Piracy Act* of 1790, Burley could be tried in Michigan, even though the crime had occurred in Ohio.

The case resumed again on January 10, when the defence formally introduced Davis's proclamation, but was adjourned for yet another day following lengthy legal quarrels. The next day William L. (Larry) Macdonald, who operated an explosives factory in Toronto and had been involved in various Confederate secret service work in Canada before Thompson's arrival, testified that he had helped to send unarmed Confederate soldiers back to the South and that he had no doubt Burley was a legitimate Confederate officer. The public mood over the issue was such that, a month later, Macdonald was attacked and beaten near the York Street Inn in Toronto by a group of Northern sympathizers who had been taunting a group of Southerners by shouting "How are you, Burley?" Around the same time, Duggan was attacked by Southern sympathizers as he walked near his home. Even the elderly wife of the late Alderman Sterling, who had been involved in the initial warrant against Burley, was approached by a man near her Church Street home who said, "If it hadn't been for your dead husband, Burley would not be where he is." The man, obviously not a practitioner of Southern chivalry, knocked her down, bruising her right shoulder as she fell on the planking.

On January 21 Recorder Duggan committed Burley to extradition, sending him back to jail pending notification to the governor general, who had the authority to surrender the prisoner to U.S. authorities. The *New York Tribune* published a sensational story claiming that rebels in Canada planned another raid to capture the Clinton State Prison at Dannemora, New York, and then to raid Plattsburg and various New England towns. It claimed the Canadian rebels would hook up with a Confederate detachment from the Confederate States Army which had worked its way north and was then hiding in New York and Baltimore.

That same day the pro-Confederate *Toronto Leader* published an account of Burley's friends, honouring M.C. Cameron "for his spirited defence of Burley." They assembled at the Terrapin Restaurant at 8 p.m. and "some in sleighs, which contained a large number of ladies, and some on foot, formed a procession." Headed by the band of the Queen's Own Rifles, they "marched up King Street and down Bay Street to the Queen's Hotel, where their ranks were augmented." From the hotel, they marched up York Street, then down King Street to Cameron's home, where the band played "that inspiring tune, 'Bonnie Blue flag,' and other Southern airs." It described the crowd as containing "several hundred people." Speaking to the assembly, Cameron said that Burley was no common criminal, but a man on "a noble mission . . . who ought to have the approbation of the people of this country rather than their condemnation."

On January 27 four judges in the Practice Court unanimously agreed with Recorder Duggan's decision to hand Burley over to the Americans. At 11 p.m. on February 3, 1865, Burley, handcuffed and chained, was taken by sleigh to Union Station and boarded on a special Great Western Railway train, ordered by the Canadian government, guarded by about two dozen soldiers from the 16th Regiment of the Queen's Own Rifles, and delivered to American Customs House authorities at the Suspension Bridge at Detroit. He spent the night without irons at the Wadsworth House in Detroit and, the next day, deputy U.S. marshals Joseph Dinnuick and James Henry of the Eastern District of Michigan arrived by train in Buffalo with Burley in custody. In June the grand jury at Port Clinton, Ohio, indicted Burley on three counts and, ironically, he was shipped to Sandusky aboard the *Philo Parsons*, where he was transferred to the *General Grant*, taken to Paster Bed on the north shore of the bay, and, finally, to Port Clinton by carriage.

Incredibly, after a trial presided over by Judge John Fitch of Toledo, the jury reported it could not agree on a verdict. Fitch had instructed jury members that, as a belligerent, Burley had every right to capture the steamer, but he had no right to rob people for his own personal benefit, and, therefore, the only act the jury could consider was the robbery charge. Burley was remanded again to prison, with bail set at $3,000. Since no bail was paid, Burley stayed in jail awaiting a second trial.

It was not a popular decision. In an editorial, the *Detroit Tribune* wrote: "The decision . . . is a judicial outrage and disgrace. It is an open and positive justification of piracy, and is in all respects atrocious. Where was Judge Fitch when all these facts were transpiring? Was he insane, was he drunk; was he in the rebel army; was he making Copperhead speeches – where was he? Judge Fitch evidently needs looking after. If he is an ignoramus he ought to be removed. If he is a rebel sympathizer he ought to be impeached."[39]

The cells in the Ottawa County Jail stood at the centre of the first floor of the Court House, near a small hall that opened into the jail hall. Sheriff James P. Lattimore and his family lived in the rooms along the hall. On Sunday, September 17, 1865, the Lattimores went for a short visit to the country, giving Burley the run of the hall. About 5 p.m. a man sent by the sheriff arrived with Burley's supper but found two things missing: the sheriff's keys and Burley, although Burley had left a note on his Bible reading: "Sunday – I have gone out for a walk – Perhaps (?) I will return shortly. B.B. Burley."

Burley quickly returned to Toronto, where he stayed for a time at the Queen's Hotel, unmolested by Canadian officials, who surely must have known of his presence. He returned to Scotland and become one of the world's most famous war correspondents for the *London Daily Telegraph*, covering two Egyptian uprisings, the French campaign in Madagascar, the Ashanti expedition, the first Greco-Turkish war, and several other conflicts. He also published several best-selling books – now spelling his last name as Burleigh – and died in London on June 17, 1914.

TEN

Blockade Busters

O N AUGUST 6, 1861, JUST FOUR MONTHS into the Civil War, U.S. officials in Halifax spotted a schooner from New Bern, North Carolina, travelling under British registry, slipping quietly into the harbour. Having never heard of New Bern, the consul, J.E. Vinton, was suspicious that the British registry was one of convenience to hide the Southern ownership and the real purpose of the visitor. He was correct: the schooner was the first of hundreds of blockade-runners that would use Halifax, a city of around 40,000 people, as a useful and highly profitable port from which to conduct business with the Confederacy. The business not only helped the Confederacy prolong the war but turned some Haligonians into wealthy entrepreneurs and generally helped the city prosper throughout the entire period.

Author Thomas H. Raddall writes that the owner of the Halifax Hotel "could hardly buy champagne fast enough, for the southerners, with old-fashioned notions of hospitality and with the official classes and the military to win over, put no restraint on their lavishness . . . one man said he held one million dollars for a southern agent who was temporarily in hiding and entrusted Confederate notes to his care . . . [another] saw a man in a large wholsesale dry goods store in Halifax ask the proprietor the price for his whole establishment, spot cash.

"Halifax was prosperous as never before in all her boom and

bust history. The city was glutted with money. In 1864 the Merchants' Bank was founded on the strength of it, and, for complete coverage, so was the People's Bank. The semiweekly auctions of stocks and bonds in the Merchants' Exchange Reading Room were lively affairs."[1]

Five days after the attack on Fort Sumter, President Lincoln declared a sea blockade of six Southern states that had seceded and, eight days later, extended it to include North Carolina and Virginia. At that point, neither of those states had formally seceded, but they did a month later – no doubt influenced by Lincoln's precipitous move.

The blockade covered 3,000 miles of coastline, from Chesapeake Bay to the Rio Grande, but at the time the Americans lacked the sea power to enforce it. The U.S. Navy had just forty vessels, and they were spread around the world, leaving only about six to enforce the blockade. Early blockade-running was therefore relatively safe and easy. As the war dragged on, however, the Union fleet grew rapidly – by late 1863 it had 500 vessels, principally steamers taken from the merchant service and converted into cruisers. By the end of the war the U.S. Navy had 670 vessels, dramatically increasing the risks of blockade-running. But then, potential profits increased exponentially as the risks shot up.

In Nova Scotia the blockade immediately affected the profitable gypsum mining industry, whose main customer was the Southern United States. It also hurt the profitable carrying trade that Nova Scotia had developed over the years between the West Indies and the Southern states. Over time, however, things changed, and a profitable system developed in which large British ships would carry cargo to Nassau in the Bahamas, Hamilton in Bermuda, or Halifax, where it would be stored in warehouses, then reloaded onto the faster, sleeker, low-draught blockade-runners and shipped through the blockade to various Southern ports. Much of the coal to run Confederate steamers went

through Halifax, particularly Cardiff coal, or anthracite, the most
sought-after fuel because it was not only efficient but gave off little smoke, making it more difficult for Union ships to detect the
enemy. But it was not just materials of war that were shipped: the
haul included everyday products that Southerners demanded,
such as soap, cigars, pepper, coffee, whisky, sherry wine, bay rum,
hams, cheeses, boots, candles, and wire frames for hoop skirts
and bonnets.

There was even more money to be made exporting products
from the South, "enough to make any opportunist drool." In
1863–64, cotton, which sold for six cents a pound in the South,
commanded from 56 to 66 cents a pound laid down in England.
That meant a steamer with an average capacity of 800 bales could
earn $420,000 on a round trip. And since the South could not
produce the iron it needed, the price during the war rose from
$25 to $1,500 a ton. "It was a common saying among the
blockade-running fraternity that a shipowner could shrug off the
loss of his vessel after two safe round trips through the blockade."[2]

The potential profit was also reflected in the pay to the crew.
A captain could expect $5,000 for a single round trip from
Nassau to Wilmington, while a pilot made $3,750, the chief engi-
neer, $2,500, and even a crewman or fireman, $250, paid either
in British gold or U.S. currency – enormous sums for the day. In
addition, officers were allowed to stow away their own cargoes
and make their own deals on each trip.

At the same time, Nova Scotians continued trading with the
North, particularly New England. In 1862 Nova Scotia became
the leading supplier of fish and coal to the North, and shipbuilders and merchants prospered as a result. That year alone,
customs revenue for the port of Halifax jumped by more than
$210,000 over 1861, and by 1865 Nova Scotian exports to the
United States increased by more than 50 percent, thanks largely
to coal, fish, molasses, cotton goods, and refined sugar.

As the illegal and highly profitable trade with the South continued and more Confederates moved to town, Confederate sympathies were so pronounced that the December 16, 1863, *Halifax Sun* described Halifax as "a hot southern town." The Confederates established an informal headquarters at Waverley House, which still exists on Barrington Street, while hosting lavish parties at the Halifax Hotel to win friends and influence the right people. Dealing with the South became so popular that even Albert Pillsbury, who was the U.S. consul in Halifax before Vinton took over briefly, was later found to have been selling arms to the Confederacy, shipping them to the South concealed in barrels of fish.

When former Wisconsin Supreme Court Judge Mortimer Melville Jackson sailed into Halifax Harbour in mid-August 1861 to replace Vinton – who was retiring because of ill health after only two months on the job – the two men walked along Water Street on their way to the consulate on Bedford Row. Vinton pointed out three ships in the harbour, all flying the Union Jack, and explained that they were owned by Yankee merchants who had registered them in Britain, a neutral country. But they had all arrived from New Bern, carrying cargoes of naval stores and tobacco – a popular dodge by Northern merchants to beat the blockade.

Jackson became the most active and most effective of all his country's consuls-general in the war. He was so successful in building a network of informers that his efforts were noted in the stridently pro-Confederate *Toronto Leader*, in an article denouncing Federal "detectives" hanging around railway stations, hotels, bars, and other places spying on the locals in Toronto and Montreal. The article also attacked Jackson in Halifax and his "despicable minions" of Washington: "It may be well for our merchants to know that certain individuals frequent the Reading Room for the express purpose of reporting their conversations to the Head of the Spy Department in this city."

In a 1981 article, former U.S. foreign service officer H. Franklin Irwin Jr. writes that Jackson's efforts made him *persona non grata* in his prosperous neighbourhood on Hollis Street. "His neighbors no longer greeted him or joined him in their daily drives to their offices. Their ladies snubbed Mrs. Jackson. Mrs. Jackson, childless and in delicate health, found the loneliness, the raw, cold, windy city, and her husband's work almost more than she could bear."[3] Indeed, Benjamin Wier, Dr. William J. Almon, and Alexander Keith, three of Jackson's most implacable and influential foes, were among his neighbours.

As Jackson continued to submit regular detailed reports on cargoes and sailing dates to Washington by military telegraph, he was having such an impact on the Halifax trade that the Confederates simply moved more of their operations to St. George's in Bermuda and Nassau in the Bahamas, where communication wasn't as advanced. For a time, Halifax diminished in importance as a blockade-running port, further alienating Jackson from many of the city's leading families who were profiting handsomely from that trade, particularly Wier, Almon, and Keith Jr. – the nephew of the prosperous brewer of the same name, but the black sheep of an otherwise noble family. Then fate intervened on Halifax's behalf: the 1863 and 1864 yellow fever epidemics in the islands frightened traders and brought many of the small ships back to Halifax, which once again became a popular Confederate haven. Jackson was so persistent in his fight to undermine the Confederates and their local surrogates that he even managed to convince Washington, for the first time in that country's history, to set up a separate account – with the princely sum of $300 in it – for him to pay informants who had "aided in several important captures." Until then, consuls-general were expected to look after that sort of thing from their own salary, so most, naturally, didn't bother.

Until late in the war, every request Jackson made to provincial authorities in Nova Scotia for detention of ships loading supplies for the South was refused, even though that was supposed to be a violation of Britain's neutrality declaration. Finally, in 1864, U.S. Secretary of State William Seward, reacting to Jackson's persistent pleas, sent a personal note to the British asking that Jackson be allowed to approach the provincial officials directly, rather than diplomatically through the British legation in Washington. Seward wrote: "Halifax has been for more than a year . . . a naval station for vessels running the blockade . . . and it has been a rendezvous for piratical cruisers which came out of Liverpool and Glasgow to destroy our commerce . . . Halifax is a postal and despatch station in the correspondence between the rebels and Richmond and their various emissaries in Europe. Halifax merchants are known to have surreptitiously imported provisions, arms and ammunition for our seaports and transhipped them to the rebels . . . Merchant shippers of Halifax are willing agents and abettors of the enemies of the United States; and their hostility has proved not merely offensive, but deeply injurious. When Nova Scotia shall cease to abet our enemy, she will find that we cherish no memories of her past injuries."[4]

After that intervention, Jackson was able to negotiate directly with Lieutenant-Governor Sir Richard MacDonnell. Even then, he often ran into bureaucratic roadblocks, but at least until the end of the war he enjoyed limited success in having contraband cargoes impounded by local officials – most of whom were openly unsympathetic to the Union. But of all the envoys the United States had abroad, none was more diligent or more effective in the cause of the Union than Jackson was at Halifax.

In all wars, of course, there are numerous stories of extraordinary adventure, human drama, and unbridled heroism, and a few people emerge with lasting fame. Perhaps the two most famous people connected with Halifax during the Civil War were, not surprisingly, two sea captains: John Wilkinson, a noted blockade-runner, and John Taylor Wood, the man who rescued the CSS *Tallahassee* from a Union trap, both of whom retired to Halifax after the war and wrote best-selling books on their exploits. They even opened a joint seafaring business together, proudly flying the Confederate flag on the Halifax wharf.

We have already met Wilkinson briefly during his role in leading the first aborted attempt by the Confederacy to free their prisoners on Johnson's Island in Lake Erie, one of the few significant projects he did not succeed in completing. Born November 6, 1821, in Amelia County, Virginia, while his father, Jesse, was at sea in the sloop-of-war *Hornet*, Wilkinson joined the U.S. Navy at the age of 16 and rose to the rank of lieutenant, before opting for the Confederacy and becoming one of the leading Confederate blockade busters in the war.

A common, somewhat cynical, blockade-runner's toast of the period went: "Here's to the Southern planters who grow the cotton; to the Yankees that maintain the blockade and keep up the price of cotton; to the Limeys who buy the cotton. So, three cheers for a long continuance of the war, and success to the blockade-runners." Wilkinson enjoyed more of that success as a blockade-runner than just about anybody, but, unlike the vast majority of his compatriots – many of whom, if they weren't caught or killed, became fabulously wealthy – he didn't do it for the money: he did it for the Confederacy, and as a Confederate naval officer, not a privateer.

As commander of the legendary runner *Robert E. Lee*, Wilkinson made twenty-one runs through the blockade, exporting 7,000 bales of cotton from Charleston and Wilmington, worth about $2 million, and returning with much-needed supplies of arms and ammunition. He gained lasting fame by devising ingenious ways of avoiding Federal gunboats through the clever use of decoy signal rockets and smoke screens. In his memoirs, Wilkinson, a lifelong bachelor, described the ideal blockade-runner as "a low, long, rakish looking lead-colored steamer with short masts and a convex forecastle deck extending nearly as far aft as the waist, and placed there to enable her to be forced through and not over a heavy head sea. These were the genuine blockade-runners, built for speed; and some of them survived all the desperate hazards of the war."[5] Many didn't, including his prized *Robert E. Lee*, which was sunk when Wilkinson was not in command – a result of his assignment to Johnson's Island.

When the war broke out, Wilkinson resigned his commission in the U.S. Navy and volunteered for service directly to Confederate Navy Secretary Stephen R. Mallory in Richmond. His first task was helping to erect naval batteries and train navy crews along the James River. Then, as an executive officer on the man-of-war *Louisiana* during the Battle of New Orleans, he was captured and confined for several months at Boston's Fort Warren. He was exchanged in 1862 and sent to England by Mallory to buy a ship for the Confederacy. He purchased the 283-foot *Giraffe* from Alexander Collie & Company for $160,000, along with arms, clothing, and munitions, and refitted her into a blockade-runner. When he sailed thirty days later, twenty-six Scottish lithographers were among the passengers, hired by the Confederate treasury to design and print paper money. He made his first run through the blockade on December 28, 1862, arriving in Wilmington, North Carolina, where the *Giraffe* was rechristened the *Robert E. Lee*.

It didn't take Wilkinson long to notice a pattern among the patrolling Union blockade-spotters along the Atlantic coastline. When a runner was sighted, the spotter would fire a rocket gun, sending up a rocket in the direction of the runner's course to tell other spotters which way to go to catch the blockade-runner. Rockets came in different colours, with each one having a particular meaning. Wilkinson decided to use the Union system against them. He ordered a set of brightly coloured rockets from a New York pyrotechnics firm, detailed an officer to stand watch, and, when a Union blockader sent up a rocket, his man would fire another of the same colour, but at an angle to his own course, thereby creating enough confusion among the pursuers to affect his escape. This simple but effective tactic was quickly adopted by other Confederate blockade-runners.

Wilkinson's most famous gambit, however, was the "smoke-screen" he devised in April 1863, a device that was so successful it was still being used by the navies of Great Britain, Germany, and the United States during the two world wars in the twentieth century. As he was pursued by the swifter USS *Iroquois*, which was gaining on him, Wilkinson ordered his chief engineer to saturate cotton in turpentine and toss it into his ship's furnace. He immediately speeded up, but, several hours into the chase, the cotton, which had not burned cleanly, had choked the flues and the *Robert E. Lee* was losing steam and in danger of being captured. Wilkinson ordered his chief engineer to manufacture smoke – as much and as black as possible – then stand by to cut off the smoke instantly by closing the dampers. At the same time, his helmsman spun the wheel hard to starboard, changed the steamer's course, and, under the cloud of thick, black smoke, his vessel escaped – the first instance of using a smokescreen to flee a pursuing ship.

During the war, Wilkinson made several trips to Halifax, which sits 800 miles north of Wilmington, to load and unload supplies. In his memoirs, he recalls somewhat wistfully that he escaped the war "dead broke," although with a clear conscience, despite countless opportunities to make money "when thousands of dollars were invested in a single venture and profits were so immense that the game was well worth the candle . . . there are times when I cannot decide whether I acted the part of a fool, or a patriot."[6]

After the war, Wilkinson was regarded as a celebrity by the local gentry, many of whom assisted him financially. The most senior among the thirty or so senior Confederate army or navy officers who settled in Halifax after the war was former Confederate Commodore Josiah Tattnall, the son of a one-time Georgia govenor. Tattnall is immortalized for his famous quote that "Blood is thicker than water," uttered to justify his violation of U.S. neutrality during the Taiping Rebellion in China, when he aided British warships trapped on the Pei-ho River. He bought Rosebank Park in the Northwest Arm in Halifax, subdivided it into 130 "high-class building lots," and constructed a magnificent manor on rising ground on a tree-lined avenue near the middle of the park. After the real estate market collapsed, however, he returned penniless to Georgia in 1870 and, until he died the following year, took a job as inspector of shipping at Savannah.

Another Confederate refugee who called Halifax home after the war – although a far more unsavoury character – was Captain Thomas E. Courtenay, the developer of the "Courtenay torpedo." This explosive devise was made to look like a chunk of coal, but, when placed among the coal used for a ship's fuel and thrown into the furnace, it produced a massive explosion. Courtenay was responsible for the destruction of at least two Union ships this way, the steamer *Maria*, killing twenty-five Union soldiers, and the *Sultana*, loaded with more than 2,000 people, most of them Union POWs returning from Southern prison camps. This explosion resulted in the death of 1,800 people, including a number of women, children, and civilian men. It killed as many Union soldiers as in Tennessee at Shiloh – a Biblical word from the Hebrew for "place of peace" – one of the bloodiest battles in the entire war.

Wilkinson also got to know another famous sea captain, John Taylor Wood, who lived the rest of his life on Morris Street. They set up a shipping business together as Halifax agents for Cromwell, a line of steamers running between Halifax and New York. Years later, after Wilkinson had returned to his old Virginia home, dying there on December 29, 1891, Wood established his own business and managed a line of steamships trading with Newfoundland. He was also secretary of the Harbor Pilotage Commission and was extremely active in yachting circles and the Church of England.

Wood had been born in Minnesota in 1830 to good stock. His father was U.S. Army General Robert C. Wood; his grandfather, the twelfth U.S. President Zachary Taylor; and his uncle, Confederate President Jefferson Davis. He joined the U.S. Navy at 17, fought in the Mexican War, switched to the Confederacy in 1861, and served on the staff of his uncle, President Davis. He was engaged in the first fight of the iron-clads, for the *Virginia* (or the *Merrimac* as she was known in the North) against the *Monitor* at Hampton Roads on March 9, 1862 – a battle that revolutionized the navies of the world, instantly making whole fleets of wooden ships obsolete.

After that battle, Wood became master of the 200-foot, 700-ton, twin-screw iron steamer *Tallahassee*, formerly the *Atlanta*. As the fastest ocean steamship in the Confederate service, she became widely feared as "the terror of the North," as both a blockade-runner and a destroyer of Northern commerce. During a nineteen-day raid out of Wilmington in early August 1864, with a crew of 120 officers and men, the *Tallahassee* destroyed twenty-six Northern vessels and captured seven others, not including a couple of dozen fishing vessels that Wood also sunk. With a total of thirteen Union war ships in pursuit, the *Tallahassee* sailed into Halifax for coal on August 18, where the Confederates had brazenly established a coaling station at Ben Wier's wharf – an obvious breach of neutrality laws – anchoring inside George's Island on a cold and rainy day, with wet fog hanging over the water. Under the terms of Queen Victoria's proclamation of neutrality – and despite continuing American complaints about it – belligerents using British ports had forty-eight hours to complete their bunkering process before leaving the protected waters of such ports.

The arrival of such a famous sea raider caused great excitement in town. Dozens of small boats surrounded the ship to get a better look, and several hundred people gathered along the water that day and the next, hoping to witness a battle between the Confederate vessel and the U.S. warships waiting just outside neutral waters. The outrage caused by the *Tallahassee* in Washington prompted Lord Lyons, the British ambassador to the United States, to warn both London and Halifax about this new and serious threat to Anglo-American relations. Jackson, for his part, appealed to Lieutenant-General MacDonnell to detain the ship. Dr. Almon entertained the ship's officers at a lavish dinner and presented Wood with a new mainmast for the *Tallahassee*. Among the celebratory guests at the dinner were Halifax Mayor P.C. Hill, a future premier, and W.A. Henry, an ardent Confederate supporter who later became one of the Fathers of Confederation (the draft of the *British North America Act* in the British Museum in London is in his handwriting) and a Justice of the Supreme Court of Canada.

Describing the event, the *Boston Advertiser* wrote: "Confederate sympathizers who form five-sixths the population of Halifax Town, were all agog, and gave the pirates a most enthusiastic reception. Leading merchants met these daring plunderers, and clapped them on the shoulders at the landing place, and cheered them lustily for their bravery." On the second night of their stay in Halifax, the Halifax-Dartmouth ferry *Micmac*, filled with Southern sympathizers, steamed around the harbour and near the brightly lit *Tallahassee*, with the Halifax Volunteer Band playing such Southern classics as "Dixie," "Listen to the Mocking Bird," and "The Bonnie Blue Flag."

Shortly after arriving in the harbour, Wood made a courtesy call to British Admiral Sir James Hope on board the flagship *Duncan* to report that as soon as he procured his coal, he would put out to sea again. In an August 31 letter to Mallory, the Confederate Navy secretary, Wood described Hope's receptions as "very cold and uncivil." In effect Hope, a gruff sort of man, told Wood that all these arrangements had nothing to do with him and that whatever Wood wished to do he should take up with MacDonnell, not him.

Next, Wood went into Halifax to meet Premier Charles Tupper, a future Canadian prime minister, at Province House, and together the two men called on MacDonnell, who was so friendly that he invited Wood to join him for breakfast the next morning. Wood reluctantly declined because of the short time at his disposal. MacDonnell's obvious solicitation of Wood greatly annoyed Jackson over at the U.S. consulate. The moment the *Tallahassee* arrived, Jackson telegraphed Navy Secretary Gideon Welles to say: "*Tallahassee* has just come into port. Will protest her being coaled here." But when Jackson complained formally about it to MacDonnell, the governor replied: "His Excellency does not consider it his duty to detain the C.S.S. *Tallahassee*, or any man-of-war of a belligerent state, on the chance of evidence being hereafter found of her having violated international law, and in the absence of proof to that effect he cannot withhold from her commander the privilege of obtaining as much coal as may be necessary to carry him to a port of the Confederate States."

Wood, seizing the moment, asked for an additional twelve hours to install the new mainmast given to him by Dr. Almon and was readily granted the request, again provoking a strong protest from Jackson. But he couldn't delay forever. Admiral Hope, wanting to wash his hands of the whole potential problem as quickly as possible, offered to provide a safe convoy for Wood to a point just outside the 3-mile limit, but Wood declined, with thanks, having already decided to avoid a fight he was sure to lose with the Union ships by sneaking out at night, an unprecedented and extremely risky exercise. To help him pull it off, Wood asked Wier to loan him his best and most daring pilot. Sure enough, 63-year-old Jock Flemming of Ketch Harbour, who, according to Wood's memoir, "knew the harbour as well as the fish that swam its waters . . . [and] was honest, bluff, and trusty," happily accepted the challenge, telling Wood, "If you will steer her, I'll find the water. You won't touch anything but eel grass."

Flemming assured Wood he could take him through the narrow Eastern Passage, between the mainland and McNabb's Island, past what Wood called the "tortuous, sandy shoals on either side of a narrow channel" near Lawlor's Island, where "at one place, by the lead, there was hardly room between the keel and the bottom for your open hand. But as he had promised, we touched nothing but eel grass." It was August 20, 1864, in what Woods called "the darkest night I have ever seen." Yet the *Tallahasse*, its lights turned off, passed Devil's Island in another hour, and there the channel broadened and deepened and "we felt the pulsating bosom of old Atlantic and were safe outside, leaving our waiting friends miles to the westward where we were able to make out their lights."

For many years afterwards, Wood's writings on his dramatic escape were required reading for Nova Scotia schoolchildren. Flemming remains the most famous pilot in that province's long and impressive marine history.

When the Confederacy fell, Wood escaped to Cuba, along with General John C. Breckinridge, the Confederate war secretary, fighting general, and pre-war U.S. vice-president. On June 23, 1865, despite an offer of permanent asylum made by Spanish Governor General Domingo Dulce in Havana, Wood booked passage aboard the *Lark* for Halifax. Breckinridge would later tour Europe and the Middle East with his family before settling in Niagara and Toronto for two years, writing his memoirs and publishing them in Toronto, then moving back to Kentucky in 1869 to practise law.

Arriving in Halifax on June 30, Wood continued on to Montreal aboard the steamer *Queen Victoria*, checking into the Doneganasp Hotel, where, on July 15, he was joined by his wife, Lola, sons Zachary and Charles, and baby daughter Lola. A few days later, his family in tow, they returned to Halifax. There the firm of Wilkinson, Wood and Company flourished, and Wood spent the rest of his life in this city, where he was admired by his neighbours as "the upright figure, [with] the quiet courtesy, the broad hat, the white hair and trim goatee of a typical Southern gentleman of the old school."[7]

Wood's younger son, Lieutenant Charles Carroll Wood, a graduate of the Royal Military College at Kingston, Ontario, was the first Canadian killed in the Boer War, fighting for Britain, while Zachary was a major with the North-West Mounted Police. His grandson S.T. Wood became commissioner of the Royal Canadian Mounted Police.

Long before the Beatles and Junius Brutus Booth, a popular actor at the Theatre Royal who emigrated to America in 1821 and fathered John Wilkes Booth, Liverpool was noted as one of the great shipping centres of the world. In the 1850s, for example, about half of Britain's total imports entered the country through Liverpool.

During the American Civil War, however, the blockade killed about 75 percent of the vital cotton trade, and the already poor downtown areas of Liverpool grew even more overcrowded and desperate. At the same time, however, great fortunes were made as speedy Mersey clippers ran the blockade and returned with cargoes sold at wildly inflated prices. When the war ended, prices collapsed. Within a few months, losses mounted to more than £12 million, bankrupting many prominent Liverpool citizens along with two of its banks.

During the war, the shipyards had been busy building ships for both the Confederacy and the Union, despite Britain's declaration of neutrality. Two of the Confederacy ships, the *Banshee* and the *Alabama*, particularly the later, were so successful in wreaking havoc on Union shipping that the United States initiated an action known as the "Alabama Claims" against Great Britain for damages – a case that also settled two major questions directly affecting Canada: fishing rights and the Canada-U.S. boundary.

Among the great English shipbuilders at Liverpool was John Laird, also a member of the British House of Commons, who, despite attempts by American officials to stop her construction, built the *Alabama* for the Confederacy and launched her in August 1862. Before she was finally sunk on June 19, 1864, by the USS *Kearsarge* off the coast of Cherbourg, France, she had captured sixty-five vessels, burned nearly all of them, captured cargo worth $10 million, and, as described by *Harper's Magazine*: "No one ship that ever floated ever inflicted such injury upon an enemy . . . [she] had well-nigh driven the American commercial flag from the ocean. She was to all intents a British vessel, built at a British dock, manned by a British crew, and sailing almost always under the British flag. Her keel was never wet in Confederate waters, and no man from her deck ever caught a glimpse of the shores claimed by the Confederates; and she rarely hoisted the Confederate flag, except when, having decoyed a prize by the show of false colors, she raised her own in the act of making a prize."[8] Two of the *Alabama* officers, Lieutenant George T. Sinclair Jr. and Lieutenant B.K. Howell, also joined their compatriots in Halifax after the war and became active in local business and social affairs.

In addition to the *Alabama*, the British-built Confederate ships included the *Florida*, *Georgia*, *Rappahannock*, and *Shenandoah*. Together they sunk more than 150 Northern ships and forced much of the U.S. merchant marine vessels to adopt foreign registry to protect themselves. Things might have been even worse if the British and French, responding to U.S. government anger, had not seized some additional ships that had been on their way to the Confederacy, particularly the September 1863 seizure by the British government of two iron-clad, steam-driven

"Laird rams" that Confederate agent James D. Bulloch had secretly arranged to be built in Liverpool.

In a 2001 article for the U.S. National Archives & Records Administration, Kevin J. Foster wrote: "The American people continued to be outraged that Great Britain had allowed Confederates to build and outfit warships in its ports. The objections had begun as the warships were being built, with demands that Britain stop these actions and pay reparations for the 'private' damages caused by the vessels that they had already allowed to outfit in their ports. The U.S. government demanded a second set of reparations for indirect or 'national' injuries caused by prolongation of the war believed to have been caused by British recognition of the South as a belligerent.

"After the war ended, these feelings grew even stronger, and the United States pressed for an international court of arbitration to decide the matter."

In December 1862, with the *Alabama* and other British-built ships causing havoc on the high seas for the Americans, Secretary of State William Seward wrote to Henry Adams, the U.S. ambassador to Britain, who would ultimately negotiate the international deal on behalf of the United States, to say: "It seems to the President as an incontestable principle, that whatever injury is committed by the subjects of Great Britain upon the citizens of the United States, either within the British dominions or upon the high seas, in expeditions thus proceeding from British ports and posts, ought to be redressed by her Majesty's government, unless they shall be excused from liability upon the ground that the government has made all reasonable efforts to prevent the injury from being inflicted." The British, of course, did not agree. In fact, they filed claims against the United States for damage caused by its navy ships against British ships during the war. All these cases came to be known collectively as the Alabama Claims.

One of the problems the British had with the American claims was that, like the Confederacy, the Union also had ships built in Britain. In addition, the Union bought arms, ammunition, and other war supplies from Britain and from British North America. An August 20, 1863, editorial in the *Tillsonburg Observer* illustrates the point:

"The inconsistency of the U.S. Government in complaining of the action of the British Government for not preventing British subjects from furnishing supplies to the Confederates is strikingly exemplified by their own actions in Canada. While complaining that the Confederates have been supplied with ships, munitions of war, medicines, etc., and demanding that the Government should put a stop to the traffic, they themselves have had and still have agents in every part of the British Isles and their North American colonies purchasing and forwarding supplies of all kinds for the use of the Northern troops. And not only this, but we learn from the New York papers that two vessels of war – the *Tulip* and *Fuchsia* – have recently left that port to attack the South; and both of these vessels were purchased and fitted out in England, the same as the *Alabama* and *Florida* were.

"The *Kingston News* of last week said, 'During the past week several thousand horses have been purchased from our farmers by the agents of the Federal Government here for the use of the Northern army. On Saturday, ninety-seven animals were shipped to the other side.' The *Hamilton Spectator*, commenting on the above says, 'In this city, also, horses are being purchased for the American service. Now, we would like to know what difference there is between the Confederates buying ships in Britain for war purposes, and the Federals purchasing horses in Canada for the use of their cavalry?'

"The *Ingersoll Chronicle* says, 'During the past two weeks, Mr. William McGregor, of Windsor, an agent for the American government, has spent, in Ingersoll and vicinity alone, between $15,000 and $20,000 on the purchase of horses.'

"In our advertising columns will be found the advertisement of Mr. Allison, calling for cattle, sheep and lambs; and we have not the least doubt that he is also purchasing supplies for the Northern armies. We are glad that the American government has sent its agents into Canada; for while the money they spend will enrich our farmers, their proceedings will hurt no one. But we do think the American government and journals should act consistently and stop the senseless outcry they have raised against England, because her merchants think proper to send their wares to the most profitable market – the South."

The Americans, of course, didn't see it that way, but the British did, and, for the first couple of years after the end of the war, several diplomatic exchanges between the United States and Britain attempted to settle their dispute over damages, but the talks went nowhere. By early 1869, however, with Europe in turmoil over what Britain regarded as the dangerous expansionist policies of German Chancellor Otto Von Bismarck, the government wanted to kiss and make up with the Americans. In January 1869 the two countries signed the Johnson-Clarendon Convention to arbitrate all claims they had against each other since 1853, specifically excluding the "Alabama," prompting Radical Republican Senator Charles Sumner, who was chairman of the powerful Senate Foreign Relations Committee, to begin a campaign for rejection of the treaty by the Senate in favour of much broader wartime claims against Britain.

Sumner, of Massachusetts, demanded that Britain pay $2.125 billion in "indirect claims." He even suggested that to pay part of the bill, Britain could totally withdraw from North America and turn Canada over to the United States as a partial payment, a proposal which found favour with William Seward, who had continued as Andrew Johnson's secretary of state, and later on with his successor Hamilton Fish, who suggested that perhaps British Columbia would be a fair trade. He also suggested at different times either the British West Indies Islands or all of British North America. And Oregon Senator Henry Winslow Corbett even tabled a motion in the Senate at the time to annex British Columbia. None of this, of course, appealed to the British, who rejected the notion out of hand, so the on-again-off-again negotiations kept getting bogged down.

In 1868, Adams's successor in London, Reverdy Johnson, concluded a convention that arranged for arbitration of the individual claims against the British, but the Senate would not ratify the Johnson-Clarendon Convention because it did not cover what the Americans claimed were indirect costs brought on by the prolongation of the war due to the actions of these British-built ships. Sumner, who was fighting the Administration for being too weak-kneed on the subject, delivered a fiery speech in the Senate which received enormous coverage in the newspapers across the country, managing to stir up national anger against the British, and the Johnson-Clarendon deal, and with it, Anglo-American tensions.

Finally, on May 8, 1871, the Treaty of Washington was completed, after five commissioners from the U.S., and five from Britain and British North America – including Canada's Prime Minister Sir John A. Macdonald, made provision for the submission by both countries of the Alabama claims to an international arbitration commission. Of the five arbitrators appointed on this commission, one was named by U.S. President Ulysses Grant, one by Queen Victoria, plus one each by the king of Italy, president of Switzerland and the emperor of Brazil.

While some disputes had been settled by reference to a single neutral arbitrator, this was a significant breakthrough in international law, the first time in dealing with international disputes that national governments agreed to settle differences by appearing before a five-man international tribunal, rather than resorting to the old ways of settling differences by joint treaty, just ignoring them, or going to war.

In 1872, the Joint Tribunal of Arbitration held hearings in a room in the Geneva town hall – later named the "Alabama Room," and since then the site of hundreds of major international arbitrations – and on September 14, 1872, it dismissed America's indirect claims, i.e., costs blamed on Britain for prolonging the war, but did award the U.S. $15.5 million in "private" damages – which Britain paid, in gold, a year later – and dismissed all claims by Britain against the U.S. for war damages. While Britain did not apologize, as the Americans had demanded, it did express "regret" for its contribution to the Confederate naval actions in dispute.

But that's not all the tribunal did.

First, it settled a boundary dispute left over from the Oregon dispute from a quarter century before regarding ownership of the San Juan Islands, which both Britain and the U.S. had claimed as their own, situated halfway between Vancouver Island and the American-owned Olympic Peninsula. The decision was turned over to the German emperor who ultimately ruled in the U.S. favour.

It also guaranteed that the St. Lawrence River–Great Lakes system, including Lake Michigan, which lies entirely in the U.S., would be open to both countries, making the waterway effectively international waters for shipping purposes, a decision which explains why today there is a greater value of shipping along this corridor than any inland waterway in the world. In addition, Canada was also given the right to the free use of the Yukon, Porcupine and Stikine Rivers connecting Canada's Klondike region with the sea, a decision which didn't have much significance at the time but gave Canada control over the region during the 1898 Klondike gold rush, the greatest gold rush in world history.

By far the most significant aspect of the treaty, however, concerned the vital and increasingly explosive issue of fishing rights. Sir John A. Macdonald's Liberal-Conservative government, Canada's first Parliament, were already upset by the U.S. cancellation of the Reciprocity Treaty – in part because of U.S. anger over Britain and Canada's pro-Confederate war-time activities – and were having serious problems enforcing their new requirement that American fishing vessels needed licences to fish in

Canadian waters. When the fees were dramatically increased in 1868, American fishermen refused to pay but continued to fish without a licence. In January 1870, Macdonald suspended the licensing system and sent police cruisers onto the water to seize American vessels.

In Washington, President Ulysses S. Grant, in his opening address to Congress in 1870, threatened to retaliate if Canada didn't back off. During March and April 1871, with Macdonald in Washington as part of the Joint High Commission trying to resolve the "Alabama Claims," the Washington Treaty was settled. It was actually signed on May 8, but since the Commons was not sitting, Macdonald made no public announcement about it, although word got out, and many Canadians, especially East Coast fishermen, were not happy. In September 1871, the *E.H. Horton*, an American schooner, was seized in Canadian waters for fishing without a licence, but a month later, left unguarded, somebody cut the ship's moorings and, much to the embarrassment of Macdonald's government, escaped to Gloucester, Massachusetts.

Macdonald did not announce his signature on the treaty until May 3, 1872, when he moved first reading of the bill, a year after the deal had been reached, telling the Commons that "an American statesman said to me, 'the rejection of the treaty now means war.'" He went on to say, "I did all I could to protect the rights and claims of the Dominion." The House ratified the Treaty by a 121 to 55 vote, but it was a bitter pill for Maritimers to swallow because it gave away Canada's exclusive inshore fishing rights for ten years without giving them a preferential trade deal in return - a clear victory for the Americans.

And all of this, which was still eliciting threats of war from the Americans, came directly from the actions of British-built ships, many of them using Halifax as a safe haven, preying on Union shipping during the war, a treaty which one American commentator wrote in 1937 was "the greatest treaty of actual and immediate arbitration the world has ever seen; and it still holds that preeminence."

Not any more, of course, with the North American Free Trade Agreement, the European Union and the General Agreement on Tariffs and Trade clearly surpassing it in importance. But it was the Treaty of Washington, a direct result of Anglo-American hostilities in the Civil War, which set up the international bureaucracy that ultimately allowed these major international agreements to be made and which had an important impact on the history of Canadian-American relations.

ELEVEN

The Queen's Hotel

IT WAS NO FLUKE THAT WHEN former Confederate President Jefferson Davis sailed into Toronto harbour aboard the steamer *Champion* from Montreal on May 30, 1867, and drew alongside Milloy's Wharf at the foot of Yonge Street, he was greeted by a cheering throng of 7,000 people – at a time when the city's population was only about 45,000. Davis, who had been captured and thrown in jail at the end of the war two years earlier and released just a few days earlier, was greeted by a large cheer as he stepped onto the gangplank. He acknowledged the adulation by removing his hat and bowing to the crowd.

Lieutenant-Colonel George T. Denison, a leading Southern sympathizer, future MP, and Toronto's chief magistrate was so excited by Davis's appearance that he rushed to the top of a stack of coal to lead the cheers for their fallen hero. He wrote later about his reaction to the sight of Davis's frail body, the result of his harsh treatment in a U.S. prison: "I was so astonished at the emaciation and weakness of Mr. Davis, who looked like a dying man, that I said to a friend near me, 'They have killed him,' and then I called for cheers which were most enthusiastically given, and nothing could have been more cordial and kindly than the welcome he got."[1]

The crowd, which included Southern refugees, along with leading business, political, and church leaders, and just plain folks, was so enthusiastic that Davis, who repeatedly bowed and lifted his hat, kept saying, "Thank you, thank you, you are very kind to me."[2] He needed the help of several police constables to get him to the carriage belonging to Major Hallam. Accompanied by James Mason, of *Trent* Affair fame, Davis was whisked away to Hallam's Church Street home for lunch.

The next afternoon, the same day Canada officially became the Dominion of Canada, he sailed on the *Rothesay Castle* to Niagara, another hotbed of Confederate sympathizers and actions during the war, where, again, the town's elite and most of its ordinary citizens turned out to greet him. At one point Davis is reputed to have looked across the Niagara River to Fort Niagara and, on seeing the Stars and Stripes, quipped, "Look there, Mason, there is the grid iron we have been fried on."[3]

The June 6 *Niagara Constitutional* reported that, in the evening, after the Niagara Band had serenaded him with Southern songs, Davis stood on the verandah of the brick cottage where Mason now lived, addressed the "vast crowd, including several ladies present," and said he had always found British manhood in sympathy with the conflicted and distressed. He concluded by "raising his voice and extending his arms, in tones that thrilled through every heart present," saying, "May the Lord bless you all, may He bless those you love, and may He strengthen and guide your glorious Confederation, the new Dominion of which you are members."

Niagara, like Toronto, Montreal, and Halifax, featured a host of senior Confederate refugees during the period from late in the war until 1869, when most of them accepted the amnesty proclamation and returned home. They found a warm welcome in Niagara because the town had been settled two generations earlier by United Empire Loyalists, whose families still shared a common hostility towards the United States and sympathy for the refugees from there. Besides Mason – who lived in the Dovre-Daly cottage built in 1839 in the Old Town of Niagara at 115

Wellington Street – General John C. Breckenridge, the former U.S. vice-president and Confederate war secretary, also called Niagara home for a time, as did Confederate Generals Jubal Early, John Bell Hood, Henry Heth, and Richard Taylor, the son of former President Zachary Taylor.

Niagara was also home to several major religious leaders from the South: the Reverend Stuart Robinson, head of the largest Presbyterian Church in Louisville, split his time between Niagara and Toronto; and the Reverend Dr. William T. Leacock, who had been forced out of New Orleans by Union General Benjamin F. Butler. This man had incensed the entire South with his infamous May 15, 1862, General Order 28, which decreed that since his officers and men "have been subjected to repeated insults from the women (calling themselves ladies) . . . hereafter when any female shall, by word, gesture, or movement, insult or show contempt for any officer or soldier of the United States, she shall be regarded and held liable to be treated as a woman of the town plying her avocation." President Davis had been so outraged that he issued a proclamation declaring Butler "a felon, deserving of capital punishment . . . an outlaw and common enemy of mankind . . . in the event of his capture the officer in command of the capturing force [should] cause him to be immediately executed by hanging; and . . . no commissioned officer of the United States taken captive shall be released on parole before exchange until the said Butler shall have met with due punishment for his crimes."

Many of the Confederates who fled to Canada stayed at the Clifton House, a lavish hotel overlooking the Niagara Gorge, notable for "its three green verandahs, its huge ballroom, and its crystal chandeliers; [it] was the center of social activity at The Falls. Balls, picnics, and parties were held, many in the handsome garden at the front of the hotel."[4] Davis's reception in Niagara was a sharp contrast to his trip by railway coach in the United States, where people had pelted it with rotten fruit and angrily shouted insults as it passed by. Two days after arriving there and visiting his friends at the Clifton House and elsewhere, Davis returned for a wedding in Toronto, then sailed back to Montreal to rejoin his family in Lennoxville. He said later that the reception he enjoyed in Niagara and Toronto saved his life, reviving his broken spirits, but despite attempts by his friends to have him settle in the area, he declined.

At one point, acknowledging the adulation of the Niagara crowd, Davis told the cheering, weeping throng: "I thank you for the honor you have shown me. May peace and prosperity be forever the blessing of Canada, for she has been the asylum of many of my friends, as she is not an asylum for myself . . . May God bless you all."

Canada had not only provided an asylum for Confederate friends and sympathizers but had also been the base of numerous undercover Confederate operations designed to undermine the Union and assist the Southern cause. Along with Montreal and Halifax, or arguably even ahead of them, Toronto served as a significant source of Southern comfort, particularly during the last two years of the war when the fashionable Queen's Hotel on Front Street was transformed into the unofficial Confederate Headquarters North.

The Toronto newspapers – with the notable exception of George Brown's *Globe*, which railed against Confederates and newspaper competitors alike – were overwhelmingly pro-Confederate in their coverage of the war. Similarly, despite ongoing disdain by the Confederates for professed British neutrality and the laws connected to it, Canadian and British officials either looked the other way or enthusiastically chipped in to help the rebel cause.

Author James Horan, writing of the arrival of Captain Thomas H. Hines in 1864 to help organize Confederate military operations in the northwest states from his Toronto base, wrote: "Toronto at the time must have been like Lisbon during World War II. Agents of the Confederacy, and detectives for the Union, walked in and out of the Queen's bar, buying, selling and trading information, much of it worthless, from the freelance agents who had run the land route via the Detroit ferry to Windsor or the sea blockade from Wilmington to Bermuda, then to Canada.

"There was no mistaking the escaped Rebel prisoners. They hung around the lobby and bar of the Queen's, trying to appear respectable in worn gray coats and cracked jackboots or in castoff clothes they had robbed from some clothesline after climbing the board fences of Camps Chase, Morton or Johnson's Island. They were gaunt, hollow-eyed men, with faces lined and tanned the color of old leather by the relentless sun which had scorched the treeless prison yards that rainless summer.

"The first morning Hines walked into the bar he was recognized. A captain with whom Hines had served walked up and introduced himself, saying he had escaped from Johnson's Island. After watching the captain wolf down a welcome breakfast, Hines asked him if he could locate some of the other escaped prisoners. The rebel officer nodded. He said he would get word to the others that Tom Hines had just arrived from Richmond and wanted to see them. Before the week was out, Hines found himself feeding and clothing more than fifty escaped prisoners."

Hines also made several trips to Montreal, "But that city made him uneasy: strangers, obviously federal detectives, appeared bedside him in the depot, in restaurants and in the lobby of the Montreal Hotel. Toronto seemed much less dangerous and Hines was glad to return to the Queen's bar."[5]

The Queen's Hotel was torn down in 1928 to make way for the Royal York Hotel. Besides being the first hotel in Canada to use hot-air furnaces for heating, the Queen's was also the first to provide a passenger elevator and running water for all its rooms; its telephone was the first to be used for business. Toronto journalist Nathaniel Benson once wrote: "I well remember dining at the gracious and restful Queen's Hotel with a rich young American businessman. He assured me that there were no such slow-paced dinners, such wine cellars, such veteran servitors or red velvet comfort anywhere else on this continent."

When the railways came to Toronto in the 1850s, many owners of the expensive homes along the waterfront moved to large lots to the north and west, while industry and hotels sprang up along the tracks. Author Michael Kluckner tells the story from that era of boys swimming from the Queen's Wharf, in plain view of the Queen's Hotel: "A stately lady used to sit at her hotel window and survey the bathers through an opera or field glass, until she made a complaint, with the result that bathing without trunks was prohibited . . . From the earliest days, the harbour was crowded with little boats, lake ships, steamers, ferries which plied the bay to jetties on the island."[6]

The Toronto mayor during much of the war period was the crusty Orangeman Francis Metcalf, who loved a strong drink and hated the city's Irish Catholics. He set off several riots because of his public tirades against the papists. However, his love of all things British led him to side with the Confederacy, and he helped to welcome and entertain the growing number of Southern refugees and operatives.

Most of Toronto's leading business, political, social, and religious elite also spent time feting the Confederates. George Denison, in his memoirs, writes that he and Colonel Jacob Thompson, who lived in the Queen's Hotel, "became very close friends and he was often at my house." Denison also invited General Robert E. Lee to Toronto. Lee accepted the invitation but took ill and died on the same day he was scheduled to arrive as Denison's guest. Little is left today of the Denison estates, but they occupied a vast area in the west end of the city, where his house, Heydon Villa, was a replica of a Southern mansion, with a neoclassical columned verandah.

Perhaps the most bizarre scheme organized out of Canada at the time was the plan by Dr. Luke P. Blackburn, a Confederate agent from Mississippi, who, despite his wartime activities – or perhaps because of them – was governor of Kentucky from 1879 to 1883. Blackburn had been born in Wood County, Kentucky, in 1816 and graduated in medicine from the Transylvania University in 1835. He opened a practice in Lexington, Kentucky, them moved to Natchez, Mississippi, in 1846, where he became an expert in the treatment of yellow fever. He toured Europe in 1857, making a study of European hospitals, and by the time the Civil War began he was recognized as one of the leading authorities in the country on yellow fever.

Blackburn served briefly as a civilian aid to General Sterling Price, and in 1863 applied for the job of medical inspector under Colonel George B. Hodge, Breckinridge's assistant adjutant and inspector general. There is no formal record, however, to indicate what happened to that application. The next we hear of him, he is staying at the Queen's Hotel and attempting to instigate a yellow fever epidemic in several major Northern cities by shipping trunks full of contaminated clothing to various localities – a forerunner to modern germ warfare. The common belief at the time was that yellow fever was contagious and that its outbreaks came in hot weather. When a patient died, doctors immediately stored away the bedclothes and bedding, and later burned them, to avoid the disease spreading to other people. In the fall of 1863 Blackburn was visited by J.W. Harris, who was living at 6 Queen Street East and working as a shoemaker in Toronto, having been dismissed from the Union Army and had his property destroyed at Helena, Arkansas. Harris had contacted Blackburn through H.C. Slaughter, a Confederate enlisting agent in Montreal who, in turn, had asked the Reverend Stuart Robinson to set up the meeting.

Blackburn enlisted Harris, promising to pay him the stately sum of $60,000 from the Confederate government if the scheme succeeded. As a show of good faith, he gave him some cash on the spot and told him to be ready to swing into action on May 18 of the next year. He said he would telegraph him with instructions through Dr. Robinson. On May 10 Blackburn wrote to Robinson from Havana and, in early June, the Reverend, having read the letter, took it to Harris's house and laid it open on the kitchen table for Mrs. Harris, saying: "This is a letter for your husband. I can have nothing to do with it myself."

The letter instructed Harris to go to Halifax. He should first call on Alexander Keith Jr. to pick up some money, or get some from Robinson – enough at least to get to Montreal, where Slaughter would give him more to take him to Halifax. Harris went to visit Robinson, who was staying with Major-General William Preston, another Confederate refugee and long-time Congressman from Kentucky, who was manufacturing tobacco in Toronto. Robinson didn't have any money, so Harris borrowed $10 from Preston and, on Monday, June 10, left for Montreal. He checked into the Doneganasp, where Slaughter was staying with his family. Blackburn had also moved to Montreal and had bought a house in Prince Royal Terrace. This time it was Slaughter's turn to plead poverty – he claimed that a Montreal brokerage firm had just stolen $7,700 from him – but he asked Harris to meet him at his office at Reed's Tobacco factory on St. Michael Street the next morning. There Harris received $25, with a promise of much more, from James Holcombe, who had just arrived in Canada to look after Confederate interests in the *Chesapeake* Affair.

Harris left for Halifax and arrived in that city on June 22. Arrangements had already been made with Captain John O'Brien of Newfoundland to smuggle three large trunks into Boston and to take them to the Farmer's Hotel there, along with another three trunks that Blackburn had left for him at the Halifax Hotel. There was also a valaise packed with elegant shirts, infested with yellow fever, which Blackburn wanted Harris to deliver personally to President Lincoln, but Harris refused. After Blackburn gave him six $20 gold pieces, one of them to pay Captain O'Brien, Harris headed off for Boston on July 25, arriving seven days later, where he checked into the Parker House under his own name. From there he hired an express wagon, delivered the trunks to the Express Office on State Street, and shipped them to Philadelphia. In total, Blackburn had infected eight large trunks, and Harris also took some to New York and Baltimore. According to the plan, the clothing would be distributed through the Sanitary and Christian commissions to Northern hospitals and out-patients, so as to infect sick and wounded soldiers too weak to fight off the virus. Once Harris returned to Toronto, Blackburn visited him and expressed his satisfaction, though he again said he was short on money and directed Harris to Jacob Thompson. Later, Thompson gave Harris $50 to pay his rent and other expenses.

Even though the trunks were delivered, the plan to start an epidemic didn't work. In May 1865 Blackburn – who had tried the same scheme in Bermuda, again without success – was arrested at the St. Lawrence Hall on a warrant for breach of Canadian neutrality laws. In the end, though he was brought to trial that October, he was discharged because of insufficient evidence.

One writer concluded that Blackburn "does not appear to have been a monster. He had a good reputation as a physician," he said, "and after the war served as governor of Kentucky. His involvement in the yellow fever operation, however, is indicative of the intensity of hatred for the enemy that pervaded the Confederate Government at this stage of the war. It also suggests that strong emotions may have prevented the Confederates from thinking as deeply as they might about the consequences of some of their operations."[7]

In 1993, eight years before the air attack on the World Trade Center, terrorists exploded a car bomb in the basement of one of the towers, killing six Americans and injuring 1,042 other people. At the time, President Bill Clinton's chief of staff, Thomas McLarty, said, "To my memory, we had never really experienced anything like this on American soil."

While McLarty was right in terms of the impact of the terrorist efforts – and that was before the 2001 attack, by far the worst terrorist assault in U.S. history – it wasn't the first organized attempt to create havoc by burning several public buildings in downtown Manhattan. A few months before the November 8, 1864, election – which, thanks to a series of impressive battlefield victories by the Union forces, it now seemed Lincoln would win – Colonel Jacob Thompson and Clement C. Clay invited two veterans of Morgan's cavalry, Lieutenant John Headley and Colonel Robert Martin – to meet with them in Thompson's room at the Queen's Hotel. There they outlined a plan that, while quite different in scale, foreshadows the tactics used by the terrorists in their World Trade Center atrocities.

Despite all the evidence to the contrary – or perhaps because their situation was so desperate – the Confederate commissioners in Canada still believed they could provoke a northwest rebellion by using the armed members of the Sons of Liberty to help free thousands of Confederate prisoners in Chicago, New York, and other major centres. They would then take over these cities and derail Lincoln's apparent re-election as well as his entire war effort – at least enough to force him to negotiate a settlement on terms acceptable to the South. In Headley's own account of the meeting,[8] Thompson said that uprisings were scheduled for election day, under the command of the aforementioned Dr. Blackburn in Boston and Captain Churchill in Cincinnati, and that things were also in place in Chicago and Philadelphia.

Thompson claimed that New York Mayor Fernando Wood, who had visited Halifax during the war to meet with various Confederates there – and earlier had openly proposed that New York City secede and become a nation-state – was also onside in this endeavour: he was supposedly able to muster some 20,000 armed men to take possession of the city on the afternoon of election day and to release the Confederate prisoners at Fort Lafayette. To complete the plan, and add to the general confusion and panic, Headley and Martin were assigned the task of using "Greek Fire" – an incendiary concoction of sulphur, naphtha, and quicklime that was supposed to burst into flame when exposed to air – to torch a number of hotels and public buildings and so create a smokescreen to allow the insurrection to occur.

Thompson gave the men a letter to James A. McMasters, editor and proprietor of the *Freeman's Journal* in New York, telling him that Martin, assisted by Headley and six other men, had been given authority for military purposes. Only a few people knew of the plans, including Captain Robert Cobb Kennedy, a Georgian who had escaped to Canada from Johnson's Island but was subsequently captured, hanged as a spy, and celebrated as a martyr in the South.

The eight rebels left Toronto by travelling in pairs, although they all took the same New York Central Railroad from the Niagara Suspension Bridge and arrived in the city about ten days in advance. Martin and Headley checked into the St. Denis Hotel, at the northwest corner of Broadway and Eleventh Street, using the names Robert Maxwell and John Williams. The rest of the gang checked into various other hotels nearby, but a few days later they all moved, separately, to various boarding houses to avoid detection by Federal officials. Headley says they were assured by New York Governor Horatio Seymour, who had become an implacable foe of Lincoln's policies, of his neutrality in the affair. And W. Larry Macdonald, among the more active Confederates in Toronto at the time, had arranged with his brother, Henry W. Macdonald, for the storage of the gang's trunks at his wholesale piano store at 73 Franklin Avenue.

As usual with these things, however, Federal authorities were tipped off, and, a few days before the election, General Benjamin

Butler arrived in New York with 10,000 troops, telling the public to remain calm even though raids similar to those that had recently occurred in St. Albans, Vermont, were planned. The next day several of the conspirators were arrested in Chicago, and McMasters and the others decided to pull the plug on the whole operation, at least temporarily. As the *New York Times* explained: "There has been widespread and ineffaceable dread that rebel emissaries would seize the exciting time of a general election to put in execution the villainous threats recently made by Richmond papers of laying New York, Buffalo, and other Northern cities in ashes."

After Lincoln's re-election and repeated attempts by Martin and Headley to get a new date for the insurrection, McMasters decided to withdraw his support completely, leaving the rebels on their own to execute their plan. Despite this setback, Headley wrote that they remained determined "to set the city on fire and give the people a scare if nothing else, and let the Government at Washington understand that burning homes in the South might find a counterpart in the North."[9] Captain Longmire of Missouri, the secret Confederate agent in New York, gave them directions to a house in Washington Place where the Greek Fire had been prepared for them by a chemist and paid for by Longmire. Martin then dispatched Headley to pick up the material: "I found the place was in a basement on the west side of Washington Place," he said. "The heavy-built old man I met wore a long beard all over his face. All I had to do was to tell him that Captain Longmire had sent me for his valise. He handed it over the counter to me without saying a word. I turned and departed with the same silence. The leather valise as about two and a half feet long and heavy . . . I had not expected . . . [it] to be so heavy."

Walking to City Hall Square, Headley boarded a streetcar for Central Park and then went to Bowery Street, where he joined the other seven men. The Greek Fire was contained in twelve dozen, 4-ounce bottles, all securely sealed. As he said: "We were now ready to create a sensation in New York." They chose the date of November 25.

For one thing, Butler had withdrawn his troops ten days before, and the 25th was already celebrated as Evacuation Day, an annual fete, highly significant at the time, marking the day the British abandoned New York City during the Revolutionary War. That same day, ironically, also marked the first, and only, time that Edwin, Junius Jr., and John Wilkes Booth, three famous stage brothers – one of whom was about to become one of the greatest villains in American history – had ever performed together on stage, appearing at the Winter Gardens Theater in Shakespeare's *Julius Caesar*, which also centres on an assassin, in a benefit to raise money for a statue of Shakespeare for Central Park.

Promptly at 6 p.m. on the evening of November 25, the men met at their Central Park cottage to launch the raid. Two had deserted, but Headley provided each of the remaining men with a black-glazed satchel, which would be passed off as luggage when they checked into the various hotels. They had already rented rooms in a total of nineteen hotels. Each man took ten bottles of Greek Fire, placed them in their coat pockets, and headed out into the night.

Headley, for example, had booked rooms at the Astor House, City Hotel, Everett House, and the United States Hotel. He first hit the Astor House, an upscale hotel on Broadway, about 7:20, where he got his key and went to his top-storey room. After lighting the gas jet and hanging bedclothes loosely on the headboard, he piled the furniture on the bed, stuffed some newspapers around it, and poured turpentine over the mound. Carefully opening the bottle and spilling it onto the pile, it blazed instantly, at which point he left the room, locked the door behind him, walked calmly down the hall and stairway to the office, which was crowded, dropped off his key, and strolled out into the street.

At 8:45 p.m. a guest at the St. James on 26th and Broadway reported smoke coming from a room rented by a John School.

Firemen quickly broke down the door and extinguished the flames. About the same time, another guest reported smoke coming from a fifth-floor room at the United States Hotel, but that, too, was quickly put out. Ten minutes later fires broke out in Rooms 128, 129, 130, and 174 of the St. Nicholas Hotel, but the hotel's fire department responded, keeping the damage to the four rooms. And so it went.

Headley describes how he returned to Broadway to find that "a hundred bells were ringing, great crowds were gathering on the street, and there was general consternation," but he was disappointed on returning to the Astor to find "no panic" there. Much to his surprise, the greatest panic occurred at nearby Barnum's Museum, where "people were coming out and down ladders from the second and third floor windows and the manager was crying out for help to get his animals out. It looked like people were getting hurt running over each other in the stampede, and still I could not help some astonishment for I did not suppose there was a fire in the Museum." What had happened was that Kennedy, having started fires in three hotels, decided on a whim to "play a huge joke" on the Fire Department by tossing a vial of the material onto a stairwell, starting a spectacular blaze, and triggering a literal stampede by the hundreds of people who were then touring the museum.

The fires continued. One was set at the Lafarge House about 9:20, then at the Belmont Hotel, and at a room at Tammany Hall around 10 p.m. A hotel worker extinguished a fire at the Metropolitan and, about 10:30, another worker at Lovejoy's Hotel opened the door to a fourth-floor bedroom to find a mattress ablaze. At 11 p.m. a man calling himself George Morse checked into the New England House and, minutes later, walked out past the desk, saying he would be right back. He left his room on fire, along with another room in the southeast wing, but both of the blazes were rapidly extinguished.

When a porter opened the door of a room at the Fifth

Avenue Hotel, the bedding suddenly burst into flames, and at the five-storey Hanford Hotel, which was close by a large lumberyard and planing mill, another fire was discovered on an upper floor. Headley headed down Broadway and turned across to the North River wharf, where he started six fires, one by tossing a bottle into a barge of baled hay.

While the fires caused considerable panic, Martin, Headley, and company met as planned at 2 a.m. to compare notes. They split up quickly and found new lodgings, but they were greatly upset that the fires had been so quickly extinguished. Their first instinct was to blame Longmire and the chemist for supplying a faulty concoction. In fact, the saboteurs had no one to blame but themselves. In locking every room, keeping the windows closed, and blocking ventilation ducts, they had deprived the fires of oxygen and of the necessary draft to fuel the flames.

When Martin and Headley met for breakfast at 10 a.m. the next day at a restaurant on Broadway near 12th Street, they bought the *Herald*, *World*, *Tribune*, and *Times*, "and to our surprise the entire front pages were given up to sensational accounts of the attempt to burn the city." The papers also reported that two of the gang members had been arrested, though that was not correct. Later that day they all gathered at the train station, where two of the men bought sleeper tickets for everybody. Headley wrote that they had tickets for an 11 p.m. train for Albany on the New York Central Railroad. Although there were several detectives at the depot, not one approached them. When they boarded the train, they went directly to their berths but did not undress, having figured out an avenue to escape in case they were confronted. They arrived without incident at 6 a.m. on Sunday, but, because no trains were running until that evening to Niagara or the Suspension Bridge from Albany, they scattered among several hotels and spent the day in their rooms. In the evening they boarded a sleeper and crossed the Suspension Bridge into Canada, nearly five weeks after the mission began. They arrived in Toronto that night and immediately crossed Front Street to give a full account of their experiences to Thompson at the Queen's Hotel.

It was shortly after that caper that Thompson and his colleagues discovered that one of their closest advisers, Godfrey J. Hyams of Little Rock, Arkansas, was a traitor. Hyams, a close confidant of Thompson, had approached John Yates Beall in the summer of 1864 with the plan to take over the USS *Michigan* and free the prisoners at Johnson's Island. At the same time he kept Lieutenant-Colonel Bennet H. Hill, Michigan's assistant provost marshall general, apprised of the rebel plans and betrayed Charles H. Cole, their point man in Sandusky.

Hyams, a quiet, well-dressed man who claimed to have escaped from Johnson's Island in 1863, was never trusted by Thomas Hines, and some of the other conspirators doubted his story and told Thompson to be careful. But Thompson, who liked Hyams's dignified style and Southern charm, ignored the warnings. Hyams made his position known late in the war when he appeared as a surprise government witness against the St. Alban's raiders, and he later testified at the Lincoln assassination conspiracy trial on May 29, 1865. "All could now understand how the other expeditions had been betrayed," wrote Headley. "There had always been a mystery about the betrayal of Captain Cole at Sandusky; and others at Chicago, Boston and Cincinnati. We found that Hyams had been mysteriously absent from Toronto. He returned the day after we arrived, but quickly discovered that he was getting a cold reception and quietly left Toronto."[10] Had Hines, Headley, and some of the other members of Dixie North had their way, Hyams would have been disposed of early on. Hines, in fact, would say later that the one thing he always regretted was that he didn't get rid of Hyams before he could do the damage he did.

Even without Hyams, it's highly improbable that the Confederate activities from Canada would have altered the tide of the war. Hyam's betrayals, however, probably shortened the conflict. Before the fall of Atlanta and Richmond completely buried the rebels' cause, they might have created enough Northern pressure on members of the administration to force them to seek a peaceful solution that the South, even in desperation, could accept.

Thompson's usefulness to the Confederacy ended with the failure of the Northwestern Conspiracy. In December 1864 Confederate Secretary of State Judah H. Benjamin wrote: "We are satisfied that so close an espionage is kept upon you that your services have been deprived of the value which is attached to your residence in Canada. The President thinks that it is better that you return to the Confederacy." Instead, Thompson took the money and ran to England.

TWELVE

The Editor

T HE THING ABOUT HORACE GREELEY of the *New York Tribune*, arguably the most famous newspaper editor in American history, is that he didn't really write his most famous line, "Go West, young man." He did nothing, however, to distance himself from the credit for it. In fact, Greeley was never shy about inserting his presence and using his formidable influence to promote any cause of his choosing, a character trait that brought him to Niagara in July 1864 when he hoped to end the bloody war through face-to-face "peace" negotiations with Confederate officials stationed in Canada. This bold – or naïve – move prompted Abraham Lincoln to write his memorable "To Whom It May Concern" letter, one of the most celebrated letters of his storied career.

Greeley had been born into hardship on a farm near Amherst, New Hampshire, on February 3, 1811. A voracious reader, the precocious reformer and political gadfly apprenticed to a Vermont printer at the age of 15, wrote for various local publications, and engaged in numerous public debates for the Whig Party. He moved to New York City five years later to pursue his career as a journalist/printer. Learning quickly how to use the political system to his advantage, Greeley convinced party bosses in Albany to finance his own print shop, where he began publishing partisan journals promoting the pro-business/anti-slavery

Whig candidates. In 1838 he edited the *Jeffersonian*, a Whig newspaper, where he published editorials arguing for more rights for factory workers and the unemployed – an extremely radical position at the time. He also wrote for the *New Yorker* magazine, and during the 1840 presidential election he edited the pro-Whig campaign weekly journal, *Log Cabin*. He dramatically increased his personal political influence by tripling the journal's circulation, giving public speeches, sitting on party committees, and helping to manage the state campaign, all of which brought him substantial credit for aiding William Henry Harrison's narrow presidential victory.

Even though Harrison died of pneumonia a month after taking office – the first president to die in office – and the Whig program subsequently died with him when Vice-President John Tyler became president and split with his own party, Greeley had already established himself as a force to be reckoned with. In 1841 he began the *New York Tribune*, one of the first "penny daily" newspapers, merging it with the *New Yorker* and the *Log Cabin*. Adopting a high moral tone and campaigning relentlessly against alcohol, tobacco, gambling, prostitution, capital punishment, and particularly against slavery, Greeley's *Tribune* was so successful that, by the eve of the Civil War, it boasted a daily circulation of more than a quarter of a million, while his weekly *Tribune* sold more than one million. In the days long before broadcasting was invented, when newspapers carried tremendous influence on public affairs, Greeley became the pre-eminent editor of the most influential newspaper in the country.

Greeley had attempted to secure various government appointments from politicians he had helped get into office, but his only actual service in government lasted ninety days. That was in 1848, when he replaced an indicted U.S. congressman from New York City, and he saw his colleagues quickly turn against him when he began publicizing the private goings-on of his fellow politicians, including exposés of legislative corruption. Seven years later, as a reporter covering Congress, Greeley suffered a mild concussion when Speaker Albert Rust, an Arkansas Democrat, hit him over the head with his cane after Greeley criticized Rust's pro-slavery politicking.

With the death of the Whigs, Greeley supported the Free Soil Party. Essentially an amalgamation of dissenting Democrats and former Whigs, this political movement was headed by former President Martin Van Buren to fight against the expansion of slavery into the new territories. But the free-soilers eventually disbanded too. Greeley was one of the most prominent opponents of the 1850 *Fugitive Slave Law*, and in February 1856 he was instrumental in the birth of the Republican Party at its founding convention in Pittsburgh. Four years later, at the Republican National Convention in Chicago, Greeley initially supported Edward Bates of Missouri, but, on the eve of the balloting, he swung his considerable influence to a gangly, Illinois politician named Abraham Lincoln. He engineered Lincoln's last-minute nomination – and earned himself an entrée into the Lincoln White House, at least for a time, which few other men enjoyed.

Leading up to the Civil War, Greeley was steadfast in his support of Lincoln and the North, although he stridently opposed war. In one of his more famous editorials on the Mexican war in 1846, Greeley had written, "Sign anything, ratify anything, pay anything . . . There never was a good war or a bad peace." But after the war actually began, he changed his tune. When the Northern armies marched off to face the Confederates during the first major battle at Bull Run, Greeley's newspaper proclaimed: "On to Richmond! Crush the rebels in blood and fire!" He also criticized Lincoln for being too cautious in banning slavery. On August 19, 1862, he published an open letter to Lincoln, accusing the president of compromising moral principles for political reasons by refusing to make slavery the dominant issue of the war. Claiming that Lincoln's supporters were "solely disappointed and deeply pained" by his policy, Greeley continued: "We think you are strangely and disastrously remiss in the discharge of your official and imperative duty with regard to the emancipating provisions of the new Confiscation Act."

Greeley's letter prompted Lincoln's celebrated August 22 reply: "If there be those who would not save the Union, unless they could at the same time save slavery, I do not agree with them. If there be those who would not save the Union unless they could at the same time destroy slavery, I do not agree with them. My paramount object in this struggle is to save the Union, and is not either to save or destroy slavery. If I could save the Union without freeing any slave, I would do it; and if I could save it by freeing all the slaves, I would do it; and if I could save it by freeing some and leaving others alone I would also do that. What I do about slavery, and the colored race, I do because I believe it helps save the Union."

As the war dragged on through 1863 and into the first half of 1864, Greeley, like many Americans, became increasingly cranky, so much so that he refused to support Lincoln's presidential renomination that year. Early that spring, before Grant opened his bloody Virginia campaign, Greeley had flatly predicted an imminent end of the war and victory for the Union. But in the thirty days after Grant ran up against Lee in the Wildnerness, Grant's Army of the Potomac had lost 50,000 men, about half as many as the North had lost in total in the previous three years of the war. As the weeks passed, Grant and Lee virtually paralyzed each other, and when the Union began its bloody siege of Petersburg, which would drag on for ten dreadful months, a complete military victory seemed more distant than ever. Lincoln's re-election prospects looked bleak. Greeley, in a July 7 letter to Lincoln – one of about two dozen letters, dispatches, or telegrams he exchanged on the subject – said: "The anxiety of the confederates everywhere for peace . . . is beyond doubt . . . And therefore I venture to remind you that our bleeding, bankrupt, almost dying country longs for peace – shudders at the prospect of fresh conscriptions, of further wholesale devastations, and of new rivers of human blood; and a wide-spread conviction that the Government and its prominent supporters are not anxious for peace, and cannot improve proffered opportunities to achieve it, is doing great harm now, and is morally certain, unless removed, to do far greater in the approaching elections. I entreat you . . . to submit overtures for pacification to the Southern insurgents, which the impartial must pronounce frank and generous . . . this should be done at once."

Besides his highly public plea for peace, Greeley had consistently urged Lincoln privately, in numerous letters and face-to-face encounters, to seek a negotiated peace with the South, and he believed that the Confederacy also wanted a way out if it was approached properly. He was upset in 1863 when Lincoln rebuffed peace overtures from Confederate Vice-President Alexander Stephens, even though Lincoln's refusal to talk was based on Stephen's insistence on Southern independence in any negotiated settlement. At the time, Greeley had endorsed Lincoln's decision on Stephens's proposal in an editorial in his newspaper, but in his July 7 letter he said that the decision "has done harm."

At this point William Cornell Jewett – "Colorado Jewett" – a wealthy, eccentric old friend of Greeley's, became a key player in what would become the Niagara peace initiative. On July 5, 1864, Jewett, a former gold-mine promoter, sent Greeley a short note telling him that "two ambassadors of Davis & Co. are now in Canada, with full powers of peace," and inviting him to a private meeting with them. Greeley also learned that various Peace Democrats – the same ones who had been conspiring against his beloved Union with the Canadian-based Confederates – had also been spending some time with the Confederate commissioners in Canada.

Perhaps blinded by his own ego, Greeley didn't seem to notice that both the Confederates and the Peace Democrats, or Copperheads, were less interested in negotiating an honourable peace than they were in derailing Lincoln's impending re-election campaign. It was a key part of Confederate strategy at the time to do everything it could to assure Lincoln's electoral defeat. Whenever the war was not going well for the North, the Copperhead peace faction of the Democrats heightened their demands for peace negotiations and grew in strength and popularity. The Confederates, especially those in Canada, had done a good job of cultivating this important group, hoping to exploit their relationship to promote their own plans to get rid of Lincoln and replace him with somebody who would negotiate a settlement that, in essence, would amount to a victory for their cause.

Jewett, having made his fortune in Colorado – although there were always questions about exactly how he made it – then settled in California. In September 1853 he purchased a huge South Beach water property, covering what is now a major part of downtown San Francisco, and decided to dedicate his life to pacifism. He appeared as a delegate from Pike's Peak at a Colorado peace convention in 1861 and, during the war, made three trips to Europe to lobby for peace on the basis of a renewed Union with slavery preserved. He also visited Canada at least twice to meet with the Jacob Thompson and his Confederate associates there. Early in 1864 Jewett made what he called a universal appeal for peace, buying large advertisements in major newspapers to publicize it. He was just the man for Greeley.

Not everyone, however, was enamoured by Jewett. Manton Marble of the *New York World* called him "that dancing wind-bag of popinjay conceit," and an "overwheening rogue."[1] And Attorney General Edward Bates, the man Greeley had withdrawn his support from in 1860 to promote Lincoln as the Republican presidential candidate, described Jewett as "that meddlesome blockhead . . . a crack-brained simpleton who aspires to be a knave, while he really belongs to a lower order of entities." None of that mattered to Greeley, as he wrote back to his old friend Jewett telling him he was interested in getting involved in the scheme. Jewett was thrilled, and the Confederates were ecstatic at the prospects of such a well-known and influential Northern publisher helping their cause, whether unintentionally or not.

When Jewett received Greeley's approval, he immediately contacted his friend George N. Sanders, one of the Confederate cabal in Canada, and told Greeley he had been authorized by Sanders to say there were two Confederate commissioners in Canada "with full and complete powers for peace" who were ready to negotiate. In fact, the commissioners had no authority to negotiate peace or anything else on behalf of the Confederacy. Jewett recommended that Greeley either come to Niagara Falls himself to meet them or obtain presidential permission for them to travel unmolested to New York City to meet with him there so that peace might be consummated "by you, them and President Lincoln." Jewett followed up with an urgent telegram the next day to Greeley, asking "Will you come? Parties have full powers."

Greeley, buying Jewett's claim that the Canadian-based commissioners had both the authority and the desire to end the war peacefully, sent an urgent message to Lincoln – including Jewett's original letter – pleading with him to immediately make "frank and generous" overtures for peace to the Southern representatives at Niagara. "Do not, I entreat you, fail to make the Southern people comprehend that you and all of us are anxious for peace. Mr. President, I fear you do not realize how intently the people desire any peace consistent with the national integrity and honor . . . I do not say that a just peace is now attainable, though I believe it to be so. But I do say, that a frank offer by you to the insurgents of terms . . . will . . . prove an immense and sorely needed advantage to the national cause; it may save us from a northern insurrection . . . I beg you to invite those now at Niagara to exhibit their credentials and submit their ultimatum."

For his part, Lincoln replied that he would provide safe conduct for anybody with a written proposal from Jefferson Davis which, whatever other suggestions it contained, agreed to the restoration of the Union and the end of slavery – two impossible conditions for the South to agree to. He also suggested that Greeley himself bring the negotiators to Washington. But Greeley, knowing that such pre-conditions would end any hope of holding talks, decided he would not mention them to the Confederates. He wrote back to Lincoln saying he had no desire "to be made a confidant, far less an agent in such negotiations," but repeating his plea that any serious Southern offer for peace should at least be seriously considered. Three days later Greeley telegraphed Lincoln again, telling him that two Confederate commissioners, with the power to negotiate peace, were at Niagara hoping to meet with him or his representatives. Lincoln wired back to say he was "disappointed" that Greeley had not brought these men to him, adding he was sending his personal secretary, Major John Hay, to New York with his full reply to Greeley's request.

At 6 a.m. on July 16 Hay checked into the Astor House and, within minutes, was informed that Greeley was already waiting for him in the lobby. Hay descended the stairs and handed Lincoln's letter to Greeley. In it, the president referred to his previous letter, setting out his terms, and asked Greeley to show it to the Confederate commissioners. "If they will come on the terms stated in the former, bring them," he wrote. "I not only intend a sincere effort for peace, but I intend that you shall be a personal witness that it is made."

Greeley was not happy. He knew that if he personally undertook this assignment under Lincoln's preconditions, it likely wouldn't work and he would become chicken fodder for his legions of enemies in both political parties and most major Northern newspapers. Still, if Lincoln insisted, he would do it, but he wanted safe conduct for four people – a request Hay wired to Lincoln and Lincoln approved. Greeley told Hay that he would leave for Niagara that night, Saturday, and, if the Confederates agreed, arrive with them in Washington by Tuesday morning. That same day, ironically, Lincoln put out a call for 500,000 more soldiers to replenish his shrinking army.

Greeley arrived in Niagara Falls that night, checked into the International Hotel on the American side, and immediately sent for Jewett, who had been staying with the Confederates on the Canadian side at the Clifton House. In a "private and confidential" letter to Greeley, Sanders wrote that he was "authorized" to say that he, Clement C. Clay, and James Holcombe "are ready and willing to go at once to Washington, upon complete and unqualified protection being given either by the President or Secretary of War."

The three men were staying at the Clifton House, but they too were unhappy because Jacob Thompson, the chief commissioner, who could claim to have some official standing with Richmond, had refused to get involved in the process and had remained behind in Toronto. Despite Thompson's absence, however, Jewett, acting as the go-between, returned from his meeting with Greeley with a letter addressed to Thompson, Clay, and Holcombe. The letter read, in part: "I am informed that you are duly accredited from Richmond as the bearers of propositions looking to the establishment of peace, that you desire to visit Washington in the fulfillment of your mission and that you further desire that Mr. Geo. N. Sanders shall accompany you. If my information be thus far substantially correct, I am authorized by the President of the United States to tender you his safe conduct on the journey proposed, and to accompany you at the earliest time that will be agreeable to you."

Greeley still had not mentioned Lincoln's hard-line preconditions. The next day, Clay and Holcombe responded – with Jewett again delivering the letter to Greeley – writing that Lincoln's safe-conduct pledge "has been tendered us, we regret to state, under some misapprehension of facts. We have not been accredited to him from Richmond as the bearer of propositions looking to the establishment of peace. We are, however, in the confidential employment of our Government and entirely furnished with its wishes and opinions on that subject, and we feel authorized to declare that if the circumstances enclosed in this correspondence were communicated to Richmond, we would be at once invested with the authority to which your letter refers, or other gentlemen, clothed with full power, would be immediately sent to Washington, with the view of hastening a consummation so much to be desired, and terminating at the earliest possible moment, the calamities of war. We respectfully solicit through your intervention a safe conduct to Washington, and then by any route which may be designated through your lines to Richmond. We would be gratified if Mr. Geo. N. Sanders were embraced in the privilege. Permit us in conclusion to acknowledge our obligations to you for the interest you have manifested in the furtherance of our wishes, and to express the hope, that in any event, you will afford us the opportunity of tending them in person, before you leave the Falls." A postscript followed: "It is proper to add that Mr. Thompson is not here, and has not been staying with us since our sojourn to Canada."

Again, Greeley was disappointed that things weren't going as smoothly as he had hoped, particularly over the revelation that the Confederates, contrary to Jewett's story, were not officially authorized by Richmond to negotiate anything. Greeley responded the same day, saying that because the facts in their letter are "materially different from that which was understood to exist by the President . . . it seems . . . advisable that I should communicate with him by telegraph and solicit fresh instructions." Greeley wired Lincoln with the new information, but he put the best spin he could on it. He argued that because these men were employed by the Confederacy and possessed inside knowledge of its goals and aspirations, the solution lay in allowing them to go to

Richmond to obtain formal authority for themselves or some other representatives. Lincoln, after talking over the situation with Secretary of State William Seward – a bitter enemy of Greeley's ever since the editor had helped defeat Seward's presidential nomination bid in the 1860 convention – wrote another note and gave it to Hay to take to Niagara Falls and personally deliver to Greeley.

At 11:30 a.m. on Wednesday, July 20, Hay arrived at the International Hotel and gave Greeley Lincoln's memorable "To Whom It May Concern" letter, which said: "Any proposition which embraces the restoration of peace, the integrity of the whole Union, and the abandonment of slavery, which comes by and with an authority that can control the armies now at war against the United States, will be received and considered by the Executive Government of the United States, and will be met by liberal terms in substantial and collateral points, and the bearer or bearers thereof shall have safe conduct both ways."

Greeley, realizing he'd been put in a no-win situation by Lincoln, tried desperately to convince Hay that it was a terrible mistake to refuse to open negotiations without firm conditions. Hay replied that Lincoln's preconditions were absolutely proper and that Greeley himself, not Jewett, should present the letter to the Confederates. Greeley, who had yet to meet these men, did not want to be introduced under these conditions. Instead, he wanted Hay to deliver the letter. Hay responded that Lincoln insisted that Greeley deliver the letter, though he would accompany him. Seeing no way out of the impasse, Greeley reluctantly got into a carriage with Hay and drove across the falls to the Clifton House. Sanders greeted them there, but Clay was away in St. Catharines and Holcombe was upstairs in his room. As Greeley, Hay, and Sanders stood at the bar, waiting for a response from Holcombe for a meeting, many people recognized Greeley and a crowd gathered. Hay would write later in his memoirs, with considerable pleasure, that "the barroom began to fill and the hall outside to bloom with wide-eyed and pretty women."

When the two men entered Holcombe's room, he was taking tea. Described by Hay as "tall, solemn, spare, false-looking man, with false teeth, false eyes, and false hair," Hay offered to wait for any reply the Confederates wished to send to Washington. Because Clay was absent, however, Holcombe said he would telegraph him immediately and give his reply in the morning. "As Greeley and Hay were about to step into the carriage to return to the other side of the falls," according to historian John C. Waugh, "Greeley told Sanders, 'I expect to be blackguarded for what I have done, and I am not allowed to explain. But all I have done has been done under instructions.'"

The Confederates, who, because of Greeley, had not been told about Lincoln's strict preconditions, were outraged by what they saw as this sudden turn of events – although it certainly suited their propaganda purposes – and immediately fired off a letter to Greeley, with copies to the Northern press, responding to Lincoln's "To Whom It May Concern" letter and accusing the president of an unconscionable about-face. The Confederates believed that the majority of Northerners would be prepared to allow the continuation of slavery if it meant putting a speedy end to the war, so felt they were on solid ground. They had good reason for that belief. On August 4, 1864, for example, after news of the affair became public, the *Columbus Crisis*, a Copperhead newspaper in Ohio, wrote: "Tens of thousands of white men must yet bite the dust to allay the Negro mania of the president . . . a half million more are called for and millions in debts are yet to be saddled upon the people to carry out this single Negro idea, while the Negroes themselves will be literally exterminated in the effort to make them equals with the white man."[2]

In their letter of reply to Greeley, Clay and Holcombe described how they interpreted the original news that Lincoln was prepared to talk as a "most gratifying change in the policy of the President." In allowing them safe passage, "exacting no condition but that we should be duly accredited from Richmond . . . it sounded to us that the President opened a door which has previously been closed against the Confederate States, for full interchange of sentiments, free discussion of conflicting opinions and untrammeled effort to remove all causes of controversy by liberal negotiations."

For these reasons, they claimed, they had felt confident that Richmond would agree to pursue the peace negotiations. Now, however, Lincoln's position "precludes negotiation and prescribes in advance the terms of conditions of peace," a return to his policy of "no bargaining, no negotiation, no truces with rebels, except to bury their dead, until every man shall have laid down his arms, submitted to the Government, and sued for mercy.

". . . We feel confident that you [Greeley] must share our profound regret that the spirit which dictated the first step toward peace has [not] . . . been continued," they wrote. "What may be the explanation of this sudden and entire change in the views of the President, of this rude withdrawal of a courteous overture for negotiations at the moment it was likely to be accepted?"

The envoys thanked Greeley for his efforts, but added that if peace was possible only by submitting to such "terms of conquest, the generation is yet unborn which will witness its restoration . . . now the war must continue." They added that they could not even submit Lincoln's "intemperate and unyielding demands" to President Davis "without offering him an indignity, dishonoring ourselves, and incurring the ill-merits and scorn of our country."

Nothing in this episode was good news for Lincoln. The newspapers and the public – and even the rebel commissioners – did not know the whole story. What they believed was that Lincoln had held out hope for meaningful negotiations, only to renege later on. The *Philadelphia Age*, for example, wrote: "Let no man forget that the Confederate agents in Canada did not make their national independence a precedent to negotiating; they said nothing about it . . . There can be no doubt that if men so violent and so opposite in their views as Mr. Greeley on the one side and C.C. Clay on the other side could think it possible that peace between the North and South could be arranged, there can be no doubt, we say, that calmer, higher-minded men, coming together with fuller powers, could have devised some means to terminate this bloody contest. Yet the grinning, chattering, autocrat, Lincoln, says there shall be no peace."

The pro-South *Toronto Leader* wrote that Greeley "appears to have borne some mission from President Lincoln looking to the negotiation of peace, but after the opening of negotiations between the two parties he seems to have been snubbed altogether by his master in Washington . . . and when Lincoln, with a wretched punctiliousness that prevented him seizing such a favourable opportunity of bringing about peace, addressed a letter to nobody in particular, but insulting to every Southerner who might read it, nothing could be done. The door remained as effectually barred as ever against negotiation for the settlement of the present difficulties and all efforts to open it proved futile."

Greeley even had to defend himself in print against accusations from other newspapers that he was breaking the law by negotiating with the enemy. He published much of the material that had flowed back and forth between the parties, but did nothing to counter the picture of Lincoln portrayed by Clay and Holcombe. In an editorial, he wrote that, as an authorized intermediary, he was merely trying to bring people together in a more "agreeable" atmosphere.

Things certainly weren't very agreeable for Greeley or, more important, for Lincoln during the following months. *New York Herald* editor James Gordon Bennett, also a leading figure of the day, scoffed "that shuffle-gaited peripatetic, old Greeley, has gone on a peace mission to Niagara."[3] With resistance to the military draft getting stronger, volunteerism stalling, and the war effort bogged down, the public was sick of the war. And news that

Lincoln, apparently, had so cavalierly thrown away an opportunity for peace was not sitting well. An August 26, 1864, editorial in the *Montreal Gazette* captured the mood of the period. "The signs of peace multiply in the Federal territory. In several Northern States resolutions have been passed, some condemning the war as unconstitutional, as waged against slavery, which each state has a right to abolish or maintain for itself, some proclaiming the right of States to secede and denouncing any attempt to coerce them as a violation of their constitutional rights.

"Two years ago, or even eighteen months ago, these men would have been arrested for treasonable utterances, and either confined to some military prison, or banished to 'Dixie' or Canada. Now, no action seems to have been taken against them."

In the South, where news of the Niagara meeting came as a general surprise, discovered only after it was published in the Northern press, most seemed to believe it would help their cause. Confederate Navy Secretary Stephen R. Mallory, a former Florida senator, wrote privately to Clay's wife, Virginia, on August 1, 1864: "Our weak brothers in North Carolina and Georgia, who have clamored so loudly that peace propositions should be made by us, cannot fail to see that at present peace with Lincoln means degradation." Reflecting the same view publicly, the July 26 *Richmond Sentinel* wrote that the Niagara documents would convince "the miserable faction existing in a neighboring state" that peace with Lincoln meant "the most abject submission with the loss of honor, property, and liberty."[4]

Not everyone was pleased by Clay and Holcombe's initiative, however. The July 26 *Richmond Examiner* wrote: "To exhibit an ex-senator and member of Congress of the Confederate States thus timidly crawling by a roundabout way to the footstool of the Emperor of the Yahoos, whining and sniveling about peace and 'liberal negotiations,' and haughtily refused even admittance to the sovereign presence will serve not the peace, but the war party; because it will be used to create the impression that the

Confederacy must be in the agonies of death when two distinguished legislators make so pitiful an attempt to reach the ear of offended majesty."

Clay wrote later that their communication with Greeley "has impressed all but fanatical Abolitionists with the opinion that there can be no peace while Mr. Lincoln presides . . . From all that I can see or hear, I am satisfied that the correspondence has tended strongly toward consolidating the Democrats and dividing the Republicans and encouraging the desire for peace . . . we have developed what we desired in the eyes of our people – that the war, with all its horrors, is less terrible and hateful than the alternative offered by Mr. Lincoln."

The *New York Commercial News* reported that George Sanders had left for Washington "with a proposition that if Lincoln will publish a proclamation of armistice, with a call for a convention of all the states, the South will agree to it and come to the convention. This not succeeding, it is understood to be the further object of these high envoys to procure, as an alternative, the nomination by the Democrats of ex-president Pierce at Chicago." The Chicago Democratic National Convention (which chose General George B. McClellan as its "peace" presidential candidate) was just a few weeks away, and it was hardly a secret that the Confederates were hoping to use their influence with the Peace Democrats to pick a candidate more compatible with their goals. After Greeley left Niagara by train, headed back to New York, the *Rochester Democrat* stated: "It is understood the Commissioners, with Sanders and Jewett, are to remain and carry on negotiations with the Democrats. A letter is to be prepared for the Chicago convention, in which the Commissioners will hold out strong assurances of a restoration of the Union under Democratic auspices. The whole movement is regarded by many as a mere scheme to entrap the administration into a false position before the country and the world for the benefit of the disunion Democrats."

Lincoln himself, in a letter to his friend Abram Wakeman in New York concerning Clay's intentions, wrote: "Does anyone doubt that what they [the Niagara negotiators] are empowered to do, is to assist in selecting and arranging a candidate and a platform for the Chicago convention? . . . Thus the present presidential contest will almost certainly be no other than a contest between a Union and a Disunion candidate, disunion certainly following the success of the latter."[5]

When the Democrats held their convention in Chicago, the prospects for Lincoln's re-election appeared bleak. The public perception of his actions at Niagara Falls – thanks largely to Greeley's stupidity – contributed to the general malaise against the president. But good fortune intervened – at least for Lincoln. Three days after the Chicago convention, and a little over a month after Greeley's fiasco, William T. Sherman captured Atlanta. Then Philip H. Sheridan won a series of major victories over Jubal Early in the Shenandoah Valley. As the *Richmond Examiner* lamented, the "disaster" at Atlanta came "in the very nick of time . . . [to] save the party of Lincoln from irretrievable ruin . . . It will obscure the prospect of peace, late so bright. It will also diffuse gloom over the South."[6]

And when the votes were tallied that fall, the Democrats, who had flirted with the rebels to undermine Lincoln and, just a few months earlier, had appeared ready to ride to victory on the strength of their "peace" platform, were devastated. Lincoln defeated McClellan by 411,428 votes, swamping him 212 to 21 in the electoral college vote. McClellan carried just three states – New Jersey, Kentucky, and Delaware – and the North was left with a single Democratic governor, Joel Parker in New Jersey.

Greeley lost some of his considerable political clout over the Niagara event, although he still remained politically active. He suffered a landslide defeat as the 1872 Democratic presidential candidate to incumbent General Ulysses S. Grant. A month later he died, and his funeral, larger than Lincoln's, filled New York's streets for three days with seemingly endless processions of both high government officials and ordinary working people.

THIRTEEN

St. Albans

O N OCTOBER 10, 1864, Kentucky-born Confederate Lieutenant Bennett H. Young, a member of the famous Morgan's Raiders, left the St. Lawrence Hall hotel in Montreal with his friend William Hutchinson, also a Confederate cavalry veteran. They boarded a train heading south to the quiet, picturesque village of St. Albans, Vermont, a community of about 1,600 people on Lake Champlain, just 15 miles from the Canadian border and 62 miles from Montreal. Young, who, as a divinity student in 1861, had raised the first Confederate flag in Kentucky, and Hutchinson (whose real name was W.H. Huntley, also a Kentuckian), checked into Room 6 at the Tremont Boarding House on Main Street, directly across from Taylor Park, the town's expansive village green. They gave their address as St. John's, Lower Canada, and told the proprietor they had arrived on a sporting vacation.

On the same day, two other members of Young's secret Confederate command arrived from Canada and checked into the American Hotel. The next day there were three more, and, on October 18, with the town's population doubling because it was Market Day, another six men arrived from Canada and booked into various hotels. They were all about to make history.

St. Albans – named in honour of Charles II's son, the Duke of St. Albans – was a small dairy-farming community on the old Central Vermont Railway line, huddled at the foot of the Champlain Valley and smack in the heart of Franklin County (after Benjamin Franklin). For nearly a century beginning in the mid-1600s, Vermont had been part of the French territory known as La Douville – giving it a French flavour that still exists. After the British defeated the French in North America, Vermont was claimed by both New Hampshire and New York. When New York won the subsequent court battle, the well-known American patriot Ethan Allen, who would become a colonel in George Washington's Continental Army, formed a defence regiment called the Green Mountain Boys to stop New York officials from surveying their land. Ethan's brother Levi was one of the founding settlers of St. Albans, where he claimed a huge part of the townsite and addressed his wife as the Duchess of St. Albans.

During the War of 1812 about eighty St. Albans volunteers fought in the American victory over the British at Plattsburgh, New York, in 1814. Leading up to that war, St. Albans became the base of the largest smuggling operation on Lake Champlain when the locally owned *Black Snake* continued to defy President Thomas Jefferson's ill-fated 1807 *Embargo Act* against trading with the Europeans by shipping local potash north of the border to Montreal, in exchange for lumber, tobacco, nails, kettles, salt, and rum. The vessel was eventually captured by the federal revenue cutter the *Fly*, after a battle in which three federal officers died. Only one of the smugglers was hanged, and the others were eventually pardoned. The last skirmish had occurred there during the 1837 Rebellion, or the Papineau War, when French-Canadian rebels against British rule were given both sympathy and refuge and, in response, Canadian officials threatened to burn the town.

Although Vermont had more than its fair share of men fighting in the Civil War and was the first state to formally offer troops to the Union, the actual battlefields were still a long way off. The war had been brought a little closer to home on July 18, 1864, during a failed bank robbery attempt in Maine by some Confederates. A band of fourteen men, led by Captain William Collins of the 15th Mississippi Regiment, CSA, a former company commander of the "Quitman Rifles, Co. C," had left Saint John, New Brunswick, on July 14 in a lead-coloured sail- and rowboat headed first for Robbinston and then for Calais, Maine, intent on plundering the town and robbing its banks, ostensibly on behalf of the Confederacy but more likely for Collins's personal benefit. Collins, born in Ireland and raised in Saint John, had adopted the Southern cause. He was a well-known scoundrel, having murdered two men in Saint John, and a braggart to boot. Unfortunately for him, J.Q. Howard, the U.S. consul at Saint John, had learned of his plans from his spies in the community – primarily William Dymond, a Union deserter from the 6th New Jersey Volunteers, who later received an honourable discharge for spying on Collins. Howard telegraphed Maine Governor Samuel Cony, warning him that the raiding party had left Saint John "to commit depredations on the Maine frontier."

On July 18 J.A. Lee, the cashier at the Calais Bank, received a telegram from Howard saying that the men intended to rob his bank. "If they have not been alarmed, you can apprehend them quietly in the bank. William Collins is the leader." Captain B.M. Flint's company of State Guards was immediately detached for service, with pickets stationed at various points in the town. About noon, Collins and two companions – Francis X. Jones and William Phillips – entered the bank on a reconnaissance mission. When Collins, pretending that he wanted to exchange some gold for greenbacks, appeared to reach for a revolver in his side pocket, the men were immediately surrounded and taken to the Municipal Court Room. Collins was also found to be carrying a Confederate flag (which is now held by the Maine Historical Society). This large blue-silk banner features eleven stars and an inscription painted in gold: THE CONFEDERACY FOR EVER / TO

DEFEND HER RIGHTS, FROM HOME AND FRIENDS WE'LL SEVER.

While the rest of Collins's party escaped, the three captured Confederates were taken to the county jail at Machias, the site of the first naval battle of the American Revolution. Jones told the sheriff that the Confederacy was about to launch a full offensive against Maine, and his story was credible enough that officials notified senior Washington officials, who in turn dispatched the assistant judge advocate general to Maine to solicit further details. As it turned out, it wasn't true, but was part of an orchestrated Confederate disinformation program. Still the story, combined with the nearby coastal exploits of the Confederate ship *Tallahassee* at about the same time, made it appear credible and created a local sensation for several weeks.

The Calais incident provides a graphic illustration of the extent of pro-Southern feelings in Saint John at the time. The city council actually passed a strongly worded motion condemning Howard, the U.S. consul, for warning Maine authorities about Collins. Eventually, Collins and his two compatriots were found guilty of conspiracy and sentenced to three years in the Maine State Prison.[1] Though hardly a success, the incident also heightened anxiety in the northeast, prompting border state governors to increase the vigilance of their various State and Home Guard units against expected raids from Confederates in Canada.

Even so, the people of St. Albans had no way of knowing that the war was about to arrive literally at their front doors.

Wednesday, October 19, began in St. Albans with a light drizzle and the promise of heavier rain in the afternoon. There was considerable activity in the town that morning, as many people who had come for Market Day on Tuesday prepared to leave by train or coach. A good portion of the local gentry headed off to Montpelier for the legislative session, to Burlington for the opening of the court, or to any number of business-related destinations. The Confederate raiders knew that the streets would be quiet and the bank vaults filled with money from the previous day's receipts.

About three o'clock that afternoon, the serenity of the town was suddenly shattered by a group of twenty-one Confederate raiders. The action was so unexpected and bold that it caused a sensation on both sides of the border and, for a time, it seemed that Canada and Great Britain would be drawn into a war against the United States.

Having raided the Governor's Stables, Young and three of his men suddenly appeared, galloping on horseback at full speed down Main Street, waving their large Naval Colt revolvers, shouting that they were Confederate soldiers, and tossing fire bombs through local store windows – in the vain hope that they would burn the town to the ground. At the same time, other men, wearing their Confederate uniforms, were robbing the town's three banks – Franklin County Bank, First National Bank, and St. Albans Bank – of $208,000, a tidy sum for the day.

At the Franklin County Bank, at Main and Kingman Streets, Confederate cavalryman Thomas Collins, a brother of William Collins of Calais fame, was in charge of the five-man raiding team. Holding a gun to the head of cashier Charles Bishop, Collins announced that they were members of John Morgan's raiders and "we shall do to you what your Sheridan is doing to us." Collins forced Bishop and clerk Martin Seymour at gunpoint to pledge allegiance to the Confederacy. When local shop owner Samuel Breck entered the bank carrying a deposit of $393, it was quickly taken from him and he too was forced to take the oath of allegiance. Shortly after that, 13-year-old errand boy Morris Roach came in to deposit $210 for his employer, and that money was stolen from him.

In the meantime, some of Young's men were rounding up the locals and forcing them to congregate under guard at Taylor Park. The group included a Canadian trapper named Frenchy

Boivin, who had been wrestling with three Confederates in an attempt to stop them from stealing his horse but was now marched at gunpoint across Fairfax Street to the park.[2] A local man named Collins Huntington, though wounded in the side, was also taken to the park. Three others were slightly wounded, but Elias J. Morrison, a visitor from New Hampshire, was seriously wounded and died two days later.

Young and his men had also stolen several more horses at both Field's and Fuller's livery stables to facilitate their escape into Canada. While their "Greek Fire" bombs had started some fires, most had fallen harmlessly against the outside of buildings, and the raiders' grandiose plan to burn down the town didn't materialize.

One of the intended targets of the raiders was the hilltop mansion of Vermont Governor J. Gregory Smith, a lawyer, railroad magnate, and lifetime resident of St. Albans. At the time of the raid, Smith was at the State House in Montpelier, America's smallest capital city, but Young had gone to the house before the raid to inspect the governor's stables. Smith's wife, Ann Eliza, warned by a neighbour's maid that the "Rebels are in town," quickly drew the shades, bolted the doors, grabbed the only weapon she could find – a large horse pistol with no ammunition – and stationed herself defiantly on the front steps, prepared to defend her home and family. Her heart raced madly as she heard the sound of a horse galloping at full speed up the hill, but, happily for her, the horse was carrying her brother-in-law, Worthington C. Smith, a member of General George Custer's staff, who happened to be home on leave. The rebels had to leave town before they got a chance to visit the Smith mansion, although troops were stationed there later that night.

In the meantime, Captain George Conger of the 1st Vermont Cavalry, on hearing the commotion and spotting smoke pouring from the downtown area, mounted his horse and rode to the local machine shops, the railroad depot, and up and down several streets shouting that "the Rebels are here" and telling the locals to get their guns and head for Main Street. Within minutes, about sixty local citizens had assembled at Taylor Park, although only twenty of them were armed.

Conger and his posse quickly pursued Young and his raiders, who took flight along the Sheldon Road. They failed in their attempt to burn the highway bridge across Sheldon Creek and headed for the Missisquoi River at Enosburg Falls, hoping to reach what they anticipated was the safe haven of Canadian soil at Frelighsburg and Phillipsburg. Two of the raiders were captured on the American side, one with $50,000 in his pocket. Once on the Canadian side, however, the others made no attempt to hide, believing that the Americans would stop at the border. They did stop, but only briefly, before continuing on and capturing six more raiders at Stanbridge on the Canadian side. Joined by a detachment of Canadian militiamen, who had been ordered to the area by Governor General Sir Charles Stanley Monck, the pursuers proceeded to Frelighsburg and captured eight more raiders, including Young, along with several horses and some of the stolen money. Young attempted to escape, but was caught and was being pummelled by the angry posse when, fortunately for him, a British major chanced on the scene. He warned the Americans to turn over their prisoner, because they were in violation of British neutrality laws. For a time the situation was tense, particularly when one Vermonter pointed his gun at the officer and said, "We don't give a damn for your neutrality." Eventually, however, the situation cooled, and Young was passed over to the British officer.

Two other raiders, C.M. Wallace, 26, and Charles Swegan, 22, had turned themselves in to George W. Wells, the bailiff at Frelighsburg. Wells and some assistants were escorting them to the Carpenter's Hotel for safekeeping for the night when they were confronted by about fifteen of the Vermonters, led by Conger, who ordered Wells to surrender his arms or be shot. A frightened Wells fled into a nearby yard, hotly pursued by Conger, but after a short chase Conger and his men dispersed for the night. Other raiders had escaped to Montreal. One of them, William Huntley (aka Hutchinson), Young's original companion at St. Albans, surrendered a few days later to Montreal police.

Young and his group were taken by the local militia commander, Colonel Edward Ermatinger, to the jail at St. John's, Canada East, a few miles south of Montreal, where a large garrison of British regulars was stationed. Within three days of the event, authorities had a dozen raiders in custody at St. John's, "and some of the money dropped on the road by the raiders was brought in later by Canadian farmers."[3] A few days later they were taken to Montreal to stand trial.

On the day of the raid, however, Governor Smith, fearing that the attack on St. Albans was a precursor for an all-out Confederate offensive on Vermont, placed the entire frontier under military guard, dispatching a total of 1,300 armed men by the next morning. Having immediately sent troops from Montpelier by special train to St. Albans, Smith telegraphed Secretary of War Edwin Stanton: "It is supposed they [the raiders] were Southerners from border of Canada. Five citizens were shot, one it is feared fatally. Having accomplished their object the band left immediately for Canada."

At this point General John A. Dix, the no-nonsense head of the Department of the East, enters the story. His father, an infantry major who died in the War of 1812, had sent his son to the College of Montreal, a Catholic institution, to expose him to another culture and language. Dix studied for fifteen months in Montreal and returned home when the war broke out. In 1861 he was secretary of the Treasury under President James Buchanan for just fifty-two days – losing the job when Lincoln became president – but long enough to utter an enduring quote that is still featured on his State House portrait. Faced with growing Southern hostilities against Washington in New Orleans, Dix telegraphed the local treasury office to say, "If anyone attempts to haul down the American flag, shoot him on the spot."

When Dix received the governor's telegram about the raid, he happened to be at the same dinner party as the British ambassador, Lord R.B.P. Lyons. Dix had sent a telegram to Stanton, saying he had ordered additional troops and directed that "a discreet officer . . . be put in command, with orders, in case the marauders are not found on our side of the line, to pursue them, if necessary, into Canada, and destroy them." When Dix told the dinner guests what he had done, claiming it was justified under the rules of "hot pursuit," Lyons asked whether Washington had authorized the order. Dix conceded he had issued it on his own, although he had considerable support in Washington. Stanton not only agreed with Dix on sending pursuing troops into Canada but wanted to tell Lord Lyons to instruct Canadian authorities to hand over the chief Confederate agent, Jacob Thompson, for war crimes prosecution. Even Lincoln was leading towards the Dix view until the secretary of state, William H. Seward, became so alarmed at the possibility of provoking war with Britain that he threatened to resign if the president did not rescind Dix's order. In the end, Lincoln did disavow Dix, but not before the widely publicized order sparked more fears both north and south of the border that more invasions were inevitable. As for the Confederacy, it lived in constant hope that war would break out between the Union and Britain, and Dix's hasty pursuit order was greeted with considerable jubilation in Richmond.

An October 20 editorial in the *Montreal Gazette* about the raid called for swift justice in the case. "It is the first duty of the Government and the people of Canada to see that the right of asylum which their soil affords is not thus betrayed and violated. The Government must spare no pains to prevent it . . . We must, we repeat, preserve our neutrality . . . and punish with the sternest severity any beach which can be discovered. If we do not we shall find ourselves dragged into the war for needless cause . . . To surprise a peaceful town and shoot people down in the streets, at the same time committing robbery, is not civilized war; it is that of savages."

With American officials livid at Canada for harbouring so many Southerners, whom they considered to be criminals, Canadian officials moved quickly to assuage American anger. First, Canada East Attorney General George-Étienne Cartier telegraphed Judge Charles J. Coursol, the police magistrate at Montreal, to "use every exertion to have them [the raiders] apprehended and brought to justice" and to go himself to the border area where they were temporarily being held "with all the force to accomplish this task." And in an October 22 telegram from Governor Smith to Secretary Stanton, Smith said that the raiders then in custody had all admitted what they had done, claiming to be commissioned by the Confederate government and therefore under the protection of the Canadian government. "My last telegram from the Governor General of Canada [Monck] says, 'You need entertain no fears but that the laws will be faithfully administered,'" wrote Smith. "He has, at my request, ordered the trial removed from before the local magistrate to Judge Coursol, of Montreal, and everything looks favorable for a fair and thorough investigation." It was anything but.

The St. Albans raid had caused considerable panic among the citizens of the northeastern border states. About 5 p.m. on Sunday, October 23, in Plattsburg, New York, for example, an engine, baggage car, and single passenger car with about thirty men arrived in town. A large number of Plattsburg people armed themselves but made no attempt to stop the train. "Fearing that another train filled with hostile Confederates might arrive, the ferryboat was pushed out from shore and the railway tracks for about five acres of length was torn up. This turned out to be a groundless panic and needless precaution."[4] Almost every community had raised a

Home Guard to fight off Confederate intruders – in St. Albans, 350 men had signed up. And Canadians were frightened by widespread public reports that the Americans, despite the treaty restricting the number of warships on the Great Lakes, were planning to "place a floating armament on the lakes."[5]

On October 25, six days after the raid, Coursol opened the preliminary hearing at the crowded courthouse in St. John's. Dozens of people, including many Southerners sporting Confederate uniforms and Southern belles in their fancy gowns, had taken the 8 a.m. train from Montreal to watch the proceedings. Many more American officials had arrived from south of the border. The only witness was Cyrus N. Bishop, a teller at the St. Albans Bank, and his examination-in-chief was held in private, although he and others were taken to the jail to identify the twelve prisoners as the same men who had robbed his bank and scandalized his town. The Americans were demanding that the raiders be returned to stand trial on six extraditable charges: murder, intent to murder, assault, robbery, attempted arson, and horse-stealing. The raiders, in contrast, argued that they were duly accredited members of the Confederate Army and were belligerents carrying out a legitimate act of war. Indeed, in the pro-Southern October 22 *Montreal Evening Telegram*, Young wrote an open letter claiming he had been commissioned by Richmond to retaliate for the destruction against the South being wrought by Sheridan in the Shenandoah Valley. Insisting that no Canadian laws had been violated, Young tweaked the Vermonters who had violated the Canadian border to capture them: "Surely the people of Vermont must have forgotten that you are not in the midst of war, and ruled by a man despotic in his actions, and supreme in his infamy."

Perhaps as a precursor to the chaos that would ensue in this case, even the routine opening stage had not gone smoothly. In Stanbridge, Justice of the Peace Henry Nelson Whitman flatly refused to give up the six prisoners in his custody. Coursol, along with officers from the Montreal Water Police and Montreal Police

Chief Guillaume Lamothe – who, along with Coursol, would become a central figure in the subsequent judicial scandal over this case – was forced to go to Stanbridge and demand that the prisoners be turned over to them. Whitman still objected, but, recognizing Coursol's superior jurisdiction, he finally agreed.

Montreal criminal lawyer Bernard Devlin, a member of Montreal City Council who later fought against the Fenian raiders, was hired by the U.S. government to represent its interests at the trial, along with George F. Edmond of Burlington, Vermont. Henry G. Eddson and E.A. Sowles represented the St. Albans banks. The Crown was represented by Edward Carter, clerk of the peace for Montreal.

One thing the Confederates had, in addition to audacity, was a lot of money. Young had telegraphed Confederate agent George Sanders, saying: "We are captured. Do what you can for us." Sanders showed up with $6,000 for their defence, money they used to hire Montreal's most prominent – and most expensive – lawyer, the Honourable John J.C. Abbott, who in 1887 would become Canada's third prime minister. A native Quebecer, Abbott was dean of law at McGill University from 1855 to 1876, where he taught Wilfrid Laurier, also a future prime minister. In 1862–63 Abbott was provincial solicitor general, during a time when mixing private and public work was routine. Shortly after his dramatic successes in the St. Albans trial, he served three months as a deputy judge of the Superior Court, but declined the offer of chief justice, "possibly because the receipts of his office were from five to eight times a judge's salary."[6]

Abbott, never shy about using his connection to pursue his financial interests, became a key figure in the 1873 Pacific Scandal, the conflict-of-interest case that brought down the Conservative government of Sir John A. Macdonald. A railway magnate himself, Abbott was also legal adviser to Sir Hugh Allan, president of the Canadian Pacific Railway, helping to negotiate a deal where Macdonald accepted campaign funds in return for allowing Allan's syndicate to build the railway. He had also been among a group of prominent Montreal business leaders to sign the 1849 Annexation Manifesto, advocating that the Canadian colonies cut their ties with Britain and join the United States.

Abbott was assisted in his defence by two lawyers, Toussaint-Antoine-Rodolphe Laflamme, one of his former McGill students, and William Warren Hastings Kerr, later the acting dean of law at McGill. The aim of the preliminary hearing was to prepare arrest warrants against the raiders under the Ashburton-Webster Treaty, the 1842 agreement between the United States and Britain which had resulted from a series of serious border disputes, including the 1839 Aroostook War between Maine and New Brunswick.[7] This treaty called for the mutual extradition of criminals between the United States and British North America.

After three days in St. John's, and with tensions high along the border, Coursol decided to shift the case north to Montreal. The American lawyers, realizing how many Southerners were then living in Montreal and how much sympathy their cause had garnered, objected to the move. But Coursol would hear none of it. The prisoners, without handcuffs, were marched to a special train at Point St. Charles that evening by Chief Lamothe, his deputy, and twelve Montreal police officers and taken to an upper ward in the Montreal jail. Throughout their stay, the raiders were afforded celebrity treatment. They were soon transferred next door to the jailer's own home, where a guard was placed, not really to stop them from escaping but to prevent what many thought would be an attempt by U.S. officials to kidnap them and bring them south for trial. The raiders were feted regularly as dinner guests by the jailer and his wife and supplied with their every need, including the finest wines, the most expensive cuts of meat, and, at night, the company of female escorts. There were also regular gatherings outside the jailer's house of Southerners and their many sympathizers, often singing Southern songs and generally creating a sympathetic atmosphere which, combined with the snail-like pace of the actual legal proceedings, was getting under the skin of U.S. officials.

Coursol opened those proceedings on November 3, 1864, before the Court of Queen's Bench, but much of the first day was spent debating a defence motion that the Crown's lawyer, Edward Carter, as clerk of the peace, had acted as clerk for the judge and, therefore, could not be involved in the case. Five days later Coursol, citing the Consolidated Statutes of Lower Canada, announced that he agreed, and Carter had to resign. In the meantime, Police Chief Guillaume Lamothe had testified that the prisoners had declared they were commissioned by the Confederate government to retaliate against the acts committed by Union generals Philip Sheridan and William T. Sherman. On November 9 Coursol indicated his annoyance at the efforts of American recruiters to enlist Canadians into the Union Army. "It is, however, a well known fact that too many Canadians have of late abandoned their allegiance and entered a foreign service and that many persons have been entrapped by American bounty-jumpers and recruiting agents, by whom the whole frontier is infested."[8]

After the Crown closed its case on November 14, Coursol, over the objections of Bernard Devlin, who represented American interests, said it was time to take the voluntary statements of the prisoners, all of whom had obviously been rehearsed. Young, first in the stand, declared: "Whatever was done at St. Albans was done by the authority and order of the Confederate Government. I have not violated the neutrality laws of either Canada or Great Britain. Those who were with me at St. Albans are all officers or enlisted soldiers, and they were under my command . . . The expedition was not set on foot or projected in Canada . . . The course I intended to pursue in Vermont . . . was to retaliate for the barbarous atrocities of Grant, Butler, Sherman, Hunter, Milroy, Sheridan, Grierson and other Yankee officers." He also asked for a thirty-day adjournment in order to obtain the necessary papers from his government at Richmond for his defence.

One by one, over the next two days, the prisoners issued similar statements. A.C. Bruce of Kentucky denied that he had killed Elias J. Morrison during the raid. "I am told that I am accused of having shot Morrison at St. Albans. If I have shot him it was my duty to do so. I am taken for a comrade who is not here."

The morning of November 16 was devoted to Abbott's argument, strongly objected to by the Crown and the U.S. representatives, that the defence needed a recess of thirty days "to pass through hostile territory, guarded at every point," to obtain the necessary documents from Richmond. These materials were critical for Abbott's defence, given his argument that the raid was not criminal but a justifiable act by belligerents in the war. Although all the raiders claimed to be members of the Confederate forces, many of them had no documents to prove it. Nor did Young possess documents to show that he had been expressly commissioned to conduct forays into the border states. After adjourning to consider the matter, Coursol returned to say, "I feel I would be guilty of an act of injustice if I deprived the accused of the opportunity to place their evidence before me." Once again, the raiders got what they wanted as Coursol adjourned the case until December 13.

On December 1 the fourteen prisoners signed a petition for Governor General Monck, saying a messenger sent to Richmond had been captured by the Union, asking him to send a messenger, and promising they would pay his salary and expenses. Monck declined, just as President Lincoln had turned down an earlier petition from Abbott seeking a presidential order of safe conduct for a messenger to Richmond "for certain documentary evidence to enable them to submit their case fully and fairly." Abbott had asked the same thing, with the same result, of Lord Lyons in Washington, so he next hired prominent Washington lawyer and politician James Mandeville Carlisle to visit Lincoln and Lyons on behalf of the raiders, seeking permission to send a courier to Richmond. They both refused to see Carlisle – Lincoln because he was in no mood to do anything that might help the raiders, and Lyons because the Americans were already furious with what they saw as Canadian waffling on the issue and he did not want to add to those concerns.

In a December 7 blockbuster speech to a joint gathering of the U.S. Senate and House of Representatives, one that was enthusiastically received by politicians of all stripes, Lincoln made his feelings clear. He announced his intention to end two major treaties – the Rush-Bagot Agreement and the Reciprocity Treaty – "in view of the insecurity of life in the region adjacent to the Canadian borders by recent assaults and depredations committed by inimical and desperate persons who are harbored there."

The 1817 Rush-Bagot Agreement between the United States and Britain restricted each nation to no more than four warships on the Great Lakes, none greater than 100 tons, setting an important policy of peace between the two countries. The agreement called for six months' notice by either side for abrogation, but, since Lincoln was assassinated and the war was over before that time, the treaty was ultimately left in place. Not so the 1854 Reciprocity Treaty. It had eliminated customs tariffs between the United States and the British North American colonies on fish, raw materials, and agricultural products. The treaty resulted in a dramatic increase in trade, but American politicians, swept up by protectionist fever, had long advocated its demise, particularly after Canada raised its provincial tariffs in 1858 and 1859, as had New Brunswick in 1859 and 1863. They were even more opposed in 1860 when Finance Minister Alexander Galt enraged American business interests by introducing a 90 percent refund on tolls charged on the Welland Canal for any ships that proceeded down the St. Lawrence River to Montreal. Not surprisingly, the Reciprocity Treaty was not renewed in 1866, a serious blow to Canadian trade and a direct result of American unhappiness with what they saw as pro-Southern activities north of the border. The death of the treaty also had a major impact on Confederation itself, forcing politicians in Upper and Lower Canada to form closer trade relationships with the other British North American colonies.

Meanwhile, back in Montreal on December 14, Abbott's assistant W.H. Kerr directly challenged Coursol's jurisdiction in the St. Albans case, saying, "I deny your right to sit at all." Citing several Imperial and Canadian acts, Kerr said that because this case involved an international treaty between Great Britain and the United States, a warrant from the Governor General was "absolutely essential" to allow Coursol to sit. Since "no such warrant, however, has been issued," he argued, Coursol "has not, nor had he at any time, jurisdiction in these cases to arrest the prisoners."

Both F.G. Johnson for the Crown and Devlin for the United States dismissed the argument out of hand, but Coursol said it was "a knotty point" and adjourned to consider it. The courtroom, as usual crowded with well-dressed Southern gentlemen and parosol-wielding ladies, burst into wild applause when Coursol returned to say he agreed with the defence and "consequently I am bound in law, justice and fairness to order the immediate release of the prisoners from custody." Lamothe, the police chief, immediately escorted the raiders out of the courtroom and gave them back their weapons, which he had been holding, along with about $90,000 of the stolen St. Albans money. Earlier that day, Lamothe had been asked by U.S. law agents, who had grown suspicious of Coursol, to execute arrest warrants on new charges against the raiders, but the chief, having at first said he needed forty-five minutes to consider their request, then refused, allowing the raiders time to go to the railway depot, accompanied by a cheering mob of supporters. They left town within the hour, most of them heading west to Toronto or east to the Maritimes.

The next day George Brown's Toronto *Globe* ran a story headlined "The Raiders Escape: The Chief of Police Accused of

Complicity: He Refuses to Re-arrest Prisoners." In a subsequent investigation by the Montreal City Council police committee, led by Devlin, this time in his role as a city councillor, Kirkman Finlay Lockhart, an accountant at the Ontario Bank in Montreal, testified that about 3 p.m. that day, just before Coursol had returned to court to announce his verdict, he had delivered a sealed carpet bag on orders from Chief Lamothe to John Porterfield, an American exchange broker on the Place d'Armes. Lockhart said, "I know him [Porterfield] as a Southern gentleman, but would not say whether he is a sympathizer to the South." He certainly was a sympathizer – and more. As a former Nashville banker, he was directly involved with subversive Confederate activities in Montreal. At one point in the war he conceived the ambitious plan to undercut Union finances by buying large quantities of Federal gold, shipping it abroad, and converting it to sterling bills of exchange, which would then be used to buy more gold to ship out of the United States. Confederate agent Jacob Thompson had provided $100,000 to finance the scheme, and Porterfield had travelled to New York and managed to export about $2 million in gold before heading back to Canada, fearing that Federal agents were onto him. Porterfield had also been introduced to Lamothe by Confederate agent George Sanders a few days earlier at Sanders's office. Before that, and just a few days after the St. Albans raid, Sanders had set the stage for subsequent events by arranging to have himself introduced to Lamothe at the Doneganasp Hotel by another Confederate sympathizer, Johnathan Brune of Baltimore, in the presence of Judge Coursol.

While both Lamothe and Coursol denied allegations of being paid off by Confederate agents, their actions belie their cries of innocence. There is little doubt too that Abbott, given his own history of fiscal chicanery, was also part of the deal to free the raiders. Coursol was suspended pending the outcome of a judicial review of his actions, and in September 1865 an inquiry by Montreal Judge Frederick William Torrence on the "failure of justice in the matter of the St. Albans raid" criticized both Lamothe and Coursol, calling Coursol's ruling "an abdication of his judicial functions." As for Lamothe, he was subjected to a lengthy public investigation by the police committee and, while maintaining his innocence, he eventually resigned from the force. By a 14 to 11 vote, the committee accepted his resignation: it noted that, while the chief had "acted precipitously and imprudently . . . nothing [has been] shown to warrant the belief of his action partaking of dishonesty or corruption." Coursol testified under oath before the police committee that he had not told Lamothe or anybody else his decision before announcing it in the court. But Porterfield testified he had been asked a few days earlier by Sanders to assist Young in making a quick getaway out of Montreal because he "expected to be released."

An editorial in the December 22 *Boston Post* claimed that the release of the St. Albans raiders "converts the Canadian border into an asylum for freebooters and assassins, under the protection of Great Britain . . . If Canada refuses to surrender rebel thieves and murderers, there appears to be no other way to secure safety from their depredations, but for the aggrieved party to pursue the criminals to their headquarters." The *New York Times* wrote: "It will be hard to convince the people who are exposed to these border robberies, that there is not a species of connivance between the robbers and those who so heartily applaud their release in a Canadian court of justice." And the *New York Commercial Advertiser* added: "If British judges do not respect treaties and the claims of international comity, it is ridiculous to expect us to respect the sacred soil of Canada, which is made a harborage for rebel rogues or rebel soldiers."

It wasn't just editorial writers who were upset. On the same day that Coursol freed the raiders, the U.S. Congress voted 87 to 57 to kill the Reciprocity Treaty. "The following day Zachariah Chandler began his campaign in the Senate by reading the report on Coursol's decision, and Senator James W. Grimes of Iowa delivered himself of a long and impassioned argument in which he contended that repeal would eliminate the necessity for border defenses by forcing annexation upon the Canadas."[9] Congress also voted to place more warships on the Great Lakes, and Chandler made two motions: for the formation of an army corps "for the protection of U.S. territory along the border of Canada," and for the United States to compile a list of damages to American ships and property and to send the bill to Britain. All these developments significantly increased fears in Canada of U.S. retaliation. The angst didn't lessen when, just three days later, Lincoln issued tough new passport rules for the British North American provinces, another move designed to restrict the flow of people and commodities between the two countries. The passport rule didn't last long, but while it was in force it added to Canadian anxieties about an impending U.S. takeover. On January 12 the Senate voted 38 to 8 to give one year's notice that the treaty would then be considered null and void.

In recognition of widespread Canadian concerns about U.S. retaliation, Monck had issued a general order on December 19 calling out the militia. He asked for thirty companies of volunteer rifles or infantry, with sixty-five men in each, plus officers, "for immediate service on the frontier." Thirteen of the companies were to be raised in Lower Canada, and seventeen in Upper Canada, including six from Montreal and two from Toronto.

While American anger over the fate of the raiders continued to rage, Canadian authorities made another stab at appeasing their neighbours by appointing two special magistrates, one to tour the frontier west of Toronto, the other east of the city. They had tough new powers of arrest and detention, backed by their own special police force, "to take cognizance of any breaches of the law bearing on international relations." The December 17 *Globe* reported: "There is much excitement throughout the Northern States on this subject. The people of Detroit are patrolling the streets, expecting every night Southern incendiaries from Canada to perpetrate acts at which, as Mr. Sanders has said, 'European civilization would shudder.' . . . In every frontier town, the same feeling exists." The *Globe* argued that if Canada really wanted to show it was serious in stopping Confederate activities north of the border, "it would immediately throw Sanders, Thompson, and their associates out of Canada."

The December 19 *New York Times*, reflecting a widely held view of the St. Albans matter, said: "It is impossible to make anything else of this than that Canada has been turned into a rebel base of operations against our Government and people, and from a base more advantageous than any other, because [it is] more secure, being under the protection of a . . . neutral flag. This state of thing is deplorable . . . Canadian territory must be respected no more than Virginia or South Carolina territory. The guerillas which attack us from the north must be hunted down with the same vigor of pursuit as when they attack us at the South, and the British flag must not deter us one whit more in the one case than the Confederate flag deters us in the other. It may be said that this will lead to war with England. So it may. But if it must come, let it come . . . We were never in better condition for a war with England . . . The red squads that are in Canada would be, before one of our corps of veterans, like yellow leaves before the whirlwind. There is nothing in Canada that could offer us serious resistance. So too of the British West Indies, which might be made invaluable appendages of our great Republic. If the Canadians persist in allowing these murderous incursions into our territory, we must protect ourselves, whatever be the consequences."

The next day, December 20, Chief John McLoughlin of the Government Police, Montreal District, and some of his men, acting on a new warrant issued by Mr. Justice James Smith of the Superior Court, rearrested five of the released raiders, including Young, near Quebec City. They brought them back to Smith's Montreal court to face a new extraditable charge of robbery, the act of robbing St. Albans businessman Samuel Breck, who had entered the bank to deposit $393. Two more raiders were arrested January 9 at Pointe-aux-Trembles, the same day that 400 troops from Montreal, Quebec, Brockville, and Belleville arrived at Windsor, greeted by a large cheering crowd and a local band playing the "Red, White and Blue." The locals, worried about the possibilities of American retaliation from across the river in Detroit, threw a large civic dinner at Hiron's House that night in honour of the newly arrived officers and men. The troops had been dispatched after Canada's senior military leaders, in a special meeting at Quebec, had called for a military force to protect our frontier. On December 27 Mayor Robert Mackenzie of Sarnia presided over a mass meeting of local citizens who unanimously condemned "the disgraceful acts of the Southern sympathizers now in the Province."

On December 28 another raider was arrested in Toronto. Two days earlier, four of the raiders were captured at the conscripts' camp at Concord, New Hampshire. Claiming to be Canadians trying to enlist, they were carrying a large quantity of St. Albans money, along with other bills from Georgia and South Carolina banks and Canadian silver. Captain James Rice, the provost marshal at the camp, arrested them and sent their pictures to Governor Smith of Vermont, who telegraphed back with instructions to hold them. Rice also arrested two other Southerners who were overheard boasting that they were at the St. Albans trial and were also flush with Confederate and Canadian money, accounting for all fourteen of the raiders who had been released by Coursol. And on December 30, 130 men from the Queen's Own Rifles, Toronto, arrived in Niagara Falls at 8 p.m. to take up positions along the border with the United States. They were joined by sixty-five men and three officers from the Simcoe Rifle Company who left Simcoe for Niagara, accompanied by what the *Globe* described as "their splendid brass band."

The same day a volunteer company of the 20th Battalion left St. Catharines for Chatham. Smith's court attracted the usual Confederate men and women, but it was also regularly crowded with MPs from all political stripes and the leading men of all professions. On January 9 John A. Macdonald, then the attorney general for Canada East and later Canada's first prime minister, spent the whole day there as the defence again argued that Smith lacked jurisdiction in the case. Smith threw out the argument but adjourned the case until February 10, to allow the raiders thirty days to gather evidence from Richmond.

In the meantime, Governor General Monck recalled the legislature on January 19, 1865, about a month before it was scheduled to resume, to introduce a new *Alien Act,* or "frontier outrages bill." The act, which Monck had personally promised to Lincoln administration officials and which was intended to remain in force for one year, pleased U.S. Secretary of State William H. Seward so much that, the next day, he wrote a letter to Charles Francis Adams, the U.S. ambassador to Britain, instructing him to tell British officials that the North would not retaliate "at present" for the acts by rebels operating out of Canada. The *Montreal Gazette* was less impressed. Calling it "one of the most discreditable acts that has ever disgraced British legislation," the newspaper complained that it gave "the Governor General absolute rights to expel an alien as he sees fit, including immediate arrest and imprisonment without bail, based on suspicions only. Have our ministers no shame that they truckle to such friendly foreign influence in this way . . . ? Have they . . . advised or suggested any measure or proceedings to prevent the gangs of Northern vagabonds who infest our towns and country from debauching our young men from their homes and selling their lives and bodies as Northern recruits to subserve their own famous cupidity, or any measures . . . to prevent these vagabonds from luring away from their colours and their regiments Her Majesty's soldiers in this Province?" The bill, championed by Macdonald, passed second reading on February 1 by a 104 to 4 vote. Five days later it passed third reading and was promulgated by Monck, who arrived at the legislative building by riding on horseback through a heavy snowstorm to give his official stamp of approval for the act.

Seward had also promised to lift Lincoln's new passport provisions, which he did on March 11, a week after Lincoln's second inauguration, but not before using it as leverage to convince the federal Cabinet to reimburse the St. Albans banks for the money Lamothe had turned over to the raiders. Despite a massive protest meeting in Toronto, and similar meetings elsewhere in the country, and after a heated debate in Parliament, Canada gave $30,000 in bank notes and $39,512.75 in gold to compensate the St. Albans bankers. Canada East Rouge leader Antoine-Aimé Dorion, the man later credited with founding the Liberal Party, strongly objected to the measure, saying that Parliament didn't really know how much money was missing and that Montreal City Council had agree that Lamothe was "free from blame; he had only acted imprudently." But Canada West Conservative leader John A. Macdonald, pushing the compensation package through the assembly, said: "Whether the act at St. Albans was one of robbery or belligerency, the money did not belong to the parties it was given up to . . . The Canadian Government, feeling that an officer . . . had improperly given up the money, [felt] it would be infinitely more dignified to come forward." Actually, it had very little to do with being dignified. It was a calculated political tradeoff and, as a result, the U.S. lifted its restrictive passport rules for Canadians and British citizens crossing the border, although it didn't remove them from the Maritimes until June.

When the court resumed on February 10 before Smith, Abbott sought a further thirty-day delay, which Smith declined, on the grounds that the first messenger, Confederate Lieutenant S.B. Davies, had been arrested by U.S. authorities, detained as a spy, tried by court martial in Cincinnati, and sentenced to hang, even though General "Fighting Joe" Hooker, commander of the Army of the Potomac, who had approved the sentence, "well knew that Lt. Davies was not a spy." A second messenger had been sent on January 14, but nothing had been heard from him (it turned out that he had drowned crossing the ice on the Potomac River); a third had left on January 17, but nothing had been heard from him since he left Washington on January 21; and a fourth had gone on January 24, the day after the court learned that Davies had been captured, and he too had not been heard from. In addition, dispatches had also been sent with an unnamed person who left Montreal for the South in early January on business of his own, but he had been captured in Wilmington, North Carolina, released on parole, and returned to Montreal. Abbott had also sent John G.K. Houghton, a Montreal advocate, to Washington, seeking permission from Lincoln for safe passage. Checking into the Ebbitt House there, he requested a meeting with Seward on January 30 and managed to meet Lincoln the next day, but the president said they were rebels and it was not his business to help them. He did, however, give Houghton a card to present to Seward with the following note: "Hon. Secretary of State – Please see this gentleman, who is the gentleman from Canada spoken of yesterday. A. Lincoln. Jan. 31/65." When Houghton presented the card to Seward's office, he was refused a meeting. He then applied to the British chargé d'affaires for help, but the chargé had no intention of getting involved. So Houghton wrote again to Seward, who replied that the government of the United States "can hold no communication or correspondence with him upon that subject." He was also ordered to leave the country.

And so, lacking formal documentation that the raiders had been acting as belligerents as opposed to common thieves, the defence called a series of Confederate soldiers then living in Canada, all of whom testified that they knew the prisoners were indeed Confederate officers or soldiers – including Brigadier-

General W.H. Carroll of Tennessee, who was living at the Queen's Hotel in Toronto and had met Young several times in both the Queen's Hotel bar and the St. Lawrence Hotel in Montreal. He testified that he recognized the signatures of Confederate Secretary of War James Seddon and Confederate Commissioner C.C. Clay on documents that Young had presented to the court. Dated June 10, 1864, Seddon had ordered Young to "collect together such Confederate soldiers who have escaped from the enemy, not exceeding twenty in number . . . and exercise such enterprise as may be indicated to you. You will take care to organize within the territory of the enemy to violate none of the neutrality laws." An October 6, 1864, note from Clay said, "Your preparations for a raid upon accessible towns in Vermont, commencing with St. Albans, are approved and you are authorized and required to act in conformity with that suggestion."

By the time the court resumed sitting again on February 16, the Reverend Stephen T. Cameron, a former chaplain in Morgan's command, had returned from Richmond with the master rolls of several Confederate units. They contained the names and rank of the five prisoners, all affixed with the Great Seal of the Confederate States, and given to him personally by Confederate Secretary of State Judah P. Benjamin.

During cross-examination of defence witness Louis Saunders, the oft-repeated claim by the raiders that they did nothing in Canada to break the neutrality laws took a serious hit and would become a significant factor in subsequent judicial events. Saunders, a former Confederate then living in Montreal, who had delivered a $400 cheque to Young from Confederate agent Clement C. Clay before the raid to help pay for expenses, testified that the pre-raid conversation between Young and Clay leading to the cheque being drawn on the Montreal branch of the Ontario Bank had taken place in a private house that Clay was renting in St. Catharines.

Despite this admission, however, public opinion at the time

was generally supportive of the raiders. The February 14 *London Morning Herald*, for example, wrote that it would be a "perversion of law" to send the raiders home under the Extradition Treaty, which was intended "to secure the surrender of ordinary criminals to the justice of their country . . . [and was] never intended on either side that rebels, traitors, deserters or political offenders should be subject to its operation. America never intended to give up Irish rebels or Chartist incendiaries; we never meant to give up fugitive slaves, abolition preachers or secessionist officers . . . If they [the raiders] are robbers and incendiaries, so is Sherman, so is Sheridan, so is Grant. . . . Have they forgotten Sheridan's devastation of the Shenandoah Valley? Here the Federal army did on a grand scale what Young and his comrades did on a small one."

All these goings-on had increased tensions in Montreal between the Confederate sympathizers and those who weren't. The February 22 *Globe* recounted a story about a group of Southerners at the St. Lawrence Hall hotel bar, after the court adjourned, turning on a young Canadian who "made some remarks" about the South. The Confederates pulled a Bowie knife and drew revolvers, but "the police appeared before any blow was struck. This is the second row of the kind lately . . . There is great excitement about it."

There was even more excitement on March 29, when Justice Smith, in a judgment that took him four hours to read, concluded that the raiders were belligerents engaged in a hostile expedition under the authority of the Confederate States of America and they were free to go. If the offences had occurred in Canada, he said, he would have committed the men for trial. He cited the infamous order by General Dix to shoot the raiders, as well as the fact the U.S. administration had never rebuked Dix, as clear evidence that the United States saw the St. Albans raid as an act of war. The March 30 *Montreal Gazette* wrote that the decision "will not much surprise . . . we have always felt that if a fair hearing was obtained on the merits of the case, if the judge would consent to receive evidence of the belligerent capacity of the raiders, he could not afterwards treat them as ordinary robbers coming within the intent and meaning of the extradition treaty."

While a crowd of 3,000 people gathered outside the courthouse greeted the raiders with loud and repeated cheers for themselves, Judge Smith, and the Confederacy, Sergeant-Major Robert Dunlop of the Toronto Police Force had executed a new warrant against the five raiders, charging them with a breach of the neutrality law. This time they would be tried in Toronto for two reasons: first, because of evidence at the Smith trial that Young and Clay had planned the raid in Clay's rented house in St. Catharines, which came under Canada West jurisdiction; second, because judicial opinion was less favourably inclined towards the South in Toronto than it was in Montreal. Indeed, the warrant arresting the raiders was issued by George Duggan, the recorder at Toronto who had rejected defence arguments about the rights of belligerents and sent Bennett G. Burley back to the United States to face the death penalty on charges of robbery and piracy in the Johnson's Island incident on Lake Erie. (Burley, as we know, had escaped, but his colleague and cousin John Beall was hanged in that case.)

The prisoners were allowed forty-five minutes to celebrate with their supporters. Then they were taken, without handcuffs, to the Bonaventure Railroad Station by police magistrates, the sheriff, twenty mounted soldiers from the Royal Artillery, and a detachment of the Government Police. Ten of these policemen, under the command of Chief McLoughlin, proceeded to Toronto with the prisoners.

On April 11, three days before the Lincoln assassination, the five raiders appeared in Duggan's courtroom. It was so crowded that all the halls leading to the room were jammed with people. Four of the prisoners were quickly discharged, and Young was returned to jail to face extradition charges.

Young, who rose to the rank of general and was awarded the Confederate Medal of Honor, was never convicted of anything. He was held in jail by the Canadian government under large bonds until 1866, when the government finally admitted it could not convict him. When President Andrew Johnson issued his amnesty proclamation in 1865, Young was one of the few people specifically exempted. In 1866 he married Mattie R. Robinson, the eldest daughter of the Reverend Stuart Robinson, the famous Louisville Presbyterian preacher who spent much of the war working for the Confederacy in St. Catharines. He then moved to Europe, living briefly with General John C. Breckinridge before Breckinridge moved his family to the Niagara Falls area. He resumed his law studies, which he had begun in 1864 at the University of Toronto, at Queen's University of Belfast, Ireland.

Young returned to Louisville, Kentucky, in the summer of 1868 and became one of the most famous jury lawyers of his time, eventually being elected as commander in chief of the United Confederate Veterans. A charismatic figure, Young's final trip to Canada came in a short visit to Montreal in 1911, when a group of local dignitaries from St. Albans, Vermont, paid him a courtesy call at the Ritz-Carlton Hotel.

FOURTEEN

The Assassins

O N AUGUST 5, 1865, nearly four months after U.S. President Abraham Lincoln was assassinated by John Wilkes Booth at the Ford Theater in Washington, Confederate agent George N. Sanders and a Montreal police detective named O'Leary were riding through Priest's farm in Sanders's carriage late at night. Suddenly, a gang of armed men rushed out of the bushes, unceremoniously tossed O'Leary out of the carriage, gagged and handcuffed Sanders, and drove off into the night with their prize.

Unfortunately for the gang, the police had been expecting them. A few days before the attempted kidnapping, O'Leary, working undercover, had been offered $10,000 to help capture Sanders and other Southerners in Montreal. When the gang reached St-Antoine Gate, it was the police who jumped out of the nearby bushes. Several shots were exchanged, but the gang ran off, leaving Sanders behind.

One man, the notorious crimp Charley Adams, was arrested at 2 a.m. in the city. Others were arrested attempting to hire boats to escape across the St. Lawrence River. Among their effects, police found pictures of Sanders, Beverly Tucker, Clement C. Clay, Jacob Thompson, William C. Cleary, and other Confederate operators working in Montreal, Toronto, and St. Catharines. Two weeks earlier, in fact, some men had broken into Sanders's home, but they were foiled when confronted unexpectedly by his son-in-law and a friend, before they could do any damage.

Why were they after Sanders? The one thing he and the other potential kidnap victims had in common – besides their geography and their sympathies – was that, in the immediate aftermath of the April 14 murder of Lincoln, they had all been named by the U.S. government as co-conspirators wanted for their part in the assassination. The authorities believed – with considerable cause – that the assassination plot had been nurtured in Canada, particularly in Montreal, and that all those senior Confederate representatives working north of the border had been "combining, confederating, and conspiring together," as the formal charges alleged, with Booth and his compatriots. With huge rewards being offered for the capture of the conspirators, it's hardly surprising that a certain class of men were quick off the mark to score a bonanza by kidnapping the wanted people and dragging them back to Washington to stand trial

Booth, in fact, made several trips to Montreal in the weeks leading up to the assassination, meeting with these men and lodging at the grand St. Lawrence Hall hotel on St. James Street. To accommodate the number of Confederates in Montreal at the time, the Doneganasp Hotel, which normally closed in November, stayed open during all the winters of the war to take the overflow from the St. Lawrence.

It's also highly possible that a warning made five weeks before the assassination by journalist Sandford Conover may have saved the president's life had his story not been suppressed by his editor, Horace Greeley of the *New York Tribune*. Conover – part con man and part correspondent, and therefore not absolutely believable – posed as a Southerner and a Confederate sympathizer in Montreal, to ingratiate himself into the active Confederate circle there. To hide his true identity he never signed his dispatches to the *Tribune*, and in Montreal he went by the name of Charles A. Dunham. During the aftermath of the assassination, Conover – a major witness at the subsequent Lincoln conspiracy trials – would claim that in early March 1865, after attending a series of meetings with Thompson, Clay, Sanders, and Booth, most of them at the St. Lawrence Hall, he sent a story to the *Tribune* outlining a plot to murder Lincoln and other senior members of the administration. But his story was turned down, he says, "because they had been accused of publishing sensational stories of that kind before, and they feared there might be nothing in it, and did not wish to be accused of publishing sensational stories."

Whatever the truth of Conover's somewhat self-serving version – and during the Lincoln conspiracy trials much of his testimony proved to be perjured – the fact remains that all these men were holding a series of meetings during that dreadful spring. It was dreadful for them, of course, because their side in the war had lost – and Booth, the victor's assassin, was a key participant in those meetings.

In a July 14, 1973, column in the *Montreal Gazette*, the journalist Edgar Andrew Collard wrote: "Montreal during the American Civil War had nests of Confederate agents and plotters. It was ideally situated for conspiracy. It was neutral territory. Confederates could come and go as they pleased. And it was close to the practically unguarded border of the United States." In fact, wealthy Southerners had been coming to the area for years before the war to escape the Southern summertime heat, particularly after the war began when they no longer felt welcomed in New England resorts like Bar Harbor, Maine, and Burlington, Vermont. So, instead of stopping on their own northeastern coast, these tourists – many of whom would keep the blinds down on their train cars as they passed through the Northern territory so as not to "contaminate" themselves by looking on "Yankee" soil, – kept going north and founded a holiday colony in North Hadley, about an hour southeast of Montreal near the border between Quebec and Vermont. They built spacious summer homes along the shore of Lake Massawippi, often copies of their grand plantation homes in the Old South. After the war, these places attracted several Confederates who were escaping prosecution south of the border.

At the start of the war, Montrealers, like most British North Americans, generally favoured the North and the abolition of slavery. But as the war went on, the *Trent* crisis occurred, and Montrealers got to know the hundreds of troops that were posted to Montreal and, wary of an American attack, formed themselves into military companies, attitudes changed dramatically. The bellicose sword rattling from Washington officials such as Secretary of State William H. Seward didn't help, nor did the equally threatening remarks by Joshua Giddings, the U.S. consul general in Montreal, described by author Kathleen Jenkins as "a tactless individual, and totally inexperienced in the niceties of diplomacy."[1]

Giddings, a Pennsylvania native, had been a schoolteacher before studying law in Ohio. A veteran of Congress and an outspoken critic of slavery, he was first elected in 1826 as a Whig, and eventually became one of the founders of the Republican Party. The 29th Ohio Infantry was nicknamed the "Giddings Regiment" when it was first mustered in August 1861 at Camp Giddings, Ohio, the same year Lincoln appointed Giddings to Montreal, where he died on May 27, 1864. By that time, however, he had made enemies of just about everyone because of his consistent arrogance and anti-British expressions.

By 1862, Jenkins continues, "many of the local citizenry, in common with their fellow Canadians, were in the process of becoming firm supporters of the Confederacy. The crude partisanship of the Northern press irritated them, while friction along the border and minor 'incidents' kept the dislike very much alive.

"Montreal, of course, actually knew the southerners, who, in more peaceful times, came to Canada as tourists to escape the summer heat of their own homes. They were usually persons of wealth, whose refinement in manner formed a pleasing contrast to the forceful Yankees; upper-class society made them welcome. When stranded in this alien country by war, the same charm was put to work on behalf of their cause. It was only a short step to the establishment of informal confederate headquarters in several Canadian cities, and notably at Montreal . . . The result of all this was that the southern secret service agents began to use Canada as a base for plotting hit-and-run raids against the north. Whatever they did was magnified by rumors along the frontier. So serious, in fact, did the situation become, that by the end of 1863 the Canadian government was cooperating with the North in an attempt to prevent any more serious occurences."

At the same time, Montreal's Griffintown, home to thousands of Irish immigrants escaping poverty and famine in the early and mid-1800s, was a hotbed for Northern military recruitment. The prospect of large bounties appealed to the working-class Irish, many of whom worked fifteen-hour days in conditions not unfamiliar to the readers of Dickens. The 30,000 residents in the Griff made the Irish the largest English-speaking minority in Lower Canada. During the war, many Boston-based Irish units made regular trips there to replenish their ranks, sometimes finding voluntary recruits, but often taking them by force or trickery.

Montreal, a thriving city of 90,000 in 1861, the financial centre of the country, was so attractive to the Confederates that, late in the war, and for about three years afterwards, President Jefferson Davis sent his wife, Varina, his mother-in-law, Margaret K. Howell, and his children to live there. When Mrs. Howell died in November 1867, she was buried in Mount Royal Cemetery. For a time the Davis family, with Jefferson still in Richmond, lived at Phillips Square, where a large Hudson's Bay store now sits, in a row of three terraced townhouses. Mrs. Davis lived at one end of the row, with well-known publisher Robert Lovall next door and prominent surgeon Sir William Hales Hingston, a future mayor of Montreal, next to him. In 1957 the Daughters of the Confederacy erected an English-language plaque at the site to mark this bit of Southern history for American tourists. Sometime during the 1970s, after Quebec's separatist party began to enforce Bill 101 and its insistence on French-only signs, the original was replaced by a French-language plaque, something few Americans could read.

In May 1867, when Davis was freed after two years of confinement in prison on a $100,000 bond posted by Horace Greeley and a group of businessmen, he, along with his son William (Billy) and daughter Winnie travelled to New York City, then Montreal, where he was reunited with his daughter Margaret and son Jefferson Jr. The two boys, Jeff and Billy, along with the sons of several prominent Confederate officials and officers, were studying the classics at the private, upscale Bishop's College Grammar School in Lennoxville, and Margaret was enrolled in a convent school in Montreal.

While there was no shortage of Southern sympathizers and Confederate activists in Montreal, numerous Northern spies also lived there, the most prominent being Dr. Alexander Milton Ross, a famous Canadian-born naturalist who had moved to New York as a teenager after the death of his father. In the 1850s Ross became a leading anti-slavery activist and a personal friend of John Brown. When war broke out, he served for a short time as a U.S. military surgeon before being employed by Lincoln, whom he had also come to know well, as a "confidential correspondent" in Canada. As a major figure in Montreal social circles at the time, Ross was well placed to pick up news of Confederate activities and, on several occasions, to travel to Washington and report in person to Lincoln and his senior officials at the White House. After the war he remained active in scientific and medical circles. Ultimately, he was knighted by the emperor of Russia and the kings of Italy, Greece, Saxony, and Portugal. He was appointed consul in Canada by the kings of Belgium and Denmark and, in 1879, received the decoration of the Académie Française from the government of France for his work in advancing natural medicines.

John Wilkes Booth had been born on May 10, 1838, at the family farm near Bel Air, Maryland, the ninth child of the English actor Junius Brutus Booth and Mary Ann Holmes, who had emigrated to the United States in 1821. Junius had abandoned his lawful Belgian wife and 2-year-old son in England. The younger Booth became a well-known stage actor too, and his pro-Confederate sympathies drew him into the secretive Knights of the Golden Circle in the late 1850s and finally into some clandestine operations for the Confederacy in mid-1863. "His ability to travel, passion for the South, and ready acceptance at various levels of society made him a perfect choice" for this role.[2]

There is considerable evidence to suggest that the Lincoln assassination actually began as a plan to kidnap the president, along with several senior administration officials, and to use the hostages as a bargaining chip to force an end to the war and to allow the South, at the very least, to maintain the institution of slavery. "It is also possible," writes William Tidwell, "that the plan to capture Lincoln may have originated in Canada during the winter of 1863–64. Patrick C. Martin, a former Baltimore liquor dealer and blockade-runner, and George P. Kane, the former Baltimore police chief, had worked together to help organize the expedition to rescue the Johnson's Island prisoners in November 1863. Both men were from Baltimore and strongly pro-Confederate. They could have conceived the idea of capturing Lincoln as a hostage and discussed it with other Confederates in Canada, including [the Reverend K.J.] Stewart, who had the geographical knowledge necessary to flesh out the concept. When Kane went to Richmond in February 1864, he may have taken the idea with him." Stewart, an Episcopalian minister related to Robert E. Lee through marriage, was active in Canada after 1863 and often in direct correspondence with President Davis. In October 1864 he left Canada and went to Baltimore, then travelled on to Richmond and met with both Davis and Lee. When he returned to Canada, he carried $20,000 in secret service funds from Davis.

Booth was registered at the Parker House in Boston on July 26, 1864, along with three men from Canada – Charles R. Hunter of Toronto, H.V. Clinton of Hamilton, and R.A. Leech of Montreal – as well as A.J. Bursted of Baltimore. "The inference is that agents of the Confederate apparatus in Canada had a need to discuss something with Booth," says Tidwell. "Capturing Lincoln? Within a few weeks Booth was in Baltimore recruiting others for just such a scheme and had closed out his Pennsylvania oil operations. The inference becomes stronger as a result of a careful search of records in Toronto, Baltimore, Hamilton, and Montreal. No trace of Hunter, Bursted, and Leech was found. Thus the names appear to be aliases."[3]

On May 28, 1864, however, a man using the name H.V. Clinton registered at the St. Lawrence Hall in Montreal, giving his address as St. Louis this time, instead of Hamilton. In fact, St. Louis was a favourite cover address during the period, since it was neither in the South or the North. Clinton again checked into the St. Lawrence Hotel on August 24.

On October 16, 1864, Booth visited the wealthy Southerner Robert E. Coxe in Poughkeepsie. Coxe was a good friend of Clement C. Clay, and it was his house that Clay and other Confederate operatives used in St. Catharines for their activities. At 9:30 a.m. on Tuesday, October 18, Booth checked into Room 150 of the St. Lawrence Hall, where he stayed for ten days, meeting both Clay and Martin. Martin, who had strong connections with the Confederate underground, died a few weeks later when his 73-foot schooner *Marie Victoria* left Montreal, ran into a storm, and capsized, losing all hands, along with Booth's theatrical wardrobe, in the icy waters of the St. Lawrence River. Booth also held several meetings with George N. Sanders, the hotheaded Southerner with a history of advocating political assassination, who was then staying at the Ottawa Hotel in Montreal. Indeed, it was Sanders whom Colonel Ambrose Stevens, head of U.S. General John Dix's secret service, had overheard advocating Lincoln's assassination during the ill-fated Niagara peace conference at the Clifton House in Niagara. Stevens had gone to the hotel dressed in civilian clothes and reported the incident to Dix. Sanders, who hated the Union at the best of times, was in a particularly foul mood because his son Major Reid Sanders, a prisoner of war, had died at Boston's Fort Warren prison several weeks earlier.

The Montreal gathering was put off track for a time when, the day after Booth arrived, a group of Confederates raided St. Albans, Vermont. Sanders left Montreal for a few days to help the prisoners, but returned on October 25 and checked into Room 169, just down the hall from Booth in 150.

Two days later, Booth deposited $455 in the Ontario Bank in Montreal and purchased a bill of exchange for £61 12 shillings 10 pence, which, with identification, could be cashed anywhere. In his testimony at the conspiracy trial after the assassination, in May 1865, bank teller Robert Campbell said he believed that Booth had been introduced at the bank by Patrick Martin. The bank, just a few doors away from the hotel, should have been friendly towards the Southerners: Thompson alone had so much money deposited to his credit there that he once withdrew nearly $300,000 within a few months. And documents presented at the Lincoln assassination trial showed that, on two occasions in late April 1864, Thompson made payments of gold under the titles "Necessities and Exigencies" and "Secret Service," the first for $100,000, the second for $900,000. The Confederate operations in Canada may have been beset by numerous problems, but money, it seems, wasn't one of them.

In November, Booth spent a few days in Toronto, staying at

the Queen's Hotel. Colonel Robert M. Martin, who was arrested in Kentucky and jailed in October 1865 for his involvement in the failed attempt, organized in Toronto, to burn down a series of New York Hotels and public buildings, testified that he drank with Booth in Toronto that November.

The following month, December 1864, General Edwin Gray Lee, a cousin of Robert E. Lee, arrived in Canada, first in Hamilton and then in Toronto, assigned to assume some of the undercover work from Thompson and Clay. These two gentlemen had not been as successful in their work as headquarters in Richmond had hoped. Lee too was involved in the earlier meetings in Richmond between Stewart and the senior Confederate officials.

As the war continued to deteriorate for the South, and the Canadian-based plotters grew more desperate in their attempts to turns things around, Thompson told a few friends that, if only Lincoln and some of his important officials were "put out of the way," it was still possible to negotiate a peace treaty the Confederates could accept. During that period, Thompson flitted back and forth between Toronto and Montreal, holding regular meetings with the Confederate cabal and growing ever more desperate as the military situation collapsed before their eyes. The journalist Conover would later claim that, at one gathering in Thompson's room at the St. Lawrence Hall, Thompson asked him if he'd read the pamphlet *Killing No Murder*, an address to Oliver Cromwell in 1657 written by an officer named Titus, arguing that there are strong grounds of public necessity in getting rid of oppressors of the people.[4]

In Toronto, Christmas was celebrated in the Queen's Hotel "with a large tree, a great deal of whiskey, brandy and tears. Men in exile thought of past Christmases at home and tried to hide their feeling by roaring out Morgan's old song 'Song of the Raiders,' or 'Here's to Morgan' and 'Duke, Drink Them Down.' But the women wept and when the songs were all ended and the braggadocio forgotten, the men did, too. They were in exile. When they would return home they didn't know."[5]

Despite the hopelessness of the military situation for the South at this time, Thompson sent two envoys – Colonel Robert M. Martin and Lieutenant John W. Headley – to Richmond to deliver a bizarre scheme to Secretary of War John C. Breckinridge. This scheme envisioned the evacuation of Richmond and a massive counterattack by Lee's forces, combined with a northern uprising by the Sons of Liberty.

Thompson was still at the St. Lawrence Hall around noon on March 8, 1865, just weeks before Lee's surrender to Grant, when Lieutenant-Colonel James Gordon and Lieutenant Robert W. Brown, giving their addresses as the Confederate States of America, checked into Rooms 145 and 149, respectfully. Gordon, the son of a wealthy planter, knew Thompson well, not only as a fellow politician from Mississippi but because he had married Thompson's niece Virginia C. Wiley in 1856. Gordon was also a close personal friend of Davis, which meant he "was immediately on the inside of whatever the Confederates in Canada were doing or planned to do."[6] Brown, though born in North Carolina, had grown up in New York City, where his father ran a profitable ship-chandlering business. In 1846 the business moved to Wilmington, and Brown married local debutante Josephine Lovett. During the last two years of the war, she was an important and successful courier for the South. Brown fled to Richmond in 1862 to avoid arrest for his pro-Confederate activities and served on the staff of General John H. Winder, before being sent to Canada in September 1864 to work with Clay in St. Catharines.

When Brown and Gordon arrived at the St. Lawrence Hall that March, Thompson, who had checked in on February 14, was there, along with George Sanders, William C. Cleary, Beverly Tucker, and several others. They were joined a few days later by General Edwin G. Lee, who arrived from Hamilton.

At this point another mysterious Confederate figure enters the picture, a woman named Sarah Slater, described as "an exotic young French-speaking Confederate agent and courier also known as Kate Thompson."[7] Slater made several trips to and from Montreal, Washington, and Richmond, spending time in the home of Mrs. Mary E. Surratt and squiring around George A. Atzerodt, two of the people hanged after the assassination. She also reportedly spent much private time with Booth. In his confessions, published in the *Baltimore American*, Atzerodt – who, as part of the plot, was assigned to kill Vice-President Andrew Johnson but was obviously smitten by Slater – wrote somewhat ruefully that while he had once rowed her across the Potomac River to Virginia, she "went with Booth a good deal. She stopped at the National Hotel." She also escorted John Surratt, Mrs. Surratt's son, who was wanted in the Lincoln assassination but initially fled to Montreal to avoid prosecution. Throughout the subsequent Lincoln conspiracy trial, there were numerous references to her and her role in the affair, but, despite an intensive search for her, she disappeared and was never found.

During the St. Albans trial in Montreal, Slater carried messages between Richmond and Montreal, including papers and money for the bank robbers being held in a Montreal jail – papers that, as we know, played a key role in their ultimate acquittal because they established their claims that they were Confederate soldiers acting under legitimate wartime orders, rather than common bank robbers caught with the money in their pockets. Now, just a month before the assassination, she was in Montreal. She arrived with dispatches for Thompson and Lee from Confederate Secretary of State Judah P. Benjamin, dispatches considered so urgent that immediate responses were required. A few days later, Slater was entrusted with those responses and, once again, set out for Richmond.

Years later, Gordon said: "We knew that we were beaten, and there was a general fear among southern men that the North would impose terms so severe that the already shattered and impoverished South could not meet them. Many plans were discussed in this country and abroad looking to the reaching of a settlement on terms the South could endure. One plan which found favor was to capture Lincoln, take him into the Confederacy, and with him as a hostage, trade for peace. I was party to this plot and did some work to promote it and carry it to a successful conclusion. The venture needed desperate men and the exercise of great caution and skill as well. Somehow the men in the plot became impatient and finally a new conspiracy was hatched which contemplated the killing of Lincoln. With that conspiracy, I had no part or sympathy."[8]

On April 13, 1865, saddened by Lee's surrender to Grant and further outraged by the joyous reaction of the North and the caterwauling against the Confederacy by the Northern press, the conspirators at the St. Lawrence Hall still hoped for revenge against what they saw as this monstrous injustice. By this time, however, Thompson, despite his grand reputation for Southern honour, had decided to slink away to England – and take much of the Confederate money with him – and on April 14, the day he was shot, Lincoln turned down a request brought by Assistant Secretary of War Charles A. Dana from Stanton seeking the arrest of Thompson, his old Senate ally. But Lincoln is said to have offered, instead, one of his famous aphorisms: "When you have got an elephant by the hind leg, and he's trying to run away, it's best to let him run." And so the provost marshal at Portland allowed Thompson to board a ship to Halifax, where he was escorted in the private carriage of Benjamin Wier, and from where, after a brief stay, he retired to the English lakes, passing his time reading volumes of William Wordsworth and other Lake poets. During the Lincoln trial a Montreal banker testified that after Slater had arrived in Montreal with the dispatches, including a letter in cipher from Jefferson Davis, Thompson withdrew $184,000 from the more than $600,000 he had in his private account.

The last note that Lincoln ever wrote, before heading off to the theatre with his wife, was to George Ashmun, his unofficial emissary to the Canadas.[9] Ashmun, a Massachusetts Congressman, had been chairman of the 1860 Republican Convention that first nominated Lincoln. According to his biography on the Lincoln Institute Web site, Ashmun had tried to obtain permits to trade in cotton along the Mississippi in February but had been thwarted by the Treasury Department. And so he met his old friend Lincoln, along with House Speaker Schuyler Colfax, in the Red Parlor, just as the Lincolns were leaving for the play. Lincoln gave Ashmun the note he wanted, then, after chatting awhile, they stood outside the parlour talking about Colfax's upcoming trip across the continent. They moved on to the main vestibule of the White House, where Colfax took his leave. Ashmun continued onto the portico with President and Mrs. Lincoln, said goodbye, and started off downtown.

Within the hour, Lincoln had been mortally wounded by Booth. Twelve days later, when Booth was tracked down to a barn and shot, the man who fired that fatal bullet was Canadian-born Lieutenant Edward P. Doherty, head of a detachment of the 16th New York Cavalry. Doherty, born in London, Canada West, had moved to New York when he was 8. He received a $5,000 reward for his act.

The reaction to Lincoln's death in Canada was so devastating that even Confederate emissary Edwin Lee described it in a note to Richmond as "universal horror." Almost every city in the country passed resolutions expressing sympathy. Many businesses were closed, and special church services were conducted. "In Toronto, the streets were choked with men and women who thronged the newspaper offices to hear the latest news. A meeting at the American Hotel was crowded with Canadians who wished to pay homage to a leader whom they had never known. Canadians streamed into Detroit to attend mourning services and to watch a huge catafalque hauled through the street behind bands playing funeral dirges. Within a day the merchants' stock of crepe was sold out."

That aside, two of the St. Albans raiders, holding forth in the bar room of the Queen's Hotel in Toronto, openly toasted John Wilkes Booth, and a group of Southerners at the St. Lawrence Hall held an impromptu champagne supper to celebrate the event. The April 15 *Globe* described it as "a noisy debauch in honor of the event, and a clergyman among them said publicly at the breakfast table at the same hotel that Lincoln had 'only gone to hell a little before his time.'" But they, of course, were the exceptions. The vast majority of people in British North America – including every newspaper except for the pro-Confederate *Toronto Leader* – were profoundly moved by Lincoln's death.

The assassination also sparked a massive manhunt in Canada, particularly in Montreal, where it was believed that Booth had escaped by rail. When American officials wired Lord Monck to say that some of the persons involved were headed towards Quebec, the governor general promised full cooperation and, all along the border, citizens voluntarily patrolled crossing points. An emergency company was formed in Malone, New York, to patrol the border east to Rouse's Point. At one point Montreal police rushed to Trois-Rivières, after being told that the assassins had been seen there.

On May 29, after Booth's death, three Montreal detectives – who, like many people, didn't believe it was the actual assassin who'd been shot – swooped down on the Garneau Hotel, believing that Booth was hiding there. Finding the "suspect" in the reading room, they locked the door and had their man cornered, confirming their belief that it was Booth by looking at a photograph of the assassin. The man denied that he was Booth, but, since the detectives refused to believe him, he agreed to go with them to the police station, where he was minutely searched, then taken to the Central Police Station in the Bonsecours Market building. There, they ran into Charles-Joseph Coursol, the inspector and superintendent of police for Montreal, who already had a pro-Confederate reputation for freeing the St. Albans raiders the year before. Coursol took one look at "Booth," said their prisoner was "not the right man," and ordered the police to let him go.

As sometimes happens in such moments of high drama and excessive excitability, Lincoln's replacement, his vice-president, Andrew Johnson, managed to undercut much of the goodwill expressed by Canadians towards their Northern neighbours – a turnabout from the previous few years of general sympathy for the Southern cause. He directly accused Canada of having "harboured" Lincoln's killers – Thompson, Clay, Tucker, Sanders, and others – who, he said, had plotted the whole thing along with Jefferson Davis. He offered substantial rewards for the capture of these men. Actually, the accusation wasn't that far off base, although, at the time, there was little public knowledge about how involved the Canadian Confederates had been in the affair.

Incredibly, both the *Montreal Gazette* and *Montreal Evening Telegram* responded with similar editorials suggesting that Johnson himself, having the most to gain, may have been involved in the murder plot. The *Gazette* hadn't been sympathetic to the Northern cause in the past. In the midst of the conflict it published an editorial saying: "For ourselves we condemn the principle of slavery entirely, but in practice, we are free to confess that it has necessarily no absolutely repugnant features. Practically, we are all slaves, more or less and the mildest form of the condition is perhaps that of the slave with a reasonably benevolent master. A great deal of humbug is mixed up with this questions as with all others . . . if accounts are to be relied upon, all of the outrageous crimes and two-thirds of the minor ones are perpetrated by the coloured people. Let every man in Lower Canada take his experience of them. Respectable men ought to be made welcome, whatever may be the colour of their skins, but the idle and vicious are unworthy of consideration. What have we to do with the institution of slavery in the

United States? It does not affect us. If they are satisfied, and after all the blustering to the contrary, they appear to be fully so, Canada has nothing to complain of, about it."

That attitude no doubt explains why, on May 4, 1865, both newspapers also published open letters from Sanders and Tucker calling Johnson's proclamation "a living, burning lie," claiming they had never met Booth and had never heard of him until the assassination, and even accusing Johnson himself of being involved in a plot to kill Jefferson Davis. In the May 5 *Globe*, Tucker published another letter, in an "Address to the People of Canada," in which he repeated that he had never heard of Booth and, he asserted, whoever accused him of being involved in the assassination "hath blackened his soul with diabolical perjury."

On May 10 Clay wrote to U.S. Brevet Major-General James Wilson in Macon, Georgia, saying he'd seen the president's proclamation offering a $100,000 reward for his, Clay's, arrest and, "conscious of my innocence, unwilling even to be seen to fly from justice, and confident of my entire vindication from so foul an imputation from the full, fair and impartial trial which I expect to receive, I shall go as soon as practicable to Macon and deliver myself up to your custody." Clay wasn't just talking a good game because he actually did voluntarily surrender and was immediately thrown into jail. The November 30, 1865, *St. Catharines Constitutional*, six days after the War Department revoked the rewards it had offered for Thompson, Tucker, Sanders, Cleary, and John Surratt, wrote that Clay's actions "evinced the true nobility of the man, [and] brought upon him a fate more cruel than that of the great majority of his comrades. He was torn from his family, subjected to uncalled for indignities, thrown into a dungeon, and there he lies to this day, the victim of his own exalted sense of honor and propriety."

The May 10 *New York Times* wrote that David Herold, regularly described as "a half-wit Confederate sympathizer" – and one of those eventually convicted and hanged for his role in the affair

– "went to Canada and conferred with the rebels about the assassination of Mr. Lincoln . . . It is positively known that [John] Surratt is in Canada and there is little doubt that he will soon be taken."

The newspapers were right about Surratt, who had acted as a messenger for Edwin Lee and whose mother, Mary, because of her role in the plot, was the first women ever hanged by the United States. He was in Montreal, hiding out in the Roman Catholic rectory at St-Liboire. A pocket handkerchief with his name on it had been found in the railway depot at Burlington, Vermont, heightening the search, but Surratt eventually escaped to Rome. He was captured in Egypt and brought to trial in 1867 in a civil court, but he won his freedom when the trial ended in a hung jury. In a seventy-five-minute lecture on December 6, 1870, in a small courthouse in Rockville, Maryland – which adults paid 50 cents to attend, and children half that price – Surratt told his story of the conspiracy. He hotly proclaimed his innocence and outlined in painstaking detail how he had escaped to Canada. Before that, on the eve of the fall of Richmond, he said that Judah Benjamin had given him $200 in gold to pay his way to Canada to carry dispatches for him, "the only money I ever received from the Confederate government or any of its agents." He said he met Booth many times, and Booth told him about his plan to kidnap Lincoln, but he had nothing to do with it.

Before the assassination, Surratt continued, and on Benjamin's orders, he arrived in Montreal by train, checked into the St. Lawrence Hall in Montreal using the name John Harrison, and shortly after that delivered the dispatches to General Edwin Lee. A week later, Lee came to his room and asked if he would go to Elmira, New York, make a sketch of the prison, and find out other details, with a view to releasing Confederate prisoners being held there. He arrived in Elmira, he said, two days before Lincoln's assassination and spent the next day sketching the prison and its surroundings. Surratt claimed he went to bed

about 10 p.m. on the night of the assassination and didn't hear
about it until somebody told him at breakfast the next morning.
This story contradicts testimony at the trial from another witness,
who swore he saw Surratt and Booth in front of the Ford Theater
on that fateful night.

In any event, Surratt, realizing that authorities would be
searching for anybody ever connected to Booth, headed for
Baltimore on horseback and, three days later, arrived at the railway depot in Burlington, Vermont. He had crossed Lake
Champlain by boat, which was four hours late, so he missed the
last train to Montreal. He slept in the depot and boarded the
4 a.m. train. Later, as the watchman swept the floor at the depot,
he discovered the handkerchief marked "J.J. Surratt 2." After
changing trains at Essex Junction and heading for St. Albans, he
arrived there for breakfast. An elderly man showed him the local
newspaper, which included his name among the suspected assassins. He also heard someone else say that Surratt must be in town
by this time, headed for Canada, because his handkerchief had
been found. He left immediately, travelling by foot across country, and finally arrived in Montreal. John Porterfield, the former
Nashville banker who had played a significant role in the trials
following the St. Albans raid, arranged for a Roman Catholic
priest to take custody of him, and he went with Joseph F.
Du Tilley to St-Liboire, about 45 miles from the city. Father
Boucher and Father La Pierre later volunteered to testify as
defence witnesses at Surratt's trial and to admit that they had hidden him, despite knowing he had been charged in the assassination, although they had conveniently forgotten the names of
anybody else involved in Surratt's escape. They kept him hidden
until mid-September, when, after colouring his hair, painting his
face, and putting glasses on as a disguise, he sailed to Quebec
with the priests and Beverly Tucker, who had publicly declared
his innocence in the whole affair. At Quebec they boarded him on
the *Peruvian* for the crossing to Europe.

As for Tucker, who had sent his four sons to Upper Canada College and the University in Toronto during his days in St. Catharines, he too had his local admirers. The November 30 *St. Catharines Constitutional*, completely rejecting any charges of propriety, said no one who knew him doubted his innocence. "There was something so upright and manly in all his actions and conversation, that it was impossible to believe he could be guilty of anything base or treacherous. However, a blood-thirsty oligarchy ruled the hour, and had he been caught there is little doubt that the wretched Court that hanged Mrs. Surratt would have likewise stained their hands with the murder of the gentleman in question. As it was, he was subjected to the vilest insults . . . so that wherever he went he might be branded an escaped assassin; while his family were subjected to indignities and outrages that would have done credit to the fiendish ingenuity of the King of Dahomey." This account appeared a few years before Tucker bought the fashionable Stephenson House spa, racked up considerable debts, and, in 1871, suddenly skipped town, leaving behind a slew of debtors and unpaid staff. Southern chivalry, like the Confederacy itself, lay in tatters.

There is little doubt that the Confederate cabal in Canada, in cooperation with senior administration officials in Richmond, played a major role in Lincoln's assassination. After the war, it was common to point the finger solely at Booth, the crazed actor, to explain one of the most cataclysmic events in American history. The Canadian Confederate contingent lucked out and never had, really, to face up to its role in the affair. Union detectives had found two witnesses – Dr. James B. Merritt and Charles A. Dunham, alias Sandford Conover – to testify to the direct involvement of these men in the plot. Both had spent considerable time in Canada gaining the confidence of the Confederates, but, unfortunately for the Union's case, they also shared another trait: they were unmitigated liars and were found guilty of perjury during the trials.

Their lies did not harm the Crown's case against the eight people on trial, but, to the delight of the Canadian contingent – who made sure the perjured testimony was well publicized – Merritt and Dunham discredited the Crown's case against Thompson and all his friends. Pity.

FIFTEEN

Circling the Wagons

W HILE THE SECTIONAL CONFLICTS in the United States during the 1850s were inexorably headed for war, the regional disputes in British North America weren't faring all that well either.

In the decade leading up to the Civil War, the Province of Canada was mired in a political deadlock. In a ten-year span, ten different governments had tried, without success, to solve the linguistic, religious, and cultural differences between the English and the French. The overwhelming sentiment in the Maritime colonies held that the people there wanted nothing to do with the feuding Upper and Lower Canadians.

In Canada East the two main combatants were the Bleus led by George-Étienne Cartier and the nationalistic Rouges under Antoine-Aimé Dorion. In Canada West it was the Tories led by John A. Macdonald and the Grits led by George Brown, the bombastic owner of the Toronto *Globe*. All four produced relatively equal groupings, which meant nobody could get a majority, and, despite attempts at various coalitions to form a government, all had quickly failed. Things were so bad that Queen Victoria felt the only answer was to shift the capital to a "neutral" location, and in 1857 she chose Ottawa, slated to open for business as the new capital during the last year of the Civil War. Underneath the unrest was growing concern over American expansionism, fears that the United States, having forcibly removed the Crown less than a century before, might take the final step and annex all of British North America.

While that notion did not have wide appeal north of the border, there were some who thought it a good idea. In 1849, for example, a group of leading Montreal businessmen – including the Molsons and the Redpaths, along with the future prime minister J.J.C. Abbott and four future Cabinet ministers – published the Montreal Annexation Manifesto in the *Montreal Gazette*, addressed rather grandly "To the People of Canada," calling for "a friendly and peaceful separation from British connection and a union upon equitable terms with the great North American Confederacy of Sovereign States." Such a move, they argued, would instantly double the current value of property in Canada and be of "incalcuable benefit" to the country. "In place of war and alarms of war with a neighbour, there would be peace and amity between this country and the United States."

War, and alarms of war, had marked the relationship between the United States and British North America ever since the American Revolution. With the War of 1812 still fresh in the minds of many Canadian and Maritime leaders, and America's Manifest Destiny a political reality, fear of an American takeover was never far from the surface as an issue for most colonists. With the outbreak of the Civil War, these concerns were about to get worse. At the same time, the fear of American reprisals, aided by some dramatic wartime events and the bellicose threats from several leading American politicians, began to break down the strong localized opposition against forming a single, united Canada. Some form of federation seemed to be the best way to stave off an American takeover.

The Americans had coveted Canada for many years. In 1775 Thomas Jefferson had anticipated that "the delegates of Canada will join us in Congress and complete the American union." Indeed, the U.S. Articles of Confederation invited an application by Canadians to be "admitted into and entitled to all the advantages of the union."

The northern colonies had always been affected by powerful external forces beyond their control. First, the power struggles between Britain and France had resulted in the fall of Quebec to the British in 1759. Then the Treaty of Paris of 1783, after the American Revolution, had recognized the United States as an independent nation. Although the treaty confirmed the continuing existence of the British colonies, they were considerably reduced in size by American claims of vast territories in the interior of the continent.

The Americans and the colonists tended to co-exist fairly well, but problems arose between Britain and the United States over British involvement in the wars associated with the French Revolution. Those entanglements led to serious disputes with the Americans over the issue of neutrality on the high seas when American sailors were forced into the Royal Navy. There were other tensions too, leading to the War of 1812, where, once again, the colonists had no say in the affair but found themselves on the front lines of the battlefields. Henry Clay, the Speaker in the House of Representatives, depicted the 1812 attack on Canada as a way to break the British alliance with the Indians and challenge the British Navy. Jefferson, speaking from retirement, said the conquest of Canada was merely a matter of "marching." The Rush-Bagot Agreement of 1817 tried to address the issue of an arms race by limiting naval armament on the Great Lakes, and, a year later, the United States and Britain agreed that the boundary would be the 49th parallel from Lake of the Woods to the Rocky Mountains, leaving the Pacific border open for future disputes. In 1844 the incumbent U.S. government wanted to extend the 49th parallel to the Pacific, but Democrat James Polk won the presidency on a campaign demanding that the boundary line be drawn so far north – "Fifty-four forty or fight" – it would block British North America off from the Pacific. That led the British to mobilize their land and sea forces in the colonies in preparation for war. But the Americans were already about to fight with Mexico, and in 1846, twelve years before the Crown Colony of British Columbia was proclaimed, the 49th parallel was extended to the Pacific coast, leaving Vancouver Island as wholly British territory.

Tensions were also heightened after the 1837 Rebellions in Upper and Lower Canada, when rebel leaders fled to the United States and solicited the aid of American sympathizers in a failed attempt to continue their fight from there. By 1869, concerned that westward expansion in the United States would result in the annexation of parts of British territory, the British Parliament decided to merge the Hudson's Bay Company territories (Rupert's Land) with its colony in Ontario, and proceedings began to allow more powers of self-government to the colony in response to what it saw as the American threat.

When Sir Charles Stanley, Lord Monck, arrived at his official post as governor general in 1861, he had to deal not only with the mutual trust between French and English in Upper and Lower Canada but with the simmering tensions between Canada and the United States. Less than three weeks into his term, the *Trent* Affair precipitated an enormous diplomatic crisis between Britain and the United States – one that seemed, for a time, likely to turn the colonies into a battleground. Monck is given great credit in helping to build the "Great Coalition" in 1863, when Brown agreed to work with Macdonald and Cartier towards political reform, and for using his formidable diplomatic skills to promote the controversial concept of unity in the Maritimes, ultimately opening the road to Confederation.

But it was the American Civil War, and the palpable fears of a military takeover, which to a large extent provided the fuel that kept the unity train on track. The war affected Canada in other important ways too, helping to determine the actual structure of our federal-provincial process. Historian Donald Creighton argues that Macdonald, Canada's first prime minister, admired the Americans, but "he was convinced the conflict was the result of a weak central government – a view that led him to advocate limits on provincial rights in negotiating terms of Confederation with Nova Scotia, New Brunswick and other colonies."[1]

Another author, E.B. Biggar, wrote that when the war began, Macdonald believed it would result in the formation of two independent nations to the south. In an 1861 speech, Macdonald said he hoped that if it happened that way, the "two great, two noble, two free nations would exist in place of one." While he sympathized with their current situation, he said it should serve as "a warning to ourselves, that we do not split upon the same rock. The fatal error which they committed – and it was perhaps unavoidable from the state of the colonies at the time of the revolution – was in making each state a distinct sovereignty."[2]

Since 1850, William Seward, who acted as Lincoln's secretary of state throughout the Civil War, had been an active annexationist, believing that British North America was destined to become a part of the United States. For the colonists, fears of an American takeover were intensified as the British began withdrawing their troops and leaving the colonies to rely more on their own defences. This policy wasn't reversed until the Civil War, after British Prime Minister Lord Palmerston, at the height of the *Trent* Affair, told Queen Victoria that Britain was ready "to inflict a severe blow upon and to read a lesson to the United States which will not soon be forgotten."

The Reciprocity Treaty, which allowed freer trade between the United States and the colonies, along with the expansion of the railway system, inevitably brought the two peoples closer together over the years. Despite their rocky history, Canadians were overwhelmingly pro-Union when the war began, largely on the strength of their recent trade history and their almost universal anti-slavery views. But as the fighting continued, attitudes changed dramatically. The *Trent* Affair angered the colonists as well as the British, and Britain's recognition of the South as belligerents outraged the Union. Lincoln's early downplaying of slavery as the central issue neutralized that issue for the colonists, and a series of high-handed American actions along the frontier, combined with growing Confederate operations in Canada, quickly undercut the cordial relations that had been developing with the North.

In the United States, more politicians and newspapers began to promote the notion of a war with Britain, one that would reunite all of North America. There was considerable talk, too, about "driving the French out of Mexico and the British out of Canada," once the Confederacy was crushed. Responding to this speculation, Brown wrote in the August 7, 1861, *Globe*: "The insolent bravado of the Northern press toward Great Britain and the insulting tone assumed toward these Provinces have unquestionably produced a marked change in the feelings of our people. When the war commenced, there was only one feeling, of hearty sympathy with the North, but now it is very different. People have lost sight of the character of the struggle in the exasperation excited by the injustice and abuse showered upon us by the party with which we sympathized." Historian Oscar D. Skelton agrees that the *Trent* Affair brought matters to a crisis: "If war broke out between the United States and Great Britain, Canada would be the battlefield. Every Canadian knew it; nothing could be clearer."[3]

When the immediate danger passed, the Canadian government brought in a bill providing for a compulsory militia, but the administration was defeated in 1862. The next ministry promoted volunteerism in an effort to shore up Canadian defences against the growing threat of American attack. Skelton cites an unnamed British lord, scoffing at Canada's feeble efforts to defend itself, saying, "If the people of the North fail, they will attack Canada as a compensation for their losses; if they succeed, they will attack Canada in the drunkenness of victory." And *The*

Times declared that if that happened, Britain had neither the power nor the will to protect Canada without considerably more aid on her part. This theme would echo throughout the period, creating grumblings in Britain from a significant political faction that felt the colonies weren't worth the trouble and the expense, particularly if they weren't prepared to help themselves.

Thomas D'Arcy McGee, a firebrand newspaperman who became one of Canada's leading politicians – before being assassinated by Fenian sympathizers in 1868 – spoke to a standing-room-only crowd in Britain, at London City Hall on September 27, 1861, of the threat of American expansionism. He stated that, because Americans were "not satisfied with the overthrow of British power in the original thirteen states, there was a periodical menace held out to British North America; not content with the subjugation of the Spanish race in Florida, Texas, and California, there was a like menace held out against Cuba and Central America. The Monroe Doctrine, as expounded at San Juan, has not been entirely forgotten by the United States." It was McGee who also said in 1861 at Quebec that the first shots fired at Fort Sumter "had a message for us," and that message was "to sleep no more except upon our arms."

The Monroe Doctrine, a unilateral U.S. policy proclaimed in 1823, consisted of four main points: no new European colonization; no extension of European political systems in the Western Hemisphere; no intervention to put down revolutions; and – the U.S. quid pro quo – no American interference in Europe's internal concerns. Later on, there was Manifest Destiny, a term coined by journalist John Louis O'Sullivan in an editorial supporting the annexation of Texas in the July-August 1845 edition of the *United States Magazine and Democratic Review*. It was a nationalistic belief, quite popular at the time, that the territorial expansion of the United States was not only inevitable but divinely ordained, and it was used by expansionists to justify the acquisition of Texas from Mexico and, later, the acquisition of

California, the Oregon Territory, and Alaska. Many expansionists also suggested it as justification for including British North America among the possessions of the United States.

Illinois Representative Owen Lovejoy, a Lincoln confidant, threatened that, once the war ended, the Americans would help the Irish rebels to foment a revolt in French Canada. Indeed, says historian D.C. Bélanger, "toward the end of the war many Americans did fund and support the Fenian Brotherhood . . . American-based Irish nationalists who sought to harass the British by launching periodic raids or 'invasions' into British North America. Poorly planned and badly led, the Fenian raids were easily repelled by the Canadian militia. Nonetheless, the unofficial American support of Fenianism was a direct consequence of the diplomatic friction generated by the Civil War. Many members of the Fenian 'army' were veterans of the Union army.

"Without a doubt, the Civil War had a profound impact on Canada's political and constitutional evolution. Fear of an American or Fenian invasion and the need for a common defence strategy was one of the major factors that launched British North America on the road to Confederation from 1864 to 1867. Many of the delegates at the three constitutional conferences that drafted the *British North America Act* of 1867 felt that the Civil War was an indictment not only of egalitarianism, democracy and republicanism, but also of a decentralized federalism, if not of federalism itself. In turn, Canadian conservatives drafted a constitution that granted most of the powers that were considered important in the nineteenth century to the federal government and contained several checks to 'excessive' democracy. Canada became a country based not on 'life, liberty and the pursuit of happiness,' but rather on 'peace, order and good government.'"[4]

In his famous Confederation speech, D'Arcy McGee said there had always been a desire among Americans to expand. "They coveted Florida, and seized it. They coveted Louisiana, and purchased it; they coveted Texas, and stole it, and then they picked a quarrel with Mexico, which ended by their getting California. They sometimes pretend to despise these colonies as prizes beneath their ambition but had we not had the strong arm of England over us, we should not now have had a separate existence." He also said earlier, in the debates leading up to Confederation, that if you are searching for reasons why the colonies should have become a Confederation under the Crown, "look to the embattled valleys of Virginia, and you will find reasons as thick as blackberries."

In August 1863, in a letter to the *Montreal Gazette*, McGee wrote, "I am no alarmist, but neither can I close my eyes to the signs of the times. At Rouse's Point, fifteen miles from this populous city, the heart of Canada, our neighbours have hurried to completion an immense new fortress, Fort Montgomery . . . designed to play no feeble part in the contemplated subjugation of our country . . . I speak upon no newspaper authority, upon no doubtful information, when I say that the plan contemplated at Washington for the invasion of Canada is to march 100,000 men up to the district of Montreal, to cut the connection between Upper and Lower Canada, to abstain religiously from meddling in our local affairs, but to force a separation of the Province, by the mere force of an army of occupation interposing a military barrier to their intercourse. What would follow such separation, rest assured, has not escaped their calculation."

The Maritimes in particular worried about being swallowed up by a united Canada, and opposition to the concept remained strong. The first constitutional conference took place in September 1864 in Charlottetown, when delegates from Nova Scotia, New Brunswick, Prince Edward Island, and Canada discussed unification and, in what has marked Canadian politics throughout its entire history, agreed to another meeting. These more formal talks were held in Quebec City in October and included a delegation from Newfoundland. The seventy-two resolutions proposed at this conference became the basis of the Confederation debates and, ultimately, the basis of the *British North America Act* that created Canada.

The Quebec Conference was interrupted by the St. Albans raid, across the border in Vermont. Many delegates later said that this explosive event, which renewed heated American threats of retaliation, convinced them that the strength-in-unity argument had merit. When the St. Albans raiders were ultimately freed by a Montreal court, the number of American voices demanding an invasion of Canada grew louder, and tough new measures requiring passports were temporarily instituted. Most significant, the Americans gave notice they would not renew the Reciprocity Treaty as of May 1866 – a free trade arrangement that had been of great benefit to Canada since its introduction in 1854. To top it off, a bill was approved in the U.S. Congress in July 2 for the "Admission of the States of Nova Scotia, New Brunswick, Canada East and Canada West, and for the organization of Territories of Selkirk, Saskatchewan and Columbia . . . as States and Territories of the United States of America." The U.S. administration also informed Canadian officials that it was abrogating the Rush-Bagot Agreement, which restricted the number of warships allowed on the Great Lakes. In the 1864 election, the Republican Party, on its way to victory, openly advocated annexation of Canada. And in April 1865, right after the fall of Richmond, Secretary of State Seward, speaking of Canada, told a celebratory crowd in Washington: "As for Earl Russell himself, I need not tell him that this is a war of freedom and national independence and the rights of human virtue, and not a war for empire; and that if Great Britain should only remain undisturbed by us so long as she proffers the authority of the noble Queen to voluntary incorporation with the United States."

On his way to London in April 1865 to help press the British government to approve the Quebec Resolutions, just after New Brunswick had voted against Confederation, Alexander Galt told a large, enthusiastic, pro-Confederation audience at the Temperance Hall in Halifax: "It is impossible to shut our eyes to the events occurring in the neighbouring States, and it is undeniable that unless we are united under the terms as agreed upon at Quebec, another union will be formed that will be found to be of an entirely different character, and under a different flag than that which we now recognize, and it becomes a question of whether we prefer the good old flag we are now under to that of the United States."

Stories were rampant that Seward had sent two representatives to Canada, financed with a large sum of money from the Secret Service Fund, to set up and promote an annexation movement. In July J.W. Potter, the U.S. consul general to Canada – in a speech both vetted and vigorously encouraged by Seward – created an international sensation when he brazenly told a large group of American and Canadian delegates at a business conference at the Board of Trade Hall in Detroit that there was a strong feeling in Canada, especially Lower Canada, "of a closer alliance with the United States than has ever existed before." He was greeted by loud cheers from the U.S. delegates and expressions of dissent from Canadians.

Saying he was "sorry" that some disagreed, he continued: "The people of the United States have seen, to say the least, the very great inconvenience of having a country on our northern borders which may be, and has been to a considerable extent, the basis of hostile operations against the United States, and therefore I say it is for the interest of the United States that a closer alliance should be entered into with the people of Canada . . . I agree with those who say we should not force the people of Canada into it . . . I tell you frankly I am more willing to excuse the people of Canada than many on this side . . . Now, we are ready to give you in Canada the most perfect reciprocity. We will give you complete free trade, but we ask you to come and share with us the responsibilities of our own government." At that point many Americans in the audience rose and cheered, while many Canadians shouted No. "We make this proposition, but not in a spirit of conquest," he continued. "When they come, let them come by their own consent . . . as brothers . . . with one flag, under one destiny." Again, the speech was interrupted by American cheers and Canadian boos.

Addressing the dissenting Canadians, Potter said, "The question is then, shall we simply be content to give Canadians all the benefit of our markets? . . . it is not the policy of our Government to continue this treaty and I believe that in two years from the abrogation of the Reciprocity Treaty, the people of Canada themselves will apply for admission in the U.S."

A member of parliament from St. Catharines, described in newspaper reports only as the "Hon. Mr. Currie," replied that he had never had an unkind thought or said an unkind word about the United States, yet the consul "would not coerce us by bayonets, but he would try to drive us into a corner by a hostile tariff, and by raising barriers against our trade and yours . . . That is not the way to bring us into the Union . . . [or] to maintain those friendly feelings between the two neighbouring countries which ought to exist between us."

Those "friendly feelings," of course, had become considerably less friendly during the war and were destined to get even worse the following year, when the Fenians launched several attacks into Canada with the clear assistance of the Americans. While the Fenians were easily defeated, their raids undermined the opposition to Canadian unity, in both Nova Scotia and New Brunswick in particular, and forged one more significant step towards Confederation. In the wake of the Fenian raids, the *Saint Croix Courier* wrote on May 19, 1866: "If there is one argument in favour of union . . . it is the necessity that exists for a good and efficient system of mutual defence . . . Now when we see how soon sudden danger can threaten us, and how our enemies may concentrate within a gunshot of our very doors, the man must be blind, infatuated, or prejudiced who can fail to recognize its force."

During the Confederation debate, John A. Macdonald said: "Ever since the [American] union was formed the difficulty of what is called 'state rights' has existed, and this had much to do in bringing on the present unhappy war in the United States. They commenced, in fact, on the wrong end. They declared by their Constitution that each state was a sovereignty in itself . . . We have strengthened the General Government. We have given the General Legislature all the great subjects of legislation. We have conferred on them, not only specifically and in detail, all the powers which are incident to sovereignty, but we have expressly declared that all subjects of general interest not distinctly and exclusively conferred upon the local governments and local legislatures, shall be conferred upon the General Government and Legislature.

"We have avoided that great source of weakness which has been the cause of the disruption of the United States. We have avoided all conflict of jurisdiction and authority, and if this Constitution is carried out . . . we will have in fact . . . all the advantages of a legislative union under one administration, with, at the same time, the guarantees for local institutions and for local laws, which are insisted upon by so many in the provinces now, I hope, to be united."

They were, of course, united in 1867. Despite the apprehensions of Canadians and the threats of Americans, who had built the largest army the world had ever known, the crisis passed, to a large extent because the American troops, after four bloody years of war, were in no mood to fight another war and quickly headed back to their homes.

Canadian parliamentarian Sir Richard Cartwright, looking back years later on Captain Wilkes and the *Trent* Affair, wrote: "As for Canada, the six weeks' suspense during which no man knew from day to day whether we would find ourselves at war, produced a most profound impression. A witty friend of the author was wont to maintain that the true father of Confederation was neither Brown, Cartier nor Macdonald, but Captain Wilkes, USN." Overstated, of course, but his comment makes the point.

And Skelton, reviewing those events in 1919, had this to say: "If the Civil War did not bring forth a new nation in the South, it helped to make one in the far North. A common danger drew the scattered British Provinces together and made ready the way for the coming Dominion of Canada."

Notes

1. Lois E. Darroch, *Four Went to the Civil War* (Willowdale, Ont.: Ampersand Press 1985), 123.
2. Ibid., 126.
3. Ibid., 276.
4. Ibid., 283.
5. Ibid., 284.

CHAPTER 2: MEN AT WAR

1. D.C. Bélanger, *French Canadians and Franco-Americans in the Civil War Era* (Montreal: Marianopolis College 2001), 42.
2. Malcolm Forbes and Jeff Bloch, *Women Who Made a Difference: One Hundred Fascinating Tales of Unsung Heroines & Little-Known Stories of Famous Women Who Changed Their World & Ours* (New York: Simon & Schuster 1991).

CHAPTER 3: REACH FOR THE TOP

1. Greg Marquis, *In Armageddon's Shadow: The Civil War and Canada's Maritime Provinces* (Montreal & Kingston: McGill-Queen's University Press 1998), 89.
2. Personal information contained in the guide to the Henry Benham Family Papers, prepared by Shirley R. Rodnitzky, March 1997, Special Collections Division, University of Texas at Arlington.
3. On April 17, 1861, after a convention of Virginians voted to have a referendum on secession, western delegates stormed out of the convention, promising to form a state government loyal to the Union. A month later, amid claims of vote-rigging by both sides, a majority of Virginians voted to secede from the Union, but a series of Union military victories allowed pro-Union delegates to form the Restored Government of Virginia, which was quickly recognized by Lincoln as the legitimate state government. On October 24, 1861, voters in thirty-nine counties in western Virginia approved a new Unionist

state, although the vote was tainted by Union troops stationed at most of the polls to prevent Confederate sympathizers from voting. After considerable more politicking – including a Lincoln-approved compromise that allowed the partial maintenance of slavery – West Virginia officially became a state on June 20, 1863.

4. Guide to the Benham Family Papers.

5. Ibid.

6. Oberlin College Catalog, 1994–95, Oberlin Online.

7. Ibid.

8. Garfield was shot twice at a Washington railway station on July 2, 1881, by lawyer Charles Julius Guiteau, who had been denied an application to become U.S. ambassador to France and believed that God had ordered him to kill the president. As a result of the shooting, Garfield died of blood poisoning on September 19. Guiteau was convicted and hanged on June 30, 1882.

CHAPTER 4: DIXIE BOUND

1. See Fred L. Logan, "Dr. Solomon Secord and the American Civil War (1861–1865)," essay, New Orleans, July 1995, for the following account of Secord.

2. Greg C. White, *A History of the 31st Georgia Volunteer Infantry* (Baltimore: Butternut and Blue 1997).

3. John Bakeless, *Spies of the Confederacy* (Mineola, NY: Dover Publications 1970), 264–65.

4. Ibid., 266.

5. Ibid., 280.

6. Ibid., 90.

7. William A. Tidwell, with James O. Hall and Winfred Gaddy, *Come Retribution: The Confederate Secret Service and the Assassination of Lincoln* (New York: Barnes & Noble Books, by arrangement with University of Mississippi Press 1997), 412.

8. Ibid.

9. Thomas H. Raddall, *Halifax: Warden of the North*, rev. ed. (Toronto: McClelland & Stewart 1971), 193.

10. Fred Landon, "Canadian Opinion of Southern Secession, 1860–61," *Canadian Historical Review* 1 (September 1920): 262.

11. W.T.R. Preston, *My Generation of Politics and Politicians* (Toronto:

D.A. Rose 1927), 25.

12. Donald Creighton, *John A. Macdonald: The Young Politician* (Toronto: Macmillan 1952), 369.

13. Wade Family Papers, Nova Scotia Public Archives.

CHAPTER 5: BLACKS AND BROWN

1. At the first battle of Kernstown on March 23, 1862, the legendary Confederate General Stonewall Jackson suffered his only military defeat. At the second, July 24, 1864, Confederate General Jubal Early gave the Confederates one of their few victories in the later part of the war. Early would later flee prosecution by escaping to Canada, living for some time at Niagara and Toronto.

2. An abridged version of the event as told by Martin Delany to his biographer, Frances Rollin Whipper – a black woman writing under the pseudonym Frank A. Rollin.

3. Daniel G. Hill, extracts from "Negroes in Toronto, 1793–1865," reprinted in *Ontario History*, no. 2, 1963.

4. From "The Canadas," West Virginia University online.

5. Ibid.

6. Ibid.

7. While the myth persists that blatant racism was confined to the South, the 1847 Black Codes of Ohio, and similar laws in other Northern states, prohibited blacks from settling in the state without proof of freedom and without a co-signer to vouch for them. These laws also prohibited blacks from attending common schools or testifying in any court where a white person was involved.

8. Black History exhibit, Guelph (Ontario) Museums online.

9. Ibid.

10. Harriet Beecher Stowe used King as the model for a fictional character in *Dred: A Tale of the Great Swamp*.

11. "The First Black Power Town," Buxton National Historic Site & Museum online.

12. Ibid.

13. "Introduction to Elgin's Black History in Southwestern Ontario," Buxton National Historic Site & Museum online.

14. *Montreal Gazette*, August 6, 1842.

15. Robin W. Winks, *The Blacks in Canada: A History*, 2nd ed. (Montreal

& Kingston: McGill-Queen's University Press 1997), 546.

16. John Kalbfleisch, in *Montreal Gazette*, January 19, 2003.

17. Fred Landon, "From Chatham to Harper's Ferry," *Canadian Magazine*, October 1919, 447.

18. James Cleland Hamilton, "John Brown in Canada," *Canadian Magazine*, 1894, 129.

19. Winks, *The Blacks in Canada*, 267.

20. Hamilton, "John Brown in Canada," 128.

21. "Re-evaluating John Brown's Raid at Harper's Ferry," *West Virginia History* 34, 1.

22. Landon, "From Chatham to Harper's Ferry," 447.

23. Ibid.

24. Ibid.

25. Winks, *The Blacks in Canada*, 267.

CHAPTER 6:

SKEDADDLERS, DESERTERS, CRIMPS, AND ASSORTED ROGUES

1. *Sarnia Observer*, November 4, 1864.

2. Robin W. Winks, *The Civil War Years: Canada and the United States* (Montreal & Kingston: McGill-Queen's University Press 1998), 181.

3. Ibid.

4. *St. Catharines Constitutional*, November 24, 1864.

5. *Brockville Recorder*, March 31, 1864.

6. This section relies heavily on Marguerite B. Hamer, "Luring Canadian Soldiers into Union Lines during the War between the States," *Canadian Historical Review* 77 (June 1996).

7. Ibid.

CHAPTER 7: TO THE BARRICADES

1. Geoffrey Ward, with Ric Burns and Ken Burns, *The Civil War: An Illustrated History* (New York: Alfred A. Knopf 1990), 81.

2. Charles Higham, *Murdering Mr. Lincoln: A New Direction of the 19th Century's Most Famous Crime* (Beverly Hills, Cal.: New Millennium Audio 2004).

3. Christopher Barth, "Averting Diplomatic Disaster: The Trent Affair," essay, Anchorage, Alaska, December 1990, quoting Ephraim

Douglass Adams, *Great Britain and the American Civil War* (New York: Russell & Russell 1924), 218.

4. Ibid.

5. Francis I.W. Jones, "A Hot Southern Town: Confederate Sympathizers in Halifax during the American Civil War," paper read before the Royal Nova Scotia Historical Society, January 21, 1999.

6. Robin W. Winks, *The Civil War Years: Canada and the United States* (Montreal & Kingston: McGill-Queen's University Press 1998), 52.

7. Thomas H. Raddall, *Halifax: Warden of the North*, rev. ed. (Toronto: McClelland & Stewart 1971), 195.

8. Originally called the *Leviathan*, the *Great Eastern*'s maiden voyage to New York City in June 1860 prompted a fourteen-gun salute, the first merchant ship ever to receive the honour. To make extra money, the owners opened the ship to the public and, during July, 150,000 people visited her. Her fame as a passenger ship was short-lived, however, as bad luck and poor engineering hampered her. In 1866, after a failed attempt the year before, she successfully laid the transatlantic cable for the Atlantic Telegraph Company. She was sold for scrap in 1888.

9. Nicholas Kiersey, "The Diplomats and Diplomacy of the American Civil War," University of Limerick, March 1997, 11.

10. Ibid., 7.

11. Ibid.

12. Ibid., 5.

13. Ibid., 7.

14. Ibid., 9.

15. Ibid., 5–6.

16. Winks, *The Civil War Years*, 72.

17. Ibid., 73–74.

18. Barth, "Averting Diplomatic Disaster."

19. Ibid.

20. Ibid.

21. Christopher Layne, "Anglo-American Crisis 1: The Trent Affair, 1861," *Washington Quarterly*, spring 2002.

22. Ibid.

23. Winks, *The Civil War Years*, 99.

24. Ibid.

25. Ibid., 100.

26. See also Donald Swainson, *Sir John A. Macdonald: The Man and the Politician* (Kingston, Ont.: Quarry Press 1989), 55.

CHAPTER 8: THE *CHESAPEAKE*

1. Greg Marquis, *In Armageddon's Shadow: The Civil War and Canada's Maritime Provinces* (Montreal & Kingston: McGill-Queen's University Press 1998), 139.

2. Robin W. Winks, *The Civil War Years: Canada and the United States* (Montreal & Kingston: McGill-Queen's University Press 1998), 245.

3. Marquis, *In Armageddon's Shadow*, 164.

4. Winks, *The Civil War Years*, 251, quoted from E.M. Saunders, *The Life and Letters of the Rt. Hon. Sir Charles Tupper*.

5. Marquis, *In Armageddon's Shadow*, quoted from the diary of Confederate Navy Secretary Gideon Welles.

6. Pat Lotz, "Halifax," speech to the Nova Scotia Heritage Trust, December 19, 1996.

7. *Halifax Herald*, "The Most Exciting Christmas Week Ever Known in the History of Halifax," December 23, 1891.

8. Winks, *The Civil War Years*, quoted from *Halifax Morning Journal*, January 13, 1864.

9. *Halifax Herald*, December 23, 1891.

10. Known as the "Wild Rose of the Confederacy," Greenhow was returning from London bearing urgent dispatches on the blockade-runner *Condor* when a Union ship gave chase, forcing the *Condor* aground on a sandbar off the coast of Wilmington, NC. Greenhow, fearing capture and an almost certain death penalty – she had already been deported to Richmond in 1862 for spying – persuaded Captain William Nathan Wright Hewett to allow her, Holcombe, and another companion to escape in a lifeboat. But the small craft overturned during a howling storm off the coast and Rose drowned, dragged down by the $2,000 in gold she carried. Holcombe barely escaped with his life, but he did manage to save the Confederate dispatches and deliver them to Richmond.

11. Marquis, *In Armageddon's Shadow*, 181.

12. Winks, *The Civil War Years*, 257.

13. Ibid.

CHAPTER 9: LAKE ERIE REBELS

1. Charles E. Frohman, *Rebels on Lake Erie* (Columbus: Ohio Historical Society 1965), 38.
2. Captain Robert D. Minor's Report, taken from the *Richmond Dispatch*, December 15, 1895, reprinted in *Southern Historical Society Papers* 23 (January–December 1895): 283–90.
3. John Wilkinson, *The Narrative of a Blockade-Runner* (1877; Alexandria, Va: Time-Life Books 1984), 252.
4. William A. Tidwell, with James O. Hall and David Winfred Gaddy, *Come Retribution: The Confederate Secret Service and the Assassination of Lincoln* (New York: Barnes & Noble Books, by arrangement with University of Mississippi Press 1997), 87.
5. Wilkinson, *The Narrative of a Blockade-Runner*, 181.
6. Ibid., 180.
7. Wilfred Bovey, "Confederate Agents in Canada during the American Civil War," *Canadian Historical Review* 2 (March 1921): 46–57.
8. Larry E. Nelson, *Bullets, Ballots, and Rhetoric: Confederate Policy for the United States Presidential Contest of 1864* (Tuscaloosa: University of Alabama Press 1980), 22–23.
9. Bovey, "Confederate Agents in Canada," 97.
10. James D. Horan, *Confederate Agent* (New York: Crown Publishers 1954), 85.
11. Bovey, "Confederate Agents in Canada," 47.
12. Nelson, *Bullets, Ballots, and Rhetoric*, 24.
13. Ibid.
14. Thomas P. Lowry, *"Don't Shoot That Boy!" Abraham Lincoln and Military Justice* (El Dorado Hills, Cal.: Savas Publishing Company 1999).
15. John W. Headley, *Confederate Operations in Canada and New York* (1906; Alexandria, Va: Time-Life Books 1984), 216.
16. Tidwell, *Come Retribution*, 129.
17. Ibid., 194.
18. Ibid., 35.
19. Ibid., 119.
20. Ibid., 122.
21. Ibid., 123.

22. Horan, *Confederate Agent*, 26.
23. Robin W. Winks, *The Civil War Years: Canada and the United States* (Montreal & Kingston: McGill-Queen's University Press 1998), 275–76.
24. Horan, *Confederate Agent*, 72–73.
25. Tidwell, *Come Retribution*, 195.
26. Horan, *Confederate Agent*, 42.
27. Ibid., 72–73.
28. Tidwell, *Come Retribution*, 195.
29. Nelson, *Bullets, Ballots, and Rhetoric*, 111–12.
30. Ibid., 151.
31. Clement C. Clay Papers, Duke University, NC.
32. *Globe*, "The Camp Douglas Conspiracy," February 10, 1865.
33. Thompson to Cole, cited by Frohman, *Rebels on Lake Erie*, 73.
34. See Frohman, *Rebels on Lake Erie*, 74–92, for details of this account.
35. John Bakeless, *Spies of the Confederacy* (Mineola, NY: Dover Publications 1970), 246.
36. Michael Kluckner, *Toronto: The Way It Was* (Toronto: Whitecap Books 1989), 202.
37. Bakeless, *Spies of the Confederacy*, 248–50.
38. Dave Swayze, "A Great Lake Pirate Ship . . . Or Not," essay.
39. Frohman, *Rebels on Lake Erie*, 120.

CHAPTER 10: BLOCKADE BUSTERS

1. Thomas H. Raddall, *Halifax: Warden of the North*, rev. ed. (Toronto: McClelland & Stewart 1971), 347.
2. Hamilton Cochrane, *Blockade Runners of the Confederacy* (Indianapolis–New York: Bobbs-Merrill 1958), 63.
3. H. Franklin Irwin Jr., *Foreign Service Journal* (June 1981).
4. Ibid.
5. John Wilkinson, *The Narrative of a Blockade-Runner* (1877; Alexandria, Va: Time-Life Books 1984), 86–87.
6. Ibid., 251.
7. Raddall, *Halifax*, 240.
8. *Harper's Pictorial History of the Civil War* (New York: The Fairfax Press 1866), 427.

Notes

CHAPTER 11: THE QUEEN'S HOTEL

1. George T. Denison, *Soldiering in Canada*
   (London: Morang & Co. 1901), 69.
2. Adam Mayers, *Dixie & the Dominion: Canada, the Confederacy and the War for the Union* (Toronto: Dundurn 2003), 19.
3. Ibid., 20.
4. Pierre Berton, *Niagara: A History of the Falls* (Toronto: McClelland & Stewart 1992), 10.
5. James D. Horan, *Confederate Agent* (New York: Crown Publishers), 79–80.
6. Michael Kluckner, *Toronto: The Way It Was* (Toronto: Whitecap Books 1989), 110.
7. William Tidwell, with James O. Hall and Winfred Gaddy, *Come Retribution: The Confederate Secret Service and the Assassination of Lincoln* (New York: Barnes & Noble, by arrangement with University of Mississippi Press 1997), 187.
8. John W. Headley, *Confederate Operations in Canada and New York* (1906; Alexandria, Va: Time-Life Books 1981), 480.
9. See ibid., 271–77, for the following account.
10. Ibid., 281.

CHAPTER 12: THE EDITOR

1. The following account is based on John C. Waugh, *Re-electing Lincoln: The Battle for the 1864 Presidency* (New York: Crown Publishers 1997), 248–53.
2. Larry E. Nelson, *Bullets, Ballots and Rhetoric: Confederate Policy for the United States Presidential Contest of 1864* (Tuscaloosa: University of Alabama Press 1980), 74.
3. Waugh, *Re-electing Lincoln*, 253.
4. See Nelson, *Bullets, Ballots and Rhetoric*, 70–73, for the quotations that follow.
5. Waugh, *Re-electing Lincoln*, 257.
6. Geoffrey C. Ward, with Ric Burns and Ken Burns, *The Civil War: An Illustrated History* (New York: Alfred Knopf 1990), 355.

Notes

CHAPTER 13: ST. ALBANS

1. The St. Albans raid is routinely described as the northernmost action of the war, but Calais, in fact, is slightly north. Calais is 45 degrees, 5 minutes, north latitude, compared to 44 degrees, 49 minutes, for St. Albans. Still, the Calais caper was not an officially sanctioned Confederate act of war, while the St. Albans raid was.
2. Timothy Short, a trooper with the 1st Vermont Cavalry. "When the South Rose Again in Vermont," essay.
3. Robin W. Winks, *The Civil War Years: Canada and the United States* (Montreal & Kingston: McGill-Queen's University Press 1998), 301.
4. *Montreal Gazette*, October 26, 1864.
5. Ibid., November 1, 1864.
6. Frederick Terrill, ed., *The Late Sir John J. Caldwell Abbott: A Chronology of Montreal and of Canada from 1752 to 1893* (Lovell & Son 1893).
7. The 1783 Paris Treaty, following the American Revolution, had not clearly defined the boundary between New Brunswick and Maine. When Maine gained statehood in 1820, it ignored British claims and granted land to settlers in the Arostook Valley. King William II of the Netherlands arbitrated the dispute: although the British accepted his ruling, the U.S. Senate rejected it. In February 1839 Canadian lumberjacks, working in the area, seized the American land agent who had been sent from Maine to expel them. New Brunswick called out its militia, Maine sent 10,000 troops, and the U.S. Congress, at Maine's insistence, authorized a force of 50,000 men and appropriated $10 million to deal with the emergency. President Martin Van Buren sent in General Winfield Scott, who averted any actual fighting by arranging an agreement between Maine and New Brunswick. The resulting compromise, the Ashburton-Webster Treaty, allowed the British to retain an overland route through New Brunswick between Montreal and Nova Scotia.
8. *Montreal Gazette*, November 11, 1864.
9. Winks, *The Civil War Years*, 345.

Notes

Chapter 14: The Assassins

1. Kathleen Jenkins, *Montreal: Island City of the St. Lawrence* (Garden City, NY: Doubleday 1966), 373.
2. William A. Tidwell, with James O. Hall and David Winfred Gaddy, *Come Retribution: The Confederate Secret Service and the Assassination of Lincoln* (New York: Barnes & Noble Books, by arrangement with University of Mississippi Press 1997), 273–75.
3. Ibid., 262.
4. Cited by Edgar Andrew Collard, *Montreal Gazette*, July 14, 1973.
5. James D. Horan, *Confederate Agent* (New York: Crown Publishers 1954), 234.
6. Tidwell, *Come Retribution*, 407.
7. Ibid., 415–16.
8. Lt.-Col. James Gordon, an avid hunter and sportsman, from an interview published in *The American Field: The Sportsman's Journal*, May 12, 1923.
9. Robin W. Winks, *The Civil War: Canada and the United States* (Montreal & Kingston: McGill-Queen's University Press 1998), 362–63.

Chapter 15: Circling the Wagons

1. Donald Creighton, *John A. Macdonald: The Young Politician* (Toronto: Macmillan 1952), 369.
2. E.B. Biggar, *Anecdotal Life of Sir John Macdonald* (Montreal: John Lovell & Son 1891), 182.
3. Oscar D. Skelton, *The Canadian Dominion: A Chronicle of Our Northern Neighbor* (Kingston, Ont.: Queen's University, July 1919).
4. D.C. Bélanger, *French Canadians and Franco-Americans in the Civil War Era* (Montreal: Marianopolis College 2001), 42.

Selected Bibliography

Ayer, I. Winslow. *The Great Treason Plot in the North during the War*. Chicago. U.S. Publishing 1895.

Bakeless, John. *Spies of the Confederacy*. Mineola, NY: Dover Publications 1970.

Bélanger, D.C. *French Canadians and Franco-Americans in the Civil War Era*. Montreal: Marianopolis College 2001.

Benjamin, L.N. *The St. Alban's Raid, 1865*. Montreal: John Lovell 1865. Reprinted by Tony O'Connor Civil War Enterprises, Newport, Vt.

Berton, Pierre. *Niagara: A History of the Falls*. Toronto: McClelland & Stewart 1992.

Biggar, E.B. *Anecdotal Life of Sir John Macdonald*. Montreal: John Lovell & Son 1891.

Blanton, DeAnne. "Women Soldiers of the Civil War." *Washington. Prologue: Quarterly of the National Archives* 25 (spring 1993): 27–33.

Blanton, DeAnne. "Confederate Medical Personnel." *Washington. Prologue: Quarterly of the National Archives* 26 (spring 1994): 80–84.

Bovey, Wilfrid. "Confederate Agents in Canada during the American Civil War." *Canadian Historical Review* 2 (March 1921): 46–57.

Brandt, Nat. *The Man Who Tried to Burn New York*. New York: Berkley 1990.

Brooks, Thomas Walter, with Michael Dan Jones. *Lee's Foreign Legion: A History of the 10th Louisiana Infantry*. Gravenhurst, Ont.: Watts Printing 1995.

Canan, H.V. "Confederate Military Intelligence." *Maryland Historical Magazine* 59 (March 1964): 34–51.

Careless, J.M.S. *Brown of the Globe*. Toronto: Dundurn Press 1989.

Clark, A.J. "When Jefferson Davis Visited Niagara." *Ontario Historical Society Papers and Records* 19 (1922): 87–89.

Selected Bibliography

Cochrane, Hamilton. *Blockade Runners of the Confederacy*. Indianapolis, New York: Bobbs-Merrill Company 1958.

Creighton, Donald. *John A. Macdonald: The Young Politician*. Toronto: Macmillan 1952.

Creighton, Donald. *The Road to Confederation: The Emergence of Canada, 1863–1867*. Toronto: Macmillan 1964.

Creighton, Donald. *John A. Macdonald: The Old Chieftan*. Toronto: Macmillan 1966.

Darroch, Lois E. *Four Went to the Civil War: A Gripping Story of a Canadian Family Caught Up in the American Civil War*. Toronto: Ampersand Press 1985.

Davis, Burke. *The Civil War: Strange & Fascinating Facts*. New York: Fairfax Press 1982. Previously published as *Our Incredible Civil War*, 1960.

Davis, William C. *Breckinridge: Statesman, Soldier, Symbol*. Baton Rouge and London: Louisiana State University Press 1992.

Denison, George Taylor. *Soldiering in Canada: Recollections and Experiences*. Toronto: Morang 1900.

Fesler, Mayo. "Secret Political Societies in the North during the Civil War." *Indiana Magazine of History* 14 (1918): 183–286.

Foote, Shelby. *The Civil War: A Narrative. Secession to Fort Henry*. Alexandria, Va.: Time-Life Books 1998.

Forbes, Malcolm, and Jeff Bloch. *Women Who Made a Difference: One Hundred Fascinating Tales of Unsung Heroines & Little-Known Stories of Famous Women Who Changed Their World & Ours*. New York: Simon & Schuster 1991.

Frohman, Charles E. "Rebels on Lake Erie." Ohio Historical Society 1965.

Gaddy, David Winfred. "William Norris and the Confederate Signal and Secret Service." *Maryland Historical Magazine* 71 (summer 1975): 166–88.

Gordon, Lesley J. *General George E. Pickett in Life & Legend*. Chapel Hill: University of North Carolina Press 1998.

Selected Bibliography

Granatstein, J.L. *Yankee Go Home? Canadians and Anti-Americanism.* Toronto: HarperCollins Publishers 1996.

Guersey, Alfred H., with Henry M. Alden. *Harper's Pictorial History of the Civil War.* New York: Fairfax Press 1866.

Hall, Richard. *Patriotism in Disguise: Women Warriors of the Civil War.* New York: Paragon House 1993.

Hamer, Marguerite B. "Luring Canadian Soldiers into Union Lines during the War between the States." *Canadian Historical Review* 27 (June 1946).

Hamilton, James Cleland. *John Brown in Canada.* Toronto: The Canadian Magazine 1894.

Headley, John William. *Confederate Operations in Canada and New York.* New York: Neale 1906. Reprinted Alexandria, Va: Time-Life Books 1984.

Hill, Daniel. "Negroes in Toronto, 1793–1865." Reprinted *Ontario History* 55, 2 (1963).

Horan, James D. *Confederate Agent: A Discovery in History.* New York: Crown 1954.

Jenkins, Kathleen. *Montreal: Island City of the St. Lawrence.* Garden City, NY: Doubleday 1966.

Kinchen, Oscar A. *Confederate Operations in Canada and the North: A Little-Known Phase of the American Civil War.* North Quincy, Mass.: Christopher 1970.

Kluckner, Michael. *Toronto: The Way It Was.* Toronto: Whitecap Books 1998.

Landon, Fred. "From Chatham to Harper's Ferry." *The Canadian Magazine* 52, 6 (October 1919).

Landon, Fred. "Canadian Opinion of Southern Secession, 1860–61." *Canadian Historical Review* 1 (September 1920).

Layne, Christopher. "Anglo-American Crisis 1: The *Trent* Affair, 1861." *Washington Quarterly* (spring 2002).

Logan, Fred L. "Dr. Solomon Secord and the American Civil War (1861–1865)." Essay. New Orleans, La. 1995.

Lowry, Thomas P. *Don't Shoot That Boy! Abraham Lincoln and Military Justice*. El Dorado Hills, Cal.: Savas Publishing 1999.

Marquis, Greg. *In Armageddon's Shadow: The Civil War and Canada's Maritime Provinces*. Montreal & Kingston: McGill-Queen's University Press 1998.

Mayers, Adam. *Dixie & the Dominion: Canada, the Confederacy and the War for the Union*. Toronto: Dundurn 2003.

McPherson, James M. *Battle Cry of Freedom: The Civil War Era. The Oxford History of the United States*. New York: Oxford University Press 1988.

Moore, Christopher. *1867: How the Fathers Made a Deal*. Toronto: McClelland & Stewart 1997.

Nelson, Larry E. *Bullets, Ballots, and Rhetoric: Confederate Policy for the United States Presidential Contest of 1864*. Tuscaloosa: University of Alabama Press 1980.

Osborne, Charles C. *Jubal: The Life and Times of General Jubal A. Early, CSA. Defender of the Lost Cause*. Chapel Hill, NC: Algonquin Books 1992.

Preston, W.T.R. *My Generation of Politics and Politicians*. Toronto: D.A. Rose Publishing 1927.

Raddall, Thomas H. *Halifax: Warden of the North*. Rev. ed. Toronto: McClelland & Stewart 1971.

Raney, W.F. "Recruiting and Crimping in Canada for the Northern Forces, 1861–65." *Mississippi Historical Review* (June 1923).

Starr, Stephen Z. "Was There a Northwest Conspiracy?" *Filson Club History Quarterly* 38 (1964): 323–41.

Swainson, Donald. *Sir John A. Macdonald: The Man and the Politician*. Kingston: Quarry Press 1989.

Tidwell, William A. *Confederate Covert Action in the American Civil War: April '65*. Kent, Ohio: Kent State University Press 1995.

Tidwell, William A., with James O. Hall and David Winfred Gaddy. *Come Retribution: The Confederate Secret Service and the Assassination of*

Lincoln. New York: Barnes & Noble Books, by arrangement with the University Press of Mississippi Press 1997.

Vandiver, Frank E. *Civil War Battlefields and Landmarks: A Guide to the National Park Sites*. New York: Random House 1996.

Vinet, Mark. *Canada and the American Civil War: Prelude to War.* Vaudreuil sur le Lac, Que.: Wadem Publishing/North American Historical Institute 2001.

Waite, P.B. *The Life and Times of Confederation, 1864–1867.* Toronto: Robin Brass Studio 2001.

Ward, Geoffrey C., with Ric Burns and Ken Burns. *The Civil War: An Illustrated History*. New York: Alfred A. Knopf 1990.

Waugh, John C. *Reelecting Lincoln: The Battle for the 1864 Presidency.* New York: Crown Publishers 1997.

White, Greg C. *A History of the 31st Georgia Volunteer Infantry.* Baltimore: Butternut and Blue 1997.

Wilkinson, John. *The Narrative of a Blockade-Runner.* New York: Sheldon & Company 1877. Reprinted Alexandria, Va.: Time-Life Books 1984.

Winks, Robin W. "The Creation of a Myth: 'Canadian' Enlistments in the Northern Armies during the Civil War." *Canadian Historical Review* 39, 1 (1958): 24–40.

Winks, Robin W. *The Blacks in Canada: A History*. 2nd ed. Montreal & Kingston: McGill-Queen's University Press 1997.

Winks, Robin W. *The Civil War Years: Canada and the United States.* 4th ed. Montreal & Kingston: McGill-Queen's University Press 1998.

Young, Bennett. *Confederate Wizards of the Saddle*. Nashville: J.S. Sanders 1999. First published Boston: Chapple Publishing 1914.

Acknowledgments

As any writer will tell you, putting words to paper is a solo exercise. But gathering the words to put to the paper requires considerable help.

Charles Medawar, executive director of the British health research group, The Social Audit, once wrote: "Librarians are almost always very helpful and often almost absurdly knowledgeable. Their skills are probably very underestimated and largely underemployed." That's certainly been my experience with librarians, easily the most accommodating people in the world. Particular thanks to the helpful staff at both the Nova Scotia and Ontario provincial archives and the research staff at the Metropolitan Toronto Research Library; also to *Hamilton Spectator* editor, Dana Robbins, and his chief librarian, Tammy Damcio, for allowing me free run of their extensive period files.

In Halifax, considerable thanks to Donald MacDonald of the *Halifax Chronicle Herald* for his help and hospitality, and in Montreal to journalist Alan Hustak of the *Montreal Gazette* for the dozens of items he sent along. In Ottawa, veteran journalist/research specialist Tom Korski not only volunteered considerable anecdotes and historical quotes but scoured the Library and Archives Canada on my behalf for both historical items and period photographs.

Thanks too to the dozens of authors listed in the bibliography whose previous works helped fill in the blanks. Special thanks to my agent, Linda McKnight of Westwood Creative Services; to my publisher, Kim McArthur; and to my experienced and highly professional editor, Rosemary Shipton.

Finally, since writers can be both grumpy and neglectful when they are preoccupied with a major project, much appreciation to my partner, Sally Orviss, for her continuing help, understanding, and encouragement.

Claire Hoy
Toronto, July 2004

Index

Index

Index

Index

Index

Index

Index

Index

Index

Index

Index

Index

Index

Index